THE ODYSSEY

HOMER

Translated by Rodney Merrill

With Introductions by Thomas R. Walsh and Rodney Merrill

Ann Arbor
THE UNIVERSITY OF MICHIGAN PRESS

THE ODYSSEY

Copyright © by the University of Michigan 2002
All rights reserved
Published in the United States of America by
The University of Michigan Press
Manufactured in the United States of America
∞ Printed on acid-free paper

2005   2004   2003   4   3   2

A CIP catalog record for this book is available from the British Library.

Library of Congress Cataloging-in-Publication Data
Homer.
    [Odyssey. English]
    The Odyssey / Homer ; translated by Rodney Merrill ; with introductions by
Thomas R. Walsh and Rodney Merrill.
         p.   cm.
    Includes bibliographical references.
    ISBN 0-472-11231-7 (cloth : alk. paper) — ISBN 0-472-08854-8 (pbk. : alk.
paper)
    1. Odysseus (Greek mythology)—Poetry. 2. Epic poetry, Greek—Translations
into English. I. Merrill, Rodney, 1940– II. Walsh, Thomas R. III. Title.
    PA4025.A5 M57   2002
    883'.01—dc21   2002020248

Dedication and Acknowledgments

I started this work over twenty-five years ago, while I was living in the camp-ground of Lisbon, Portugal, with not much else to do and nobody to tell me I was mad. Over the years, there would be enough of both sorts of distraction, but many people have been helpful and supportive. Of these, the ones I note first are those to whom I dedicate the translation: Alfredo C. Costa, my companion from 1973—including the year in Lisbon, *Olisipo*, the city of Ulysses—until his un-timely death in 1994; Bruce Burton, my companion since 1994; and my parents, LaVaun S. Merrill (now deceased) and Ivanelle Harpster Merrill, whose finan-cial support helped give me the leisure to pursue this long labor of love.

I must then acknowledge all the editors, commentators, scholars, and trans-lators of the past who have contributed to my understanding of the Homeric epics and the circumstances of their production; some of them are named in the introductory essays in this book, but they and I have drawn freely on their pre-decessors, so that a full list would be quite unwieldy. Next, I record my deep ap-preciation to all the friends and colleagues who have responded to my version in its various stages. Frederic Amory, J. K. Anderson, Elizabeth Ditmars, and Michael Tillotson have been especially generous in carefully reading and learnedly commenting on various aspects of this project. They and the other members of the Berkeley Greek Club—Louise Chu, Mark Griffith, Gary Holland, Leslie Kurke, Kathleen McCarthy, Christopher Simon, and Andrew Stewart—have listened to me read much of the translation and have given me valuable suggestions for improvements. Other friends who have given me advice and support include Alex Billeter, Jean-Bernard Billeter, Leonard Cottrell, John Galvin, Terry Lee, Raymond and Mary Anne Oliver, Daniel and Ana Waissbein, and William and Gay Wiser. I also thank the many other friends and acquaintances who have listened and responded to my readings and expressed interest in the progress of the work.

I want also to express my appreciation of the patient and careful treatment this project has received from the editorial staff of the University of Michigan Press. Finally, I am most grateful for the learned and stimulating contribution of Thomas R. Walsh; our collaboration on the first of the introductory essays has proved more exciting and fruitful than either of us could have predicted. Of course, I bear the responsibility for the errors and infelicities that remain in the translation despite the best efforts of my counselors.

Contents

THE *ODYSSEY* OF HOMER

CONTENTS

The *Odyssey*

The Tradition, the Singer, the Performance

Thomas R. Walsh and Rodney Merrill

READING THE *ODYSSEY*

The city of Troy fell over three thousand years ago, at the end of the second millennium before our era. Yet the story of the Trojan War still holds us in its grip, as does the account of those who returned from the war and of those others who maintained their world during the twenty-year absence of fathers, husbands, and sons. That these narratives, in the forms of the *Iliad* and the *Odyssey*, endure across cultures and across times is a remarkable fact of literary and intellectual history that raises a fundamental question: what qualities of the Homeric poems keep alive a story that might otherwise have concerned merely handfuls of scholars instead of the crowds of readers who turn to the Homeric poems for pleasure, for understanding, and for the contemplative solace of high literature?

To answer this imposing question to any satisfaction is a life's work; here, we can give only a brief sketch focusing on the *Odyssey*. The possible responses to the question vary with the perspective from which it is posed. Those looking for entertainment turn to the geographical sweep of Odysseus' journey and see the poem as an adventure tale, related to the many others that fill our shelves, from the Greek legend of the Argonauts, to the tales of the explorers in the early modern period, to the stories of the space explorers, real and fictional, of contemporary life. Moralists from pagan and Christian antiquity to the present may see the voyage of Odysseus from Troy to his home on Ithaka as an allegory for life's "journey homeward," through perils both out in the world and inside the soul, to peace, harmony, and self-reconciliation. The Western literary historian, in turn, draws a line from Homer to Virgil to Dante to Milton to Joyce to argue for the grandeur of the tradition of epic, the genre that attempts to convey an all-inclusive sense of the human predicament. Similarly, the scholar who compares outwardly diverse cultures will bring into consideration such epic works as the *Mahabharata* and the *Ramayana* from India, the *Táin Bó Cúalnge* from Ireland, or the *Sunjata* from Africa, and numerous other non-Western narratives that strike similar chords in human experience.

Such comparative studies may bring even more attention to the myth, legend, and folklore at the heart of the poem, where the one-eyed giants and clashing rocks, the Sirens and cannibals, the sun god and the denizens of the underworld put on an exhibition of the fantastic and grotesque. Scholars delight in tracing versions of these tales in cultures from all over the world. For example, Circè, from book 10 of the *Odyssey*, resembles many other witches in the woods who transform men into birds or beasts; Denys Page (*Folktales in Homer's* Odyssey 58) summarizes versions from Corsica, Germany, and India. The Sirens, past whose beguiling song Odysseus can sail only by stopping up his crewmen's ears and having himself bound to the mast (*Od.* 12.154–200), are like the mermaids of northern Europe, who lure passing sailors to destruction; the bird-women of Java, who bewitch men; or the ogresses in the birth stories of the Buddha, who lure men to their death by their sweet singing (see Page, *Folktales in Homer's* Odyssey 87–88). Such widespread currency of these stories testifies to their power in giving entertainment to ordinary readers looking for a sense of the marvelous or for an embodiment of fears or wishes otherwise left unexpressed.

Those readers for whom "literature" largely means the novel notice especially how the *Odyssey* brings together the demands of fantastic fiction and realistic narrative. Lovers of the novel of fantasy and romance find satisfaction in Odysseus' liaisons with amorous females, in his visits to such ideal places as Scheria and to such nightmarish ones as the land of the Laistrygonians, and in the unremitting sense of dangers to be overcome through his cunning and his courage. The more "naturalistic" novel's development and resolution are prefigured in the way that the stories of Telémachos' maturation, of his reunion with his father, and of his mother's stalwart defense of home and hearth lead to Odysseus' carefully prepared return to his palace and build up to the final battle against the suitors. Furthermore, since the *Odyssey* often focuses on servants and common people (e.g., Eumaíos the swineherd, Eurykleía the nurse, and Melánthios the goatherd and his sister, Melántho the housemaid), showing how they participate for good or evil in the outcome of events, it vigorously anticipates the novel's portrayal of different classes and social types. These same elements bring to the text scholarly readers bent on pursuing the historical crises of antiquity, the struggles between genders, classes, and social groups.

For these scholars and other readers, the ethical issues raised by the drama of a marriage threatened by a husband's absence, heightened by the vulnerability of Penelope as she fends off the suitors, may well hold center stage. Thus, Odysseus' vengeance reinforces the moral tale by violently reasserting the basic social bonds against the severest odds. Indeed, ethical dilemmas inform the plot from Zeus's opening speech at the beginning of the poem, in which he deprecates mortals' tendencies to evade their own responsibility by blaming the gods for their misfortunes, to the conclusion's truce between Odysseus and the townsmen who had sought to avenge their slaughtered kinsmen. How should a son act when he does not know what has happened to his father—should he just wait for his father to return, or should he take over his position as master? To whom do servants owe their loyalties, to a master absent for almost twenty years or to the demanding habitués of the palace who are in a position to punish and reward them?

Perhaps the most loyal readers of the *Odyssey* see the poem's central tensions as crucial to any life: the relationship between Odysseus and Penelope stands for the careful negotiation that attends all relations and especially those based on erotic bonding. So too, the conflicts among the suitors, Penelope, Telémachos, and the goddess Athena (in book 1, disguised as Mentes, a male friend of Odysseus, and sometimes thereafter as Mentor, an even closer comrade) are fraught with a tension that seems an irreducible part of any relationship. Portrayals of the way individuals relate to their society come up over and over again—in Telémachos' speeches before the suitors, especially in books 1 and 2; in Odysseus' strained relations with his sometimes rebellious crew in books 9 through 12, as he strives to keep them from destroying their own chance to return home; in the behavior of the Phaiákian youths in book 8, for whom the authority and age of their unknown visitor are a problem; and even, in one of the most startling examples, in Odysseus' dealing with a crowd of ghosts in Hades' domain as a politician might deal with a dubious citizenry, careful to listen to one at a time and eager to gratify them. In this light, Penelope's management of her importunate suitors is as much a political as a domestic conflict, because the well-being of the community depends on her ability to make the right decision in desperate circumstances. Even the appeal of the blinded Polyphémos to his fellow Cyklópes toward the end of book 9 highlights the problem of how a person fits or does not fit into society, a question that will come to inform Western thought, whether in historical, philosophical, or literary terms. So the conflicts in the *Odyssey* present a vision of what it is like to live a life constrained by the political terms inherent in being an individual within a group.

Each of these answers—focusing on the travel tales; constructing allegories or moral tracts; examining the psychological, social, and even political aspects of the work in almost novelistic terms—has its own truth, partial but contributing to a greater whole. Perhaps the answer to the question of why the *Odyssey* commands the attention of the ages lies in the very multiplicity of possible answers. The plot itself involves aspects of human experience that cross cultural boundaries, if not in their treatment, then certainly in their substance: all cultures modulate the relations among classes and genders, among the people and groups of people who share a community; every human community confronts the maturation of the young and the progress of age; all cultures confront deep conflicts of interest among social groups. No culture is without its elements of folklore and fantasy, as even our positivistic, technological age dwells on such fantasies as Star Wars and Star Trek and continues to be ever more fascinated by myths of the premodern cultures. In sum, Homer has been and continues to be many things to many people.

THE *ODYSSEY* AS CULTURAL ARTIFACT

Epic Scope

Whatever our main perspective on the *Odyssey* may be, the detailed episodes of the poem are what hold our imaginations through twenty-four books, from the first glimpse of Zeus and Athena on Mount Olympos to the final encounter between the house of Odysseus and the citizens of Ithaka—in such scenes as Odysseus escaping from the Cyklops by clinging to the belly of a huge ram (9.424–72) or delivered from the temptation of the Sirens by being bound to the mast of his ship (12.154–200). We are moved by the death of a devoted dog when he sees his master return after an almost twenty-year absence (17.290–327), by a faithful nurse's recognition of a scar on the thigh of the lord she nurtured as an infant (19.361–494), by Penelope's dream of pet geese slaughtered by an eagle, prefiguring Odysseus' slaughter of the suitors (19.535–58).

As we have already suggested, such episodes have their roots partly in the ages-old and worldwide folk inheritance of the *Odyssey*. But the particular cultural heritage of this story begins in the Mycenaean age, for it may well have emerged perhaps three millennia ago in the performances of oral bards before enthralled audiences. Over the course of four centuries, across the Greek Dark Ages (ca. 1150–700 B.C.) and up to the Archaic period (ca. 700–500), the folk tradition kept alive such scenes, developing new movements within an old structure. But can we say anything more precise about how these details were woven into the fabric of a narrative that dealt with the most important of human events, the movement of a people through its history? We can at least try to hold in mind an image, however dimmed by the distance of time and place, of those moments when the poem was most fully alive, when its audience and its composer were engaged together in an oral-poetic performance, in its essence both public and intimate. Precisely this image eludes our sight, just as the ghost of Odysseus' mother in Hades' domain eludes her son's grasp as he seeks to hold onto her so that they can "both take comfort in cold lamentation" (*Od.* 11.212). The vision of the sung performance that we get from merely reading the poem must remain fleeting.

Nevertheless, a clearer image of such an event is just what readers in the twenty-first century ought to ask for when we read a new translation of this most-translated poem. How much can we say about what this experience was like for its first audiences? One way to sketch that experience is to explore what we mean when we call the *Odyssey* a Homeric epic. The terms *Homeric* and *epic* have connotations for us that are virtually the same as those they had for listeners in the ancient world—they suggest vast extents of time and space and deep engagement with fundamental issues of life. A "Homeric epic" must have monumental reach if it is to fulfill the expectations brought to it by both ancients and contemporaries.

First, as to time, the events recounted in the *Iliad* and *Odyssey* themselves are of large temporal scope, the war in Troy lasting for ten years, the return of Odysseus for another ten. Though neither epic covers the full period in detail, both often evoke that length of time as signifying the immensity of the effort and the suffering incurred in both the Trojan War and the warriors' returns. Beyond that, the poems refer to many other events that occur before and after those central ones. For example, we hear the stories of Eurykleía and Eumaíos and of the birth and childhood of Odysseus; both Odysseus and Meneláos learn what will happen to them later on.

Even more important, the very antiquity of these poems was for the ancient Greeks and is even more for us a witness to endurance in time, the nearest human beings can come to immortality. The victory over Troy from which Odysseus is returning situates the dramatic date of the narrative at the end of the second millennium B.C., when historians and archaeologists have noted large-scale destruction of the major centers of cultural activity including Mycenae (Mykénè in the translation in this book), Pylos, and Tiryns, as well as Troy itself. Of the numerous cities unearthed at Hisarlık, in northwestern Asia Minor, those labeled "VIh" and "VIIa," from about the mid–thirteenth century B.C., are the ones in which archaeologists have detected the most probable ghost of ancient Troy (for a recent discussion, see Luce 93–109). The Mycenaean period preceding these destructive events appears strikingly in such features of the Homeric poems as the names of the characters. *Achilles, Nestor, Agamemnon,* and *Odysseus* are quite different from the Greek names familiar to us from classical times, such as *Plato, Demosthenes,* and *Socrates.* The Mycenaean period was indeed antiquity for these later Greeks, and the tragedians Aeschylus, Sophocles, and Euripides evoked that past by staging many dramas with Mycenaean characters (e.g., Ajax, Philoktétes, and Odysseus himself): they clearly thought of it as remote but accessible, to be bodied forth in artistic representations that helped them define what it meant to be Greek.

Thus, the sense of a temporal expanse traversing the history of a culture is firmly rooted in the notion of the epic. So too is the geographical sweep of the poems, especially of the *Odyssey,* in which Odysseus' return takes him far across the sea, just as the Trojan War had brought warriors from everywhere in the Greek and Trojan world (as listed in the famous catalogs of book 2 of the *Iliad*) to join their respective confederations in battle over the fate of the city. Moreover, this geographical sweep appears in both legendary and realistic terms. Odysseus' voyage takes him to the furthest extent of Greek mythical distance, Hades' domain, the land of the dead, as well as to the legendary lands of the Lotus-eaters, the one-eyed monster Cyklops, the witch Circè, the sun god, Kalýpso, and the Phaiákians. Then, when Odysseus lands on Ithaka, he contrives realistic stories about his fictional origins in the distant but quite worldly regions of Egypt and Crete.

But beyond the quantitative scope of time and space that constantly informs the Homeric narrative, the poems have what we might call great qualitative breadth. That is, they—especially the *Odyssey*—touch on most of the common features of human existence: from family and domestic arrangements to the highest heroism and tragedy and to the ways the immortal gods interact with mortals; from dialogues between intimates to speeches in the assembly; from accounts of real habitations, such as the palace of Ithaka and the farm of Laërtes, to imaginative constructions of ideal ones—Scheria's ever-productive fields and splendid court and the perfect climate of the dwellings of the gods on Olympos.

Wide ethical understanding, too, can emerge from our encounter with these events and characters. Take the fate of the suitors as an example. We must confront the cruelty of Odysseus' revenge in book 22 and the fact that some suitors clearly deserve their fate more than others. Amphínomos, notably, appears to be a good man, attempting to restrain the excesses of his fellow suitors. Yet he has participated in the unseemly pursuit of Penelope in her own home and thereby in the devastation of the household, so Athena and Odysseus will not exempt him from the final slaughter. Shall we take this as a model of justice or as a stimulus to discover more nuanced ways of dealing with degrees of wrongdoing? Whatever we decide, this culminating episode deepens the moral questions posed by the *Odyssey*. In this case and others, the poem provides a clear image, perhaps even a provisional decision, but leaves the final judgment to its audience.

Origins

This broad scope of the epic is as significant for us as it was for the ancient Greeks, who regarded Homer as the foundation of their culture. But just how, in concrete terms, did the Homeric tradition arouse such admiration? How did the audience, to begin with and later on, receive these songs so as to secure them as the bedrock of cultural experience? These questions lead to further questions about both the genesis and the transmission of the poems, questions to which there are no uncontested answers. As to genesis, we know that some elements of the Homeric narratives extend back to Mycenaean culture, while other elements antedate them, reaching toward the pre-Greek Indo-European past (see Nagy, *Best of the Achaeans*). Still other elements derive from the rich cultures of the ancient Near East (see Burkert). For Mycenaean material, the names of the major palace centers, Pylos, Tiryns, and Mycenae itself, correspond to the evidence from the archaeological record, whereas the medium of dactylic hexameter verse and such story elements as the episode that starts off the whole epic cycle—the Trojan boy Paris' choice of the most beautiful among the three goddesses Hera, Athena, and Aphrodítè—may stem from the time when the speakers of the original Indo-European language formed one unified people.

However, scholarly debate has lately tended to emphasize the more recent features to be found in the Homeric texts, especially as they provide evidence for the successive ages through which the earlier material was transmitted, elements from the Greek Dark Ages and from the Archaic period, which we have come to call the renaissance of the eighth century. Such transmission must have encompassed generation after generation of performers—young ones learning from their masters, singers in their prime exchanging ideas and innovations within their tradition, aged and respected elders in the singing community passing the torch to a new generation—until a fixed text came to be transmitted securely, first through memorization and then through writing, or even perhaps through a combination of both. More remarkable than the bardic fluidity that we moderns have labored so hard to divine is the fact that such a robust and vital tradition has somehow been captured and bequeathed to us in these two poetic monuments. Perhaps to repay that bequest, we cannot help but ask: What is meant by the name *Homer?* Who finally composed these great epics out of the mass of material the tradition gave him? The way we experience the poem may be affected by the answer we give, just as we expect different things of Dickens and Austen, of Tolstoy and Faulkner.

The twentieth century saw a great advance in our understanding of the way epic poetry was produced in ancient Greece. But as Adam Parry shows in his introduction to his father's collected papers, that advance had been anticipated by the suspicion that the Homeric poems were somehow different from other texts. When Herodotus, the first Greek historian (ca. 484–ca. 422 B.C.), asserted that "Hesiod and Homer are four hundred years older than I and not more" (2.53), he gave evidence of a controversy surrounding these early Greek traditions; we may call what he says the earliest assertion about the "Homeric question," which has caused so much ink to be spread over so many pages. Much later, Josephus, the Jewish historian of the first century A.D., contrasted the Greeks unfavorably with the ancient Hebrews by contending that the literacy of the Hebrew texts made them superior to an oral Homer. That first assertion of Homeric orality came to an abundant harvest in the modern period, when, for example, the Abbé d'Aubignac, a French scholar of the seventeenth century (1604–76), suggested that our *Iliad* and *Odyssey* were collections of earlier songs pasted together in a haphazard manner. Perhaps more congenial to our sense of the process was the claim of Giambattista Vico, an Italian philosopher (1668–1744), that there was no Homer and that the "Greek people" had produced the texts. Following the assertion of the English scholar Robert Wood (1717–71) that Homer need not have been literate, Friedrich August Wolf (1759–1824) systematically argued that there was no written text until the sixth century, so that Homeric "texts" were on this score at least different in kind from later texts.

By the nineteenth century and into the early twentieth, the controversy centered on sorting out the elements of Homeric texts in such a way as to locate the "real" Homer and segregate "accretions," elements that do not belong to the "central core." For the *Odyssey*, such a method can yield, for example, separate authors for the story of Telémachos (books 1–4), the tales Odysseus tells Alkínoös in Scheria (books 9–12), and the revenge of Odysseus (books 13–24, with some excisions). In response to this challenge to the unity of the *Odyssey*, some scholars in the early twentieth century—the so-called unitarians—tried to show how the travels of Telémachos, those of Odysseus, the revenge on the suitors, and the reunion of Odysseus and Penelope fit together in an organically unified work.

These controversies were fundamentally altered in what can be characterized as a major paradigm shift in Homeric studies, one of the most dramatic advances in the humanities in the twentieth century. Beginning in the 1920s, Milman Parry, a young scholar from California, determined to discover the nature of Homeric tradition by joining his own fine aesthetic sense to the linguistic methods he learned when studying with Antoine Meillet and others in Paris. He found that Homeric poetry not only reflected an oral tradition but did so systematically, basing this conclusion not on surmise or historical inference, as had been the case

since Josephus, but on the meter and language of the verse itself as these are com-
pared with works of other cultures that ethnographers classify as "oral." Parry
applied a rigorous analytical method to this data, examining systematically the
way that meter and phrasing regularly interact to yield the most salient feature
of Homeric poetry, its repetitive and formulaic diction. The result was to iden-
tify Homeric poetry as *oral-formulaic*, a term that has caused much controversy
but that can easily be elucidated through the sample of Homeric language that
provided the core of Parry's original research.

In Homeric poetry, nouns and adjectives come to be associated in formulas. Ex-
amples of similar associations from modern idiom are *heavy hitter, worthy colleague*,
and *bed of roses*. *Heavy hitter* not only is a regular formula but also calls to mind the
entire subculture of baseball. *Worthy colleague* is unlikely to be heard at the family
dinner table but occurs often in speeches about fellow managers or legislators. *Bed
of roses* has both a literal and a metaphorical meaning; which one is meant is de-
termined by the context in which the phrase appears. Those who use such ex-
pressions feel the security of a familiar locution applied to a familiar situation.

But whereas we may consider such expressions clichés, perhaps to be avoided
in writing or speaking to a discriminating audience, such phrases as *polýtlas díos
Odýsseus*, translated "much-suffering noble Odysseus" (*Od.* 5.171, etc.); *períphron
Pénelopeía*, "Penelope, thoughtful and prudent" (1.328, etc.) or "prudent Pene-
lope" (4.787, etc); and *nephelégeretá Zeús*, "the cloud-gathering god Zeus" (1.63,
etc.), occur frequently and in regularly recurring metrical contexts. They are fun-
damental to the very existence of the Homeric poems. Parry's definition of the
formula is famous: "The formula in the Homeric poems may be defined as *a group
of words which is regularly employed under the same metrical conditions to express a
given essential idea*" (Parry 272). Thus, *polýtlas díos Odýsseus* occurs thirty-seven
times, always as the second half of a line, of which the first half also is usually for-
mulaic. Similarly, both *períphrón Pénelopeía* and *nephelégeretá Zeús* occur only in
the last part of a line. (In the translation in this book, "prudent Penelope," the
alternative rendering of the former phrase, occurs at the beginning of the line
when English syntax would be unpleasantly distorted by placing the subject late.)
Sometimes, the particular qualities denoted by these "epithets" bear little im-
mediate emphasis: Odysseus might be called "much-suffering" in contexts where
his sufferings are less prominent than, for example, his wiliness, because the for-
mula for the latter—*polymétis Odýsseus* ("Odysseus of many devices")—may not
fit the metrical context. Thus, the "essential idea" of Parry's definition is in these
cases the full identity (not merely the name) of the person or god in question.

Many have objected that a poetic procedure so defined must greatly limit a
composer's creativity—if he must confine himself to such rigid compositional el-
ements, he has little opportunity for the free play of his artistry. But within an

oral-traditional context, the interaction of formula and meter is conditioned by another element, that of theme. In such a tradition, the idea that Odysseus is "much-suffering noble Odysseus" or that Penelope is "thoughtful and prudent" does not depend on any individual performance or text. In rhetorical terms, these aspects of the Homeric language do not rise from the "invention" of the poet but rather come to him as part of the language, the "vocabulary," with which the poet makes the poem, with which the singer sings the song. In essence, each of these expressions derives from a larger theme, which it encapsulates briefly and memorably: the suffering, or endurance (*polýtlas* could also be translated "much-enduring"), of the hero is central to his existence in this poem, just as identifying Penelope as "thoughtful and prudent" typifies her whole behavior with respect to the suitors and to Odysseus himself. Both expressions come straight out of the traditional conceptions of these characters, as do the other epithets that so strike the notice of a modern reader—for example, "thoughtful Telémachos," "the goddess bright-eyed Athena," "the great earth-shaker Poseidon."

This notion of theme, so important as a control on our view of formula and meter, was a development of Parry's work by his colleague and successor Albert Lord, as set forth especially in Lord's *The Singer of Tales*. Though the word *theme* is used in different ways, it refers, for purposes of Homeric criticism, specifically to what Lord calls a "group of ideas," such as the feasting theme that occupies so much of the *Odyssey*. We can debate exactly how the singers conceptualized such themes; but that recurring themes are fundamental to Homeric epic is clear. For example, as we shall show later in this essay in some detail, the important theme of guest-friendship courses through the entire *Odyssey*, from Telémachos' warm and polite reception of Athena disguised as Mentor in book 1 to the late scenes in which the suitors confirm their unworthiness by abusing Odysseus, who is disguised as a beggar looking for hospitality. Another sort of theme appears in the *nóstos*, "song of return," as one type of tale, parallel to the *aristeía*, "song of a hero's battle-exploits," so prominent in the *Iliad*. The *nóstos* theme is realized not only in the homecoming of Odysseus himself but also in passages recalling the homecomings of Agamemnon, Nestor, Meneláos, and other heroes of the Trojan War.

The Parry-Lord hypothesis about the oral-formulaic character of Homeric language and story construction leads to the wider conclusion that what we have of the tradition—the *Iliad* and the *Odyssey*—are at each level traditional. Meter, diction, themes, characters, and the basic story all have living roots deep in the tradition. What has led to some confusion is the modern preconception that what is traditional is not shaped by a mind with a view to producing art but merely tends to reproduce received knowledge. In answer to such a pedestrian view of the vitality of this traditional medium, it can be said that Homeric language is an "art language" within and because of its traditional features but that, in the words of one critic, "the art language cannot compose for the poet" (Nagler 61). The language of meter, formula, phrase, and theme provide what any language provides its speakers: units of discourse fraught with such connotations and associations as to allow meaningful utterances between speakers—in the oral-poetic context, between singer and audience. The traditional nature of these elements in Homeric song gives rise to and reinforces the audience's familiarity with the medium, and this can in turn encourage great inventiveness in a particular singer's management of the elements, since he can be sure that his audience fully understands the basic nature of his composition.

The consequences of Parry's conclusions are being felt even to this day, though not without controversy as to their exact bearing. What he discovered is crucial to a reading of the translation in this book, whose main claim is its sensitivity to the oral-formulaic medium, by virtue of which it tries to re-create as far as possible the poetic conditions of the *Odyssey*'s original performance. In "Translating Homeric Song," the translator discusses this formulaic method of composition in somewhat more detail and tells how he has responded to the high degree of repetition inherent in this medium, including the way it can reinforce the narrative structure of this long and complex work by means of "musical" echoes. The more one reads the epic, the more one admires the singer's virtuosity and subtlety in using these traditional elements to make a song as accomplished as any novelist's work in its exploration of characters and situations.

Transmission

The original audiences of Homeric epic would surely have appreciated the aptness of the singer's combination of phrase, rhythm, theme, and tale to compose (literally, to "put together") a song; sensitized to the medium from childhood, singers and audiences alike could respond as readily to such matters as can contemporary Balinese villagers to a shadow-puppet master's virtuosity in presenting his age-old stories to them in word, image, and music. The epic scope of the songs must have motivated some of these listeners to preserve and transmit them. But how did these monumental works reach their present state? How did they come to be written down? Scholars still do not agree on responses to these questions, but new and persuasive ideas are emerging.

One reason for disagreement is the murky history of the period succeeding the events narrated in the poems. After the fall of the Mycenaean palace cultures and the destruction of Troy, from the end of the twelfth century to the beginning of the eighth, Greek civilization crosses the period that historians call the Dark Ages because of what appears to be a general decline in cultural vitality. Instead of featuring the large palaces of Agamemnon's Mycenae and Nestor's Pylos, where scribes kept records of palace accounts and where royal functionaries administered the organization of the palace and the surrounding community, life in the Dark Ages was lived in small communities for whom writing seems not to have existed and grand social systems were only a memory.

Yet communities still existed, as did culture, however insensitive our historical instruments are in measuring it. Indeed, in maintaining the tradition, the Greeks who lived in that period made the next stage possible. Beginning in the eighth century B.C., there occurs a renaissance, called the Archaic period in most historical accounts, which stretches roughly to the end of the sixth century. This period sees many changes: a rise in population, especially marked by increasing emigration from the established centers; a growing challenge to older forms of social organization by a new social structure, the polis, or city-state, which allowed increased numbers of people to live together; a corresponding increase in the tempo of colonization in places as far apart as Massilia (present-day Marseilles), Syracuse in Sicily, and Asia Minor, providing homes and sustenance for the burgeoning numbers; and the development of such cultural institutions as the Olympian Games and other festivals, which gave coherence to these scattered Greek settlements. The Homeric epics play a crucial role in this new world. Like the rise of the polis and the adoption of a common Greek alphabet, these works are a hallmark of Panhellenism, the sense that all Greeks belong to the same cultural world despite their separation in space. Just as the establishment of the polis marks an achievement of archaic Greek social organization, so Homeric narrative is the supreme achievement of early Greek poetic artistry. All Greeks, from city to city and from region to region, readily saw Homer as belonging to Hellas, which they accordingly perceived as a cultural unity.

From our modern perspective, the Archaic period is the foundation for the Classical period (490–323), with which we are most familiar. For Panhellenism enabled the city-states to see themselves as part of a unified, if varied, social structure. Thus, when toward the end of the sixth century the Persians seek to destabilize Greece, the Ionian cities of Asia Minor, with some help from Athens, join in an unsuccessful revolt against the empire (499–494 B.C.). But when in the next generation the Great King Xerxes launches a massive and determined invasion, he is defeated by contingents from thirty-one city-states (480–479). The alliance that emerges (the Delian League) finally works to Athenian advantage, especially by accumulating in its leading city, Athens, the wealth that makes possible the achievments of her great age. Under these circumstances arise the hallmarks of Athenian society: the splendid architectural monuments on and around the Acropolis, the state-sponsored theater (tragedy and comedy), the philosophical thought of the sophists and Socrates, the brilliant beginnings of prose history (Herodotus and Thucydides), and, conditioning all of them, the startling Athenian experiment in social organization that the Greeks themselves name *demokra-tia*, democracy. Athens stands out because its great achievements bring to fruition the development we have been describing. For the tragedians in the fifth century, Odysseus, Achilles, Agamemnon, Helen, and the other figures of Archaic art and narrative are still—some 600 years after the fall of Troy—the focal points for thought about power and love, sorrow and joy, despair and hope.

After these heady times came a period of strife, the Peloponnesian War, one of whose major results was to transform the power structure of the Greek world and open the way for its conquest by rulers from the provincial north, Philip II and his son, Alexander the Great of Macedonia. Alexander's military prowess, inspired as it partly was by his admiration of the Homeric hero Achilles, led to a territorial expansion that enlarged yet further the scope of Panhellenism, from North Africa through the vast territories of the former Persian Empire and as far as northwest India. It also resulted in the seemingly paradoxical fact that we owe much of our information on the epics to a city far distant from the Greek homeland, Alexandria in Egypt, and to the scholars in the great ancient library there. The very cognomens of these scholars—Zenodotos of Ephesus (in Asia Minor), Aristophanes of Byzantium (modern Istanbul), Aristarchos of Samothrace (an island in the northern Aegean Sea)—betoken the movement from the Greek north to the Egyptian south. These men were just as intent on preserving the great epic tradition as their predecessors and contemporaries in Athens were, and they labored indefatigably to keep it "genuine" as they understood it, even launching the habit of distinguishing the "true Homer" from "interpolations" or "accretions."

This history offers a range of hints concerning the recording and preservation of the *Odyssey* as we know it. One possibility often suggested is that the new technology of writing was responsible. According to the theory of the "oral dictated text," our text of the poem originated, perhaps in the middle to late eighth century B.C., when an amanuensis patiently recorded a master singer's long performance of the Odyssean story. This text is then presumed to have been passed down through the Athens of the sixth century B.C. to scholars of the third and second centuries B.C. in Athens, Alexandria, Pergamon, and elsewhere, who did much critical work on the text, codified it, and handed it down to the compilers of the surviving medieval manuscripts that are our main sources, supplemented by some ancient papyrus fragments and citations in ancient authors.

Another school of thought insists on the primacy of the text commissioned by the Athenian tyrant, Peisistratos (d. 527). On this view our text is ultimately based on this version, one of this ambitious ruler's many public and artistic projects. Later, even more decisively, Hipparchos (d. 514), Peisistratos' son and successor, decreed that the Homeric poems be recited in order in relays by reciters called "rhapsodes" at every yearly celebration of the Panathenaic Festival. This tidy approach usually assumes that writing, now a firm part of the cultural landscape, helped produce a stable Athenian version, which was passed down through the later critics to become essentially the poem we have now.

In perhaps the most creative theory, Gregory Nagy proposes an evolutionary model to account for what he thinks must have been a lengthy process, from oral song to fixed text. Such a model takes fully into account the importance of the Panhellenism we noted earlier and gathers under its wings the other features we see by positing different stages in the development of our text across the traditional historical periods. The following five steps from fluid oral performance to rigid text are based on Nagy's account of his research (*Homeric Questions* 42; cf. also *Poetry as Performance*):

1. An oral period when live performances by singers, with no written text, vitally produced myriad versions of the *Iliad*, the *Odyssey*, and other songs like them—including the poems of the so-called Epic Cycle—concerning the Trojan War, as well as epics about Jason and the Argonauts and other subjects from Greek mythology. These performances could have been of whatever length the singer, his audience, and the circumstances required, from an hour's entertainment to large-scale recitations over perhaps several days.

2. A Panhellenic period, from the eighth to the mid–sixth century, when social forces were drawing together the local Greek traditions and when the performances of singers or reciters all over the Greek world inspired a demand for Homeric poetry, as far-flung listeners began to feel that their participation in such manifestations of Hellenic culture would be validated by hearing authoritative Panhellenic versions.

3. A definitive, or "transcript," period, from the middle of the sixth century (the time of the Peisistratean Rescension and the decrees of Hipparchos in Athens) through the later fourth century, when transcriptions of performances of the *Iliad* and *Odyssey* played a part and when rhapsodes would use transcripts as supplements to oral recitation, especially at great festivals like the Panathenaia.

4. A standardizing, or "script," period, from the end of the fourth century, when Demetrios of Phalerum reformed Homeric performance in Athens, to the middle of the second century, when Homeric performances would have been based on authoritative texts that tended more and more toward uniformity. To this period belong the initial Alexandrian attempts to make definitive written texts of the two main epics.

5. A "scripture" period, from the middle of the second century, when Arist-
archos completed his work on the Homeric texts. The Alexandrian editions
and others from Greece and Asia Minor made the epics into fixed texts copied
and recopied for schools and other public institutions all over the Greek-
speaking world; these formed the basis for the medieval manuscripts on which
our texts are based.

Such a scheme will not satisfy the positivist's desire for Homeric dates, for the
facts of publication of our *Odyssey*. An evolutionary model proposes for Homer
what such a model proposes for nature, an overall pattern of development—we
know or think we know the oral beginning and the fixed text at the end, but the
middle is out of focus. Where do we place the minds that made the astounding
artifacts we possess? Do we place them in the age before writing was widely prac-
ticed, or after writing became the civilized norm? To some extent, the model al-
lows the partisans of writing to sit Homer at a desk with pen in hand, since the
narrative might have undergone "literate" sorts of manipulation at the time it
was written down. But the evolutionary model makes it more likely that the
Homeric tradition was fortunate in taking shape, substantially as we see it em-
bodied in the two great epics, before it disappeared into the major cultural de-
velopments that led to the Classical period—most importantly, the unification of
Greek culture known as Panhellenism and its cultural flowerings in the poleis,
or city-states, where writing was firmly established. Homer anticipated the po-
lis, and in fact, the polis recognized Homer as its ancestor. Thus, though the
phrase *oral text* may seem a contradiction in terms, it captures the movement
from oral tradition to scripture that seems to have occurred.

READING THIS *ODYSSEY*: RE-CREATING THE PERFORMANCE

The Homeric poems, once purely oral, became over time the text whose transla-
tion you hold in your hand. In a real sense, that text, especially when read aloud
and listened to (as the translator strongly recommends for this version), is a per-
formance—the only kind left to us from the ruins of history. Though, like many
Greek lyrics, the *Odyssey* is only a fragment of a large body of traditional material,
it is a whole as a performance on its own, showing the unity and uniqueness that
Albert Lord ascribed to the performance of oral texts: "The author of an oral epic,
that is, the text of a performance, is the performer, the singer before us. . . . A per-
formance is unique; it is a creation, not a reproduction, and it can therefore have
only one author" (Lord 101–2). The *Odyssey* can best be considered, then, as a per-
formance; here, the diehard partisan of writing and the advocate of fluid orality can
find common ground, asking what distinguishes this particular performance.

As Gregory Nagy (*Homeric Questions* 111–12) has put it, the "Homer" who is a culture hero of Hellenism and the great teacher and who comes to life in every performance of the poem is our consolation for our ignorance of the author. Even beyond accepting it as mere solace, however, we might welcome such a solution, since the question of the author has been such a problem, plaguing almost every text, from Gilgamesh and the Bible to Shakespeare and Joyce. Consider the varying endings for *Great Expectations*, the revisions of Yeats' poems, or the questions raised by a work so intertwined with its author's life as is Proust's *Remembrance of Things Past*. What were the respective authors' "intentions"? Will knowing or guessing those intentions aid our understanding or cloud it? Even the magisterial *Aeneid* comes to us with the knowledge that its author, Virgil, wanted it destroyed. Thus, the authorial problem dogs us even—and perhaps especially—when birth certificates, diaries, biographies, and a wealth of detail make it possible to pinpoint the authors in space and time, when we can make reasonable inferences about how they lived and what they thought. Perhaps the modern reader of Homeric epic is at least absolved of the authorial problem.

Nonetheless, the performer of a Homeric song is the functional equivalent of its author, so this creature, whom we may as well call "Homer," remains a kind of controlling mind that selects and orders the traditional material to create this performance, even as Odysseus performs this role for the Phaiákians in recounting his adventures. As Albert Lord has shown (68–98), as we learn more about oral traditions now and in the past, we can see that oral performers can be identified as individuals by such features as their particular use of themes—each performer has his or her own performance style. In what follows, we will look at some of the significant features of this *Odyssey* that distinguish the performance that is our text. While the main story of the return of Odysseus is traditional, every performer will both select certain features for emphasis and use additive techniques—repetition of situations (e.g., feasting or sailing a ship) or of similar characters (e.g., women, crew members, or monsters) to convey a particular slant on the tale. By examining the ways such techniques are used within the traditional narrative grammar, we can reach some conclusions about the significance of this *Odyssey*.

First, let us consider the core story of the return of the ancient Greek warrior and hero Odysseus from the destruction of Troy to his home on the island of Ithaca. Like any tale, it can be told in chronological order. After the Achaians destroy Troy, the Greek warriors who have survived the ten years of war strive to make their way home. Some of them, such as Meneláos and Nestor, return safely to their homes; others, such as Ajax, meet their end on the way back; and in the case of Agamemnon, the return culminates in treachery at home, when he is slain by his wife, Klýtaimnéstra, and her paramour, Aigísthos, who have usurped his throne. Odysseus' return is obstructed by encounters with such monsters as the Cyklops, Skylla and Charýbdis, and the Laistrygonians, and by temptations to stay abroad offered by the Lotus-eaters, Circè, Kalýpso, and the Phaiákians. His very life is threatened by the gods—especially Poseidon, who is wrathful because Odysseus blinds his son, Polyphémos, the Cyklops—and he loses all his comrades. In his absence, his wife, Penelope, barely keeps at bay the young men from Ithaka and the surrounding islands who are courting her. His son, Telémachos, smolders with impotent resentment, but acting on Athena's advice, he journeys to Pylos and Sparta to seek news of his father, discovers that he is alive, and returns, escaping an ambush set by the suitors. Finally, Odysseus, with the help of the goddess Athena and the friendly Phaiákians, in whose country he is cast on shore, achieves passage home to Ithaka and meets the loyal swineherd Eumaíos and Telémachos. But he finds the suitors in his palace, assuming that his disappearance will force Penelope to marry one of them. In disguise as a beggar, Odysseus scouts out the situation and takes advantage of a contest that Penelope sets for her hand in marriage, so that, armed and aided by loyal servants and Telémachos, he defeats and slays the suitors. Odysseus and Penelope, now reunited, are still threatened by the vengeance-seeking relatives of the suitors, but Athena and Zeus decree a truce between the feuding factions.

This account of Odysseus' return summarizes the tale much in the way that Odysseus himself tells his story to the Phaiákians in books 9–12, beginning with the fall of Troy and relating his sea adventures until he arrives at Scheria, the Phaiákians' home. But the Homeric *Odyssey* that has compelled attention for three millennia does not begin at the chronological beginning. Indeed, each performer in a tradition faces his or her first challenge in selecting a clear "beginning" from a tradition of multiple versions of any given tale. On this performance occasion, this particular *Odyssey* puts us into the middle of the story, or, as the Roman poet and critic Horace styled it, "in medias res" [into the middle of things] (*Ars poetica* 148). It then elaborates the story so as to highlight certain features of the hero's return, features that complicate and deepen our experience of the traditional tale.

Tradition is far from merely a lockstep set of narratives repeated endlessly until some bard innovates or until a restive audience finally stops listening. It is hard for modern readers to understand that tradition is not just a holding place for the repertoire of narratives used by traditional poets in their own compositions. It includes the means by which those stories are shaped: the selection of what needs to be used in a given context; the ordering or arrangement of the items selected in ways that point to certain kinds of meanings; and the repetition of some items to heighten those meanings. The result—the composition in performance of a version of the traditional story—rewards both performer and audience for their long training in habits of listening.

Before we further consider selection and repetition of narrative and thematic elements, a note on the work's manifest structure can bring us nearer to its actual performance. Any discussion of an oral poem's structure needs to take account of this problem, for an epic as long as the *Odyssey* probably would not have been performed in one sitting. It is unlikely that any audience, even an ancient Greek one, would want to sit and listen for the eighteen to twenty continuous hours that singing or reciting this whole epic might require. Indeed, Aelian, a writer of late antiquity, says that at an early stage, the poems were sung in much shorter episodes—"The Happenings in Pylos," "The Story of the Cyklops"— which were collected to make the epics (see Nagy, *Homeric Questions* 78). This is perhaps a reminiscence of the fluid oral state, when a singer could choose what he thought appropriate from a vast body of tales—as Penelope says in book 1, asking Phemios to change his subject from the returns of the Achaians.

> Phemios, since you know much else that to men is enchanting,
> deeds both of gods and of mortals, that bards make famous in story,
> sing them now one of those . . .
>
> (1.337–39)

But any time there was an extended performance of the *Odyssey* (e.g., at a festival), there must have been multiple internally coherent sessions making it up. Indeed, as we shall see, the epic can be divided into six roughly equal four-book sections, each of them comfortably performable in one sitting.

In the translator's audio performance of the translation in this book, the recitation of the four-book sections takes around two and a half hours each (more precisely, between two hours and twelve minutes for the shortest section, books 5–8, and two hours and fifty-two minutes for the longest, books 9–12). Reciting the Greek original would probably take somewhat longer. Moreover, music would add more to the performance time. We know that other epic traditions make use of music in their performances. For example, in the Russian *bylina*, a medieval tradition from Kiev, melodies played an important part. So too the South Slavic traditions that Parry and Lord studied had musical accompaniment. In the *Odyssey*, both Phemios, performing at the court of Odysseus in books 1 and 17, and Demódokos, the blind singer performing at the court of the Phaiákians in book 8, have lyres in their hands as they sit to compose their songs. Though no historical verification is possible, these scenes suggest Greek oral performance—at the very least, the portrayal of these two bards is consistent with what the early audiences of our *Odyssey* must have considered authentic. Without knowing the music to Homeric song, we cannot know if it was simple accompaniment, if musical elaboration was used to mark transitions, or even if the epic text was performed in recitative mode, as a song, or as words spoken with the barest musical accompaniment. But there is much fertile ground, especially through comparative evidence from the world's cultures, for speculation as to the part that music might have originally played in a Greek oral performance. It can at least be said that musical interludes may have lengthened a performance session and that singing a text usually takes longer than reciting it.

As for the sections themselves, it has until recently been common to assume that the "books" of our *Odyssey* were divisions made in the ancient library at Alexandria as our written manuscripts were taking shape in the second century B.C. But performance complicates and enriches the question. Many scholars now are studying the book divisions as perhaps deriving from performance contexts that may not be recoverable but that have nonetheless left their mark on the structure of our text. In the spirit of such speculation, let us turn to the structure of the *Odyssey* as a whole to see how thinking about such a six-part performance division can help make the poem coherent for us. We can envision the actual performance as taking place in these six sessions, perhaps over two or three days, between which there would be breaks for eating, for sleeping, and for other festive events. Each session would probably last between three and four hours. Here is a rough sketch of the six sections, with titles for reference.

Books 1–4. The Telemacheia
After the proem and a council of gods, Athena rouses Telémachos, who reproves the suitors both in the palace and in assembly; he then travels to Pylos and Sparta and questions Nestor and Meneláos concerning his father's return; both tell him lengthy stories. The suitors plan to ambush Telémachos; Penelope grieves.

Books 5–8. From Ogygia to Scheria
Acting on the gods' orders, Kalýpso sends Odysseus from Ogygia on a raft; after a storm, he arrives in Scheria and meets Naúsikaä, daughter of the Phaiákian king Alkínoös. She escorts him to the palace, where he receives hospitality from the king and his wife, Arétè—feasts, songs, and athletic contests.

Books 9–12. The Adventures of Odysseus
While on Scheria, Odysseus relates to the Phaiákians his adventures before arriving at Ogygia, involving the Kikonians, the Lotus-eaters, the Cyklops, Aíolos, the Laistrygonians, Circè, Hades' domain (the realm of the dead), the Sirens, Skylla and Charýbdis, the cattle of the sun on Thrinakia, and the final shipwreck.

Books 13–16. At the Farm of Eumaíos
Having been conveyed by the Phaiákians, Odysseus lands on Ithaka; stays with the swineherd Eumaíos and exchanges stories with him; meets Telémachos, who

has escaped from the suitors' ambush on his way home; and makes plans with Athena to punish the suitors.

Books 17–20. The Beggar in the Palace
Odysseus, disguised as a beggar, goes to his palace with Telémachos and Eumaíos and suffers abuse from the suitors and others. He is recognized by Eurykleía and, while disguised, talks to Penelope about himself, her troubles, and a prophetic dream she has had.

Books 21–24. Requital, Reunion, Resolution
Penelope sets up the contest of Odysseus' bow for the suitors, and Odysseus, with help, slaughters them, reunites with his wife, reveals himself to his father, and faces the vengeful wrath of the suitors' relatives; Zeus and Athena impose an end to the conflict.

This bare-bones summary cannot begin to convey the rich variety of incident and character in the *Odyssey* or the shifts in scenes that occur within each part, but it can be useful in showing how the singer of this epic structured his narrative and why he began it where he did. In this performance, "the middle of things" means the time when Odysseus is grief-stricken on the island of Ogygia and about to return home and when his wife and maturing son no longer find the conditions in the palace in Ithaka tolerable. By beginning here, the singer raises strong interest. How did Odysseus' long absence and the dreadful situation in Ithaka come to be? What will be the outcome of the tensions portrayed? From there, it goes forward in time for two sessions, the first one relating Telémachos' travels, the second one telling the final part of Odysseus' travels, beginning with the last days of his seven-year sojourn with Kalýpso.

But within the first session, we already see the flashback technique, first in book 2, when the suitors defend their long presence in the palace by telling of Penelope's deceptive evasions, then in books 3 and 4, when Nestor and Meneláos tell of their own voyages home, their *nóstoi*. The latter accounts give perspective to Odysseus' much longer story of his adventures in the third section, for the other returns occur in the known world, even if with occasional supernatural interventions. Odysseus' complete account of his wanderings, beginning as Nestor and Meneláos did at the end of the Trojan War, explains how he finds himself in the twentieth year still far from home. The last three parts of the epic can then proceed directly forward, bringing the strands of the plot together and building to the destruction of the suitors and its aftermath. Now we are back in Ithaka with a complete understanding of the situation and of the states of mind of all the major actors.

The preceding summary also points to the versatility of the performance in modulating between the "ordinary" events on Ithaka and fantastic events as told in the Adventures. A similar vitality carries the performance from the high context of the ceremonious feasting and guest-friendship in the palaces to the humble hospitality of Eumaíos' hut, where the same social values appear among the peasantry. Moreover, these divisions suggest that, though the epic is continuous from one section to the next, an audience would have a different poetic experience in each session of the performance. Thus, they would think of each as a provisional unity, much as we think of the parts of a serial—for example, the installments of one of Dickens' novels as originally published, the operas in Wagner's *Ring* cycle, or even the episodes of a television sitcom or soap opera. One can easily imagine that moments of suspense ("cliff-hangers") provided a kind of transition between one section of a performance and another.

These six sections also provide for the coherent development of important themes of the work, so that listeners would come to each successive performance session prepared for learning something new about the various themes or for seeing them in a new light. We might compare these compositional procedures to those of our classical music, in which musical matter first appears in an exposition, then undergoes development to bring out its harmonic and rhythmic implications, and reappears finally in a recapitulation, a restatement deeply informed by all that the development has unveiled in it. In this epic, of course, this matter is narrative and thematic, and the performer's techniques of selection, arrangement, and additive repetition allow listeners to understand progressively its layers of resonance, its larger potential meanings. As we look at the overall form, we can see that, as in a musical composition, the "exposition" in books 1–4 of the *Odyssey* presents each theme in a normal setting, that is, in the world such as we can all experience it either at home or nearby. The themes themselves have this same character. The "development" occurs largely in a world quite outside of ours, where everything encountered is at extremes—the utopias of Ogygia and Scheria, the horrors of the Cyklops' cave and the Laistrygonians' country. As these settings help us understand our own, so the themes also reveal their potential by being taken to extremes. It is as if a composer took his or her basic statement of musical matter and explored it by slowing it down, speeding it up, and putting it through harmonic convolutions and melodic inversions. Then, the "recapitulation" of the *Odyssey* happens back in the "real world," in Ithaka, in books 13–24, where we see the same thematic elements as presented in the first books, again in "normal" form, yet greatly enriched, with their implications brought out by the development they have undergone in the "fantasy world."

Here, we can only begin to suggest the wealth of thematic meanings in this performance. To do so, we shall focus on three "themes," of three different sorts: (1) the theme of hospitality (in Greek, *xenía*), which has to do with typical situations, or "type scenes," in which any and all of the characters participate in one way or another (this goes to the ethical center of the poem); (2) the use of female characters to define the way gender affects the hero's striving and the issues with which the epic deals; (3) storytelling as showing most directly how the *Odyssey* singer's techniques work out certain themes according to the principles we have already discussed, by selection, arrangement, and repetition. For each of these topics, we can only suggest how the six sections add to the listener's understanding and total experience, leaving it to those who read or listen to the epic to work them out in greater detail and to find other, perhaps even more suggestive and interesting ways of seeing these themes and others. The *Odyssey* is far too rich to be interpreted finally by any one commentator.

Xenía

In Greek legend, the Trojan War originated when Paris, the Trojan prince, induced Helen to accompany him back to Troy, deserting her husband, Meneláos and thereby instigating the alliance among the Greek princes to recover her. This act of Helen and Pairs desecrated two hallowed institutions—most obviously, to our eyes, the marriage of Meneláos and Helen. But the other crime was equally if not more troubling to the Homeric Greeks: the violation of guest-friendship, in Greek, *xenía*. Paris was the guest of Helen's husband when the fateful liaison began, and the violation was more than a matter of etiquette or custom: to the society presented in the Homeric texts, the institution of guest-friendship is as fundamental as marriage for regulating social relations. Though many cultures have rituals associated with the relationship between guest and host, the reciprocal relationship of guest-friendship is structured in a unique manner in early Greek society, as Moses Finley and other scholars have shown. This institution is so ubiquitous in the *Odyssey* as to make it seem that our performance sets out to explore the subject comprehensively. In particular, the suitors' threat to Odysseus' household, as to his marriage, is a test case for the significance of this social practice.

The Greek word meaning "guest," *xénos*, also means "stranger" and "friend," showing the cultural complexity of the corresponding institution, *xenía*. For us readers of Homer, it is important to see how this institution plays out in the narrative. From the opening of the Telemacheia to the death of the last suitor, guest-friendship is portrayed as an ideal human relationship that one violates only at great peril. And each of our six performance sessions puts the theme in a new light, displaying remarkably well the classical pattern of exposition, development, and recapitulation with added complexity.

In the first session, the Telemacheia (books 1–4), our performance gives a clear exposition of the theme, with preliminary development, in three different locales:

Ithaka, Pylos, and Sparta. The very first scene on earth, when Athena arrives in Ithaka in the form of Mentes, chief of the Taphians, presents the basic elements of guest-friendship: the host, Telémachos, acknowledges the guest, welcomes him, then offers tokens of hospitality, which here, as oftentimes, include being seated, feasted, and entertained by a singer. Only then can the question of identity come up. This part of the custom is neatly summarized in Telémachos' first words: "Welcome, stranger—with us you will have kind greeting, and only / when you have eaten a meal shall you tell what you are in need of" (1.123–24). Then, at parting, Telémachos offers a guest-gift as a token of the relationship, with the understanding that his guest has a reciprocal obligation to become the host in turn at some future date, when the roles will be enacted again in reverse. Here, "Mentes" declines it, but in doing so, he explicitly recognizes the mutuality of the relationship: he will accept it on his way back home, and "it will bring an exchange to be valued" (1.318). The entire sequence gives coherence to social relationships beyond the familial bonds within the household. Thus, one's guest-friend is part of a network of such people whose relationships cross both space (household to household, territory to territory) and time (generation to generation).

The importance of such an engine of social cohesion is powerfully invoked throughout the *Odyssey*, as much as the familial bonds among Penelope, Telémachos, and Odysseus. In the additive style of Homeric narrative, books 3 and 4 extend this exposition of the pattern already discussed: in them, guest-friendship institutes a bond between the son of Odysseus and the latter's comrades from the Trojan campaign. At the very beginning of book 3, Telémachos shows his inexperience by his shyness on approaching the household of Nestor in Pylos. He need not have worried, as Athena (now in the form of Mentor) advises him, for "[s]eeing the strangers arrive, they all came crowding around them, / held out welcoming hands, and invited them both to be seated" (3.34–35)—the custom ensures a welcome even for strangers. After Peisístratos, Nestor's son, seats them, the guests are given food and drink, and only after they have been hospitably treated does Nestor, their host, ask, "Strangers, who are you?" (3.71). After more hospitality and a sacrifice, Nestor sends Telémachos on his way to Sparta in a chariot with his son Peisístratos as his companion—not explicitly a guest-gift, but a signal extension of his welcome and the first occurrence of an important facet of the theme: a good host helps his guest continue his journey.

Thus, in the Telemacheia, guest-friendship functions as a kind of rite of passage, as Telémachos engages in the guest-host relationship with the previous generation, that of his father. So, in Sparta, we can expect to see the ritual enacted once again. But here, our performance develops the presentation of the ritual, for Eteóneus, a court attendant, sees the approaching guests and asks Meneláos whether they should be sent away or not (4.20–29). "Sorely displeased" at this question (4.30), Meneláos offers a poignant reason for observing the custom.

> Certainly Helen and I ate many hospitable dinners
> others provided for us as we came here, hoping that Zeus would
> sometime soon put an end to our grief. Unharness the strangers'
> horses, and bring the men into the hall to partake of the feasting.
>
> (4.33–36)

As we have seen, the original violation of Meneláos' marriage was accompanied by a violation of *xenía*, and the couple have relied on the institution in their voyage homeward. Thus, Meneláos wants all conventions adhered to, and from lines 37 on in book 4, the guest-friendship ritual is enacted: the guests are led to the house, bathed, placed on chairs, and given food, and the all-important point concerning the inquiry as to identity is stressed by the host: "when you have finished / eating your fill of the meal, we will ask you who among mankind / both of you are" (4.60–62). In the event, however, Meneláos mentions Odysseus seemingly in passing, bringing Telémachos to tears; then Helen enters (4.120–37) and also guesses that this young man might be Odysseus' son (4.138–46), a fact that Peisístratos confirms. This elaborated version of the motif of the guest revealing his name after dining depends on the understanding of the custom already established in this performance. The ritual, in other words, is put to poetic work by the singer.

Another aspect of this theme given strong exposition in the first performance session is its violation by the suitors who eat up their host's possessions by staying in his house as permanent "guests." Their excuse for this excess, given especially in the assembly Telémachos calls in book 2, is that even though Odysseus must surely be lost, Penelope refuses to choose a new husband. One of the suitors, Antínoös, tells the famous story of the shroud that Penelope wove and unwove to delay her decision (2.85–128). But no such reason can offset the blatant disregard of reciprocity in their actions; they never propose any compensation, as Telémachos complains—"with never a thought about payment" (1.377)— in a passage in book 1 that is repeated verbatim in book 2 (1.375–80 = 2.140–45).

The poetic elaboration, or development, of *xenía* continues even more strongly and in a more nuanced fashion in the next session (books 5–8), where we begin to hear of Odysseus' return home. Kalýpso has hosted Odysseus for seven years, providing lavishly for his wants and desires; but the situation does not meet the requirements of custom, because the host has been unwilling to let the guest go home. For a traditional return poem, the reluctance of the host to send the guest forward denies a salient assumption of the relationship—that the guest will leave the household and even be helped to depart, as Telémachos was by Nestor and will be by Meneláos, who later puts the assumption with aphoristic succinctness: "offer your love to a guest who is present and speed him at parting" (15.74). In this case, it takes the god Hermes, at Zeus's insistence, to make Kalýpso send Odysseus on his way.

A similar problem arises in the seeming utopia on Scheria. The threat to Odysseus' *nóstos* in that idyllic place is that he might not be given a conveyance to his home; he has to win his hosts' sympathy for his plight. This situation is played out against the background of guest-friendship ritual: after Naúsikaä comes across Odysseus shipwrecked on Scheria, she takes care of him—in effect, hosts him—and invites him into her parents' household. There, Odysseus is treated as a guest—dined and bathed, treated to games and songs—without being asked his name. This feature of the ritual is played on to great effect in this performance, for Odysseus is not asked for his identity until after the three songs of Demódokos, during two of which, concerning Odysseus' own past, his tears all but give him away to Alkínoös. This entire sequence, from Odysseus' encounter with Naúsikaä in book 6 to the end of book 8, is a variant of the ritual structure of guest-friendship, and it climaxes in book 9 with Odysseus' resounding declaration "I am Odysseus, the son of Laërtes" (9.19). The story of Odysseus in books 9–12 forms a kind of reciprocating "gift" to the Phaiákians, whom he has never seen before and will never see again. When the Phaiákians themselves convey Odysseus home with gifts, the requirements of the institution have been not only met but elaborated on in the grand Homeric style, especially the precept to "speed him at parting," which they take to its extreme—just as they do the lavish gift giving ("treasures of bronze and of gold in abundance and garments," 5.38, 13.136)—in a kind of wish fulfillment. But in effect, the return of Odysseus depends on the convention of reciprocity at the heart of Homeric culture.

This idealized version of guest-friendship is taken to the opposite extreme—even inverted—in the next session, The Adventures of Odysseus (books 9–12), especially in his encounter with the Cyklops. In this episode, we see clearly how important it is to attend to the culture-specific details concerning guest-friendship, for the institution seems violated in most of its important features. When they enter the cave of the Cyklops Polyphémos, the intruding Greeks take the Cyklops' food, eat it, and prepare to steal more, with Odysseus going so far as to say he would not be persuaded to leave, "not till I saw him and found whether he might give me some guest-gifts" (9.229). His conception of the relationship seems to have degenerated to mere acquisitiveness, not much higher, ethically, than the rapacity he recently unbridled in looting the Kikonians' country. Ironically, his actions here closely parallel those of the suitors, who are consuming his own substance without payment—and both sets of transgressors will suffer requital, Odysseus right away when his men are eaten, the suitors at the climax of the epic. When Polyphemos returns from his daily rounds, he finds the intruders, only to ask them immediately: "Strangers, who are you . . . ?" (9.252), thus violating the rule we saw so often earlier concerning the guest's name. In this instance, reciprocity seems to have become mutual rudeness.

That the issue of *xenía* concerns Odysseus becomes clear when—despite the fact that, even before he entered the Cyklops' cave, he knew he was about to meet a "savage, with no true knowledge of justice or civilized customs" (9.215)—he says to the "host" whose space he has violated:

> Come now, honor the gods, good man: we are suppliants asking.
> Zeus himself, the protector of suppliants, keeper of strangers,
> god of encounters, accompanies strangers to honor and guard them.
>
> (9.269–71)

Such a naïvely brazen demand could come only from a man who has not yet developed a sense of the deeply human significance of the custom, and only such a person could be surprised by the total refusal that follows (9.273–80). Indeed, the Cyklops' signature horror, his cannibalism, inverts the host's duties: instead of feeding his guests, he eats them. Finally, the ritual's concern with revealing the guest's identity also takes a subtle turn when Odysseus gets the Cyklops drunk and tells him, "Nobody is my name" (9.366), with consequences that are comic in part because this naming plays against the expected ritual action. In these and other features, the Cyklops episode takes the guest-friendship ritual to its negative extreme. Both host and guest stumble at every step.

Later on in this session, the ideal of guest-friendship also helps define the visit to the Lotus-eaters, during which eating—always an important feature of the host's entertainment—causes those who feed on the lotus to forget about home, thus symbolizing excessive hospitality. Something similar happens with Circè. Her initial reception of Odysseus' comrades shows a nearly Cyklopean violation of the custom, when she invites them in but gives them a drink that transforms their bodies into those of swine. Only the intervention of the god Hermes, who gives Odysseus the counterdrug moly, keeps her from visiting the same fate on the hero. But once Odysseus has "tamed" her, Circè displays a hospitality as excessive as the Lotus-eaters', allowing Odysseus and his men to stay on eating and drinking without any thought of a reciprocal obligation—unless Odysseus' sexual liaison with her could be considered such. They remain a whole year, until his comrades, less well supplied with fleshly pleasures, remind Odysseus of his purpose, to go home.

If Telémachos' voyages to Pylos and Sparta show the ideal of guest-friendship at the highest levels of society, the Scheria episode displays it as totally perfected, and the Cyklops episode shows it at its most dysfunctional, the encounter between Odysseus as beggar and Eumaíos in the fourth performance session (books 13–16) further develops the theme by displaying a humble but equally attractive version of this aristocratic institution. Though guest-friendship is idealized in the *Odyssey*, we can put it in historical context by pointing out that in democratic Athens, the institution was viewed with suspicion as a last holdout of aristocratic privilege. In this light, the *Odyssey*'s display of a fully functional guest-friendship between a beggar and a swineherd advances the ritual as good for everyone; as we shall show, it portrays the suitors as almost inhuman by contrast.

At the farm of Eumaíos, Odysseus becomes the guest, ironically, of his own slave. The pattern is familiar: Eumaíos sees the beggar (14.33–35), leads him to his cabin (14.45–48), seats him (14.49), welcomes him as a stranger and beggar who has the protection of Zeus (14.56–59; cf. what Odysseus said about Zeus in the Cyklops' cave, quoted earlier), and provides him a humble feast—"Eat now, stranger, the food that a servant is able to give you" (14.80)—all without asking his name or any other circumstances of his arrival. The reciprocity of the relationship between host and guest is then cemented, significantly, by the most extensive exchange of stories in the epic. Odysseus tells his story to identify himself, and Eumaíos later introduces his own story with a direct reference to their mutual pleasure: "we two now will enjoy each other's afflictions and sorrows / as we recall them" (15.399–400). Eumaíos understands that his enactment of guest-friendship differs from what the suitors are doing in Odysseus' household. Moreover, he joins their maltreatment of Penelope to their violations of the reciprocal bonds of guest-friendship:

> . . . they do not want in the proper
> manner to court his wife nor to go back home, but at ease they
> eat up his goods in arrogant wantonness, stopping at nothing . . .
> (14.90–92)

The contrast could not be more starkly put: the fundamental institution of guest-friendship is upheld between the lowly swineherd and his downtrodden guest, while it is abused by the elite in the palace of Odysseus.

In the recapitulation of the theme of *xenía* in the fifth performance session (books 17–20), we once more see the suitors' abuse of hospitality merged with their importunate courting of Penelope. But another element becomes even more prominent, for while the suitors only neglected "Mentes" in book 1, they here descend to outright abuse of Odysseus as beggar. Thus, they transgress against the hero in two different but complementary ways, both defined by the institution of *xenía*. The *Odyssey* has prepared us well to evaluate the suitors by the standards, positive and negative, developed in the earlier sessions. We see that the suitors' behavior is in harmony with that of the Cyklops and dissonant with the idealized behavior of the Phaiákian royal household. The greeting that the beggar gets from Antínoös in book 17, for example, presents exactly the kind of behavior toward guests that at the beginning of book 4 Meneláos abhorred when Eteóneus offered to send the visiting youths onward. Antínoös chides poor Eumaíos for bringing the beggar to the door.

> Oh most notable swineherd, and why have you brought this fellow
> here to the city? Are there not vagrants enough for us, other
> wretched importunate beggars who scavenge at meals and defile them?
> Or do you take it so lightly that men are devouring your master's
> livelihood, gathering here, and invite this man in addition?
>
> (17.375–79)

Antínoös here compounds his violation of the Greek rules of hospitality by citing them to criticize Eumaíos and the beggar even as he acknowledges his own excesses against Odysseus' household.

Telémachos rightly takes umbrage at Antínoös' behavior, and as he did earlier with Athena/Mentes, he orders that the "guest" be taken care of: "Take food; give to him; I do not grudge it; indeed, I command it." (17.400) This scene swiftly moves to its climax as Odysseus tells his lying tale about his high estate falling on bad times (17.415–44). Now occurs another strike against Antínoös, since he is not only a bad host but a bad hearer of tales, for he calls the beggar "this pain, this spoiler of dinner" (17.446) and rejects his request. Strike three comes when Antínoös hurls a stool at Odysseus and hits him on the back. The violence is of course a harbinger of the slaughter to come in book 22.

To make the violation even clearer in additive style, Homer gives another example in book 18—the entire scene, with some variation, is replayed again, with Eurýmachos taking over the aggressive role from Antínoös. In this case, Eurýmachos has taunted Odysseus with the perennial taunt of well-off people against the poor, "Get work!" (18.357–64). When Odysseus the beggar meets the challenge by claiming to be able to outwork and outfight the likes of Eurýmachos, he cannot—any more than he could when leaving the Cyklops—resist adding a taunt: "But if Odysseus should come and arrive in the land of his fathers, / quickly indeed would the doors, although in fact very broad ones, / be too narrow for you as you took flight out through the forecourt" (18.384–86). Just as Polyphémos hurled a boulder at the departing Odysseus, Eurýmachos, following Antínoös' lead, launches a footstool at Odysseus. But this time, in the manner of a Homeric battle scene, the missile misses its target and hits the wine server (18.394–98). An image from this sequence of inhospitable acts, "onto the ground fell clanging the pitcher"(18.397) reminds us of the dining ritual whose violation the suitors have been flaunting.

This motif has one more significant recurrence, in book 20, where a minor suitor, Ktesíppos, is seemingly introduced to show how clumsy one can be in treating the beggar (20.287–302). When he hurls an ox hoof (20.299), the stage is set for the final battle. Violations of guest-friendship have culminated in violence in the household.

The women in this part also illuminate the theme. One of them, the maid Melántho, who has been sleeping with the suitor Eurýmachos, illustrates the way servants can be perverted from their duties. She abuses Odysseus twice, first in book 18 (321–36), then in book 19 (66–69); both times, she directly violates the canons of hospitality by scolding the beggar for not going outside. Penelope, however, reinforces the customary ethic by expressing displeasure at the treatment of the beggar (17.492–94) and even reproving her son for allowing such foul acts (18.215–25)—though we in fact know that he has gone as far as he could to insure good treatment (17.400), given that his father has told him not to try to stop the suitors' abusive behavior (16.274–77). More positively, Penelope herself entertains the stranger; and though she does not go through the whole ritual before asking his name, one of its features—the offer of a bath—becomes the occasion for the nursemaid Eurykleía to recognize him from his scar when she washes his feet (19.357–475). Moreover, we see in the scene between Penelope and Odysseus as beggar the same reciprocity that we saw at Eumaíos' cabin: the two exchange stories, Penelope leading with the tale of the shroud she wove and unwove (19.124–63), thereby encouraging the "beggar" to tell her of himself, despite his reluctance.

In the next performance session (books 21–24), the suitors receive requital for their violations of *xenía*, as they are all slaughtered, avenged by the man they have been abusing by attacking his marriage, exhausting his household, and mistreating the "beggar." The performer of the *Odyssey* shows his individual power by producing a death for Antínoös symbolizing subtly but directly the suitors' transgressions.

Thus he [Odysseus] spoke; at Antínoös then he aimed a sharp arrow.
He was in fact just starting to lift up a beautiful goblet,
twin-eared, fashioned of gold—in his hands already he held it—
so he could drink of the wine; and he took no thought in his heart of
slaughter; for who could imagine that one sole man among many
men then banqueting there, even if he were mighty in power,
ever would bring upon him so evil a death and such black fate?
He was Odysseus' target—his throat he hit with the arrow
so that the point, penetrating the delicate neck, passed through it.
Off to the side he slumped, and the cup fell out of his hand . . .
(22.8–17)

This moment of truth is illuminated by the symbolic gold goblet: when Antínoös, about to drink from it, is cut down, the image draws together the frequent scenes of feasting throughout the epic, even as it recalls the downfall of the drunken Polyphémos. The arrow passes through his "delicate neck," grimly perpendicular to the course wine follows from gullet to belly. Finally, the beautiful Homeric touch in the phrase "the cup fell out of his hand" subtly points to the brutal fact that the suitors' way of being "guests" is at an end. The return of Odysseus means the restoration of decorous hospitality in the traditional manner.

Such restoration occurs especially in a triumphant final permutation of the theme, the recognition scene between Penelope and Odysseus, when the renewal of the marriage bond is accompanied by an affirmation of proper hospitality. Before Penelope is convinced of Odysses' identity, she gives him some of the defining features of the *xenía* ritual, a bath (by Eurýnomè, the housekeeper), good clothes to wear, and, above all, a place to sleep: the bed that he himself constructed is to be moved out of the chamber for him. The last gesture becomes the means by which his identity is confirmed, as he abandons his reserve and angrily tells the story of the bed's construction. So the observance of *xenía* becomes the catalyst for the couple's reunion, where the most intimate kind of reciprocity takes place—emphasized once again by an exchange of stories, she telling of her troubles and he of his travels (23.300–343).

There is even a sort of "coda" for this theme, a final brief restatement, when again we see Odysseus in a household of peasants, this time the farm of Dolios, where Laërtes has been living. Now the master mingles openly with his servants, yet the hospitality is just as unconstrained as it was when Eumaíos regarded him as a beggar. We even see a subtle and humorous treatment of the name-giving feature: when the servants recognize him, Odysseus tells Dolios to put his amazement out of his mind so that they can eat (24.394–96)—as if it is premature to worry about mere identity before the "ravenous belly" has been appeased. Needless to say, they ignore his order and welcome him heartily before they start the dinner. So we see an affirmation of hospitable concord just before the final scene, when it will take Zeus and Athena to impose peace on Odysseus and the relations of the suitors.

In these ways and in many others that readers can discover for themselves, the *Odyssey* highlights social harmony through one of its major defining institutions. Guest-friendship is as important to this vision of the return of Odysseus as is the marriage between Odysseus and Penelope. The theme goes straight to the heart of one of the Western world's central ethical principles: the respect that all people, regardless of origin or condition, should feel for each other simply on the basis of their common humanity. It falls outside the scope of this essay to discuss how far this is the revolutionary idea of our singer and how far it was implicit even in the aristocratic tradition of guest-friendship on which he drew. But there can be little doubt that the prominence of this performance in our own literary tradition has contributed mightily to the development of this principle of universal mutual respect, in Greek thought and in all that rose out of it. The society our singer portrays is not democratic; but one seed of democracy, we might hazard, was first planted on the swine farm of Eumaíos, where a master came on a servant who was at least his equal in the ethical humanity represented by the guest-friend relationship, and recognized his excellence.

Women

For many people, the *Odyssey* is so familiar a text that we might forget how surprising some of its features are. Most scholars would say that early epic, typified especially by the *Iliad*, puts men, warriors, in the major roles, but in this text Penelope, Athena, Circè, and even the nurse Eurykleía are at the heart of most readings. How should we conceive their function in an epic of a warrior's return from laying waste to a city? Our first attempt at understanding might begin by evaluating the female figures. Though some have tried to domesticate Penelope into merely a faithful wife, she dominates the motives central to Odysseus' return—his marriage, his continued kingship, and the order of the society he rules. Eurykleía's importance to Odysseus' return approaches that of Eumaíos the swineherd. Neither Circè nor Kalýpso, dread goddesses though they are, is demonized by the narrative. The "female" monsters, such as Skylla and Charýbdis, are right out of the cauldron of folk literature—they say as much about "women" as the Cyklops or the Laistrygonians say about "men," defining them only by negative extremes. The relationship between Athena and Odysseus is more complicated than that between any pair of male characters in this epic. So anyone trying to assess the role of women in the *Odyssey* needs to step carefully, not merely to avoid removing gender from its social context, "essentializing" it, but also to account for the vital complexity of the way Homeric narrative thinks about women, men, and the world they navigate together.

No reader can finish this poem without having confronted questions of gender, at least unconsciously. How do women relate to the men who, at least outwardly, dominate them? How do they carve out a space for themselves in this male world? How far, indeed, are they in control, despite appearances? Happily, the performance sessions that we hypothesize for the *Odyssey* can help bring some order to the answers we might tentatively give to these questions. Each of these sessions advances our sense of women's place and their peculiar kinds of consciousness. They help us to see progressively how men's sense of themselves depends largely on the women in their lives, even when they think they are operating quite alone.

The Telemacheia, as exposition of this material, presents a wide range of women, both divine and human: the goddesses Athena on Olympos and Eídothéa (who rescues Meneláos in book 4) in the sea, Penelope and Eurykleía in Ithaka, Helen in Sparta, and Helen's sister, Klýtaimnéstra, in Nestor's tale of wanderings. In book 1, Athena provides a pattern for mortal women by deferentially but firmly taking over the conversation from her father, Zeus, after he complains of the way men blame the gods for the consequences of their own recklessness. Not only does she turn the talk to the plight of her favorite Odysseus, but she imposes her agenda for rousing Telémachos and rescuing Odysseus.

However, when Athena descends to encounter Telémachos, she appears as an authoritative man, Mentes, chief of the Taphians; even if Telémachos eventually realizes who she is, her male form surely makes the advice she gives more palatable. It is also as a man, this time Mentor, that she accompanies Telémachos on his voyage to Pylos. Her male guise sets the keynote for this session, where we see men firmly in ultimate control, however clever or determined the women are. When Penelope in Ithaka tries to exercise authority by asking the singer Phemios to stop singing of the returns of the Achaians, a song that causes her sorrow by reminding her of her absent husband, she runs into the burgeoning male self-consciousness of her son, who rudely orders her back to her room: "The men will attend to the talking, / . . . I above all, since mine is the rule of the household" (1.358–59). Before this moment, Penelope has already discovered how helpless a woman can be in a male world, even when she has the intelligence to shape a situation to her desires. We see this in book 2 when the suitor Antínoös blames her for postponing the question of marriage and tells the famous story of the shroud she wove by day and unwove by night (2.85–128). This ruse worked for three years, but she was finally betrayed to the suitors by one of her own women—no doubt, one of those women who, we find out later, have been sleeping with the suitors—and she finished it "unwillingly, under compulsion" (2.110). Here we see also how the theme of male power as reinforced by the betrayal of a woman's natural allies, other women, is an ancient one.

The question of a woman's power to influence events is raised also by Eurykleía, "the old wise-counseling woman" (1.438), who in book 2 tries unsuccessfully to get Telémachos to renounce his journey; indeed, in later appearances also we see her trying, largely without success, to influence the menfolk. She shows the traditional role of women: persuasion is the only weapon they have, and their own notions of correct action, however wise, are usually ignored. Two other women, Klýtaimnéstra, the wife of Agamemnon, about whom we hear briefly in Nestor's story in book 3, and her sister Helen, the wife of Meneláos, who plays an important part in book 4, seem to have been more successful—destructively so—in their attempts to seize control. Yet in book 3 (255–75), Nestor elaborately tells the story of how Klýtaimnéstra was seduced by Agamemnon's murderer Aigísthos against her own excellent judgment—thus pointing directly to another way in which male dominance asserts itself. As we have already seen, Klýtaimnéstra's sister Helen takes us to the very center of the Homeric story, for Paris' violation of her marriage to Meneláos started these events in motion. She too was the victim of seduction, but in book 4, we see her at first in control of the situation—she identifies Telémachos; she throws a drug in the wine so that painful stories of the past can be told (4.219–26); and she begins the tales told to celebrate Odysseus, so she seems more successful than Penelope in shaping narrative choice. But as we shall show in more detail later, these stories convey something quite different from admiration for the absent hero; moreover, her husband has the "last word," telling how his own wife tried to betray him and the other Greeks to the Trojans when they were sitting in the wooden horse inside Troy. Taken together, the stories suggest how infatuation with a woman can override considerations of prudence and justice, for though Meneláos ostentatiously mourns for the comrades who died in the war, he has not renounced the woman for whose sake he made it all happen. He goes to some length to humiliate her before his youthful guests, however, thus flaunting his male superiority.

The female figures of the second performance session (books 5–8) take up some of these themes and develop them at the extremes such imaginary places allow, for Odysseus' fate there falls entirely into the hands of females. The goddess Kalýpso shows a woman in control of an unwilling mortal man, Odysseus— a reversal of the theme of male seduction—until the Olympians, at the instigation of Athena, intervene. Kalýpso then utters a lengthy complaint concerning just what a candid mortal woman might complain about their promiscuous husbands—how the male gods begrudge female goddesses their mortal consorts (5.118–28). Moreover, the god to whom Kalýpso must defer is not Athena, who has instigated the order, but Zeus, as both Hermes (5.103–4) and she herself (5.137–38) say in identical lines, thus affirming the hierarchy of power. Kalýpso also displays the other side of a Homeric woman's nature, its nurturing sympathy, since she helps Odysseus on his way despite her disappointment. This side appears again in the sea nymph Ino, who spontaneously gives Odysseus a scarf to save him as he swims from his wrecked raft to Scheria.

The other two women in this session, the mother and daughter Arétè and Naúsikaä, live in the idealized land of Scheria and present idealized patterns of how women and men can relate to each other in this world of desire, passing encounters, and power relationships. One of Homer's great triumphs is his success in conveying the charm of the daughter, a young girl just coming of age; there could be no better foil for the conniving Helen, the murderous Klýtaimnéstra, or even, at this point, the conflicted Penelope. By means of a dream, Athena sends

Naúsikaä to help Odysseus and to provide for his journey to the palace. In her generosity and beauty, Naúsikaä presents even more of a temptation to Odysseus—who devotes to her some of the loveliest lines of praise in all of literature (6.150–69)—than had Kalýpso, who had promised him youthful immortality; the girl's admiration of him makes the temptation even stronger. Yet like her equally admiring father, she gracefully eschews any attempt to hold him, once he has expressed his determination to return home. Arétè, however, shows to perfection how a strong and vital woman of experience can exercise real power while allowing her husband to keep his role. According to both her daughter (6.303–15) and Athena appearing as a young girl (7.48–77), Odysseus must direct his entreaties for conveyance to his home to Arétè, and the goddess tells how even men have their quarrels settled by the queen. She is the one who begins questioning the stranger and who instigates the giving of gifts. Yet, in every case, her husband gives the orders and has the outward authority. Thus, she models in human terms the paradigm set forth by Athena's management of Zeus in the proem (1.44–95).

Such paragons of Homeric womanhood—who excellently exemplify, at their different stages of life, the virtue called by the later Greeks *sophrosúne,* "temperance," or "self-control"—point to enduring ways of negotiating gender relationships. They show how the *Odyssey* gives us in additive manner example after example of the way life can be lived in a world where desire and sexual relationships constantly accompany the hero. In the next session (books 9–12), the female figures present the opposite extreme, male fantasies in which female figures dominate or destroy men. In Télepylós, some of Odysseus' comrades meet the "comely daughter" of the Laistrygonian king, who takes them to meet her mother, an enormous woman "as huge as the peak of a mountain," who calls home her cannibal husband, after which destruction promptly ensues for all of the galleys except that of Odysseus (10.103–32). This brief encounter has the quality of a nightmare, an enticing girl leading to a monstrous woman who betrays rather than nurtures.

The same sort of response is evoked by the most important encounter in this section, that with Circè, who transforms Odysseus' comrades into swine, while Odysseus himself can only resist her with the aid of the herb moly provided by Hermes. Yet Circè also shows, in dreamlike fashion, a male fantasy of how such a woman can be brought under control, in a scene as stark as any unreconstructed male chauvinist could wish for: Odysseus draws a sword and threatens her life, and she submits and invites him to bed. Afterward, she meekly releases his men from their enchantment and entertains them with feasting for a full year. Perhaps Odysseus' dramatic (though in actual fact easy) conquest of the goddess contributes to his willingness to remain on the island, forgetful of home, until his comrades remind him of his goal. At any rate, we see here the fantasy pattern of conquest of a powerful woman—even if the real power remains with the goddess. This discreetly ironic sense is confirmed at the end of book 10, when we see Circè providing Odysseus with full instructions for his trip to Hades' domain, and again in book 12, where she advises him at length on the rest of his trip homeward, including a strong admonition to leave the cattle of the sun uninjured.

The other female supernatural beings in this section have little bearing on women in the world, but they luridly represent male fears. The Sirens' song has in our world come to symbolize the temptation to yield to the attractions of destructive females, though in the case of Odysseus, it represents more the possibility of limitless knowledge ("we know all that is on the much nourishing earth generated," 12.191). Even so, it is significant that this lure is presented as a feminine distraction from the male business of getting on with a voyage. Then come two figures quite at the opposite extreme of self-presentation from the enticing Sirens: Charýbdis is the goddess of a whirlpool that threatens to swallow up hapless mariners ship and all, while Skylla is a six-headed monster who seizes in her mouths at least six men from every passing ship. Such nakedly nightmarish fantasies of being swallowed up by females reveal a dark extreme of the psychological world in which the Homeric hero moves.

That world receives illumination also from the heroines of old whom Odysseus meets in his journey to Hades' domain, the land of the dead, in book 11—a catalogued encounter with mythical history, so to speak, in which the forebears of the Achaians speak to the uncertain possibilities of Odysseus' present. These women itemize the fortunes of marital life. Some were taken by gods and brought forth heroes: Tyro bore Neleus and Peleus to Poseidon, and Alkménè bore Herakles to Zeus (11.235–59, 266–68). Others, such as Epikástè, who in ignorance married her own son Oidipous, brought disaster by their liaisons (11.271–80). The last woman Odysseus here mentions, Eriphýlè, betrayed her husband (11.326–27). These and other possibilities of marital life, however, are overshadowed by the heroine Odysseus only hears of, directly from the husband she helped to murder: Klýtaimnéstra now appears as a full partner with Aigísthos, killing Kassandra and refusing even to shut her dead husband's eyes and mouth (11.405–34). If Agamemnon unwittingly suggests Klýtaimnéstra's resentment at her husband's betrayal of their marriage bed, the horror of her actions, though explicitly contrasted with the situation Odysseus will face with his faithful wife (11.441–61), dominates his imagination as he goes on to Ithaka, for he will follow Agamemnon's advice not to be trusting of women.

Thus, these two performance sessions have defined the full range of feminine potential in the Homeric world, going far beyond the scope of the reality most people know. In the fourth section of the epic (books 13–16), Odysseus finds himself firmly back in that reality. Just after his arrival, he has an interview with Athena

herself, who assures him of her solicitude in his behalf; finally, she can appear the
nurturing helper, after having abstained out of proper patriarchal fear of the wrath
of her uncle Poseidon (13.339–43). When Odysseus goes to Eumaíos' farm, he
encounters no women, but there we hear of Penelope's desire for messages con-
cerning her husband (14.373–74), as well as Eumaíos' story of the treacherous
maidservant who led him into slavery (15.389–484). So two alternatives for a
woman's behavior, fidelity or betrayal, remain in our minds from this session.

Not until the next performance session (books 17–20) does our singer bring
Penelope back on the scene. Despite the long history of the *Odyssey*, we are only
beginning to understand Penelope's role. A flurry of books at the end of the twen-
tieth century (see, e.g., those by Katz, Cohen, Felson-Rubin, and Segal listed in
the bibliography) marked critical interest in Penelope as a character pivotal to
the meaning of the epic. Regarding Penelope in this way serves as a belated re-
sponse to the misogyny in so much Western literature, especially, perhaps,
among the Greeks. For example, in Hesiod's depiction of Pandora and her box
of evils or in Semonides' long diatribe against women, misogyny is not only a so-
cial pathology but a literary motif. That motif is best represented in the *Odyssey*
by the advice Agamemnon gives Odysseus in Hades' domain, not to trust women.
Despite that advice and Odysseus' apparent agreement with it, Penelope is a full
partner with Odysseus in effecting his homecoming. We listeners or readers are
prepared to see how this should be: with our minds so stored with images of fem-
inine possibility, we can place Penelope. Which characteristics of the clever and
masterful Athena will she have, which of the charming Naúsikaä, which of the
discreetly authoritative Arétè? How can a woman in such a vulnerable predica-
ment negotiate the fine line between keeping her feminine sensitivity and being
exploited, between exercising firmness to achieve what she wants and becoming
over-assertive or treacherous? How can she affectionately yield to her long-ab-
sent husband while letting him know that he is to take nothing for granted about
her affection? Such questions still resonate with many women. In these last two
sections, we see Penelope taking a leading role in what must finally be done.

Yet her entrance at the beginning of this fifth section recapitulates her earlier
appearance. Again, as in book 1 (330), she descends from her upstairs chamber;
again, Telémachos sends her back when she asks him for news (17.45–51). But
her son is now not so harsh, and he later gives her the full story of his travels,
thus recognizing her right to an answer. We next see her at the end of the book,
when she hears that Antínoös has struck the beggar. Her reaction, to pray for An-
tínoös' death (17.494) and to summon the "beggar" Odysseus to speak to her,
shows her beginning to assert decisive power. But her summons is not heeded
for two whole books, with much suspense building for the encounter. Will she
recognize Odysseus? Will he, in his disguise, be able to restrain himself?

Meanwhile, we get an answer to one of the questions we asked earlier, for in book 18, Athena inspires Penelope to appear again to the suitors, and the goddess enhances Penelope's appearance so that she exceeds even the youthful Naúsikaä in charm (18.192–96). When Penelope goes downstairs—on a verbatim recapitulation of the scene in book 1, complete with accompanying handmaids (18.207–11 = 1.331–35)—the suitors are correspondingly moved: "Then were the men's limbs loosened, their hearts enchanted with passion; / they all loudly were praying to lie in the bedding beside her" (18.212–13, the second line exactly echoing 1.366). Eurýmachos tells her that if other Achaians could see her, she would have even more suitors. But she belongs in another world than the Phaiákian maid, and she shows herself a true wife to Odysseus by taking firm and crafty control of the situation, exploiting the suitors' responses to extract gifts from them—at which Odysseus himself rejoices.

In book 19, the beggar finally has an audience with Penelope. Putting forward his false identity as a Cretan of even higher birth than he pretended to be for Eumaíos, he says that Odysseus had visited his house. But the beggar's cunning intelligence is matched by Penelope's, for after an emotional response, she tests the beggar, asking him what apparel Odysseus was wearing during his visit (19.215–19). This reminiscence of Arétè's probing about the clothing Odysseus wore on Phaiákia shows Penelope to be the equal of that queen in controlling the situation. She does not relinquish her control even when she weeps at finding that the beggar knows the garments Odysseus wore. Her immediate reaction is to accept the stranger as a welcome reminder of Odysseus without believing in his homecoming.

The question of Penelope's control comes up again in an even more intimate exchange. Penelope asks the beggar to interpret her dream of domestic geese slaughtered by an eagle, though the eagle itself, in the voice of Odysseus, had interpreted its significance: the geese were the suitors, and the eagle was her husband who would be coming to kill them (19.536–53). For us, the dream gains added meaning in conveying Penelope's complex attitude: in it, she rejoices at the living geese and mourns insistently for the dead ones; yet when she awakens, she notices that her real geese are still "feeding on wheat from the trough"—a marvelous image of domestic tranquility. When Odysseus confirms the dream eagle's interpretation, however, Penelope is elaborately skeptical, and she goes on to tell of the test of the bow and axes that she has decided on as a way of choosing a suitor for the marriage she sees as inevitable. What is happening? Why does she ask a stranger for an interpretation of a dream so transparent and then reject what he says? Is her intention here to convey a message to the husband she already recognizes? Has she decided that everyone's best interests are served by a postponement of outward recognition?

In thinking of Penelope's role here, many have wondered if she secretly or perhaps subconsciously recognizes Odysseus without revealing it—Sheila Murnaghan has written perceptively about this question. For Penelope to conceal such a recognition would be consistent with a masterful use of cunning intelligence on her part, and it would resonate with Odysseus' own restraint in maintaining his disguise. But her welcoming treatment of the beggar and her intimate conversations with him are also psychologically consistent with the narrative moment. She has just been given gifts by the suitors; Telémachos is fully of age, which is when Odysseus told her she should get another husband; she is about to set the contest of the bow and axes for her hand in marriage; and she has just been told by the prophet Theoklýmenos that Odysseus is already on Ithaka: this combination of events in her life causes such tension in her predicament as to make her need this intimate exchange, even with one she thinks of as a stranger. In any case, the singer shows his own skill in arousing our suspicions but not letting us be sure.

Whatever we decide, Odysseus and we now know clearly that though Penelope will have no part in the actual killing of the suitors, that outcome is precisely the one she expects. Even if she will mourn the loss of their attention, her grief, she seems to be saying, will pass just as completely as it did when she awoke from her dream, once domestic harmony is restored by this drastic cleansing. Yet her soliloquy at the beginning of book 20 still assumes that Odysseus is dead and assumes also that another dream of Odysseus she has had was an evil illusion (20.87–90): she would rather be dead than have an inferior husband (20.79–82).

Two other women have significant roles in this session. One, Eurykleía, the old nurse, we have seen already in book 1. As she is washing Odysseus' feet, she sees the scar on his thigh and becomes the first household servant to know who he is. The lengthy digression on how he got this scar became famous when Eric Auerbach used it as the starting point for a seminal essay on the poetics of Homeric narrative. But for the present discussion, the image of the old woman holding her master's naked foot and almost blurting out his identity to Penelope is more important. Here, as in book 2, Eurykleía is unable to affect the course of events, for Odysseus immediately stops her with the threat of death——thus showing how intransigent his distrust of women still is and how even an old nurse's life matters less than his scheme. The other woman with a significant role in this session is Melántho, a maid who has repaid Penelope for her kind treatment by sleeping with one of her main suitors, Eurýmachos. Now we see how the maid's submission to a rapacious male has affected her character (as it did that of the serving woman in Eumaíos' story), for she abuses the "beggar" twice within two books, equaling the suitors themselves in her contempt for canons of hospitality.

Melántho's major importance, however, lies in preparing us for one of the most ferocious images of the epic, which occurs in the final performance session (books 21–24), as one aspect of the requital there depicted. Ordered by his father to put to death "with the fine-edged swords" (22.443) the twelve maids who betrayed their master and mistress by sleeping with the suitors, Telémachos obeys. But when the time comes, he rejects the idea of a "neat clean death" for women who have been "heaping disgraces" on himself and his mother; so he strings them up in nooses, like birds in a snare, and they dangle there until a pitiful death comes (22.461–73). Not soon will the other maids forget that they must choose carefully the males to whose importunities they succumb. Telémachos leaves no doubt about his descent from an implacable father.

Also in this section, we see Penelope moving with sure mastery among the competing demands on her, showing herself the equal not merely of Arétè but of Athena herself, adding wily devices to discreet control. First, she sets a contest whose terms, she must know in her heart, none of these suitors can satisfy: after all, her powerful husband, in the prime of life, last achieved what seems impossible, stringing the great bow and shooting one arrow through twelve axes (or their helve holes) in a line (19.572–81)—and moreover, as he had boasted to the Phaiákians, only Phíloktétes surpassed him as an archer (8.219). Then, when she has provided this opportunity for the beggar to get his hands on the bow, she herself intervenes to make them let him try the contest, assuring the suitors that he will not expect to marry her if he wins (21.311–42). In a recapitulation of the scene in book 1, with four almost exactly repeated lines (21.350–53 = 1.356–59), Telémachos takes over the masculine role and orders her upstairs, and she goes, exactly the same as in book 1 (21.354–58 = 1.360–64). But the speech has made it clear where her sympathies are, and it spurs her son to action and makes him yet more unwilling to yield to the suitors' reluctance to give the bow to the beggar—especially since his mother has recently scolded him (18.214–25) for sitting by as the beggar was abused. We see how recapitulation, far from being mere repetition, gives this mother-son relationship new depth and complexity.

But it is in the famous recognition scene of book 23 that Penelope's circumspect control and crafty intelligence appear most admirably. After the suitors have been dispatched, when Odysseus has every right to be welcomed back as her husband, he expects the recognition token that revealed his true identity to the suitors (the bow contest) to convince her too. Instead, Penelope surprises her son and us by hesitating:

> Long in silence she sat, and a daze came over her spirit;
> sometimes full in the face she would gaze at him, thinking she knew him,
> sometimes failing to know him who wore foul clothes on his body. (23.93–95)

Even after a good bath and the divine help of Athena have transformed him, Penelope holds back, saying,

> You strange man, I am not being proud, nor at all do I slight you,
> nor am I overimpressed; I know very well what you looked like
> when you departed from Ithaka once on the long-oared galley.
> (23.174–76)

Odysseus' own craftiness, one might say, has served him too well—he looks like himself, but it might be a trick. Penelope outbraves Odysseus' craft by doing exactly what she said she would in 23.109–10: she refers to a token that only husband and wife can know. When Odysseus gives up for the evening and asks to sleep alone (23.171–72), Penelope orders that the bed he himself built on the living trunk of an olive tree be moved outside their bedroom so that he can sleep in it. Odysseus falls for the trick, protesting in anguish, telling the story of the bed's construction and thus confirming his identity. The bed simultaneously, if symbolically, confirms Penelope's fidelity; for the bed is still in its place, it has not been cut from the olive tree.

We see in Penelope an intelligence that, unlike that of her husband, does not boast of itself but achieves astutely and exactly what the occasion demands. Beneath it lie firmness of purpose and determination not to be swayed by mere emotion at least equal to his: when both of the males in her life scold her, partly in identical words, for her unyielding heart (Telémachos at 23.96–103; Odysseus at 23.166–72; 100–102 = 168–70), she does not give in until she herself is fully satisfied that it is time to do so. When she finally explains why she waited, she first expresses her distrust of fair-seeming words—she was afraid "that a man might someday come and beguile me / merely by speaking" (23.216–17).

Penelope then shows a consciousness of "the lessons of history" that takes us once more to the heart of the Homeric story, the abduction of Helen by Paris.

> Neither in fact would Helen of Argos, the offspring of Zeus, have
> mingled in love and in bed with a man from an alien people
> if she had known that the warlike sons of Achaians would bring her
> back once more to her home, to the much loved land of her fathers.
> It was a god who aroused her to do so shameful an action;
> never before she had laid in her heart such hateful and reckless
> folly, from which first came for us also affliction and sorrow.
> (23.218–24)

In comparing her own predicament with that of Helen, Penelope shows the complexity of her mind: as Helen did not know that she would be brought home by force of arms, neither has Penelope known that Odysseus would come back to his home—indeed, she has repeatedly expressed the conviction that he has been lost. Yet the bare possibility of his return has been enough to keep her faithful, for she has learned from the lesson of Helen what general calamity may follow an act of folly, even one aroused by a god in an otherwise virtuous woman. So she has had to hold out for the highest degree of certainty before recognizing this man who has claimed to be her husband.

Perhaps Penelope gives Helen too much credit. But in comparing her own obstinate fidelity to the Homeric tradition's central symbol of the fragility of relationships, she raises the question of whether Helen is to be blamed or exonerated, scorned or forgiven, whether, indeed, we must blame the gods or ourselves for what happens to us and to those around us as a result of our actions—the very same question Zeus raised in the proem of the epic. If any answer to this difficult question is ever to be found, the example of Penelope herself may come nearest to it. No Athena has been standing by her in her troubles; no Zeus has been sending a messenger god to make the suitors desist from their importunities. She has been told that Odysseus is alive, but how could she trust the tellers when so many of them have proved to be deceivers? Yet she has endured. Her postponement of action is the most courageous and intelligent action in the whole Homeric tradition. It challenges listeners and readers to take equivalent responsibility for their acts.

Another parallel too is important: as Helen was absent in Troy for many years and caused much devastation, so Odysseus has been away from Ithaka for twenty years, leaving a household and a society in disarray. We know better than Penelope ever will how much of that long absence was due to his own impetuous folly, just short of Helen's. Yet he, like the Helen we saw so comfortably situated in Sparta, must be greeted with joy; his return must be adequate consolation for all that loss. Penelope knows enough to take the good when it comes, however great the regrets. So after Odysseus informs her of the journey Teirésias decreed for him, she says in the last words we hear from her:

> If it is true that the gods bring forth an old age that is better,
> then there is hope that for you there will be an escape from afflictions.
> (23.286–87)

No one has ever earned more completely the right to utter words of such qualified optimism.

Storytelling

Finally, we come to the theme of storytelling, a key to "Homer's" sense of his task and the way he carries it out. Once again we can see a clear development across the performance. In the first books, the stories mainly convey the credible facts of the "normal world," sometimes moralized. In the Adventures, Odysseus recounts his marvelous travels as sober truth, expecting his listeners to believe what seem extravagant fictions and stimulating deeper cogitation on the moral implications of actions. In the final books the stories again concern the world we know, but now many of them are outright fictions calculated to put the teller in a certain light and to have specific effects on those who hear them. Each of the six performance sessions advances our understanding of the manifold powers of storytelling as explanation, celebration, moral education, entertainment, and, not least, deception.

The explanatory function—recounting what has happened before as a key to understanding the current situation—begins early in the first session. Zeus himself alludes to the murder of Agamemnon at the hands of Aigísthos, whom Orestes then killed (1.35–43), a story that will be greatly developed but that is here merely sketched to show how men bring disaster on themselves despite knowing better. Then, Athena and Zeus together tell a brief story explaining why Odysseus is still in Ogygia rather than at home (1.48–75), a parallel to the first one: Odysseus brought his exile on himself by putting out the Cyklops' eye and thus incurring the wrath of Poseidon. This bare statement will not be fully developed until book 9, when Odysseus himself tells the story—then we will find out whether it is fully parallel: should Odysseus have known better? The next story in this first performance session is similarly explanatory: in book 2, the chief suitor, Antínoös, tells how Penelope put off the suitors by weaving and unweaving a great fabric until a maid informed the suitors, who forced her to finish it (2.93–110). Like the stories of Zeus and Athena, this one, though factual, has a moral dimension, for Antínoös uses it to prove that Penelope is to blame in deceiving the suitors and evading a necessary decision. For us, of course, it also shows how far she will go to maintain her loyalty to Odysseus. Unlike the earlier stories, this story has its full exposition here, but like them, we shall meet it later in other contexts with other resonances.

In books 3 and 4 occur two far more extended narratives, both coming in answer to Telémachos' inquiry concerning his father. In Pylos the aged warrior Nestor tells of his own return and the returns of several other Greeks to explain why he knows nothing about the fate of Odysseus. Though this elaborate passage may humorously characterize the old man's garrulity, it also serves to place Odysseus' homecoming in a wider context of *nóstoi* (returns) of the Greek heroes, thus filling out the bare allusion to them in book 1 when Penelope asks the bard Phemios not to sing of them (1.325–27, 337–44). Nestor also adds to our knowledge of the Agamemnon story. Like Athena in book 1 (298–302), he offers Orestes, the avenger of the murder of his father, Agamemnon, as a model for Telémachos (3.193–200), and he makes the story a warning not to wander too long lest the suitors destroy his patrimony (3.313–16). Then in Sparta Meneláos tells an even longer story of his own *nóstos*, his wanderings as he came homeward, this time explaining how he came to hear about Odysseus from Proteus, an old man of the sea. Being even more closely concerned for his brother Agamemnon, Meneláos adds to the resonance of that story the sense that his own careless neglect of proper sacrifices, resulting in his not being at home to aid his brother against the usurper Aigísthos, was largely responsible for the tragic event (4.512–40). Thus, the central theme of absence, a wandering that brings about terrible upsets for one's native country, is reinforced by a story parallel to that of Odysseus. Moreover, though Meneláos' travels take place in the known world, he prepares us to hear the tale of Odysseus by introducing supernatural characters, Eídothéa the sea nymph and her father, Proteus.

Two other stories in book 4, told by Helen and Meneláos, show how stories can have multiple implications and effects, even when they narrate facts. The explicit intent of these stories is to celebrate Odysseus for the sake of his visiting son, by telling of the deeds that "the strong man dared and accomplished" (4.242) in Troy. But in each tale, its teller has another less explicit but essential aim: to present Helen herself in a certain light. In her story (4.240–64) Helen says that when Odysseus entered Troy disguised as a beggar, she recognized but did not reveal him, and that when he slaughtered many Trojans—the people who had received her—she "only rejoiced," for her heart had turned toward going home to her excellent husband. As if in deliberate response to her, Meneláos tells (4.266–89) of Odysseus' steadfast resourcefulness later, inside the wooden horse. When at this last moment of the war, Helen tried, by imitating their wives, to make the Achaians—including her own husband, to whom she has just professed to have been so devoted— reveal themselves to their enemies, Odysseus restrained them and saved the day. From these stories, Helen appears hopelessly duplicitous, her husband hopelessly infatuated: this is the woman for whose sake he caused so many Achaians to be destroyed. Moreover, by their juxtaposition, these stories give us a glimpse of a household whose outward splendor is undermined by unreconcilable marital tensions.

In the second session (books 5–8), storytelling occurs only late, since the early parts are direct narration of the way Odysseus came to be among the Phaiákians. But once he is received in the royal palace, in answer to Queen Arété's question concerning the clothes her daughter Naúsikaä gave him to wear, he begins to tell of his travels (7.236–97). His aim here is adequately served by relating only how he set off from Ogygia, was shipwrecked, arrived in Scheria, and was aided by Naúsikaä, who lent him the clothes the queen and her women made. We know he tells the tale with factual exactness, because we have recently heard it directly from the narrator. Again, the explanatory function of storytelling seems uppermost, but the story also accomplishes another even more important aim: it elicits the listeners' sympathy for the teller's plight.

The story is also entertaining, and as we might expect of a society so given to the pleasures of life, this is the power we mainly encounter in the stories told in these three books. Even the two stories about Odysseus that the singer Demódokos sings have this primary function, for neither of them so much celebrate the hero as recount how he was involved in the Trojan War. This is especially true of the first briefly summarized tale of the quarrel between Odysseus and Achilles that heralded the war (8.72–82). The song entertains the hosts, but it causes Odysseus to weep. Then, at the end of the session, Odysseus himself—as yet unidentified—asks for the story of the wooden horse, which will highlight his own courageous craft (8.492–520). Once again he weeps to hear of the events. What he requested as a song to exalt himself results in grief for the loss of his comrades and even for the destruction of Troy. Later, we will again see these unexpected effects of stories—what is wanted is not always what is achieved.

Between these two Trojan stories occurs one that seems even more to be sheer entertainment: Demódokos' famous account of how Hephaistos exposed the love affair of Ares and Aphroditè by trapping them in his own bed (8.266–366). Even the "morals" drawn in the story—for example, "Bad deeds never succeed, for the slow man catches the swift one" (8.329)—seem calculated more to amuse by their patness than to illuminate by their depth. But on further thought, the story raises questions about the truth and the significance of narrative. We know the two lovers in the tale as powerful and deadly—in her patronage of Helen and Paris, Aphroditè was at the very root of the destruction visited on Troy, while Ares is the ferocious god of war—yet they are shown here as feckless participants in a comic interlude, almost as the victims of a jealous husband. What authority can the singer claim for such a portrayal of them? Is he simply inventing, and are stories like this the only sort of revenge we mortals can take on the gods who victimize us? Or should we adopt the perspective of these peaceful Phaiákians, for whom neither of these gods seems to present a real problem? We are told before this episode how they care little for the "martial arts" of fistfighting and wrestling, preferring to run, dine, sail, sing, dance, bathe, and sleep (8.246–49). As for Aphroditè, no such temptations as assailed Helen (and Klýtaimnéstra in Nestor's story in book 3) even occur to the mind of the vital young woman Naúsikaä—she wants a husband, but only and strictly on the terms that her beloved parents approve, as she makes clear to Odysseus in book 6 (286–88). For these people, then, if this beguiling tale of adultery is cautionary, it is so in the sunniest way, employing laughter rather than tragic pity and fear to discipline the violations of marriage.

Aside from this story, those in the second section are apparently sober truth. However, at the end of his story of his arrival in Scheria, Odysseus gives a brief but significant foretaste of a talent that will become prominent in the Ithakan sections: he can improvise on the spur of the moment, changing or inventing facts to suit his purposes. When Alkínoös blames his daughter for not bringing Odysseus with her to the palace, Odysseus tactfully says that he himself was afraid of being found offensive if he came with her (7.293–307), whereas we know that it was she who feared being taunted when officious Phaiákians saw her with a man like him (6.255–99). Thus, he not only "covers" for Naúsikaä but also endears himself to her parents as sensitive and careful—to the point that the king immediately wants to marry him to his daughter.

But the factuality of most of the stories in the second performance session prepares the audience and us to receive as truth the astonishing adventures in the third session (books 9–12). Here, Odysseus becomes an accomplished performer in his own right: King Alkínoös signals as much when he says in book 11, "like some singer of tales, you have skillfully told us the story / showing the piteous woes of yourself and of all of the Argives" (368–69). That Odysseus succeeds gloriously as an entertainer is testified by the listeners and readers of almost three millennia, who have made this sequence of tales probably the best-known in the literature of the West. So entertaining are these tales, some would say, that, taking his cue from the Phaiákians' love of pleasure, Odysseus must have set out to win them by extravagant inventions. The monsters he meets seem to have just that value—they give much pleasure, but are not of great human significance.

We cannot elaborate further here on the kinds of story that Homer puts together in this tale of wanderings: we referred to them briefly at the beginning of this essay when discussing the folkloric elements in the *Odyssey*. But we may recall that in the section on women, we suggested that just because they are fantasies, these stories can evoke deep psychological truths that we do not confront so directly in normal life—indeed, that is the very reason they entertain. As to the factuality of his account, Zeus himself (1.68–75) provides evidence for one of its most spectacular and grotesque episodes, that concerning the Cyklops. Moreover, Alkínoös says that Odysseus cannot be supposed to be "one of the cheats or insidious charlatans" (11.364) who fashion lies and inventions. Most important, perhaps, Odysseus comes across as a teller of truths because he does not try to hide or mitigate his own culpability in many of the episodes: he alone was responsible for the decision to explore the Cyklops' cave, for the even more drastic decision to blind the Cyklops (thus incurring the fatal wrath of Poseidon), and for the reckless taunt, using his real name, which added magical efficacy to the Cyklops' curse (book 9). It was he who, not having told his crew what was inside the bag of winds Aíolos gave him, fell asleep within sight of Ithaka, with the result that the crew opened the bag to find treasure, let the winds loose, and condemned them all to further wandering (10.1–79). His was the idle self-indulgence on Circè's island, lasting a full year, from which only his comrades roused him (10.466–74). Even more than with his earlier story of arriving in Scheria, his purpose in telling this story—beyond providing the explanation King Alkínoös has asked for—is to gain the sympathy of his listeners, so that they will give him conveyance back home. In this respect, his account succeeds admirably, for he shows himself a man who has learned from facing his own failures, who has used his wily intelligence and courage to achieve ends that his rebellious crew too often thwarted, and who finally has the gods on his side. But it cannot be denied that, above all, he has given his listeners a splendid entertainment, equaling or outdoing even the professional singer Demódokos: twice we hear that "all of the people were hushed in silence, / held by the charm of the tale all over the shadowy chamber" (11.333–34, 13.1–2).

Also in this section, in his account of the voyage to Hades' domain (book 11), Odysseus tells how he heard from Agamemnon himself the fullest and most authoritative account of that warrior's demise, one notable for emphasizing the part of his wife, Klýtaimnéstra, in the murder (11.405–34). By doing so, Agamemnon turned the tale to account as a lesson for Odysseus (much as Athena, Nestor, and Meneláos had done for his son, Telémachos)—in this case, that women are not to be trusted, even Penelope, who, by Agamemnon's insistence, is nothing at all like his own murderous wife. Therefore, Odysseus must proceed cautiously, secretly, when he returns to Ithaka. Agamemnon's inconsistency here may seem extreme, but it outlines exactly the state of mind in which Odysseus approaches his wife: he sees incontrovertible proofs of her devotion and loyalty, yet he keeps her from knowing him until the very end. So we observe how an exemplary story may affect the minds of those who hear it.

Agamemnon's recommendation of secrecy (11.455) provides the keynote for the whole of the next performance session, At the Farm of Eumaíos (books 13–16). On Scheria, Odysseus began his long tale of adventures with the intention of establishing his identity unequivocally, beginning with the ringing assertion "I am Odysseus the son of Laërtes, who am among all men / noted for crafty designs, and to heaven my fame has ascended" (9.19–20). Now, his purpose is to hide his identity, using fictions to establish a new one while explaining how he has come to be in Ithaka. Yet entertainment, the charm of the tale, remains a powerful means by which Odysseus accomplishes his ends. In both deceiving and entertaining, he remains the performer *par excellence*, and his stories also show us how selection and repetition can add force to a narrative point or direct a specific appeal to a listener.

In his performances at Eumaíos' farm and later in the palace, instead of telling true stories about experiences that are hardly credible, Odysseus concocts false stories about quite believable life events. The response he gets is equally contrary: whereas the Phaiákians had no problem believing him, his listeners in these books stop well short of swallowing his stories whole. The first of those listeners is Athena, and her skepticism is that of a goddess. But after he gives her (disguised as a young man) a tale of his Cretan origin, his murder of Idómeneus' son, his hasty departure from Crete, and his landing on Ithaka (13.256–86), she reveals herself and rightly characterizes the storyteller as getting pleasure from his fabrications, saying that even in his native land, he would not stop "telling the fraudulent tales that are dear to your soul from the ground up" (13.295).

In this first tale, Odysseus' intention was to establish his identity as a Cretan who fought at Troy and to explain his arrival on Ithaka. The same intent informs the long story he tells Eumaíos in the next book—the additive technique is clearly at work, since many of the same elements enter the story (14.199–359): he is a Cretan, the son of a lord, and a warrior at Troy. But he adds to this account an involved story of piratical wanderings with men who were not fully under control, and tells how he was shipwrecked (in a passage that echoes, often line-for-line, the narrative of his real shipwreck after his comrades had eaten the cattle of Helios) and how he was driven to Thesprotia, where he heard of Odysseus as returning home and whence he was brought to Ithaka and escaped from sailors who intended to sell him as a slave. While this story goes well beyond its immediate purpose of establishing his identity, it fully achieves one equally important end: his listener, Eumaíos, is moved by it, so that he later tells Penelope, "Such good stories he tells, he would charm the dear heart in your bosom" (17.514). Moreover, this tale suggests by thematic echoes and repetitions what the wanderings of Odysseus (as told in books 9–12) might have been like if they had happened in the known world: both narratives show how bad fortune and bad weather, the teller's own folly, rebellious comrades, and encounters with hostile or treacherous people and with kind and helpful people have interwoven to bring him where he is. But the present story fails to convince Eumaíos that Odysseus is returning, and he in fact accuses the "beggar" outright of lying (14.364–65) even though his return is the only substantially true fact in the whole story. Eumaíos, like Telémachos in book 1 (413–16) and Penelope in book 23 (215–17), is skeptical because of the proven falsity of previous reports concerning Odysseus. He and they know that unscrupulous men use such tales to charm their listeners into giving or doing something, and Eumaíos explicitly says that Odysseus should not attempt it —"make no effort to please me with lies or to charm me" (14.387).

Nevertheless, Odysseus does exactly that at the end of the book, when he tells a story of the time he, the fictional Cretan, was third in command with Odysseus in ambush under Troy (14.462–506). His aim is to get the swineherd to give him a warm cover, so he tells how since he had come out without warm clothing, Odysseus cleverly obtained some for him. The story succeeds in its aim, for Eumaíos praises him for the story and gives him a mantle for "now: but again in the morning your own rags you will be flaunting" (14.512), strongly implying that he need not believe the beggar's story about having been a chieftain of the Achaians at Troy to get its point. Probably a simple request would have gained the same end, but both men have gotten pleasure from the story.

Despite Eumaíos' skepticism, both of these stories have made him even readier to entertain the beggar in his cabin, and in book 15 (398–484), he signals that hospitable spirit by telling his own tale: "we two now will enjoy each other's afflictions and sorrows / as we recall them" (15.399–400). Significantly, the epic's clearest examples of reciprocity in the guest-host relationship appear in exchanges of stories. Moreover, like the first tale of Odysseus, Eumaíos' tale establishes his identity as the child of a lord and explains how he happens to have come to Ithaka, through the treachery of a servant woman who led him out of his father's house to be taken away by Phoenicians who sold him to Laërtes. As will happen to his master, Eumaíos, after all his afflictions, has ended up in a good place, as Odysseus himself says: "after suffering much, you came to the house of a kindly / man who in fact has provided you plenty for eating and drinking" (15.489–90). Such repetitions of story patterns implant them in our minds, making us sense the variations within the common overarching trajectory of human life.

Though both tellers of these stories derive from noble stock, their present identities place them in the lower classes, and in this too they feel a commonality. In the next performance session (books 17–20), the scene moves to the palace, and Odysseus as beggar confronts men who are arrogantly conscious of their nobility. One important concern of these books is to show how thoroughly the suitors and their collaborators among the servants deserve the fate they are going to suffer. So though the story Odysseus tells them at 17.419–44 shows some of the former deceptive aim, to establish a false identity, it has an equally strong "moral" intent, to challenge them to recognize the principles of *xenía* we discussed earlier. In begging for food, he supports his plea by telling Antínoös that he also was a prosperous man and gave freely to vagrants but that now he is down on his luck after misfortunes suffered on his travels. Antínoös' response is to reject the example offered, repudiate the teller as a "bold-faced beggar" (17.449), and throw a stool that hits Odysseus' right shoulder. Even the other suitors are horrified at the way Antínoös tempts fate, lest this man should be some god coming in disguise among them.

Another feature of this tale excellently shows how selected repetition advances its teller's moral intent. Of its thirty-six lines, fifteen (17.427–41) reproduce exactly the Egyptian episode of the tale he told Eumaíos (14.258–72), which recounted the fate incurred by the men who "yielded to wanton excess" in pillaging the country: they were killed or taken slaves. The end of the story is very brief and quite different from the end of the one he told Eumaíos; but it suits Odysseus' purpose here to hasten to the end. It would be hard to imagine a clearer cautionary tale for the present company of wanton revelers who are pillaging the household of the king.

Something similar happens in the brief excerpt Odysseus tells Melántho, the housemaid who has been sleeping with Eurýmachos, when she scolds the "beggar." He selects only enough of the previous story to achieve his aim—six lines (19.75–80), which reproduce exactly the first six lines of the story he told the suitors (17.419–24), in which he tells of his past wealth and generosity and how it disappeared. So he explains why he is a beggar, but in the moral that follows, he admonishes the maid to beware of an equal change of fortune, the loss of her beauty, and not to anger her mistress, who might cast her out. Penelope immediately reinforces this moral by scolding the maid.

An even more important exchange of stories occurs just afterward, when Penelope finally talks to the beggar, as she has requested. This first meeting of man and wife after almost twenty years of separation is charged with drama, and Odysseus heightens it by his seeming reluctance to tell his story lest he be reproached for wine-soaked weeping (19.115–22). So Penelope begins with her story of sorrows, its centerpiece being the account of how she put off the suitors by weaving and unweaving a great shroud, repeated line-for-line from Antínoös' telling in book 2 (19.139–56 echo 2.94–110, with some minor changes). Earlier, the story was aimed at blaming Penelope, but here it demonstrates her crafty fidelity to her husband—the man who is listening—and explains why now, having been caught at her evasion, she must marry.

In response, the "beggar" tells her a fiction whose main thrust is to assert his personal knowledge of Odysseus and to assure her that he is returning. He gives himself a Cretan origin again, but here a more exalted one—he says he is Aithon, the brother of King Idómeneus himself. He tells her that he met Odysseus when the latter was blown off course on his way to Troy. This part of his story ends with Odysseus' ships parting for Troy, and Penelope's response is the twofold one we have encountered before with Eumaíos: she is so moved that she dissolves in tears, but she distrusts the story's truthfulness and decides to test the storyteller. Odysseus easily answers her questions about what clothes the "beggar" saw her husband wearing and about his comrades; having won her trust, he can reassure her about Odysseus' return. In doing so, he tells the story he purports to have heard about Odysseus, mentioning the incident involving the cows of the sun god, the destruction of his comrades at sea, and his visit with the Phaiákians, all facts, but going on to the fictions he told Eumaíos about how Odysseus went to Thesprotia and Dodóna. Even for us, "So did the numerous falsehoods he told seem like a true story" (19.203) that the boundary between "truth" and "false-

hood" becomes blurred. We see Odysseus in disguise mingling factual and in-
vented happenings as if both to evade and to invite detection and focusing not
on his fictional persona's life but on that of Odysseus. It is no wonder that some
readers have thought that Penelope begins to recognize Odysseus at about this
time. Our sense of how fictions are made and of what they accomplish has be-
come very complex.

Formally, both Penelope's and Odysseus' stories in book 19 are recapitula-
tions, for they each incorporate earlier material in a new context, with enriched
meanings. This is even more the case with the stories told in the final perform-
ance session (books 21–24). After Odysseus wins the contest by stringing his bow
and shooting an arrow through the axes, then slaughters the suitors, his reunion
with Penelope is partly consummated by the story he tells of his travels in re-
sponse to a very brief summary of her tribulations, in indirect discourse
(23.302–5)—a full account is hardly needed after her talk with the "beggar" in
book 19. Odysseus' longer story (23.310–41), also a summary in indirect dis-
course, though it covers his whole voyage, invites two quite opposed interpreta-
tions. For some people, it may indeed be merely a summary: its omission of de-
tails simply shows that the narrator does not feel the need to go over the ground
carefully, and if we were hearing Odysseus' own words, we would see him as quite
open in letting Penelope know what happened. Others, however, would say that
even as a summary, this recapitulation of Odysseus' adventures is highly selec-
tive, unlike the frank confession he made to the Phaiákians, and is tailored for
this occasion and listener just as much as his outright fictions have been. The
summary gives no hint of the disastrous consequences of his very first raid, the
death of many men—on which the original story enlarges far more than on any-
thing that could be called conquest——but says, "he began how first he had
quelled the Kikonians" (23.310). There is no word of his foolhardiness in ap-
proaching the Cyklops, but he tells "all that the Cyklops had done, then how he
[Odysseus] had taken revenge on / him" (23.312–13), omitting also the calami-
tous outcome of that revenge, the deadly wrath of Poseidon. The mention of
the Aíolos episode leaves out Odysseus' own sleep, which allowed his comrades
to free the winds; it says, rather, that he "was not destined as yet to arrive in his
own dear / fatherland" (23.315–16). As to the female figures he met on his voy-
age, about the goddess in whose charms he remained for a year, he apparently
lets Penelope know only "the guile and the many devices of Circè" (23.321),
while he goes into more detail about Kalýpso, closely quoting three significant
lines:

> . . . how he had reached the Ogygian isle and Kalýpso the nymph who
> kept on holding him fast—she wanted to make him her husband—

there in her spacious cavern, and gave him nurture, and told him
she would make him immortal and ageless forever and ever;
nevertheless, she never persuaded the heart in his bosom . . .

(23.333–37; cf. 7.257–58, 9.33)

As to the Phaiákians, the summary devotes three lines (23.339–41) to the honor
"as if he were a god" and the gifts they gave him—there is not a word about the
two women on whose gracious sympathy depended the homecoming of a man
reduced to total nudity. Many listeners or readers may conclude that Odysseus
of many devices, the accomplished storyteller, knows and says what is best suited
to a returned husband's purpose, especially in emphasizing that he resisted one
goddess's lavish promises rather than confessing that he willingly stayed with an-
other. He might do this not so much because he is devious but because he does
not want to cause his dear wife useless pain. Since we have been primed by his
own earlier fictions to notice how the selection of details is crucial to a story's
meaning, we might not be unjustified in thinking that this summary points to
Odysseus' desire to present himself in the best possible light, here as in any
episode when his behavior was not such as to rouse admiration. But we remain
unsure that this brief account fairly represents "all" that Odysseus said during
that long night's narration. Perhaps the only certain conclusion to be drawn con-
cerns Homer's mastery in making this story a sort of mirror, stimulating us to
look into our own hearts for what we prize in the marriage bond and how best
to maintain it—total frankness whatever the cost or tactful forgetfulness of
painful episodes.

In the final book, which begins with a recapitulation of the scene in Hades' do-
main in book 11—this time it is the spirits of the suitors who go there—we hear
other stories, some of them also restatements. Responding to Achilles' commis-
eration over Agamemnon's "death most shameful," the latter tells an extended tale
(24.35–94) of the glorious burial of Achilles, almost as if he were answering that
hero's earlier repudiation of the idea that glory should be a consolation for being
no longer alive (11.482–91), but even more as a contrast with his own ignomin-
ious slaughter, explicitly drawing the comparison again at the end of his story. In
another clear counterpoint to Agamemnon's shame, the shade of the suitor Am-
phimédon tells of the events leading up to the slaughter of the suitors. In the
course of his tale, he recapitulates once more, line for line, the story of Penelope's
ruse to put off the suitors by weaving and unweaving the shroud (24.128–48).
Again, the new context gives it new resonance, for now it has its proper place in
the whole narrative of resourcefulness that led to the suitors' punishment, and it
demonstrates Penelope's equal participation in the overall achievement. This
judgment is highlighted even by the suitor's own underestimation of her, for at

24.167, he attributes the plan of the contest with the bow and axes to Odysseus, while we know that it was her own idea and that Odysseus merely took advantage of it. After such a tale, Agamemnon has even more reason to congratulate Odysseus on his wife, in comparison with his own: here, he does not so much re-capitulate his earlier account as evoke it vividly, at 24.199–202, and he gives Penelope the highest accolade possible for a singer of tales.

> And so the renown of her virtue
> never will die: about constant Penelope will the immortals
> make for the people on earth a delightful song in her honor.
>
> (24.196–98)

The song he mentions, it need hardly be said, is the great epic to which we have been listening. It is hard to think of an ancient prediction that has been more completely realized than this one.

But Penelope is not the last person with whom Odysseus has been anticipating reunion; in his encounter with his aged father, we see one of the most moving occurrences of storytelling in the epic. Odysseus chooses deliberately, but without any possible justification, to test the father who has been so grieved by his absence. Indeed, we can see his pleasure in fraudulent tales working itself out in this most inappropriate setting, for he seems to enjoy the approach to his self-revelation. After criticizing the old man's dilapidated condition, he says (24.266–79) that he once met a man who claimed to be the son of Laërtes. Then, when his sorrowful father questions him, he tells how he himself has been driven to Ithaka from his native land, Sikania, and describes the good omens he had seen when Odysseus had departed from there five years ago. Far from preparing his father for the truth, this tale causes an entirely unnecessary emotional crisis: what are good omens against the five years since Odysseus left, presumably for home? The resulting "black cloud of distress" that "enshrouded his father" (24.315) cuts through even Odysseus' self-control, and he leaps up, embraces his father, and reveals himself. True to his lineage, his father demands tokens, which Odysseus easily provides. But through the ensuing joy, we cannot forget how Odysseus has given unseasonable rein to his love of shaping a response by concocting a story. Unlike us, he is a hero beloved of the gods; but like us, he is still a human being who can too easily yield to his impulses.

Looking at these stories has shown us how conscious our performer, "Homer," was of the way fiction works and of how people make use of it. Thus we can be even surer that his management of the complex material in his larger performance, our *Odyssey*, is equally self-conscious and skillful. Like Odysseus in his tales, he draws on story materials offered by the tradition which has shaped him, but he uses them for ends that are his own, transcending the tradition even as he remains rooted in it. The more we look at the *Odyssey* as a whole, the more we see how the bardic tradition supported a work of enormous and unique power, one whose performance, first by singers and then in written form, became itself a major foundation of the great tradition of storytelling in the Western world.

CONCLUSION

This introduction has dwelt on the particular features of the *Odyssey* that has come down to us, to emphasize the ways it may have been distinctive as a performance within its tradition. The traditional elements that this *Odyssey* brings to the foreground include the rituals and ideology of guest-friendship; issues connected with women (gender, power relations, erotic bonding); the way stories can tell the truth, can be manipulated to bring about some effect, or both; the disruption to the social order caused by a leader's absence and an undisciplined group's presumptuous ambitions; and the relations among persons at different social levels (beggars, servants, farmers, aristocrats, kings). Though we have necessarily been selective in highlighting how the poetic artistry of the *Odyssey* presents these problems, readers who look more closely at this particular performance of a traditional tale will see how it puts these issues at the core of the epic.

The translation in this book, which attempts to convey the traditional language of Homer as far as a strict English hexameter can do so, provides the readers of the English Homer with a way to explore these topics on their own beyond this introduction. As the next introductory essay shows in some detail, the translator has tried to make more visible the way repetition brings out these significant features of this performance of an early Greek narrative. A particular performance is as much a part of the tradition as an individual sentence is a part of its language. What distinguishes sentences as good or bad is not that they are "against" their language but that the language has been made into something so fine as to be itself worthy of note. So too, if we imagine ourselves as audiences at performances of the *Odyssey*, we can scarcely help feeling that the tradition has bodied forth in this singer and this song a stunning exemplar. To make that imaginative leap is both rational and inspiring, whether we subscribe to an oral dictated text or to an evolutionary development. The text that you are about to read is both traditional and extraordinary at the same time. To read the *Odyssey*, we too must use *mêtis* (cunning intelligence), like that of its hero, disguising the twenty-first-century self to participate in the best fiction we have for an oral performance, so that we can sit by the hearth and hear the singer sing.

Translating
Homeric Song

Rodney Merrill

Every translator of a classic must have two main hopes for the version he produces: that it convey as nearly as possible the poetic sense and significance of the original and that it be accessible and pleasing to his readers. The potential conflict between these two aims appears most strikingly in the case of an ancient classic like the *Odyssey*, composed by oral bards in a preliterate tradition with poetic means quite alien to poets of literate ages. In the twentieth century, heeding Ezra Pound's injunction to "make it new," most translators chose rather to bring the version close to the presumed literary tastes of contemporary readers than to make an attempt—a dubious one, they might have said—to reproduce the oral qualities of the original.

Dubious or not, my effort here has been to come as close as possible to the oral poetics of the Homeric epic, with as much reproduction of the formulaic and repetitive elements of the medium as I have been able to achieve. The preceding introductory essay shows how important these elements were to the performance and to the narrative structure; my discussion here aims to show somewhat more intimately how the medium works and how it can be conveyed even in a modern translation. Perhaps the time is ripe for such a version: we have pointed to the way wide-ranging scholarship on the world's oral traditions has made us aware of strengths unavailable in "literate" work, strengths that are well worth trying to capture in a modern version of this ancient oral epic. Moreover, the taste for "authenticity" in our encounter with older cultures, aroused in part by the broad popular appeal of archaeology and anthropology, has put down deep roots, and we are eager to come as close as we can to the lives and experiences of people quite unlike ourselves. One way of doing so is to understand and appreciate the art of such people on its own terms. Thus, the movement to re-create the music of the medieval, Renaissance, and Baroque eras using historical modes of performance and original instruments or careful reproductions of them reveals much about that music that before could be heard less fully, and so we are brought closer to the minds and lifestyles that produced it.

This example is not adventitious, for I first came to my own task with the ambition of making available in English something like the dazzling music of the dactylic hexameter line as it appears in Homer (in the following transcription, the acute accents ['] indicates a long syllable, not a stress, in Greek):

Ándra moi énnepe, Moúsa, polútropon, hós mala pólla
plángthe, epeí Troíés hierón ptoliéthron epérse;
póllón d' ánthrópón iden ástea kaí noön égnó,
pólla d' ho g' én póntó pathen álgea hón kata thúmon,
árnumenós hén té psúchén kaí nóston hetaírón.
                                                            (1.1–5)

Although we lack the melody to which the words were sung, even a Greekless reader who reads these five lines aloud should detect the essentially musical elements that do survive—the rhythmic vitality, the variety in the arrangement of long and short syllables and in the placement of pauses, all within strict metrical bounds—and that make the hexameter such a great formal meter, such great "music."

Total "authenticity"—performing and listening to the Greek original—is not possible for any but the few who can learn Greek well enough to follow and respond to such a performance. But we can come closer to the experience of that music than past translations have allowed: if the English dactylic hexameter does not equal the Greek in sonority and weight, the English line has its own virtues, in part because the dactylic rhythm itself has a strength and a beauty transcending particular manifestations in Greek, Latin, or English. Longfellow's uneven performance in *Evangeline* and *The Courtship of Miles Standish* has too often been seen as evidence that the meter cannot work in English. But it need not be the last word, any more than the thumping iambic pentameters, the "blank (unrhymed) verse," of *Gorboduc,* Thomas Norton and Thomas Sackville's early tragedy, prove that blank verse is not a good medium for English drama: Thomas Kyd and, after him, Christopher Marlowe, Ben Jonson, and William Shakespeare happily did not take that possible lesson to heart when they adopted the line for their great plays. Much the same thing might be said of such earlier dactylic-hexameter versions of the *Odyssey* as those of H. B. Cotterill and Brian Kemball-

Cook. Though the meter of neither one seems to me fully successful, their very problems—especially those of Cotterill, whose translation I encountered at the outset of my project—helped me understand how I could make the English hexameter work for a Homeric translation that seeks to convey the formulaic nature of the original. My rendering of the first five lines of the epic will suggest how I have responded to the Greek example (here, the acute accent ['] represents primary metrical stress; the grave accent [`] represents "natural"—that is, normally spoken—stress when it differs from metrical stress).

Téll mé, Múse, of the mán vèrsatíle and resoúrceful, who wándered
mány a seá-míle áfter he ránsácked Tróy's hòly cíty.
Mány the mén whóse tówns he obsérved, whóse mínds he discóvered,
mány the paíns in his heárt hé súffered, travérsing the seáwáy,
fíghting for hís ówn lífe and a wáy báck hóme for his cómràdes.

My verse does not do the same thing as the Greek, but it attempts to use English language patterns in equally energetic and varied ways within the bounds of a stress-based metrical norm, with such "counterpoint" (tension between the metrical and the "natural" stress) as appears in the words *versatile* and *holy* in lines 1–2 and in the first *his* in line 5.

Whatever the final judgment on the English hexameter may be, I have become more and more aware that in Greek, the strict but flexible dactylic hexameter forms the essential basis of an overall structure that is musical in a broader sense, a structure defined in part by free repetitions of such oral-formulaic features (discussed shortly) as noun-epithet combinations, half-lines, lines, and entire passages. Moreover, these musical repetitions not only afford great pleasure of a kind unique to oral epic, they are also central to the meaning of this epic, giving an almost ritual resonance to the narrative and adding other sorts of significance that are virtually invisible in most translations. I became increasingly convinced that conveying this music, derived from oral-formulaic composition but not dependent on it for its effect, should be my major aim. The English version of the dactylic hexameter, however unlike the Homeric hexameter it may be in its accentual as opposed to quantitative measure, seems, for reasons I hope to make clear, by far the best medium for such an effort. No other English poetic line can even approach a fairly strict hexameter for providing the sort of music appropriate to this undertaking.

As I advanced, I also came to believe that any version predicated on this sense of the poem must be intended for reading aloud and hearing, not for reading silently in one's chamber—except so far as the lonely reader imagines a fully voiced performance of the work, as a reader of Shakespearean drama needs to imagine a stage performance. This should not be surprising; after all, the epic—or, at any rate, its constituent episodes and formulas—was originally produced by singers who probably could not write, for an audience whose members could not refer to any written or printed text. Whatever they got from the song, they got "on the wing," so to speak, as the words came to them from the singer and then vanished. Such a song does not admit of highly sophisticated or complex syntax. Nor can it demand unremitting concentration on the poetic substance over long stretches of time. In oral performance, the formulaic speech openings, for example, which often seem protracted and even tedious in prose translation, make for a pleasing and useful transition between one block of substance and another. They allow the singer and the hearers alike to relax for a moment, while taking pleasure in a familiar musical line—there is no "dead space," but listeners need not concentrate on what is happening. For example, the formula "thoughtful Telémachos then spoke out to him/her, giving an answer" occurs forty-seven times in the epic and becomes a familiar cadence. This formula and other formulaic features of the epic allow auditors to listen closely, yet without straining, to a narrative in which familiar formulas mingle with new substance. As was pointed out in the previous essay and as my later discussion of the oral-formulaic tradition will amplify, the singers who brought these stories into being could rely on a secure "language" to support their creative efforts, which they might well have considered as "re-creations" of the songs they had heard, rather than as "original" productions.

Beyond its advantages for doing, following, and enjoying such a performance, the music of repetitions—which has so little value for a silent reading that translators usually minimize it or even plume themselves on finding "fresh" ways of handling the same narrative idea—adds significantly to our understanding of the story. To begin with, the literal repetitions can reinforce and illuminate the narrative, as hearers perceive (to varying degrees of consciousness) connections on the musical level both within episodes and between them, whether close together or widely separated (as has already been set forth in the preceding essay). An especially subtle example of significant near repetition within an episode occurs near the beginning of book 22, when Odysseus is starting to kill the suitors (again, in the following transcription, the acute accent marks long syllables).

Hós dé sphín kái pásin oléthroú peírat' ephépto.

(22.33)

Nún húmín kái pásin oléthroú peírat' ephéptaí.

(22.41)

Reading these lines aloud should give a sense of the strong rhythmic component of this repetition: the lines are unusually spondaic (i.e., they include many long syllables) and are therefore highly emphatic. The first line occurs just after the suitors have berated Odysseus for shooting one of the suitors' leaders, Antínoös, and have threatened with dire revenge the man whom they think is a mere beggar, whereupon the narrator reflects:

> So each man of them guessed, for in fact they thought that he had not
> willfully slaughtered the man; and the poor fools never suspected
> *how on all of the suitors the grim death bindings were fastened.*
>
> (22.31–33; italics mine)

The passage continues:

> Looking from lowering brows said Odysseus of many devices:
> "Oh you dogs, you believed I would have no return and would not come
> home from the land of the Trojans, and so you have pillaged my household;
> so you have taken to bed by force those women, the handmaids;
> so though I was alive my wife you illicitly courted;
> neither the gods you feared, the immortals who hold the broad heaven,
> nor any vengeance that men might bring upon you in the future.
> *Now on all of you suitors the grim death bindings are fastened!*"
>
> (22.34–41; italics mine)

Odysseus' pregnant echo of the narrator is obscured or lost in translations that do not reproduce such repetitions. For example, Pope changes the lines totally. He has the narrator say,

> Blind as they were; for death even now invades
> His destined prey, and wraps them all in shades.

He has Odysseus say,

> The hour of vengeance, wretches! now is come;
> Impending fate is yours, and instant doom.

The repetition is equally invisible in a more recent translation, that of Robert Fitzgerald; he has the narrator say, "fools! not to comprehend / they were already in the grip of death," and Odysseus, "Your last hour has come. You die in blood." Even Richmond Lattimore, who is much more intent on conveying a specifically Homeric feeling, seems to play down the rhythmical and verbal echo. He has the narrator say, "they had not yet realized / how over all of them the terms of death were now hanging," and Odysseus, "Now upon all of you the terms of destruction are fastened." Albert Cook's literal translation makes it clear that the repetition might be significant. His narrator says "the fools did not perceive / That already the bonds of destruction were fastened on them all," and Odysseus, "Now the bonds of destruction are fastened on you all." But the force conveyed by the echoing meter is not very strong, and a reader might easily miss the close interplay between character and narrator. My aim here is less to criticize these translations than to suggest that the "literate" habit of mind can make such repetition effects seem either inessential or "untranslatable."

More extensive narrative connections between episodes also rely on musical repetitions for their full force. A good example occurs in the first two books of the epic. In book 1, Athena, disguised as Mentes, ruler of the Taphians, gives Telémachos advice on how he should handle the problem of his mother's marriage.

> Early tomorrow, convoke to assembly the hero-Achaians;
> say your word to them all, with the gods themselves to be witness;
> lay your commands on the suitors to scatter and go to their places.
> But for your mother, if now her heart should urge her to marry,
> let her return to the house of her wealthy and powerful father;
> they will make ready the marriage, arranging the gifts for her dowry,
> many and rich, as are fitting to go with a much loved daughter.
>
> (1.272–78)

She goes on to advise a voyage; and later on, Telémachos responds gratefully to her counsel and begins to carry it out almost to the letter. But in the assembly that he convokes in book 2, the suitors remain unyielding. The noblest among them, Antínoös, gives advice that resembles Athena's:

> send your mother away from the palace and urge her to marry
> him whom her father commands and whoever to her is most pleasing.
>
> (2.113–14)

Antínoös ends his speech by asserting that the suitors will never leave the house until Penelope is wedded. Telémachos, responding to the hint of compulsion in the suitor's advice, rejects the suggestion out of hand.

> Never, Antínoös, could I thrust from my house unwilling
> her who bore me, who raised me; my father in some other land yet
> lives or has perished; and it would be bad for me, paying a heavy
> fine to Ikários, if I should willfully send away Mother.
> For from her father will I suffer evils, and others a god will
> send upon me, since Mother will call down cursèd Avengers
> when she departs from the house; then also from men there will be much
> censure for me; therefore that word I never will utter.
>
> (2.130–37)

Later, another suitor, Eurýmachos, carries Antínoös' suggestion further and echoes Athena's lines in the exasperated advice he gives Telémachos.

> I myself among all will now offer Telémachos counsel:
> let him order his mother to go back home to her father's;
> *they will make ready the marriage, arranging the gifts for her dowry,*
> *many and rich, as are fitting to go with a much loved daughter*
>
> (2.194–97; italics mine)

The exact repetition underlines the way Athena's reasonable advice for dealing with his mother's marriage—taking into account her own desires—has been recast in terms of an order to be given her: Telémachos cannot accept such a suggestion without both yielding to the suitors and tyrannizing over his mother. Thus, the repetion helps us to see how Telémachos, in responding to such demands, is moving beyond the helplessness he showed only a few hours earlier and becoming capable of strong and risky decisions concerning the welfare of his mother and his house.

Often, such repetitions are much more widely separated. One example appears in books 1, 16, and 19. In a passage somewhat earlier in book 1 than that just cited, Athena-as-Mentes inquires of Telémachos why there are so many arrogant men dining in his palace; in his answer, the boy tells about his misfortunes, and one passage sums up his helplessness.

> All of the highborn chieftains who lord it over the islands,
> over Doulíchion, Samè, and also wooded Zakýnthos,
> those men too who in rock-strewn Ithaka govern the people,
> all these seek my mother in marriage and wear out the household.
> She will neither reject this odious marriage, nor can she
> make herself carry it through; meanwhile they eat and destroy this
> household of mine. And indeed they will soon put me to the slaughter.
>
> (1.245–51)

Inspired (or so it appears) by such indignity to the son, "Mentes" suggests that he visit Nestor in Pylos and Meneláos in Sparta to seek news of his father, and in books 3 and 4, Telémachos follows this advice. After he has taken this voyage of maturation, escaped from the suitors' ambush on the way home, and returned to Ithaka, he meets his father, still unknown to him, at the cabin of the swineherd Eumaíos. During the meeting, he says this same passage verbatim (16.122–28). But this time, his own father listens; and this time, Telémachos directs the swineherd, in a manner quite worthy of that father, to go inform Penelope in secret of her son's return. He even orders him not to tell his grandfather

Laërtes, despite the latter's pain. The repetition underlines musically both the similarity and the difference in Telémachos' situation: he is still faced with arrogant and scheming suitors, but now, fully adult in his astuteness, he can return plot for plot. Soon after, Athena directs Odysseus to reveal himself to his son, and together they begin laying their plans to recover the household.

Some of this passage recurs yet again in book 19, this time when Penelope speaks to her own husband, who is disguised as a beggar, when she tries to overcome his (feigned) reluctance to speak of himself by telling of her own misfortunes.

> All of the highborn chieftains who lord it over the islands,
> over Doulíchion, Samè, and also wooded Zakýnthos,
> also those who dwell around Ithaka, bright in the sunshine,
> seek me in marriage against my wishes and wear out the household.
>
> (19.130–33)

She goes on to express her great longing for Odysseus and tells of the wiles by which she has avoided the suitors' importuning. This repetition emphasizes how despite Telémachos' earlier impatience with his mother's seeming indecisiveness (1.249–50 above)—perhaps because his youth prevented him from grasping the perils of a lone woman beset by rapacious men—she is much like him in seeing the numerous suitors as a threat to her family rather than as a tribute to her own attractions.

Sometimes it appears that the singer has even constructed his story according to musical principles as much as narrative logic. For example, in book 4, Meneláos tells the visiting Telémachos a long story of his travels, including what he found out from Proteus, on old man of the sea, about Odysseus' survival on Kalýpso's island. He thereby fulfills Telémachos' main purpose in traveling, to find out whether his father is yet alive. Then in book 17, after Telémachos has sailed back to Ithaka, met his father, and returned to the palace, his mother naturally asks him to tell her what he found out (17.44). Instead of complying with her request, as we might expect in such a story, Telémachos tells her not to arouse his emotions but rather to bathe and go to her room while he deals with the prophet Theoklýmenos, who has come with him to Ithaka. Later, Penelope complains that he has not told her any news concerning his father's return, and this time, Telémachos gives her not merely the facts of the case but an abridged account of his travels. In particular, he repeats Meneláos' exact lines concerning Odysseus, moving to what the old man of the sea told him—twenty-three lines of recapitulation, which in the epic performance must have come across much like the reprise of a song or an aria in a modern music drama, made even more memorable by the powerful image of the revenge that Odysseus is to bring on the suitors.

Shameful to think what strong-hearted man is the one whose bed they
want to be bedded in, they themselves being spiritless cowards!
So when a doe having fawns newborn, still sucking her sweet milk,
lulls them to sleep in a thicket, the lair of a powerful lion,
then goes off to the grassy ravines and the spurs of the mountain,
seeking her forage, and then, when he comes back into his covert,
both on the brood and the mother he visits a hideous doomsday,
so upon those men Odysseus will visit a hideous doomsday.

(4.333–40 = 17.124–31)

The reprise is dramatically apt as it comes from Telémachos to his mother, so reinforcing the sense they both have of Odysseus' excellence and of the need to punish the suitors. But its placement may well have arisen in part from this particular singer's skill in using musical repetitions. Such a full recapitulation would not suit the earlier context, the immediate greeting; too much else is happening to stop the action there. So the singer raises our expectations and postpones their fulfillment until the characters are more at leisure, just as a skillful opera librettist might do. The postponement also allows us to see Telémachos as both commanding and devious, quite like his father: he knows firsthand that Odysseus has returned, but he can keep it a secret—and we may perceive that the strain of this concealment makes him at first seem inconsiderate, even rude, to his mother. When he finally consoles her with his powerful "hearsay," Theoklýmenos is on the scene, and we get another bit of dramatic irony when he says of Telémachos, "no clear knowledge he has" (17.153), and then tells her, by his prophetic powers, that Odysseus has not only survived but is already at hand and preparing destruction for the suitors. Thus, Penelope both knows and does not know that Odysseus is alive and returning—a psychological ambivalence that the singer skillfully develops in the next few books.

We see here, as the preceding essay suggests, how a master of his craft can work with traditional compositional techniques to give depth to his narrative. Of course, any translation that renders word-for-word recurrences can make such connections visible. But they do not come so vividly to mind if the medium is less strongly rhythmed and formularized, partly because the strict rhythm itself is a powerful stimulus to the listener's memory—as we all know from such mnemonics as the familiar "Thirty days hath December . . ." And even though, despite the strength of such repeated passages as those I have examined, first-time listeners may not be consciously aware of narrative connections so far apart, as they come to know the work in performance, with its rhythms and repetition techniques, they will perceive how recapitulations in new contexts can add to their sense of the story's significance. In this respect also, the oral epic resembles musical composition: we begin by hearing rhythm and melody, and as we listen more closely, we perceive variations and recapitulations that become a major source of our overall pleasure.

Other features of the work gain even greater meaning from the rhythmical regularity and formulaic phrasing in passages that recur not merely two or three times, emphasizing narrative connections, but many times, to underline the ritual or repeated aspects of life itself. Among these passages is the famous line describing the sunrise, which occurs only twice in the *Iliad* but twenty times in the *Odyssey*:

émós d' érigeneía phanè rhododáctylos Éos . . .
Soon as the Dawn shone forth rose-fingered at earliest daybreak . . .
(2.1)

The sunset too has its formulaic expressions, one of which occurs seven times in the *Odyssey*:

dúseto t' ééliós skioónto te pásai aguíaí.
Then did the sun go down and the ways were all shadowed in darkness.
(2.388)

For the recurring events of daily life, more extensive formula systems were available to the singer of tales, as is illustrated by the following lines about eating a dinner, which first appear in book 1.

Into the house then came the presumptuous suitors, who straightway
took their seats in orderly rows on benches and armchairs.
Heralds at once poured over their hands clean water for washing;
bread they were served by maids, who had heaped it high in the baskets;
young men filled to the brim great wine bowls, ready for drinking.
They put forth eager hands to partake of the food lying ready.
When they had quite satisfied their appetites, drinking and eating,
into the minds of the suitors came other affairs to attend to,
singing and joining in dance, since these are adornments of dining.
(1.144–52)

The formal rhythm of the lines heightens our sense of the occasion itself—of the orderly way in which it is carried out, the pleasure, and the opulence—thus making us experience musically the other aim of the suitors besides winning Penelope: taking their pleasure at another man's expense.

Some of these lines and some shorter formulas within the lines would be familiar to an audience acquainted with the epic tradition, which reached far back before this particular performance (as is shown in the preceding essay) and included songs on other matters, such as the *Iliad*. For example, the originals of the seventh and the fifth lines from the preceding quotation appear (in that order) in *Iliad* 1.469–70, ending a dinner in the house of Chryses, to whom Odysseus has returned his daughter; the sixth and seventh lines appear together three times in the *Iliad*, and the seventh three more times. The third and fifth lines occur (with a slight change) at *Iliad* 9.174–75, describing the dinner from which Ajax, Odysseus, and Phoinix are sent on their embassy to Achilles. There were surely many examples in other oral epics we no longer have. Thus, the singer was setting the perverse decorum of this banquet against an extensive body of associations in the minds of ancient listeners, strongly evoked by the rhythm and the formulaic phrasing.

As the translator of a single epic in this book, I cannot expect to awaken such associations in my readers; but I can try to convey the formality, the decorum of word and act, that ancient readers would have perceived. Moreover, the rhythm of the lines just quoted sets the stage for bringing the feelings evoked by the passage to bear on later occurrences of the same lines in the epic, sometimes in the same order, sometimes mingled with other, equally formulaic elements. The recurrences of these lines are far too numerous to catalog, and there is little use in abstracting them from their context: they come to listeners in the natural course of the narrative, re-creating musically the pleasure and decorum of dining in company. Two examples will suffice. Two of the lines occur in book 3, introducing a libation in the house of Nestor.

> Heralds at once poured over their hands clean water for washing;
> young men filled to the brim great wine bowls, ready for drinking,
> then poured wine into all of the cups to begin the observance;
> throwing the tongues on the fire, they stood up and poured libations.
> When they had made libations and drunk whatever their hearts wished, . . .
>
> $\qquad\qquad\qquad\qquad\qquad\qquad\qquad\qquad$ (3.338–42)

Here, the repetition underlines the deeper decorum of the observance, in contrast to the sheer pleasure the suitors are seeking in the earlier passage. Much later, however, in book 21, four lines of this second passage appear when Antínoös, attempting to divert attention from the failure of the suitors to bend the bow of Odysseus, suggests that the current holiday of Apollo makes it unfitting to try, so that a libation is appropriate.

> Heralds at once poured over their hands clean water for washing;
> young men filled to the brim great wine bowls, ready for drinking,
> then poured wine into all of the cups to begin the observance.
> When they had made libations and drunk whatever their hearts wished, . . .
>
> $\qquad\qquad\qquad\qquad\qquad\qquad\qquad\qquad$ (21.270–73)

Again, the repetition emphasizes how the suitors turn the decorum of the observance to their selfish ends. Immediately afterward, Odysseus proposes that he himself be allowed to attempt stringing and shooting the bow—and the climax of the epic, the slaughter of the suitors, is not long in coming.

Other such repetitions occur with formulas for setting sail on a voyage, arriving and disembarking, arming, and fighting, just to name a few. The actions whose constant recurrences make up the texture of these people's lives are appropriately linked in musical repetitions that evoke a corresponding recognition and satisfaction in the listeners, a sharing in the experience that has an almost ritual quality.

Another feature of Homeric epic—the famous fixed epithets for people, places, even things—can provide pleasure as much in adding to the musical texture, the pattern of rhythmical repetition, as in what they say about the person or thing so modified. Sometimes, they do not seem to fit at all in terms of meaning: more than once the suitors are called the equivalent of "valorous" or "noble" by someone who has little reason to admire them. Even such epithets, like the more apt ones, are important rhythmically in filling out the half-lines, many of them interchangeable, that are so prominent a feature of the epic verse. Such phrases, more so than individual words, are the basic musical units of the work, and noun-epithet combinations provide a potent means of instilling the rhythms in the ears—that is, the consciousness—of listeners. Thus, even many readers who know nothing of the oral-formulaic tradition will remember the formulas "prudent Penelope," "wine-dark sea," and "swift-footed Achilles." Not all these familiar examples are the metrical equivalents of the Greek phrases, but they show how rhythmic units can take hold of the auditory imagination, so to speak, even in cultures far removed from the one in which their originals were first used.

None of this will be new to readers of epics in Greek or to readers without Greek literacy who know about the work in oral-formulaic composition begun about 1928 by Milman Parry and pursued, after his death in 1935, by Albert B. Lord and many other scholars. To the discussion of these matters in the preceding essay, I need only add some notes on aspects that are relevant to this translation. These songs are the fruition of a long tradition of bards who received their stories, their themes, and their very language by oral transmission from their predecessors, elaborating on them, improving them, selecting the best—most appropriate, euphonious, grammatically adaptable—formulas from among an enormous stock, all of them devised to suit one powerful meter, the dactylic hexameter. Some scholars argue indeed that the meter arose from early formulas; but however it originated, it became a decisive factor in the elaborated epic fulfillment. Parry and Lord, who investigated a similarly preliterate oral-formulaic tradition in Yugoslavia still flourishing in the early twentieth century, remarked that the elegance and sophistication of the Homeric epic were in great part products of the demands and the potentialities of the hexameter. Yugoslav bards were far less challenged by their comparatively simple and easily manipulated line, and the results were correspondingly less advanced in complexity and interest. This is not to ignore social conditions—Homer and his predecessors were probably composing their songs at a time when these works constituted the highest literary art of a courtly society, patronized by its most sophisticated members, whereas the Yugoslav bards sang when this niche of high art was occupied by the works of literate men writing for an audience of readers. But the ancient line itself invites, even requires, more complex development.

I need not recapitulate here the controversy over how these monumental epics came to be written down and transmitted. What concerns me rather is the source of the meter's power, a power so great as to make it the standard line for compositions short and long in both Greek and Latin for a millennium—or, indeed, for more than two millennia, if we take into account medieval and Renaissance Greek and Latin productions. It is worthwhile to describe this line as a musical phrase independent of its Greek or Latin embodiment. Even if its value depends largely on its particular linguistic realization, we may be able to see why the rhythm itself is so attractive.

The quantitative dactylic hexameter line as used in Homeric epic is analyzed as being divided into six feet according to the length of the syllables ("quantity"), the first four freely alternating between dactyls (long-short-short, i.e., – ⌣ ⌣) and spondees (long-long, i.e., – –), the sixth either a trochee (long-short, i.e., – ⌣) or a spondee, and the fifth usually a dactyl, though with numerous exceptions. It often has a caesura—a break or sense pause—in the third foot, after either the first long syllable or the first long plus first short, but sometimes this comes in similar places in the fourth foot, and there are occasionally two caesuras. A dieresis—when the end of a word corresponds with the end of a foot—occurs fairly often after the fourth foot, setting off the last two feet; and sometimes the first one or two feet are similarly set off. Enjambment, or "runover"—when the syntax, the phrasing, runs over without pause from one line to the next—is not uncommon. But while it increases narrative continuity and adds rhythmic variety, it seldom compromises the unity of the line, especially since so many of the lines are co-extensive with the formulas of which they are composed. Thus the first five lines of the epic, quoted near the beginning of this essay, scan as follows (ā = long *a*, etc.; ă = short *a*, etc.; | = foot division; ‖ = caesura; |: = dieresis):

Āndră moĭ | ēnnĕpĕ, |: Moūsă, ‖ pŏ | lūtrŏpŏn, |: hōs mălă | pōllă
plāngthĕ, ĕp | eī Troī | ēs ‖ hĭĕ | rŏn ptŏlĭ | ēthrŏn ĕ | pērsĕ;
pōllōn | d' ānthrō | pōn ‖ ĭdĕn | āstĕă |: kaī nŏŏn | ēgnō,

pōllă d' hŏ | g' ĕn pōn|tō ‖ păthĕn | ālgĕă |: hōn kătă | thūmŏn,
ārnŭmĕn|ŏs hēn | tē psū|chēn ‖ kaī | nōstōn hĕ|taīrōn.

Even this short example shows how the meter gives rise to many rhythmic variations within the bounds of a strict measure. Such a quantitative line could be set to quite a regular "beat," yet it can move slow or fast and be light or weighty, smoothly continuous or disjunctive. Its divisions are sufficiently regular to bring the pleasure of expectations fulfilled but are sufficiently variable to allow for many shades of emphasis and meaning. Perhaps most important of all, it is ample enough to embrace substantial formulaic elements that transcend single words, especially as these fill out one of the two half-lines—as is the case with many formulaic noun-epithet combinations. Even phrases that, as far as we can tell from extant verse, are not formulaic take on the strength of those polished units of thought by being cast in such a powerful meter.

As to the actual sound of the hexameter in Greek, the wide variety of consonantal and vowel sounds make an agreeable music in themselves, apart from meaning and the instrumental music that the *Odyssey* itself portrays as accompanying the song (a bard plays the lyre in, e.g., books 1, 4, and 8). Moreover, the polysyllabic words of Greek make the line coherent. The pitch accents of written Greek, provided by Alexandrian editors beginning in the third century B.C., indicate variations in pitch—we are not sure exactly how they are to be interpreted—that would have provided a counterpoint to the strict quantitative rhythm. Though the shape and rhythm of the line derive from oral composition, especially from the formulaic habit of mind, they could and still can be enjoyed by people who have no clear idea of that process. The Athenians of antiquity were probably in precisely that situation: at the Panathenaic festival, they would hear a fixed version of the epics declaimed by a series of rhapsodes who had neither the skill nor the license to improvise—or, rather, "re-create"—in the manner of oral poets. Later, literate poets could take the basic rhythm of the line, dropping formulaic elements as archaic, redundant, and prolix, and use it for a wide variety of compositions, from short lyrics to long philosophical and scientific treatises or quasi-Homeric epics, such as the *Argonautica* of Apollonios Rhodios.

It should be clear by now why a translator of the *Odyssey* might wish to reproduce some of this music, so crucial to the meaning and so implicated in the very existence of the epic. The English hexameter has been the occasion of much controversy, and I am not concerned to defend it as a medium of general poetic composition, though a defense might be made. Once Longfellow has been dismissed as the standard, we should judge success with this meter as with any, according to the way it is managed. Open-minded readers will want to judge the matter quite independently of critical orthodoxies, especially in terms of its suitability for translations of ancient epic poetry.

I make no claim to have reproduced the Greek hexameter in the English translation in this book. Such an attempt would fail before it started; there is no agreed-on or aurally evident system of quantitative syllabic measures in English to correspond with those in Greek, and English does not provide the sonorous polysyllables that give the Greek line its euphony. Though it is inevitably a translator's lot to be compared unfavorably with the great original, I disclaim the presumption of trying to provide the "equivalent" of the Greek line. Even the basic rhythm cannot be quite that of Homer; one critic has said that the English accentual hexameter is more like waltz time than the march time of a quantitative dactyl or spondee. This exaggerates: few Greek readings can have been as strictly measured as a march is—indeed, M. L. West maintains on the basis of good, if scanty, evidence that in Greek epic meter, longs and shorts are in a five to three, rather than a two to one, proportion. Moreover, even if English words have no agreed metrical quantity, syllable length—which word accent often prolongs—makes a significant difference in the rhythm of any line, so that there can never be a real "waltz time" in English. But the two meters are manifestly not the same.

Nevertheless, the English hexameter verse can be beautiful in some of the same ways the Homeric line is, strictly formal and yet highly flexible, adaptable to many situations and levels of style, so to speak, while never losing its fundamental poetic decorum. The English line is composed of shorter words, but these need not make a long line incoherent. Whereas a Greek line contains comparatively few long words, as well as the short articles, particles, and prepositions that go closely with them, the equivalent units in English are phrases: prepositional and appositive phrases, adjective-noun combinations, short dependent clauses. Such word groupings affect the rhythm of any speech in English, and they can be given special value in a long line, either coinciding with or overriding foot boundaries to provide variety.

By the same token, caesura and dieresis can occur in the English line in much the same way as in the Greek line; attentive readers will find that most of my hexameters have just such metrical divisions as I have described with respect to the Greek quantitative line. Most often, a line in my translation will have a caesura in the third foot, not so much because this is the Greek practice as because it makes the most natural division. But many occur in the fourth foot; and there are perhaps more secondary divisions in these lines than in Homeric verse, simply because the long English line can accommodate and profit from more pauses. As in Homer, a dieresis after the fourth foot is not uncommon in my translation. One line division I have found especially useful, even necessary—for

example, to accommodate English versions of Greek names—is the dieresis af-
ter the second foot (e.g., after "thoughtful Telémachos"); the greater frequency
of this break and the very rare division of the line into two equal parts are prob-
ably the main ways in which the basic metrical groupings of my line depart from
those of the Homeric line. To my ear, such variations increase the variety and in-
terest, especially when the verse is read aloud.

Reading aloud will also, I hope, give value to the various ways I have realized
the basically dactylic rhythms with their spondaic alternatives. I think the
difficulty of introducing spondees into English dactylics is sometimes exagger-
ated, but it is true that a trochee with a strong second syllable (i.e., ´ `) sometimes
has to do duty for a spondee. It is not possible to be uniform in this; for exam-
ple, possessive pronouns sometimes provide a short syllable in a dactyl and at
other times are the second element of a spondaic foot, depending on the metri-
cal needs of the place. I know that not all readers will agree with my sense of the
allowable latitude in these and other ambivalent feet, but I hope the overall
strength of the line will override such disagreements.

One other case that may cause discomfort in some readers is my use of a strong
adjective-plus-noun spondee at the end of a line, as in "beautiful bright eyes,"
which seems to contravene the prevalent falling feeling of the final cadence. To
my ear, this variation aptly emphasizes the adjective and brings out the mono-
syllabic strength of English. It happens rarely; other line endings composed of
monosyllables, which are fairly frequent, maintain the cadential fall, that is,
movement from strong to weak. (It is interesting, though not decisive as a ra-
tionale, to notice similarly rare cases in Homeric verse—which also gives most
line endings a clearly falling cadence. For example, in both *nepheleígeretá Zeús*
and *póntoporós neús*, the final monosyllable is more emphatic in both meaning and
sound than the syllable before.) In these cases, as in others, my judgments are
based on reading aloud and listening; "bright eyes" or "sweet wine," to name two
examples, sound right in final cadences.

Names pose a few problems. I have adopted the standard English pronunci-
ations, especially of famous names, and whenever possible, I have followed the
index in H. J. Rose's *Handbook of Greek Mythology* for less common names, often
using diacritical marks to make pronunciation clear. Most such pronunciations
fit well into English dactylics, though some names (e.g., *Ámphitrítè*) require more
latitude. As for the name of the hero, though many Americans would pronounce
it as four syllables, I have assumed Rose's pronunciation of the *-eus* ending as a
diphthong, sometimes filling out a spondee—"O/dýsseús"—but more often the
first short syllable of a dactyl—"O/dýsseus of/ mány de/víces." I have assumed
the same for other names ending in *-eus*.

Let us revisit the English translation of lines 1–5 with this more analytical approach in mind (´ = metrical stress, ˘ = unstressed syllable, ` = natural stress when different from metrical stress, | = foot division, ‖ = caesura, |: = dieresis).

Téll mé, | Múse, ŏf thĕ | mán ‖ vèrsă|tíle ănd rĕ|soúrcefŭl, whŏ |
wánderĕd
mánў ă | seá-míle |: áftĕr hĕ | ránsácked |: Tróy's hòlў | cítў.
Mánў thĕ | mén whóse | tówns hĕ ŏb|sérved, ‖ whóse | mínds hĕ
dĭs|cóvĕred,
mánў thĕ | paíns ĭn hĭs | heárt ‖ hé | súffered, tră|vérsĭng thĕ | seáwáy,
fíghtĭng fŏr | hís ówn | lífe ‖ ănd ă | wáy báck | hóme fŏr hĭs |
cómrádes.

These lines are similar to those of the Greek epic in their overall rhythmic shape, though as I remarked earlier, English has its own kind of counterpoint, that is, tension between the metrical and the natural stresses. Also, the same virtue of wide variation within a strict metrical norm, a "singable" line, appears in English as in Greek.

Though I do not claim to have made every line a perfect hexameter, even of the English kind—the exigencies of conveying the sense closely would make that ideal impossible to attain—I hope that the metrical norm is strong enough, the result distinct enough to the ear, to maintain the exhilarating and powerful forward motion so essential to the epic as a performance. Moreover, while I recognize the differences between the English and the Greek line, I have paid attention to ways in which they are or can be made similar. One underlying similarity derives from the fact that both languages have a "rising" rhythm—that is, moving from weaker to stronger emphasis—in ordinary speech, because both have articles before many nouns, as well as significant unstressed prepositions, pronouns, and other features that often come before the sense stresses. Even verbs in Greek often begin with relatively less emphatic augments determining tense or aspect. So it is not surprising that in both languages, iambic verse—pentameter in English, trimeter (somewhat like an English iambic hexameter) in Greek— is used in the verse drama for most dialogues: speech, however stylized, follows the basic rhythms of the languages. In both languages, therefore, the dactylic meter reverses normal speech rhythm to evoke special language and special uses of language and seems to be governed more by musical principles. Therefore, its speech patterns are even less to be judged by standards of colloquial speech than are those of dramatic dialogue. In the hexameters of both languages, almost every line begins and ends with a "falling" rhythm (i.e., strong to weak): while this puts a strain on the ordinary resources of the languages, it produces a clear and compelling musical effect.

It follows from this view of the hexameter that any attempt to be colloquially idiomatic in such a translation would run counter to the very genius of the medium. Indeed, only twentieth-century critical orthodoxies, reacting against late Victorian artifice, could have made such insistence on colloquial speech patterns seem fitting to Homeric translation. Nobody would maintain that anybody ever spoke in anything like the Homeric idiom; in terms of ordinary speech, it must always have seemed otiose to say "see with my eyes," "grasp with my hands," "in his heart and his spirit," or many other quite usual Homeric locutions. Even less idiomatic are the fixed epithets and other formulaic ways of saying things, the drawn-out speech openings, the repeated passages I discussed earlier. However well the twentieth-century passion for bringing every sort of poetry into the idiom of its intended readers may succeed in other genres, it can seriously limit a reader's sense of the Homeric epics. At best, it brings about a total recasting of the original, a "reinterpretation" in modern terms. Fitzgerald's translation has been very successful in that respect; Richmond Lattimore tried much harder—with a good deal of success—to recognize the special nature of the Homeric idiom, and I have profited as much as possible from his example. Robert Fagles' recent translation is more like Fitzgerald's in seeking its own quite modern flavor, and its success in finding one congenial to many contemporary readers is apparent. Stanley Lombardo's version tries even harder to present Homer in modern dress, and his diction is often colloquial, even at times slangy—as in "arrogant bastards" and "Hey, everybody," to quote random examples.

The words I have chosen come from a more traditional stock, just as Homeric diction was deeply traditional. Though I do not at all claim to have produced a genuinely formulaic translation—such a version would have to draw on a huge body of traditional formulas like that available to the Homeric bard—this essential feature of the original has had a considerable effect on the diction of my translation. Far from trying to find "original" words or locutions, I have seized on such formulaic ways of putting things as English offers. At its best, this procedure can reveal the musical potency of familiar modes of speech. A similar consideration has governed my translation of the fixed epithets. Some are inventions, responding to considerations of meter and euphony as much as to sense. But as often as I could, I have used a phrase that is anchored in our tradition of Homeric translation—one notable case being "wine-dark sea" (sometimes, for the meter, varied to "wine-dark seaway") for the Greek *oínopa pónton*. As in Homeric verse, the meter itself determines the choice of some words, especially such manifestly "poetic" ones as *sea-brine* and *scion*, which occur where a spondee or a trochee is required. Though such usages depart from normal English, I make no apology; in the original also the tradition and the rhythm override considerations of "normal" diction or even grammar in many places. I hope that such words and phrases will come to seem quite normal in this epic context, especially when the translation is read aloud with full attention to the rhythm.

Such a reading should also confirm the accuracy of Matthew Arnold's pronouncement in his famous essay *On Translating Homer* that Homer is among the most direct and straightforward of poets in his narrative style. Our greater understanding of the conditions of oral performance has made it clearer why this is so: no audience of an oral epic would put up with involved or circumlocutive singing, even if a bard wanted to do it. The diction in my translation reflects this Homeric directness; I do not think it would be appropriate to try for an archaic effect, for Homeric Greek is too much its own poetic idiom to be turned into a quaint version of English, even if a contemporary audience would tolerate it. Thus, I have striven to make non-idiomatic, "poetic" words and phrases fit into a medium that does not require major adjustments of the reader. For the same reason, though inverted syntax—phrasing not in the normal order of spoken English—sometimes appears in my translation, I have tried to use it only in ways that do not interfere with listeners' immediate grasp of the sense, aided as they are by the strong rhythm of the verse.

The strict meter at the basis of this rhythm recurs in every particular poetic line, and my aim, to make available in English as much as possible of the musical repetition of the original Greek, has enforced a close line-for-line equivalence. Sometimes a line that first occurs in a two-line sentence occurs alone later on, and I have occasionally had to recast my earlier rendering to make such a line independently intelligible and therefore repeatable in isolation from its "mate." Line-for-line translation means also that I have had to "fill out" some lines whose sense could be rendered more briefly; I hope I have done so in reasonably "Homeric" ways. An obvious advantage of this approach is that my translation can be used in conjunction with any standard commentary on the work, as the line numbers in the translation will coincide exactly with those of the commentaries. Finally, keeping to the Homeric line has made me preserve the Homeric syntactical movement as closely as English allows. Wherever the syntax seems incoherent, the reader can assume that the received text of the original has much the same effect, often helping to characterize the speaker of the passage.

For all these reasons, "originality" could not be my major aim. I seek to connect this work with as many elements of both traditions—the Homeric and the English—as I can. Therefore, I gladly acknowledge my debt to my many predecessors in the field of Homeric scholarship and translation, whom I have freely plundered to find the best interpretations and the most suitable words. I mention the most important here. I have used the text and the commentary of W. B. Stanford. *A Commentary on Homer's* Odyssey, by Alfred Heubeck and his associated editors, has illuminated my understanding, as have the editions of books 6–8 by A. F. Garvie and of books 19–20 by R. B. Rutherford. R. J. Cunliffe's *Lexicon of the Homeric Dialect* has provided an indispensable word-hoard. My ambition to reproduce the many repetitions of lines and even half-lines would have been hard, if not impossible, to envision without the aid of Henry Dunbar's *Complete Concordance to the* Odyssey *of Homer.* My most constant companions among the translations have been those of A. T. Murray, revised by George E. Dimock, in the Loeb Classical Library edition; Albert Cook, valuable for the very literalness of its readings; and Richmond Lattimore, which has yielded many a lovely turn of phrase, for some of which I might have to face the accusation of plagiarism—though I cannot be sure that he himself did not take them from his predecessors. To reject the right phrase just because somebody else has used it first would be to ignore the very nature of our enterprise. I can only thank Lattimore and the others and hope that the resulting translation is of sufficient interest and beauty to exonerate the deed. Translation of a great work of literature must always be as much a matter of cooperation as of competition with those who have come before. In this respect at least, I claim kinship with the ancient singers of tales, since not originality but fidelity to the sense and the experience of the song has been my aim, and I draw on a long tradition in trying to achieve that aim.

Though a translator must always be ready to weather the scorn of those who know and love the original epic, I can hope that even for them, this translation may make more vividly manifest the music of repetitions that would appear only dimly, if at all, from a slow and painstaking reading in one's study. In such a situation—which is surely the situation that most readers of Greek encounter—attention to vexed problems of text and interpretation prevent the sort of continuous auditory experience by means of which this music can best be heard. Only the most advanced Homerists, who could bring to the experience a close knowledge of the language and the epic, could respond to an oral performance in Greek—others would naturally be unable even to follow the narrative. After hearing the English version, scholars may perhaps return to the original with more appreciation of its undeniably greater music. A few Greekless readers or hearers may gratify one of the translator's highest ambitions: that his work inspire others to seek more direct access to the poem by learning the language in which it was written. As to whether my regard for the music of the epic has brought me nearer the attainment of another high ambition, to approach the nobility that Matthew Arnold rightly pronounced the most elusive of Homer's qualities for the translator to convey, others must decide.

Bibliography

This list both provides references to the works, including translations, mentioned in the two introductory essays and suggests books and essays for further reading. Nonspecialists can read and enjoy most of the latter, and some, like those of Butler and Severin, show lively nonscholarly approaches to questions raised by the *Odyssey*. For those who want to read more deeply on particular Homeric questions, more comprehensive lists can be found in such books as those of Schein, Segal, and Olson.

TEXTS, COMMENTARIES, WORDBOOKS, AND TRANSLATIONS

Allen, T. W., ed. *Odyssey*. 2nd ed. 2 vols. Oxford, 1917–55.

Cook, Albert, trans. and ed. *Homer: The* Odyssey. New York, 1993.

Cotterill, H. B., trans. *Homer's* Odyssey. London, 1911.

Cunliffe, R. J. *A Lexicon of the Homeric Dialect*. Norman, OK, New ed. 1963.

Dunbar, Henry. *A Complete Concordance to the* Odyssey *of Homer*. New ed. Revised by Benedetto Marzullo. Hildesheim and New York, 1971.

Fagles, Robert, trans. *Homer: The* Odyssey. New York, 1996.

Fitzgerald, Robert, trans. *Homer: The* Odyssey. New York, 1961.

Garvie, A. F., ed. *Homer,* Odyssey*: Books VI–VIII*. Cambridge, 1994.

Heubeck, Alfred, Manuel Fernandez-Galiano, J. B. Hainsworth, Arie Hoekstra, Joseph Russo, and Stephanie West, eds. *A Commentary on Homer's* Odyssey. 3 vols. Oxford, 1988–92.

Jones, Peter V. *Homer's* Odyssey*: A Companion to the Translation of Richmond Lattimore*. Carbondale and Bristol, 1988.

Kemball-Cook, Brian, trans. *The* Odyssey *of Homer*. Hitchin, Eng., 1993.

Lattimore, Richmond, trans. *The* Odyssey *of Homer*. New York, Evanston, and London, 1965.

Lombardo, Stanley, trans. *Homer: The* Odyssey. Indianapolis, 2000.

Murray, A. T., trans. *Homer: The* Odyssey. Revised by George E. Dimock. Loeb Classical Library. Cambridge, MA, and London, 1995.

Pope, Alexander, trans. *The* Odyssey *of Homer.* London, 1725.

Rutherford, R. B., ed. *Homer,* Odyssey: *Books XIX and XX.* Cambridge, 1992.

Stanford, W. B., ed. *The* Odyssey *of Homer.* 2nd ed. 2 vols. London and Basingstoke, 1958–59.

ESSAY COLLECTIONS

Atchity, Kenneth. *Critical Essays on Homer.* Boston, 1987.

Bloom, Harold, ed. *Homer: Modern Critical Views.* New York, 1986.

———, ed. *Homer's* The Odyssey. New York, 1988.

Bremer, J. M., I. J. F. de John, and J. Kalff, eds. *Homer: Beyond Oral Poetry, Recent Trends in Homeric Interpretation.* Amsterdam, 1987.

Buitron, Diana, and Beth Cohen, eds. *The* Odyssey *and Ancient Art: An Epic in Word and Image.* Annandale-on-Hudson, NY, 1992.

Carter, Jane B., and Sarah P. Morris, eds. *The Ages of Homer: A Tribute to Emily Townsend Vermeule.* Austin, 1995.

Clarke, Howard, ed. *Twentieth-Century Interpretations of the* Odyssey: *A Collection of Critical Essays.* Englewood Cliffs, NJ, 1983.

Cohen, Beth, ed. *The Distaff Side: Representing the Female in Homer's* Odyssey. New York and London, 1995.

McAuslan, Ian, and Peter Walcot. *Homer.* Greece and Rome Studies. Oxford, 1998.

Morris, Ian, and Barry Powell, eds. *A New Companion to Homer.* Leiden, 1997.

Myrsiades, Kostas, ed. *Approaches to Teaching Homer's* Iliad *and* Odyssey. New York, 1987.

Nelson, Conny, ed. *Homer's* Odyssey: *A Critical Handbook.* Belmont, CA, 1969.

Schein, Seth L. *Reading the* Odyssey: *Selected Interpretive Essays.* Princeton, 1996.

Steiner, George, and Robert Fagles, eds. *Homer: A Collection of Critical Essays.* Englewood Cliffs, NJ, 1962.

Taylor, Charles H., Jr., ed. *Essays on the* Odyssey: *Selected Modern Criticism.* Indianapolis, 1963.

Wace, Alan J. B., and Frank Stubbings, eds. *A Companion to Homer.* London, 1962.

BOOKS AND INDIVIDUAL ESSAYS OF SPECIAL INTEREST

Arnold, Matthew. *On Translating Homer.* London, 1861. Reprinted in *On the Classical Tradition.* Ed. R. H. Super. Ann Arbor and London, 1960.

Auerbach, Eric. "Odysseus' Scar." *Mimesis: The Representation of Reality in Western Literature*, chapter 1. Trans. Willard Trask. Princeton, 1953. Reprinted in the essay collections of Bloom, Nelson, and Steiner and Fagles.

Austin, Norman. *Archery at the Dark of the Moon: Poetic Problems in Homer's* Odyssey. Berkeley, Los Angeles, and London, 1975.

Beye, Charles R. *The* Iliad, *the* Odyssey, *and the Epic Tradition.* New York, 1966.

Bowra, C. M. *Heroic Poetry.* London, 1952.

Burkert, Walter. *The Orientalizing Revolution: Near Eastern Influence on Greek Culture in the Early Archaic Age.* Cambridge, MA, 1992.

Butler, Samuel. *The Authoress of the* Odyssey. London, 1897. 3rd ed. Chicago, 1967.

Camps, W. A. *An Introduction to Homer.* Oxford, 1980.

Clarke, Howard. *The Art of the* Odyssey. Englewood Cliffs, NJ, 1967.

———. *Homer's Readers: A Historical Introduction to the* Iliad *and the* Odyssey. Newark, DE, 1981.

Clay, Jenny Strauss. *The Wrath of Athena: Gods and Men in the* Odyssey. Princeton, 1983.

Dimock, George E. *The Unity of the* Odyssey. Amherst, 1989.

Doherty, Lillian Eileen. *Siren Songs: Gender, Audiences, and Narrators in the* Odyssey. Ann Arbor, 1995.

Engelmann, R., and W. C. F. Anderson. *Pictorial Atlas to Homer's* Iliad *and* Odyssey. London, 1892.

Felson-Rubin, Nancy. *Regarding Penelope: From Character to Poetics.* Princeton, 1994.

Finley, John H., Jr. *Homer's* Odyssey. Cambridge, MA, and London, 1978.

Finley, Moses. *The World of Odysseus.* 2nd, rev. ed. Harmondsworth, 1979.

Foley, John Miles. *Traditional Oral Epic: The* Odyssey, Beowulf, *and the Serbo-Croatian Return Song.* Berkeley, 1990.

Griffin, Jasper. *Homer: The* Odyssey. Landmarks of World Literature. Cambridge, 1977.

Katz, Marilyn A. *Penelope's Renown: Meaning and Indeterminacy in the* Odyssey. Princeton, 1991.

Kirk, G. S. *Homer and the Epic.* Cambridge, 1965. Abridged version of *The Songs of Homer.*

———. *The Songs of Homer.* Cambridge, 1962.

Lord, Albert B. *The Singer of Tales.* Cambridge, MA, 1960. New ed., 2000.

Louden, Bruce. *The* Odyssey: *Structure, Narration, and Meaning.* Baltimore, 1999.

Luce, J. V. *Celebrating Homer's Landscapes.* New Haven and London, 1998.

Martin, Richard. "Telemachus and the Last Hero Song." *Colby Quarterly* 29 (1993): 222–40.

Moulton, Carroll. *Similes in the Homeric Poems.* Göttingen, 1977.

Murnaghan, Sheila. *Disguise and Recognition in the* Odyssey. Princeton, 1987.

Nagler, Michael N. *Spontaneity and Tradition: A Study in the Oral Art of Homer.* Berkeley, 1974.

Nagy, Gregory. *The Best of the Achaeans: Concepts of the Hero in Archaic Greek Poetry.* Rev. ed. Baltimore and London, 1999.

———. *Homeric Questions.* Austin, 1996.

———. *Poetry as Performance: Homer and Beyond.* Cambridge and New York, 1996.

Olson, S. Douglas. *Blood and Iron: Stories and Story-telling in Homer's* Odyssey. Leiden, New York, and Cologne, 1995.

Page, Denys. *Folktales in Homer's* Odyssey. Cambridge, MA, 1973.

———. *The Homeric* Odyssey. Oxford, 1955.

Parry, Milman. *The Making of Homeric Verse: The Collected Papers of Milman Parry*. Ed. Adam Parry. Oxford, 1971.

Peradotto, John. *Man in the Middle Voice: Name and Narration in the* Odyssey. Princeton, 1990.

Rubens, Beaty, and Oliver Taplin. *An Odyssey Round Odysseus: The Man and His Story Traced through Time and Place*. London, 1989.

Rutherford, R. B. *Homer*. Oxford, 1994.

Scully, Stephen. *Homer and the Sacred City*. Ithaca, NY, and London, 1990.

Segal, Charles. *Singers, Heroes, and Gods in the* Odyssey. Ithaca, NY, and London, 1994.

Severin, Tim. *The Ulysses Voyage: Sea Search for the* Odyssey. New York, 1987.

Stanford, W. B. *The Ulysses Theme: A Study in the Adaptability of a Traditional Hero*. Oxford, 1983.

Stanford, W. B., and J. V. Luce. *The Quest for Ulysses*. New York and Washington, 1974.

Symeonoglou, Sarantis. "The Homeric Geography of Ithaka." *Proceedings of the Fourth Congress on the* Odyssey, *September 1984*. Ithaca, 1986. 91–111.

Thalman, William G. *The* Odyssey: *An Epic of Return*. New York, 1992.

———. *The Swineherd and the Bow: Representations of Class in the* Odyssey. Ithaca, NY, 1998.

Thornton, Agathe. *People and Themes in Homer's* Odyssey. Duneden, NZ, and London, 1970.

Tracy, Stephen W. *The Story of the* Odyssey. Princeton, 1990.

Vivante, Paolo. *Homer*. New Haven and London, 1985.

Walsh, Thomas R. *Fighting Words and Feuding Words: Anger and the Homeric Poems*. Lanham, MD, 2002.

West, M. L. *Ancient Greek Music*. Oxford and New York, 1992.

Whitman, Cedric H. *Homer and the Heroic Tradition*. Cambridge, MA, and London, 1958.

Woodhouse, W. J. *The Composition of Homer's* Odyssey. Oxford, 1930. Reprint, 1969.

Maps

Almost all the geographical names mentioned in the *Odyssey* can be found on one of the following maps drawn by Bruce Burton. Most of them are on the map of Greece and its environs, depicting mainland Greece, the Aegean Sea and its islands, and Asia Minor, where many of these locations have been called by the same name since antiquity. But a few of them are uncertain, and some may be imaginary. Even the identification of Ithaka has been questioned, though most scholars now think the island called Ithaki in modern Greek to be that of the epic. Samè is the modern Kefalonia. The identity of Doulíchion, assigned here to the modern island of Lefkada, is uncertain, as is the location of Taphos.

The main purpose of the map of Ithaka is apparent in the relief drawing: to give an image of the island itself in all its hilly, "rugged and rocky" (10.463) beauty so cherished by Odysseus and so suggestive of his own character in that respect, as in the way the sea interpenetrates the land. The location of Odyssean places is controversial; this map shows what British archaeological investigations have proposed, as most recently set forth in J. V. Luce's *Celebrating Homer's Landscapes* (165–230), which interested readers should consult. Luce's views are contested by Prof. Sarantis Symeonoglou of Washington University in St. Louis, who says he has strong archaeological evidence for siting the palace of Odysseus and the city of Ithaka south of Mount Aetos on the southern end of the isthmus connecting the two parts of the island. He places Laërtes' farm where the palace of Odysseus is on this map. For him, Rheithron Harbor is the water between the two parts of the island, and Phorkys Bay is the long bay leading southeastward from it. He agrees with Luce on the locations of Mount Nériton, the cave of the nymphs, Eumaíos' farm, Ravens' Rock, and Arethoúsa Spring, but he places Mount Neion in the southern part. He thinks that Ásteris, where the suitors wait in ambush for Telémachos, is the island off the southeast coast of Ithaka, not far from Ravens' Rock. Symeonoglou's views are available in Greek, with a summary in English, in his "The Homeric Geography of Ithaka."

The outline map of the Mediterranean gives sites of Odysseus' adventures as conceived by ancient tradition and conveyed by such writers as the Roman geographer Strabo; it has no claim to authenticity of any sort. Even if these ideas had their origin in ancient nautical lore, they have been so transformed by the poetic imagination as to be unidentifiable. We can say that the Lotus-eaters must have been southwest of Cape Máleia, since the winds blew Odysseus' ships past Kýthera in that direction. But Odysseus' other wanderings are not so clear. In *The Ulysses Voyage*, Tim Severin claims to have recovered a sense of Odysseus' route—radically differing from the one this map would indicate—by actually taking a voyage in such a ship as Odysseus might have captained and following the indications in the text carefully, but his conclusions, while of considerable interest, are probably no more "authentic" than those of the many others who have tried to trace Odysseus.

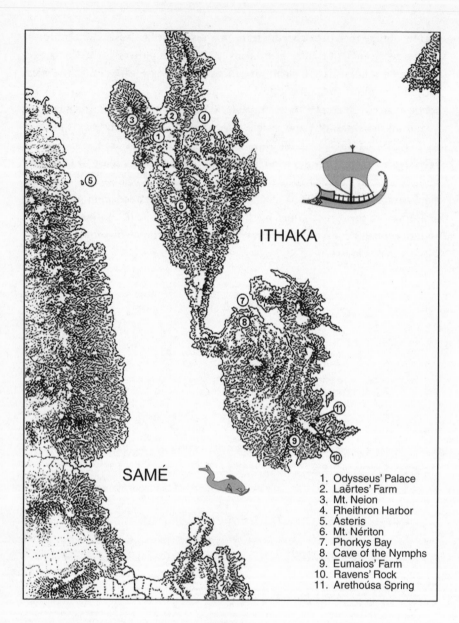

ITHAKA

SAMÉ

1. Odysseus' Palace
2. Laërtes' Farm
3. Mt. Neion
4. Rheithron Harbor
5. Ásteris
6. Mt. Nériton
7. Phorkys Bay
8. Cave of the Nymphs
9. Eumaios' Farm
10. Ravens' Rock
11. Arethoúsa Spring

Ithaka

Greece and its environs

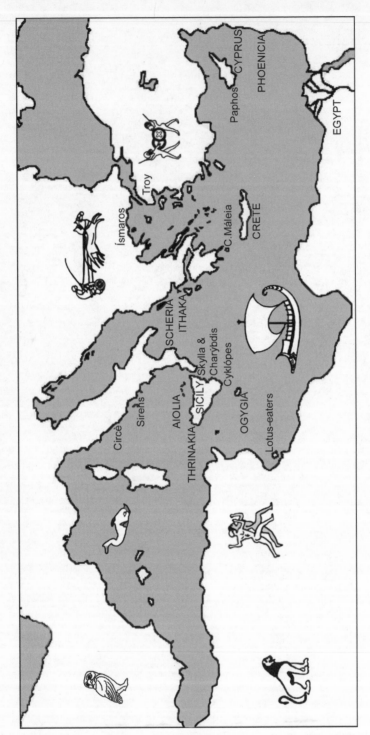

The Mediterranean Sea of Odysseus' adventures

THE *ODYSSEY* OF HOMER

BOOK 1

Tell me, Muse, of the man versatile and resourceful, who wandered
many a sea-mile after he ransacked Troy's holy city.
Many the men whose towns he observed, whose minds he discovered,
many the pains in his heart he suffered, traversing the seaway,
5 fighting for his own life and a way back home for his comrades.
Not even so did he save his companions, as much as he wished to,
for by their own mad recklessness they were brought to destruction,
childish fools—they decided to eat up the cows of the High Lord,
Helios: he then took from the men their day of returning.
10 Even for us, holy daughter of Zeus, start there to recount this.

    Then were the others, whoever escaped from the sheer destruction,
all in their homes, since they had escaped from the war and the deep sea;
only the one still yearned to go home, still wanted his woman;
queenly Kalýpso, a nymph and illustrious goddess, was holding
15 him in her spacious cavern; she wanted to make him her husband.
But when the year came round in the course of the seasons' revolving
wherein the gods had spun as his destiny making the journey
homeward to Ithaka, once he was there he did not escape trials,
even among his own friends. All the gods took pity upon him,
20 all but Poseidon, who hated with deep unquenchable anger
godlike Odysseus, until he arrived at last in his country.

    But to the far Ethiopians now that god had departed—
these Ethiopians, farthest of men, are divided asunder;
some of them dwell where the High Lord sets; near the others, he rises.
25 He was with them to partake of their hecatomb, bulls and mature rams;
there he rejoiced as he sat at the feast; but the other immortals
were in the house of Olympian Zeus all sitting together.
Speaking among them opened the Father of gods and of mankind,
for in his heart he was moved to reflect on faultless Aigísthos, ← *zeus thinks he's an idiot*
30 whom Agamemnon's child had killed, far-honored Orestes.

Mindful of him, Zeus spoke these words there among the immortals:
    "Strange to behold, what blame these mortals can bring against godhead!
For their ills, they assert, are from us, when they of themselves by
their mad recklessness have pain far past what is fated.

35 So even now has Aigísthos, beyond fate, married the lawful
bedmate of Atreus' son, then murdered the man as he came home,
though he knew of his ruin, because we told him beforehand—
sending as messenger Hermes, the keen-eyed slayer of Argos—
neither to murder the man himself nor to marry his bedmate:

40 'For from Orestes will come the requital for Atreus' scion,
when he reaches adulthood and feels a desire for his country.'
So spoke Hermes but did not prevail on the mind of Aigísthos,
though so kindly disposed; now all has been paid for together."
    Speaking to him then answered the goddess bright-eyed Athena:

45 "Father of all of us, scion of Kronos and sovereign ruler,
surely indeed that man most fittingly lies in destruction.
So let all be destroyed, whoever may work such malice.
But for ingenious Odysseus the heart inside me is troubled.
Wretch! Faraway from his friends, he has long been suffering sorrows,

50 off on a tide-washed island the broad sea has at its navel.
There on the forested isle in her home is a goddess residing,
daughter of Atlas the murderous-minded, who knows of the deepest
chasms in all of the seas and himself holds up the enormous
pillars that hold in their separate places the earth and the heaven.

55 His is the daughter who keeps that man, unhappy and weeping,
always in speeches of tender cajolery tries to beguile him,
so that he might put Ithaka out of his mind. But Odysseus,
longing to catch at the least some glimpse of the smoke as it rises
out of his land, wants rather to die. Yet even for this no

60 care is your heart now taking, Olympian. Did not Odysseus
please you, offering victims beside the Achaians' vessels
there in the broad Troäd? Why is he so odious now, Zeus?"
    Answering her in return spoke forth the cloud-gathering god Zeus:
"Oh my child, what a word has escaped from the fence of your teeth now!

65 How could I ever indeed be forgetful of godlike Odysseus,
who in his mind is beyond all men, and beyond them he offers
sacred gifts to the gods, the immortals who hold the broad heaven?
No, it is earth-upholding Poseidon who feels a relentless
wrath on account of the Cyklops, deprived of his eye by Odysseus—

70 that godlike Polyphémos, who is among all the Cyklópes

86

greatest in power and strength. He was born to the nymph Thoösa,
who is the daughter of Phorkys, a lord of the desolate sea-brine—
deep in the hollow caverns, she mingled in love with Poseidon.
Since that deed of Odysseus, although the earth-shaker Poseidon
75 does not kill him, he leads him astray from the land of his fathers.
But come now, let us all take thought and consider together
how he may go back home; and Poseidon will have to renounce his
wrath at the man: he cannot, against all of the other immortal
gods who now are unwilling, alone go on with his wrangling."
80   Speaking to him then answered the goddess bright-eyed Athena:
"Father of all of us, scion of Kronos and sovereign ruler,
if to the fortunate gods it indeed is agreeable now that
various-minded Odysseus return back home to his palace,
let us at once send Hermes the messenger, slayer of Argos,
85 to the Ogygian isle, so that he may swiftly deliver
this our certain decree to the nymph with the beautiful tresses:
'Send home steadfast-hearted Odysseus, that he may return now.'
Meanwhile I will go down into Ithaka, so as to rouse his
son about him much more and to put more strength in his spirit.
90 When to assembly he summons the long-haired men, the Achaians,
he will speak out the case against all of the suitors, who keep on
killing his thick-thronged sheep and his swing-paced crooked-horned cattle.
I will dispatch him to Sparta as well as to sandy-soiled Pylos
asking about his father's return, if he hear of it somewhere,
95 so that a noble renown among men may hold him in honor."
    So she spoke; on her feet she fastened her beautiful sandals,
golden, undying, divine, which carry her over the water,
over the measureless surface of earth with the breath of the storm wind.
Then she took up the powerful spear, well pointed with sharp bronze,
100 heavy and huge and compact, that she uses to shatter the close-pressed
ranks of the fighters who rouse her wrath whose Father is mighty.
Speedily she came down from the summit of lofty Olympos;
there in the Ithakan land, she stood at the doors of Odysseus,
on the threshold of the court—in her hand still holding her bronze spear—
105 making herself like a stranger, the chief of the Taphians, Mentes.
There she discovered the suitors, presumptuous nobles, who then were
playing at draughts to amuse their minds in front of the doorway,
sitting on hides of the cattle that they themselves had slaughtered.
They had heralds attending on them, and efficient retainers,
110 some of them mixing the wine and the water together in wine bowls;

others were cleaning the tables with many-holed sponges, and then they
set them ready for dining and carved much meat for the suitors.
     Godlike Telémachos now was the first by far to observe her;
for in the midst of the suitors he sat, much troubled in spirit,
115 seeing in mind his glorious father, if coming from somewhere
he might cause those suitors throughout his palace to scatter,
then have honor himself and be lord of his own possessions.
Thinking of this he sat with the suitors, but seeing Athena
went straight out to the porch; in his heart he was vexed that a stranger
120 stood so long a time there in the doorway; standing beside her
then, he gripped her right hand and received from the other the bronze spear;
raising his voice he spoke, and in these winged words he addressed her:
     "Welcome, stranger—with us you will have kind greeting, and only
when you have eaten a meal shall you tell what you are in need of."
125   So as he spoke he led her; with him went Pallas Athena.
When these two had arrived in the high-built hall of the palace,
first then, taking the spear, he stood it against a tall pillar,
inside the well-polished holder for spears, in which there were others,
many a spear left there by steadfast-hearted Odysseus.
130 He led her to a seat in an armchair, covered with linen,
beautiful, skillfully made; and beneath for her feet was a footstool.
Nearby, his own painted chair he set, well apart from the other
diners, the suitors, for fear that his guest, in disgust with the tumult,
have no taste for the meal, coming so among arrogant idlers—
135 also that he might ask him concerning his faraway father.
Hand-washing water a maid then carried to them in a lovely
gold-wrought pitcher, and over a basin of silver she poured it,
so they could wash; nearby, she set out a well-polished table.
Carrying food, the revered housekeeper approached them and set it
140 close to them, many a dish she gladly supplied from her storage.
Platters of meat an attendant lifted and set there beside them,
every sort, then close to their hands placed gold drinking goblets;
often the herald who poured out wine came round to the diners.
     Into the house then came the presumptuous suitors, who straightway
145 took their seats in orderly rows on benches and armchairs.
Heralds at once poured over their hands clean water for washing;
bread they were served by the maids, who had heaped it high in the baskets;
young men filled to the brim great wine bowls, ready for drinking.
They put forth eager hands to partake of the food lying ready.
150 When they had quite satisfied their appetites, drinking and eating,

into the minds of the suitors came other affairs to attend to,
singing and joining in dance, since these are adornments of dining.
Therefore a herald delivered a beautiful lyre to the hands of
Phemios, who by compulsion would sing his tales for the suitors.
155 Straightway he struck up a beautiful song by playing a prelude.
      Meanwhile Telémachos spoke of his troubles to bright-eyed Athena,
keeping his head near hers, so as not to be heard by the others:
"Stranger and friend, will you blame me for what I am going to tell you?
These men turn their attention to such things, harping and singing,
160 lightly, because they consume without payment the goods of another,
one whose glistening bones are now somewhere rained on and rotting,
lying upon the firm earth, or else rolled by the billowing sea-brine.
Should they ever behold him return to his Ithakan homeland,
all of them then would pray to be far more nimble in running,
165 rather than richer in gold or in clothing or other possessions.
But as it is, he has died by a terrible death, and there is no
comfort remaining for us, even if some earth-dwelling man should
say he will yet come back. Quite lost is his day of returning.
But come now, tell me this and recount it exactly and fully:
170 Who are you? Whence do you come? What city is yours, and what parents?
Then, upon what sort of ship did you come here? How did the sailors
bring you to Ithaka? What did they claim as their names and their nation?
For it was certainly not on foot, I suppose, that you came here.
Truthfully speak to me now about these things, so that I know well
175 whether indeed you arrive for the first time or are an old-time
friend of the family, since there were numerous men who would come here—
others, when he was among men too, still coming and going."
      Speaking to him made answer the goddess bright-eyed Athena:
"These things I will indeed now tell you exactly and fully.
180 It is my boast to be Mentes, sagacious Anchíalos' offspring;
I rule over the Taphian folk, those lovers of rowing.
Just now I have put in for a call with my ship and my comrades,
sailing the wine-dark sea toward peoples of alien language,
carrying lustrous iron to trade for Temesian copper.
185 Out by the fields my galley is anchored, away from the city,
inside the harbor of Rheithron, beneath dark-forested Neion.
We can indeed make claim to be family friends of each other
long since, if you would now go question the elderly hero
Lord Laërtes; no longer, they say, he comes to the city,
190 but far out in the fields he suffers affliction, with only

one old woman attendant, who places the drink and the victuals
next to him when the exhaustion of labor has taken his limbs as
he creeps over the ridge of his orchard planted with grapevines.
I have come now, for they said he really was back in the country,
195   your dear father; but always the gods block him from his pathway,
since nowhere on the earth can the noble Odysseus have perished,
but he is somewhere alive still and kept in the midst of the broad sea,
off in a tide-washed isle, where cruel and harsh men hold him,
savages, who somehow, though he is unwilling, have kept him.
200   But now I will deliver a prophecy, as the immortals
send it into my mind, and I think this will be accomplished,
though I am no soothsayer nor skilled at interpreting bird flights.
No very long time now will he yet be away from his own dear
fatherland, even if he should be bound in fetters of iron.
205   He will contrive his return, since he is so full of devices.
But come now, tell me this and recount it exactly and fully,
whether, as big as you are, you can be the own child of Odysseus.
Marvelously, in your head and your beautiful eyes, you resemble
that man, since very often we visited each with the other;
210   that was before he parted for Troy, when also the other
Argive nobles and kings went away in their hollow galleys.
Since then, neither have I had sight of Odysseus nor he me."
      Thoughtful Telémachos then spoke out to her, giving an answer:
"These things, stranger and friend, I will tell you exactly and fully.
215   Yes, my mother has told me that I am his son, but in fact I
do not know; for a person can never be sure of his father.
How I wish now that I were the fortunate son of a man whom
old age came upon dwelling contented amidst his possessions!
But as it is, he was born to be most unlucky of mortals.
220   His they say I was born, since you are inquiring about it."
      Speaking to him made answer the goddess bright-eyed Athena:
"Yours is a race that the gods, for the men of the future, have not made
nameless, seeing Penelope bore you to be of such mettle.
But come now, tell me this and recount it exactly and fully:
225   What is the feast, this throng, that you have here? Why do you need it?
Wedding or festival? Since it is no shared communal dinner.
Such unabashed arrogance I see! How rudely they strut it,
feasting around this palace! A man would feel indignation
seeing so much that is shameless, whoever discreet came among them!"
230   Thoughtful Telémachos then spoke out to her, giving an answer:

"Friend, as about these things you are asking and making inquiry,
there was a time this house would have been both wealthy and faultless,
during the years that man still dwelt in the land with his people.
Now have the gods' wills changed, now they are devising us evil—
235　him they have made disappear without trace, in a way never any
other man did—since, though he was dead, I would not so much mourn him
if among comrades he was brought down in the land of the Trojans
or in the arms of his friends after he had wound up the warfare.
Then would a funeral mound have been heaped by all the Achaians;
240　so also for his son had he won great fame for the future.
But ingloriously he has been snatched up by the stormwinds,
taken away, out of sight, out of mind, and he left to me only
sorrows and wailing; nor yet are my mourning and lamentation
only for him, for on me have the gods wrought other afflictions.
245　All of the highborn chieftains who lord it over the islands,
over Doulíchion, Samè, and also wooded Zakýnthos,
those men too who in rock-strewn Ithaka govern the people,
all these seek my mother in marriage and wear out the household.
She will neither reject this odious marriage, nor can she
250　make herself carry it through; meanwhile they eat and destroy this
household of mine. And indeed they will soon put me to the slaughter."
　　　Letting her wrath break out, thus Pallas Athena addressed him:
"Oh, what a shame! How great is the need you have of Odysseus,
now faraway, who could lay his hands on these insolent suitors!
255　If he could come this moment and take his stand in the outside
doorway, bringing along two spears, with a shield and a helmet,
such as he was at the time when first I made his acquaintance,
when in my family's house he was drinking and taking his pleasure
as he returned from Ephýrè, from Ilos, Mérmeros' scion—
260　for to that land in a swift-sailing galley Odysseus had traveled
trying to get a man-killing elixir, that he might anoint his
bronze-tipped arrows with it; but to him King Ilos would not give
any of it, for he dreaded the wrath of the gods who live always;
but my father did give it to him, so sorely he loved him—
265　would that Odysseus in such a condition could mix with the suitors!
Then they all would become quick-dying and bitterly married!
Nevertheless, on the knees of the gods these matters are resting,
whether he is or is not to return and exact a requital,
here in his house. As for you, I urge you to ponder the problem
270　how you will finally drive these suitors away from the palace.

Come now, listen to what I say, take heed of my counsel.
Early tomorrow, convoke to assembly the hero-Achaians;
say your word to them all, with the gods themselves to be witness;
lay your command on the suitors to scatter and go to their places.
275 But for your mother, if now her heart should urge her to marry,
let her return to the house of her wealthy and powerful father;
they will make ready the marriage, arranging the gifts for her dowry,
many and rich, as are fitting to go with a much loved daughter.
You yourself I will offer some crafty advice, if you trust me:
280 fit out a galley, the one that is strongest, with twenty good oarsmen;
set forth then to inquire of your father, who long has been absent,
if someone among mortals can tell you or if you can hear some
rumor from Zeus, which best bears fame and report among mankind.
First then voyage to Pylos and question illustrious Nestor;
285 thence go onward to Sparta to see light-haired Meneláos—
he was the last to return out of all of the bronze-clad Achaians.
If you hear that your father, in fact, is alive and returning,
though you are quite worn out, you should bear it yet one year longer;
if however you hear he has died and no longer is living,
290 straightway, when you return to the much loved land of your fathers,
heap a memorial mound and provide him funeral honors,
many and rich, as is fitting, and get your mother a husband.
Finally, when these things you have done to the end and accomplished,
then indeed you should lay down schemes in your mind and your spirit,
295 by what means, right here in your house, you will slaughter the suitors—
either by treacherous guile or by open attack. You should not be
practicing childishness, since you are no longer of that age.
Have you not heard what fame was acquired by noble Orestes
throughout all of mankind when he slaughtered the father-destroyer
300 subtle and scheming Aigísthos, who killed his glorious father?
You too, friend—for I see you sufficiently handsome and grown-up—
be bold now, so that those born later may speak of you fitly.
As for myself now, I will return to my swift-sailing galley
and to my comrades, who I suppose are impatiently waiting;
305 you take care for yourself and be mindful of what I have told you."
    Thoughtful Telémachos then spoke out to her, giving an answer:
"Friend, it is plain you speak of these matters with kindly intention,
as to a son his father, and I will never forget them.
But come now, stay awhile, though eager to get on your journey,
310 so after taking a bath and allowing your spirit some pleasure,

you can return to your ship with a present, rejoicing in spirit,
something of worth and great beauty—for you it will serve as a keepsake
out of my hand, such a token as hosts give guests that they care for."
     Speaking to him then answered the goddess bright-eyed Athena:
315 "Now no longer detain me, as keen as I am for the journey.
As for the gift your courteous heart might bid you to give me,
when I return through here, then give me a present to take home,
choosing a very fine one—it will bring an exchange to be valued."
     So having spoken departed the goddess bright-eyed Athena;
320 she flew up and away like a bird, but she put in his spirit
confident purpose and courage and made him think of his father
more than before he had done. In his mind he noticed the changes,
wondering deep in his heart, for a god it was, he suspected.
Straightway then did the godlike man go back to the suitors.
325   There still singing to them was the far-famed singer; in silence
they sat listening yet, as he sang the Achaians' homecoming,
wretched returning from Troy inflicted by Pallas Athena.
     Noble Ikários' daughter Penelope, thoughtful and prudent,
up in her room was impressing the sacred song on her spirit.
330 After a time, she descended the long stairway of the palace,
not by herself, for together with her came two of her handmaids.
When she had come down there to the suitors, the splendor of women
stood by the pillar supporting the roof beams, stoutly constructed,
holding in front of her cheeks as a veil her shimmering head scarf;
335 standing with her there, one at each side, were the virtuous handmaids.
As the sad tears ran down, she spoke to the godlike singer:
     "Phemios, since you know much else that to men is enchanting,
deeds both of gods and of mortals, that bards make famous in story,
sing them now one of those as you sit here, and they may in silence
340 go on drinking the wine. But of this do not sing any longer.
Hateful it is, and it always wears out the heart in my bosom,
since unforgettable, ceaseless, the grief comes on as I listen,
such is the glorious person I long for, remembering always
one whose fame through Hellas has spread, and the middle of Argos."
345   Thoughtful Telémachos then spoke out to her, giving an answer:
"Mother of mine, why do you object when the trustworthy singer
pleases, however his mind may prompt him? For never should singers
bear any blame, but the blame somehow is on Zeus, who apportions
what he wishes to give each man among grain-eating mortals.
350 Do not accuse him for singing the Dánaäns' evil misfortunes;

for it is true that the song most honored and praised among men is
that which is newest in coming around to the people who hear it.
So within you let the head and the heart be chastened to listen,
since not only Odysseus was robbed of his day of returning;
355 others at Troy there were, great numbers, who came to destruction.
But go back to your room and devote more care to your own work,
weaving and spinning, the loom and the distaff, bidding your handmaids
busy themselves with their labor. The men will attend to the talking, *Story -*
all of them, I above all, since mine is the rule of the household."   *telling*
360   Struck with astonishment then, she went back up to her chamber,
for to her heart she had taken the thoughtful remarks of her offspring.
Going upstairs to her chamber along with her women attendants,
there she lamented Odysseus, the husband she loved, till a pleasant
slumber was cast down over her lids by bright-eyed Athena.
365   There in the shadowy hall were the suitors arousing an uproar—
they all loudly were praying to lie in the bedding beside her.
Speaking among them, thoughtful Telémachos started the discourse:
    "Suitors who court my mother, of such overbearing presumption,
let us attempt to enjoy this dinner of ours now and leave off
370 shouting, for it is an excellent thing to give ear to a singer,
noble as this one is, most like to the gods in his singing.
Going tomorrow at dawn, let us take our seats in the council,
all of us, where unsparingly I may speak out my wishes,
tell you to leave these halls, go away and provide other banquets,
375 eat up your own possessions, proceed in turn through your houses.
If this seems to you better and more to your own selfish profit,
one man's living to ruin, with never a thought about payment,
lay mine waste: but then I will cry out to the gods who live always,
hoping that somehow Zeus might grant to us deeds of requital;
380 then you too would be ruined, destroyed in this house without payment."
    So he spoke; and they all kept biting their lips with their teeth in
wonder at hearing Telémachos now, he was talking so boldly.
    Then in reply to him spoke Antínoös, son of Eupeíthes:
"Surely, Telémachos, you have the gods themselves as your teachers,
385 making you proud in speech, instructing you how to talk boldly.
Never may Zeus son of Kronos in sea-washed Ithaka make you
king over us, though you have inherited it from your fathers."
    Thoughtful Telémachos then spoke out to him, giving an answer:
"Even if what I say, Antínoös, rouses resentment,
390 I would indeed be willing to take it from Zeus, should he give it.

Or are you thinking that this among men is the greatest of evils?
Ruling as king is surely no evil, for quickly the riches
pile up high in the house, and the king himself is most honored.
But in truth there are yet other princes among the Achaians,
395   many of them in sea-washed Ithaka, younger and older;
one of them might have this, since noble Odysseus has perished.
Nevertheless I will be the lord over our own household
and of the slaves, who were captured for me by noble Odysseus."
    Speaking to him made answer Eurýmachos, Pólybos' scion:
400   "Surely, Telémachos, these things rest on the knees of the gods now,
who will as king in sea-washed Ithaka rule the Achaians.
May you keep your possessions and govern in your own household.
Never may any man come who against your will and by force would
take your possessions from you, while Ithaka still contains people.
405   But I would like, noble sir, to inquire concerning the stranger,
whence that man has arrived. What land does he claim to have come from?
Where does his family live now, and where are the fields of his fathers?
Has he brought you a message about your father's returning?
Or has he come thus hoping to meet some need of his own here?
410   He was so hasty to get on his way, he did not even linger
so we could meet him, and yet he does not seem base in appearance."
    Thoughtful Telémachos then spoke out to him, giving an answer:
"Surely, Eurýmachos, any return of my father is lost now;
I will no longer believe any message, wherever it comes from,
415   nor will I busy myself about prophecies such as my mother
gets when she calls some soothsayer into the palace to question.
This was a stranger, a guest and a friend of my father, from Taphos;
it is his boast to be Mentes, sagacious Anchíalos' offspring;
,he rules over the Taphian folk, those lovers of rowing."
420   So did Telémachos speak, but he knew her divine and immortal.
They then turned their minds to the dance and delectable singing,
playing to please themselves, and awaited the evening's onset.
While they were taking their pleasure, the evening gloom came upon them;
then they departed to rest for the night, each one to his own house.
425   Meanwhile Telémachos went to the part of the beautiful courtyard
where, in a place well-guarded, was built his lofty apartment;
there he went to his bed; in his mind many worries kept working.
Carrying fiery torches for him went astute and devoted
old Eurykleía, the daughter of Ops, offspring of Peisénor—
430   once long ago Laërtes had used his resources to buy her

95

when she was still quite young; twenty oxen he gave to acquire her,
honored her then in his palace as much as his virtuous bedmate;
never he took her to bed, but he shunned his wife's jealous anger—
she now carried the fiery torches, for she, of the housemaids,
435 always loved him the most; she had nurtured him when he was little.
He now opened the doors of his bedroom, strongly constructed,
sat down within on the bed, then took off his soft woolen tunic,
putting it into the hands of the old wise-counseling woman.
Then, when she had received and had carefully folded the tunic,
440 she hung it on a hook by the bedstead corded for bedding,
then went out of the chamber; and closing the door by the silver
handle, she fastened the bolt by pulling a strap made of oxhide.
There he rested the whole night long, wrapped up in a sheepskin,
pondering plans in his mind for the journey Athena had counseled.

BOOK 2

Soon as the Dawn shone forth rose-fingered at earliest daybreak,
out of the bed where he slept then arose the dear son of Odysseus,
put on his clothing, and hung his keen-edged sword on his shoulder;
under his glistening feet he fastened his beautiful sandals,
5   then went out of the chamber, resembling a god in appearance.
Straightway he ordered the clear-voiced heralds to make an announcement
summoning to the assembly the long-haired men, the Achaians;
they gave out the announcement; the men very quickly assembled.
Then when they had collected and all were gathered together,
10 he went out to the meeting and held in his hand a great bronze spear,
not by himself, for together with him went two of his swift hounds.
Marvelous then was the grace poured down over him by Athena;
all of the people were gazing in wonder at him as he entered,
taking the seat of his father; the old men yielded before him.
15   Then did the hero Aigyptios speak to them, opening counsel;
bent as he was in old age, he knew about things beyond counting.
He had a much loved son who had gone with godlike Odysseus,
sailed in the hollow galleys to Ilion, land of fine horses,
Ántiphos wielder of spears; but the ravening Cyklops had killed him
20 there in his hollow cavern, prepared him last for his supper.
Three other sons he had, and of them, Eurýnomos now was
joined with the suitors, and two kept on with the family farm work;
nevertheless, he had never forgotten to mourn and lament him.
Shedding his tears over him, he addressed them, giving them counsel:
25   "Listen to me now and heed me, Ithakans, while I am speaking.
Never have we held session nor called the assembly together
since when noble Odysseus went off in the hollow galleys.
Who now summons us thus? What need so urgent has risen
either of some young man or of one of the older among us?
30 Has he been hearing a message about some army invading

97

which he would tell us plainly, as soon as he learned its import?
Or would he broach and discuss some other affair of the people?
Noble he is, I would say, and enjoys much favor. For him may
Zeus achieve excellent fortune, whatever his heart may be wanting."

35   So he spoke, and the omen rejoiced the dear son of Odysseus,
nor did he stay in his seat very long: he was eager to speak out.
He now stood in the midst of the meeting; the herald Peisénor,
knowing in counsel, sagacious, to his hand transferred the scepter.
First among them he spoke to the old man; thus he addressed him:

40   "Old sir, not far off is this man—quite soon you will know him—
who has summoned the people: on me above all has come trouble.
I have been hearing no message about some army invading
which I would tell you plainly, as soon as I learned its import;
nor would I broach and discuss some other affair of the people.

45   This is a need of my own—upon my house evil has fallen,
twofold: first, I have lost my excellent father, who once held
power as king over you; like a father he was in his mildness.
Now yet a worse has arrived which soon will entirely destroy this
household of mine and will utterly lay waste all of my living.

50   Suitors beset my mother, though she herself does not wish it;
they are the own dear sons of the best men, leaders among us.
They now shrink from the trip to her father Ikários' palace,
so that the man himself could provide his daughter a dowry,
give her to him he preferred, the most pleasing of those who arrived there;

55   day after day in our house they keep on coming and going,
killing for victims the sheep and the sleek fat goats and the oxen;
drinking the glistening wine, they revel in festival fashion
heedlessly, idly, and much has been wasted, for now there is no man
such as Odysseus was to defend this household from ruin.

60   We are not able to mount a defense now, and if we attempt it,
we will be wretchedly feeble and quite unskillful in prowess.
Otherwise I would defend us, if I were endowed with the power.
For these deeds no longer are bearable, nor is there any
decency left as my house gets ruined. And you of yourselves, feel

65   shame for these deeds, be mindful what others are thinking, the neighbors
dwelling around this country, and dread the gods' wrathful resentment,
lest in disgust at such infamous deeds, they turn them against you.
Here I plead with you all by Olympian Zeus and by Justice,
who dismisses the councils of men, as she calls them to session,

70   hold off, friends, yes, leave me alone to be worn by my wretched

grieving and sorrow, unless my excellent father Odysseus,
hostile in mind, brought about great ills for the well-greaved Achaians;
these you requite on me and with hostile minds commit evils,
urging ahead these men. Much better for me it would be if
75 you yourselves would devour my stores and consume my cattle;
if it were you who ate them, at some near time would come payment—
so long we would importune and tell our tale through the city,
claiming our goods' restitution, until they all should be given.
But as it is, you load on my heart incurable sorrows."
80   So he spoke in his wrath; to the ground he dashed down the scepter;
tears burst forth from his eyes; compassion held all of the people.
Thereupon all of the others remained in silence, for no one
ventured to use harsh words on Telémachos, making an answer;
only Antínoös spoke and addressed him, giving an answer:
85   "Tongue-proud Telémachos, reckless in temper—for so have you spoken,
laying on us such shame, for to us this blame you would fasten—
they do not merit your blame, these suitors among the Achaians,
rather, your own dear mother, who well knows how to be cunning.
For already the third year passes and soon will the fourth go
90 since when she has been cheating the hearts in the breasts of the Achaians.
Holding out hope to us all, to each man she offers her promise,
sending us messages, while her own mind holds other intentions.
This is another deception that she in her spirit invented:
putting her great loom up in her chamber, she set about weaving
95 delicate fabric of amplest measure, and thereupon told us:
'Young men, suitors for me, since noble Odysseus has perished,
wait, hold off from the marriage you urge upon me, until I can
finish the mantle, lest all of the yarn be uselessly wasted.
It is a burial robe for the hero Laërtes, for when he
100 falls in the ruinous doom of his death so long in the mourning,
lest in the town some woman among the Achaians reproach me
that this man who acquired so much should be lying unshrouded.'
So she spoke, and the valorous spirits in us were persuaded.
Then each day she would weave at the loom, enlarging the fabric,
105 while each night she undid it, when torches she had set beside her.
So three years by her craft she fooled and convinced the Achaians,
but when the fourth year came with the passing of hours and of seasons,
finally one of the maids spoke out who knew of it plainly,
so that we came upon her undoing the glorious fabric.
110 Thus she completed the cloth unwillingly, under compulsion.

Therefore the suitors return this answer to you, so that you may
know it in your own heart and that all the Achaians may know it:
send your mother away from the palace and urge her to marry
him whom her father commands and whoever to her is most pleasing.

115 If yet longer the time she vexes the sons of Achaians—
thinking of this in her heart, that Athena has lavished upon her
skill unsurpassed in the crafting of beautiful things and a noble
mind and astuteness, as we never hear of a woman of ancient
ages, the earlier-living Achaians with beautiful tresses,

120 Tyro, nor yet Alkménè, nor diadem-circled Mykénè—
not one woman among them could rival Penelope's judgment—
nevertheless this thing she devised was not fitting or proper,
since so long they will eat up your livelihood and your possessions
as she keeps to this purpose, whatever it is that the gods now

125 put in her breast to pursue. Great fame she achieves for her own self;
yours is the harm she causes, and grief for the loss of much substance.
Never will we go back to our earlier farm work nor elsewhere,
not until she be wed to whichever Achaian she wishes."

     Thoughtful Telémachos then spoke out to him, giving an answer:

130 "Never, Antínoös, could I thrust from my house unwilling
her who bore me, who raised me; my father in some other land yet
lives or has perished; and it would be bad for me, paying a heavy
fine to Ikários, if I should willfully send away Mother.
For from her father will I suffer evils, and others a god will

135 send upon me, since Mother will call down cursèd Avengers
when she departs from the house; then also from men there will be much
censure for me; therefore that word I never will utter.
If in your own hearts now you are feeling the shame and the scandal,
then you should leave my halls, go away and provide other banquets,

140 eat up your own possessions, proceed in turn through your houses.
If this seems to you better and more to your own selfish profit,
one man's living to ruin, with never a thought about payment,
lay mine waste. But then I will cry out on the gods who live always,
hoping that somehow Zeus might grant to us deeds of requital;

145 then you too would be ruined, destroyed in this house without payment."

     So did Telémachos speak, and for him wide-thundering Zeus sent
forth two eagles who came soaring high from the peaks of the mountains.
These for a time on the breath of the wind kept flying together,
staying beside each other and stretching abroad their great wingspans;

150 but when at last they arrived in the midst of the many-voiced council,

wheeling above it and rapidly beating their powerful wings they
glared at the heads of them all a malign stare threatening ruin;
each of them tore with his talons the cheeks and the neck of the other,
then they sped to the right, through the houses and town of the people.
155 So at the birds they wondered as with their eyes they observed them,
turning it over in mind what things might come to fulfillment.
    Then spoke also among them a hero, the old Halithérses,
Mastor's son, who alone excelled, far over the other
men of his age, in his knowledge of birds and interpreting portents;
160 he with benevolent wisdom addressed them, giving them counsel:
"Listen to me now and heed me, Ithakans, while I am speaking,
bringing to light for the suitors especially what I will tell you.
For an enormous disaster is rolling upon them: Odysseus
not much longer will be faraway from his friends but already
165 nearby nourishes schemes for the death and destruction of these men,
all of them: there will be hardship also for others, for many
people who dwell in sun-bright Ithaka. Let us consider,
far in advance, how to cause them to stop this—rather, the men must
stop of themselves, since even for them that surely is better.
170 For I am not unproved to speak prophecies—no, very skillful.
So for him too, I am certain, are all things brought to fulfillment
as I predicted, the time that to Ilion all of the Argives
started the journey; with them went Odysseus of many devices.
Having endured many ills, I said, and with all of his comrades
175 utterly lost, he would finally come unknown to us all back
home in the twentieth year: now this is all being accomplished."
    Speaking to him made answer Eurýmachos Pólybos' scion:
"Old man, you would as well play prophet to your own children,
going away to your house, lest later they suffer disaster.
180 I far better than you can now serve as a prophet in these things.
Birds there are in great numbers beneath bright Helios' sunbeams,
flying about, nor do all bring auguries. Surely Odysseus
has been lost far away: how I wish you also with him had
perished, for then you would not be speaking so much revelation,
185 nor would you be inciting Telémachos, feeding his anger,
hoping to get some gift for your house, if perchance he should give it.
But I say to you plainly, and this thing will be accomplished:
should you, who are so learnèd in old lore, manage to rouse this
man who is younger and talk him around to a rage by your speeches,
190 first, for the man himself it will be most wearisome trouble:

he will in any case be unable to act on his anger.
Then upon you, old man, we will levy a fine that will surely
grieve your spirit to pay: much bitter distress it will cause you.
I myself among all will now offer Telémachos counsel:
195 let him order his mother to go back home to her father's;
they will make ready the marriage, arranging the gifts for her dowry,
many and rich, as are fitting to go with a much loved daughter.
Never before, I believe, will the sons of Achaians desist from
this most troublesome suit, since anyhow we fear no man—
200 no, not Telémachos, though he indeed has become a big talker—
nor do we take much heed, old man, of the prophecy you have
spoken, so idle and vain, which makes you all the more hated.
Miserably will his goods be eaten up—nor will requital
ever be made—while she puts off the Achaians, delaying
205 marriage; for all of our days, we stay here waiting and wrangling,
raising contentions over her excellence; nor after others
do we go, such women as each might suitably marry."
       Thoughtful Telémachos then spoke out to him, giving an answer:
"Noble Eurýmachos, also you other illustrious suitors,
210 these things I will no longer beseech nor address you about them;
they already are known to the gods and the other Achaians.
But come now, give me a swift galley and twenty companions
who may accomplish a voyage with me one way and the other.
For I am going to Sparta as well as to sandy-soiled Pylos
215 asking about the return of my father, so long on his journey,
if someone among mortals can tell me or if I can hear some
rumor from Zeus, which best bears fame and report among mankind.
If I hear that my father, in fact, is alive and returning,
though I am quite worn out, I will bear it yet one year longer;
220 if however I hear he has died and no longer is living,
straightway, when I return to the much loved land of my fathers,
I will then heap up a mound and provide him funeral honors,
many and rich, as is fitting, and get my mother a husband."
       Thus having spoken, he sat back down, and among them stood up
225 Mentor, the man who had been to Odysseus an excellent comrade;
when in the ships he had gone, he entrusted to him the whole household,
told him to heed the old man and to guard all the goods steadfastly.
He with benevolent wisdom addressed them, giving them counsel:
"Listen to me now and heed me, Ithakans, while I am speaking.
230 Let no king with a scepter be kindly of heart any longer,

never compassionate, nor of a mind that is skillful in justice;
let him instead be ever malignant and do what is not just,
since not one of the people is mindful of godlike Odysseus,
even among those people he ruled like a father in mildness.
235   Yet even so I do not begrudge the presumptuous suitors
doing their violent deeds with the evil devices their minds weave;
their own heads they hazard in violence, eating away this
house of Odysseus; the man, they say, will no more be returning.
Rather, the rest of the people I blame, so stolidly you all
240   sit here in silence and do not address with words of reproval
these few suitors and make them stop, though you are so many."
        Answering him spoke forth Leiókritos son of Euénor:
"Mentor, stubborn and stupid, in mind half-mad that you utter
words like these and incite them to stop us! An arduous exploit,
245   even for men more numerous, waging a war for a dinner!
Even supposing Odysseus the Ithakan came on the noble
suitors himself, while they in his house were enjoying their banquets,
then in his heart he were eager to drive them all from the palace,
much though she may desire it, his wife would never enjoy him
250   when he returned; right here he would meet with a hideous doomsday
if he fought with so many; you speak not wisely nor fitly.
But come now, let the people disperse, each one to his own work;
this man Mentor will urge on his path and so too Halithérses,
who from the very beginning have been his father's companions.
255   But I am sure he will listen to messages yet for a long time
sitting in Ithaka: this is a trip he will never accomplish."
        So did he speak, then quickly he caused the assembly to break up.
Those of the country dispersed; each one went away to his own house.
Into the palace of godlike Odysseus entered the suitors.
260   Meanwhile Telémachos, going away to the shore of the deep sea,
washing his hands in the silvery sea-brine, prayed to Athena:
"Listen to me, you god who yesterday came to our palace,
told me that I in a ship on the seaway misty and murky,
asking about the return of my father, who long has been absent,
265   soon should depart—now all these things the Achaians are thwarting,
worst by far in presumption the wickedly arrogant suitors."
        So he spoke as he prayed, and beside him there came Athena,
making herself like Mentor in speaking as well as appearance;
raising her voice she spoke, and in these winged words she addressed him:
270   "Never, Telémachos, you will be feeble or thoughtless hereafter

if indeed is instilled in you the great force of your father—
such was the man he was to achieve both action and speeches—
then your journey will not be fruitless or lacking fulfillment.
If however you are not his and Penelope's offspring,
275 then no hope do I have that you bring what you wish to completion.
Few indeed are the sons who turn out the same as their fathers;
most of them turn out worse than their fathers, and few any better.
But since never will you be feeble or thoughtless hereafter,
since the ingenious mind of Odysseus has not wholly failed you,
280 there is indeed some hope you will bring these tasks to completion.
Therefore take no heed of the suitors' intentions or counsels,
ignorant men, since they know nothing of wisdom or justice;
nor do they know anything of the death and the blackest of doomsdays
which is in fact near them: on the same day, all will be slaughtered.
285 Not much longer will you be kept from the journey you yearn for;
such a companion to you I am as I was to your father,
I will arrange a swift galley for you and myself will attend you.
Meanwhile, you go back in the palace and join with the suitors;
there make ready provisions and pack these all into vessels:
290 pour wine into the two-handled urns, then into the tight-sewn
skins put barley, the marrow of men, while I in the country
quickly collect volunteers to be comrades. Many the ships which
harbor in sea-washed Ithaka, some of them new, some older;
I will look over them all and decide which one is the stoutest;
295 speedily fitting it out, on the broad seaway we will launch it."

So spoke Athena the daughter of Zeus, and for no very long time
yet did Telémachos wait, for the voice of a god he was hearing.
He went back to the house, much troubled and heavy in spirit;
there in the halls he discovered the arrogant suitors engaged in
300 flaying some goats in the court and from hogs too singeing the bristles.
Then Antínoös came straight up to Telémachos, laughing,
took his hand in his own and said these words, calling upon him:
"Tongue-proud Telémachos, reckless in temper, no longer let any
evil affliction of action or utterance be in your spirit.
305 Join me instead in eating and drinking, the way that we used to.
All these things you seek the Achaians will surely accomplish,
furnish a ship and choice rowers, that you may swiftly arrive in
sacred Pylos, pursuing reports of your glorious father."
Thoughtful Telémachos then spoke out to him, giving an answer:
310 "No, Antínoös, there is no way that among such reckless

men as you are I can sit here dining in quiet contentment.
Is it not much that in earlier years you suitors could waste these
many and precious possessions of mine, while I was a child yet?
Now when I have grown up and have heard what others are saying,
315 learning from them, and the spirit at last grows stronger within me,
I will attempt some way to fix evil destruction upon you,
either by leaving for Pylos or else right here in the country.
Yes, I will go—and the journey I speak of will not be fruitless—
though on another man's ship, since neither a galley nor rowers
320 do I command, for to you, I suppose, this seemed to be better."
　　So he spoke, and withdrew his hand from Antínoös' handclasp
lightly; the suitors were busy preparing the meal in the palace.
They kept scoffing and jeering at him in words of derision;
such are the words which one of the arrogant youths would have spoken:
325 "Well now, surely for us does Telémachos meditate murder!
Soon he will come back leading defenders from sandy-soiled Pylos,
even, it may be, from Sparta, for he is so dreadfully eager.
Yes, and perhaps he wishes to go to Ephýrè the fertile
plowland, whence he could carry away some fatal elixir,
330 throw it into the wine-bowl, and bring us all to destruction!"
　　Thus might somebody else of the arrogant young men answer:
"Who is to know if himself, when he goes in the hollow galley,
far from his friends, will be lost while wandering, just like Odysseus?
That is a way he would greatly increase our trouble and labor;
335 we would divide up all his possessions, and as for the palace,
we would give that to his mother to keep—and to him who should wed her."
　　So as they spoke, he went downstairs to the spacious and lofty
room of his father in which gold treasures and bronze lay collected,
clothing as well in coffers, and olive oil, ample and fragrant;
340 inside, great earthen jars full of old wine, sweet in the drinking,
stood in a row, containing within unmixed the divine drink,
orderly, close to the wall, made ready should ever Odysseus
come back home, even though after suffering many afflictions.
Closing the room was a door made of planks joined tightly together,
345 folding in two; inside was a woman, the housekeeper, keeping
watch over all by night and by day with intelligent spirit,
old Eurykleía the daughter of Ops, offspring of Peisénor.
Straightway Telémachos called her out of the room and addressed her:
　　"Come now, Mamma, and draw for me sweet wine into the wine jars,
350 that most pleasing to taste, just after the one you are guarding,

thinking of that unfortunate man, if he ever should come back,
Zeus-descended Odysseus, avoiding his death and destruction;
fill up twelve altogether, on all of them fastening stoppers.
Barley as well pour into some sacks, well sewn out of leather;
355 let there be twenty measures of meal, mill-ground out of barley.
Only yourself must know; have all of this ready, collected;
later at night I will carry them out of here, after my mother
goes to her room upstairs in the house and is mindful of sleeping.
For I am going to Sparta as well as to sandy-soiled Pylos
360 asking about my father's return, if I hear of it somewhere."

So he spoke, and the nurse, well-loved Eurykleía, lamented;
sorrowing then she spoke, and in these winged words she addressed him:
"Why oh why, dear child, has a plan like this ever entered
into your mind? Why do you desire to go out in the great world,
365 being the only and much loved son, while far from his country
Zeus-descended Odysseus is lost in a country of strangers?
When you are gone, these men will at once plan evils for later,
so that you die by their cunning, and these things they can divide up.
Rather, remain right here and among your possessions: you need not
370 suffer afflictions or wander about on the desolate seaway."

Thoughtful Telémachos then spoke out to her, giving an answer:
"Take heart, Mamma, for not unknown to a god is this purpose.
But now swear me an oath to say nothing of this to my mother,
waiting until some time has elapsed, the eleventh or twelfth day,
375 or until she herself will have missed me and heard of my leaving,
so that she might not injure her beautiful skin with her weeping."

So he spoke; a great oath by the gods the old woman then swore him.
But then, when she had sworn and had brought her oath to completion,
straightway she began drawing the wine out into the wine jars,
380 also pouring the barley in sacks well sewn out of leather.
Going back into the palace, Telémachos mixed with the suitors.

Then other things were devised by the goddess bright-eyed Athena:
taking Telémachos' form, she went all over the city;
standing beside each man, she uttered a word and addressed him,
385 giving him orders to gather beside the swift galley at nightfall.
Phronios' glorious scion Noëmon then did the goddess
ask for his swift ship; he with a good will promised to give it.

Then did the sun go down and the ways were all shadowed in darkness;
down to the sea she dragged the swift galley and into it loaded
390 all of the tackle and gear that are carried on well-benched galleys.

There at the mouth of the harbor she moored it; around it the noble
comrades gathered together, and each did the goddess encourage.
    Then other things were devised by the goddess bright-eyed Athena:
she set off to return to the palace of godlike Odysseus;
395 once she was there, she poured sweet sleepiness over the suitors,
muddled the wits of the drinkers and knocked their cups from their fingers.
They rose up to go rest in the city, and not very long yet
did they sit when the sleep came fluttering over their eyelids.
Then to Telémachos words like these spoke bright-eyed Athena,
400 when she had called him forth from the house well built as a dwelling,
making herself like Mentor in speaking as well as appearance:
"Now have the well-greaved comrades, Telémachos, taken their seats out
there at the oars already, awaiting your word for departure;
come now, let us be off, no longer delaying the journey."
405   So having spoken to him, then speedily Pallas Athena
led him forward, and he came on in the goddess's footsteps.
But when they had arrived down there at the sea and the galley,
then on the shore they discovered the long-haired men, the companions.
Thus did the sacred strength of Telémachos speak and address them:
410 "Come now, friends, let us take the provisions, for all have already
been piled up in the hall. My mother knows nothing about this,
nor do the women; of them, one only has heard of the matter."
    So having spoken to them, he started ahead and they followed;
carrying all the supplies out onto the well-benched ship they
415 stowed them there in the way the dear son of Odysseus commanded.
Straightway Telémachos boarded the ship, and before him Athena
went to sit down in the stern of the galley; Telémachos took his
seat there close to her side, and the men cast off the stern cables;
going aboard themselves, they took their seats at the oarlocks.
420 Then was a favoring wind sent down by bright-eyed Athena,
Zephyr, the fresh wind roaring abroad on the wine-dark seaway.
Then to arouse them to action, Telémachos bade the companions
lay their hands on the gear. They listened to him as he urged them;
lifting the pine-hewn mast, they fitted it into the hollow
425 mast box, stood it upright, then bound it fast with the forestays,
hoisted the glistening sail with the ropes well plaited from oxhide.
Wind poured into the sail's white belly, a wave purple-foaming
thundered loudly around the curved keel as the ship sailed onward;
so with the wave she was running and so was achieving the journey.
430 When they had fastened the tackle in place on the swift black galley,

wine bowls they set up; to the brim they filled them with wine and
poured drink-offerings out to the gods everlasting, undying,
most to the bright-eyed daughter of Zeus, out of all the immortals.
All that night she was cleaving her journey, and into the morning.

BOOK 3

Helios rose now, leaving the beautiful water of Ocean,
into the bronze-bright heaven, to bring light to the immortals,
also to mortals, the men who dwell on the grain-giving plowland.
They then arrived in Neleus' well-built citadel, Pylos,
5   where on the seashore the people were making a sacred oblation,
offering all-black bulls to the dark-haired lord, the earth-shaker.
There nine cities were gathered: in each of the bands five hundred
people were sitting, with each group proffering nine of the black bulls.
While these ate of the innards and burnt thigh flesh to the great god,
10 those came straight to the land, then, furling the sails of the balanced
ship by brailing them up, they moored her and then themselves landed.
Out of the galley Telémachos stepped, but Athena was leading.
First then spoke and addressed him the goddess bright-eyed Athena:
   "Now you should not be bashful, Telémachos, even a little,
15 since in fact you have sailed on the seaway so as to find out
news of your father, the land which hides him, the fate he encountered.
Come now, go straight forward to Nestor, the tamer of horses;
let us discover whatever advice in his breast lies hidden.
You go pray him yourself that he tell you the whole and exact truth—
20 no false tale will he tell you, for he is remarkably thoughtful."
   Thoughtful Telémachos then spoke out to her, giving an answer:
"Mentor, how can I go? How can I be the one to make greeting?
Never have I been proven in words close-woven and crafty.
Shameful it is for a youth to interrogate one who is older."
25 Speaking to him made answer the goddess bright-eyed Athena:
"Some things, Telémachos, you will discover yourself, in your own mind;
others again some god will suggest: I cannot imagine
it was against the gods' wills you received such birth and upbringing."
   So having spoken to him, then speedily Pallas Athena
30 led him forward, and he came on in the goddess's footsteps.

They went into the meeting of Pylians gathered on benches;
here sat Nestor amidst his sons, and around them his comrades
readied the feast; some flesh they were roasting, and some they were spitting.
Seeing the strangers arrive, they all came crowding around them,
35   held out welcoming hands, and invited them both to be seated.
First Peisístratos, Nestor's son, came up and approached them,
took them both by the hand, and assigned them seats at the banquet
on soft fleeces of sheep laid out on the sand of the seashore,
there beside Thrasymédes, his brother, as well as his father.
40   Straightway servings of innards he gave them, and into a golden
goblet he poured them wine; in welcome he spoke to them, pledging
Pallas Athena the daughter of Zeus who carries the aegis:
      "Raise your prayer now, stranger and friend, to the lordly Poseidon;
his is the feast you have happened upon in journeying hither.
45   When you have poured a libation and uttered a prayer, as is fitting,
give him also the goblet of honey-sweet wine, so that he may
pour a libation, for he also, I am certain, directs his
prayers to the deathless ones. Of the gods all mortals are needful;
he however is younger, a fellow to me of my own age.
50   Therefore you are the first to whom I will present the gold goblet."
      So he spoke, and he placed in her hand that goblet of sweet wine.
Much did Athena rejoice in the man so thoughtful and civil,
seeing that she was the first to whom he would present the gold goblet.
Straightway many a prayer she uttered to lordly Poseidon:
55   "Listen to us, earth-holding Poseidon, and do not begrudge us
making our plea nor refuse to achieve these things that we pray for.
First, give Nestor and all of his sons good fame to attend them;
then also on the others bestow some pleasing requital,
all these Pylians here, the reward of a splendid oblation.
60   Grant to Telémachos then, and to me also, to return when
what we came here to do in the swift black ship is accomplished."
      So she prayed—and herself she was bringing it all to fulfillment—
then to Telémachos gave that beautiful two-handled goblet.
So to the same intent then prayed the dear son of Odysseus.
65   When they had roasted the outermost flesh and had taken the spits out,
then they divided the portions and dined on a sumptuous dinner.
When they had quite satisfied their appetites, drinking and eating,
speaking among them opened the horseman Gerenian Nestor:
      "Now indeed it is much more seemly to question and ask these
70   strangers and guests who they are, since they have been cheered with a dinner.

Strangers, who are you? And whence do you sail on the watery pathways?
Have you affairs in trading, or do you recklessly wander
over the sea in the manner of pirates who wander at random,
putting their lives in danger and visiting evil on strangers?"

75   Thoughtful Telémachos then spoke out to him, giving an answer,
confident now, for Athena herself had put in his spirit
courage, that he might ask him concerning his faraway father,
so that a noble renown among men might hold him in honor:
"Nestor, Neleus' son, the Achaians' preeminent glory,

80 you ask where we are from, and to you I now will give answer.
Hither from Ithaka we have arrived, from the isle below Neion;
it is a private affair, not public, that I would discuss here.
I seek news of my father, if somewhere abroad I will hear it,
noble Odysseus the steadfast-hearted, who once, as the tale goes,

85 fighting at your side, conquered the town of the Trojans and sacked it.
For about all those others, the men who battled the Trojans,
we know well where each of them perished in wretched destruction;
that man's death has been made unknown by the scion of Kronos,
since no man can declare with certainty where he has perished,

90 whether he was brought down on the land by enemy fighters,
whether he died on the sea, in the surges of Ámphitrítè.
Therefore have I come here to your knees now, thinking you might be
willing to tell of his wretched destruction, in case you perhaps have
seen it with your own eyes or have heard the report of another

95 wandering man; for his mother indeed bore him to be woeful.
Spare me nothing, extenuate nothing, nor show any pity;
tell me all to the end, however it came to your notice.
Here I implore you, if ever my father, the noble Odysseus,
brought to fulfillment in word or in deed anything he had promised

100 when in the land of the Trojans Achaians were suffering sorrows,
now call them to remembrance and tell me the truth of the matter."
        Speaking to him then answered the horseman Gerenian Nestor:
"Friend, since you have recalled to my mind the afflictions we suffered
in that land, undaunted in might, we sons of Achaians,

105 first those while in the ships on the seaway misty and murky,
roaming about after loot wherever Achilles would lead us;
then those when we were fighting around Lord Priam's enormous
citadel—there then perished whoever among us was greatest.
There lies Ajax the warlike hero, and there is Achilles;

110 there also is Patróklos, the peer of the gods as adviser;

there is my own dear son Antílochos, mighty and faultless,
swift beyond others in running, distinguished too as a fighter.
But above these, many evils besides we suffered, and who of
men who are mortal could tell all those things fully and truly?
115 Never, if you should remain five years, even six, here beside me,
asking of all those evils the noble Achaians endured there—
sooner would you be tired and return to the land of your fathers.
     "Nine years we were devising them ills by busily weaving
stratagems, every kind, that at long last Kronion compassed.
120 There no man ever wished to be likened to him for astuteness
openly, since by a long way noble Odysseus excelled in
stratagems, every kind, your father, if it is the truth that
you are the child of that man: I am held in wonder, observing.
For those words you have spoken are like his, nor would you ever
125 think that a man so youthful could speak as adeptly as he could.
All of the time we were there, myself and the noble Odysseus
never expressed disagreement in either assembly or council;
keeping to one mind rather, with wisdom and prudent advice we
guided the Argives, planning the best way matters could happen.
130 But when at last we ransacked the steep-built city of Priam,
we went away in the ships, and a god dispersed the Achaians;
then in his mind did Zeus meditate for the Argives a baneful
homeward return, since they did not all know wisdom or justice;
therefore many of them met terrible doom from the deadly
135 ruinous wrath of the bright-eyed one whose Father is mighty.
She stirred up a contention between the two scions of Atreus;
after they called on all the Achaians to meet in assembly—
rash was the summons, without due order, and just at the sunset;
heavy with wine were the sons of Achaians who came to the meeting—
140 both of them said their say as to why they had gathered the people.
Then Meneláos gave order for all the Achaians to turn their
minds to the homeward return on the great broad back of the deep sea;
not in the least this pleased Agamemnon; he was for holding
back those people; he wanted to offer up sacred oblations,
145 so as to placate Athena and calm her terrible anger—
fool that he was, not knowing that she would not be persuaded,
since not swiftly are altered the minds of the gods who live always.
So did the two lords stand there and fling harsh words at each other,
speaking in turn; with astonishing clamor the well-greaved Achaians
150 sprang to their feet—two different plans found favor among them.

That was a night we passed meditating harsh thoughts of each other
deep in our minds, for the bane of our misery Zeus was devising.
Some of us dragged our ships to the luminous sea in the morning,
put on board our possessions, as well as the deep-girdled women;
155 half of the people, however, remained, still waiting in patience
there with Atreus' son Agamemnon, the shepherd of people.
Half of us going on board pushed off, and the ships very quickly
sailed, while a god made level the sea with its monstrous abysses.
Going to Ténedos, there to the gods we offered our victims,
160 eager to hurry on home. Not yet Zeus planned our returning,
merciless one, who roused yet a second calamitous quarrel.
Those with the lordly Odysseus, ingenious, various-minded,
turned their tractable galleys around once more and departed,
going to Atreus' son Agamemnon, and carried him comfort.
165 I however and those of the ships which crowded behind me
fled, because I was aware that a god was devising us evils;
Tydeus' warlike son fled also and urged his companions.
.Afterward, joining with us, light-haired Meneláos departed,
coming to Lesbos as we were debating about the long voyage,
170 whether we should make sail above rugged and rock-strewn Chios,
keeping it there on our left, while coasting the Psyrian island,
or below Chios, beside the windblown promontory of Mimas.
There we prayed for the god to accord us a sign, and to us he
showed one, giving us orders to cut through the midst of the seaway
175 into Euboía and thereby swiftly escape from disaster.
Whistling, the wind came up to a gale, and the ships very quickly
ran straight over the fish-thronged pathways and then in the nighttime
made it to land at Geraistos, and there we offered Poseidon
many a bull's thighbone, having measured the width of the vast sea.
180 It was the fourth day then when the comrades of Tydeus' scion,
tamer of steeds Diomédes, could anchor their evenly balanced
galleys in Argos; but I held on toward Pylos; the wind was
never abated from when that god first set it to blowing.
So I arrived, dear child, quite ignorant; nothing I knew of
185 those who among the Achaians were saved nor of those who have perished.
Those things I have discovered while settled at home in our palace
you shall be told, as is right, nor from you will I hide any knowledge:
safely, they say, have the Mýrmidons come, those passionate spearmen,
led back home by the glorious son of greathearted Achilles.
190 Safe Philoktétes returned, the illustrious offspring of Poias.

Idómeneus to their homes in Crete brought all of his comrades,
those who escaped from the war, and of none did the seaway deprive him.
You have yourselves heard, far as you live, about Atreus' scion,
how he returned, how Aigísthos devised his wretched destruction.

195 Nevertheless he too most grievously made a requital.
So it is good for a man, even when he is dead, to have left his
son to survive him, for that son punished the father-destroyer
subtle and scheming Aigísthos, who killed his glorious father.
You too, friend, I see you sufficiently handsome and grown-up;

200 be bold now, so that those born later may speak of you fitly."
     Thoughtful Telémachos then spoke out to him, giving an answer:
"Nestor, Neleus' son, the Achaians' preeminent glory,
truly the son has requited the deed; the Achaians will henceforth
carry his glory abroad as a song for the men of the future.

205 Would that the gods might put about me such vestments of prowess,
so I could punish the suitors for their vexatious offenses,
arrogant men, who plot against me such reckless devices!
But it was no such fortune the gods spun out as my portion,
not for my father nor me; now nevertheless we must bear it."

210   Speaking to him then answered the horseman Gerenian Nestor:
"Friend, since you have recalled to my mind these matters and spoken,
men do talk of the suitors who seek your mother, the many
there in your house who against your will are devising you evils.
Tell me, are you subdued quite willingly, or do the people

215 hate you there in your land in response to a god's injunction?
Who is to know whether he will return some day and requite their
violence, either alone or with all the Achaians to aid him?
For if bright-eyed Athena so wanted to favor and love you
as at the time she cared for Odysseus the glorious hero,

220 when in the land of the Trojans Achaians were suffering sorrows—
never have I seen gods so openly showing their favor
as beside him stood openly, aiding him, Pallas Athena—
if in her heart she wanted to love you and care for you that much,
then at least some of those men would surely forget about marriage."

225   Thoughtful Telémachos then spoke out to him, giving an answer:
"Old sir, I do not think these words will at all be accomplished;
what you say is too grand; awe grips me. Never would these things
happen for me as I hope, not even if gods should desire it."
Speaking to him made answer the goddess bright-eyed Athena:

230   "What word, Telémachos, this that escapes from the fence of your teeth now!

114

Lightly a god, if he wanted, could save a man, even from far off.
I would prefer, even though after suffering many afflictions,
yet to arrive back home and to look on the day of returning,
rather than come to be killed at my hearth, in the way Agamemnon
235 died from the treacherous act of Aigísthos and his own bedmate.
Death however is common to all; not even the gods can
keep it from even a man they love, when finally he must
fall in the ruinous doom of his death so long in the mourning."
      Thoughtful Telémachos then spoke out to her, giving an answer:
240 "Mentor, as sad as we are, let us talk no longer of these things.
His homecoming no longer is possible, but the immortals
have already devised his death and the blackest of doomsdays.
Now of a different matter I wish to inquire and to question
Nestor, since beyond other men he knows justice and wisdom.
245 Three generations of men they say he has governed as ruler;
as an immortal appears he seems to me, gazing upon him.
Nestor, Neleus' son, now tell me the truth of a matter:
How died Atreus' son, wide-governing Lord Agamemnon?
Where was the lord Meneláos? What manner of death was devised by
250 subtle and scheming Aigísthos? He killed one greatly his better.
Was Meneláos not in Achaian Argos but elsewhere
wandering yet among men, so the other found courage to murder?"
      Speaking to him then answered the horseman Gerenian Nestor:
"Certainly, child, the whole tale I will tell you fully and truly.
255 You can imagine yourself, in fact, how this would have happened
if yet living Aigísthos had been found there in the halls when
homeward from Troy came Atreus' son light-haired Meneláos—
then no burial mound would have been piled up when he perished:
rather, the dogs and the birds would have eaten him up as he lay far
260 out on the flatland away from the city, nor would the Achaian
women have wept over him, so huge was the deed he had plotted.
For as we sat in the siege and accomplished many a contest,
he meanwhile, at his ease in the heart of horse-nourishing Argos,
kept on trying to charm Agamemnon's wife with his speeches.
265 She would at first not give her consent to the scandalous action,
glorious Klýtaimnéstra, for she used excellent judgment.
There was a singer with her, moreover, whom Atreus' son when
leaving for Troy had strongly enjoined to watch over his bedmate.
But when at last the decree of the gods entangled and tamed her,
270 then, having taken the singer away to a desolate island,

there as a victim and prey for the birds Aigísthos forsook him.
Then he took her, desired and desiring, away to his own house.
Many a thighbone then he burnt on the gods' holy altars,
many a glorious gift hung up, both of gold and of fabric,
275 having achieved a huge deed that at heart he had never expected.
    "For at the time, on the journey from Troy we were sailing together,
Atreus' son and myself, each holding the other in friendship;
but when at last we reached holy Sounion, headland of Athens,
Phoibos Apollo, attacking the steersman of Lord Meneláos,
280 killed him, visiting him with his mild and benevolent missiles,
while, as the ship ran forward, he held his hands on the tiller,
Phrontis the son of Onétor, surpassing the nations of men in
steering a ship on her course whenever the stormwinds were blasting.
There Meneláos was held, though eager to get on his journey,
285 so he could bury his comrade and celebrate funeral honors.
But when at last, as he went on the wine-dark sea in the hollow
ships and was running ahead, he reached the precipitous mountain
jutting at Máleia, hateful the way wide-thundering Zeus then
fashioned for him, for he poured out blasts of the whistling stormwinds,
290 waves too, swollen so monstrously huge as to equal the mountains.
There, separating the galleys, to Crete he drove one division,
where the Kydonians live, by the streams of the river Iardános.
    "There is a smooth stone cliff, a precipitous crag in the sea-brine,
farthest of Gortyn's domains, in the seaway misty and murky,
295 where on the left-hand headland the south wind pushes a huge wave
Phaistos-ward, but a small rock keeps the huge wave from advancing.
There did the galleys arrive, and the men just barely avoided
ruin, but billowing surf quite shattered the ships as it drove them
onto the reefs. In the meantime, currents of wind and of water
300 carried the other five blue-prowed galleys and took them to Egypt.
While he was there, much gold he collected and many provisions,
roaming about with his ships among people of alien language.
Meanwhile, at home, Aigísthos devised these odious actions;
then seven years he ruled in Mykénè, the gold-rich city—
305 having killed Atreus' son—with the people subjected beneath him.
Then in the eighth year, noble Orestes, returning from Athens,
came as an evil upon him and killed that father-destroyer
subtle and scheming Aigísthos, who killed his glorious father.
When he had killed him, he ordered the Argives a funeral banquet,
310 both for his odious mother and for unmanly Aigísthos;

116

that same day to him came the great crier of war Meneláos,
bringing his treasures, as mighty a load as the galleys could carry.
You too, friend, do not wander a long time far from your palace,
leaving behind your possessions and such men there in the household
315 so overbearing as those, lest they be dividing and eating
everything you possess, so you will have fruitlessly journeyed.
Nevertheless I urge and exhort you to see Meneláos,
pay him a visit, for he has returned from abroad just lately,
having departed from men whence no one would hope in his spirit
320 ever to come, who had once been driven astray by the stormwinds,
into a sea so vast not even the birds in their passage
come back within the same year, so enormous it is and so fearful.
But now go to that country, along with your ship and your comrades;
if by land you would go, this chariot here and these horses
325 I will provide, and my sons, to accompany you as your escorts
into divine Lakedaímon, where dwells light-haired Meneláos.
You go pray him yourself that he tell you the truth of the matter;
no false tale will he tell you, for he is remarkably thoughtful."
      So did he say; and the sun went down, and the dusk came upon them.
330 Then spoke also among them the goddess bright-eyed Athena:
"Old man, you have informed us of these things fitly and fully;
but come, cut up the tongues of the victims and mingle the sweet wine,
so having poured out wine to Poseidon as well as the other
deathless gods, we may think about sleep; for the hour is upon us;
335 now already the light goes under the dark: it is seemly
not to be seated too long at the feast of the gods but to go home."
      So said the daughter of Zeus; they listened to her as she said it.
Heralds at once poured over their hands clean water for washing;
young men filled to the brim great wine bowls, ready for drinking,
340 then poured wine into all of the cups to begin the observance;
throwing the tongues on the fire, they stood up and poured libations.
When they had made libations and drunk whatever their hearts wished,
then did Athena at last and Telémachos, godlike in stature,
both make ready to go back down to the hollow galley.
345 Nestor detained them there and addressed them words of remonstrance:
      "Now may Zeus and the rest of the gods undying forfend that
you should depart from my palace to go back down to the swift ship
as from a man so lacking in clothes, so poverty-stricken,
that in his house he has no blankets and rugs in abundance,
350 so neither he himself nor his visitors slumber in comfort.

No, for I have an abundance of rugs and of beautiful blankets.
Never, I hope, will the child of that man, the dear son of Odysseus,
lie down to sleep on the deck of a ship while I am alive yet,
nor thereafter if here in these halls my children are staying,
355 offering welcome to visiting friends who come to my palace."
    Speaking to him made answer the goddess bright-eyed Athena:
"Well you have spoken of these things, dear old man; it is surely
right that Telémachos heed you, for that indeed is much better.
But now he will accompany you, so that here in your palace
360 he may enjoy his sleep; to the black ship I will return now,
so as to raise his comrades' courage and tell them of all this;
for among them there is only myself who can claim to be older;
younger the other men are who accompany him out of friendship,
all of a similar age, greathearted Telémachos' comrades.
365 There I will take my rest by the hollow and dark-hued galley
now; then early at dawn I will start on the way to the great-souled
Kaúkones; there is a debt they owe me, and it is not recent,
nor is it little; but since this man has arrived at your palace,
send him ahead with your son and a chariot. Furnish him horses
370 which are the nimblest in running as well as the noblest in power."
    So having spoken departed the goddess bright-eyed Athena,
making herself like a vulture, and awe seized all the Achaians;
then did the old man wonder, as he saw this with his own eyes,
taking Telémachos' hand, and said these words, calling upon him:
375 "Friend, I cannot believe you will ever be base or a coward,
if you, young as you are, have gods who attend you as escorts.
For no other was this among those with Olympian dwellings:
this was the daughter of Zeus, spoil-plundering Trítogeneía,
who in the Argive host most honored your excellent father.
380 Listen to me now, Lady, and grant me excellent glory;
give it to me myself, to my sons, to my virtuous bedmate;
I will make offer to you then, a heifer, a broad-browed yearling
not yet broken, that no man has ever led under the plow yoke;
her I will offer to you with her horns all covered with gold leaf."
385   So he spoke as he prayed; he was heard by Pallas Athena.
Straightway the horseman Gerenian Nestor led the procession
back to his beautiful house, of his sons and his daughters' husbands.
But when they had arrived at the glorious house of the ruler,
they took seats in orderly rows on benches and armchairs;
390 then for the men who were coming the old man mixed in a mixing

bowl wine sweet in the drinking, that never until the eleventh
year did the housekeeper open and loosen the mantle around it.
This did the old man mix in a bowl, and he prayed to Athena,
pouring out much to the daughter of Zeus who carries the aegis.
395   When they had poured libations and drunk whatever their hearts wished,
then they departed to rest for the night, each one to his own house;
there on the spot was the bed that the horseman Gerenian Nestor
gave to Telémachos then, the dear scion of godlike Odysseus,
out in the echoing porch on a bedstead corded for bedding,
400   close to the leader of men Peisístratos, excellent spearman,
who was alone unmarried among the offspring in the palace.
As for himself, he slept in a room inside the high palace;
there did the lady his wife make ready the bedding and share it.
    Soon as the Dawn shone forth rose-fingered at earliest daybreak,
405   out of his bed then started the horseman Gerenian Nestor;
going outside, he took his seat on the stones, well-polished,
which were arranged for him there in front of the high-raised doorway,
glistening white with a polish of oil; in an earlier time had
Neleus sat upon them, that peer of the gods as adviser;
410   but he had now been quelled by his doom and departed to Hades;
there sat Gerenian Nestor then, the Achaians' protector,
holding a scepter; his sons all gathered together around him,
coming away from their rooms: first Stratios came and Echéphron,
Perseus too and Arétos, and then godlike Thrasymédes;
415   joining with them was the hero Peisístratos, sixth of the children;
leading Telémachos, godlike in form, they sat him beside them.
Speaking among them opened the horseman Gerenian Nestor:
    "Quickly achieve for me now this thing I desire, dear children,
so that the first of the gods I may sue for the grace of Athena,
420   who came openly here, to the great god's plentiful banquet.
Come then, one of you go to the field for a cow, so that she may
get here quickly—the herdsman, tender of cattle, should drive her.
Then one of you go down to greathearted Telémachos' black ship,
all of his comrades bring to the house—leave only a couple.
425   One of you then go after Laërkes the goldsmith and bid him
come here so he can cover the horns of the heifer with gold leaf.
All you others remain here together and order the servants,
those inside of the house, to make ready a glorious banquet,
also to set up benches and bring clear water and firewood."
430   So did he speak; they all got busy; and soon did a heifer

come from the field; soon came from the swift balanced galley
great-souled Telémachos' comrades; and soon also did the bronzesmith
come with a bronzesmith's tools in his hands, that art's apparatus,
well-wrought tongs for his work in the fire and a hammer and anvil,
435   which he would use to accomplish the gold-work. Then did Athena
come to partake of the rites. Old Nestor the chariot driver
gave out gold, and the smith then covered the horns of the heifer,
working with care, so the goddess would see and rejoice in the splendor.
Taking the cow's horns, noble Echéphron and Stratios led her;
440   out of the house came Arétos; he brought in a flowery basin
water to wash their hands, and he held in a basket the barley
meal to be used. In his hand, Thrasymédes courageous in battle
held a sharp ax; he stood by the cow, made ready to strike her.
Perseus held the blood bowl; old Nestor the chariot driver
445   washed his hands and commenced by sprinkling the meal; to Athena
he prayed much, and to start threw hairs on the fire from the cow's head.
    But then, when they had uttered a prayer and had sprinkled the barley,
straightway Nestor's son Thrasymédes lofty of spirit,
standing beside her, struck; and the ax cut right through the neck thews,
450   severing them and releasing the cow's strength. Loud ululations
rose from the daughters, the wives of the sons, and the virtuous bedmate,
Nestor's Eurýdikè, who was the oldest of Klýmenos' daughters.
Then they, lifting the head of the cow from the earth of the broad ways,
held it; the leader of men Peisístratos severed the throat veins.
455   After the black blood poured from the cow and the life left the bone frame,
swiftly dismembering her, they cut out all of the thighbones,
fitly, according to custom, in thick fat covered them over,
making two layers; and morsels of flesh they fastened upon them.
These did the old man burn on the split wood, over them pouring
460   glistening wine, and the youths held five-pronged forks there beside him.
After the thighbones burned and the people partook of the entrails,
then they cut up the rest, and on stakes they spitted the pieces;
holding the sharp spits firmly in hand, they finished the roasting.
    Meanwhile Telémachos had been bathed by fair Polykástè,
465   who was the lastborn daughter of Nestor, Neleus' scion.
When she had bathed him and rubbed him richly with oil of the olive,
she threw garments about him, a beautiful cloak and a tunic;
he came forth from the basin, in form most like the immortals;
going to Nestor the shepherd of people, he sat down beside him.
470   When they had roasted the outermost flesh and had taken the spits out,

they sat feasting, and excellent men rose up to attend them;
serving the wine, they poured it out into gold drinking goblets.
When they had quite satisfied their appetites, drinking and eating,
speaking among them opened the horseman Gerenian Nestor:

475 "Come, my sons, for Telémachos lead out the fair-maned horses
and to the chariot yoke them, that he may accomplish his journey."
    So did he say; they carefully listened to him and obeyed him;
speedily then they yoked to the chariot swift-running horses.
Wine and provisions were put inside by the woman who kept them,

480 meats too, such as are eaten by rulers belovèd of heaven.
Straightway Telémachos stepped in the chariot, matchless in beauty;
also the leader of men Peisístratos, scion of Nestor,
climbed in the chariot; taking the reins in his hands, he drove by
wielding the whip, nor against their wishes the horses were speeding

485 out on the plain, so leaving the steep-built city of Pylos.
All that day they were shaking the yoke they carried about them.
    Then did the sun go down and the ways were all shadowed in darkness;
soon thereafter they came into Phérai, to Díokles' palace;
he was the son of Ortílochos, whom great Álpheios fathered.

490 There they rested the night, and he gave them guests' entertainment.
    Soon as the Dawn shone forth rose-fingered at earliest daybreak,
yoking the team, they climbed in the chariot, bright with adornment,
out of the courtyard gate and the echoing portico drove it,
wielding the whip, nor against their wishes the horses were speeding.

495 Into the wheat-bearing plain they came, there striving to finish
that whole journey, so swift were the horses to carry them onward.
Then did the sun go down and the ways were all shadowed in darkness.

BOOK 4

Then they reached Lakedaímon, the land of ravines, in its valley,
driving ahead to the house of the glorious lord Meneláos.
They found him with his numerous kinsmen and friends in the palace,
feasting the marriage of both his son and his beautiful daughter.
5 Her he was sending away to the son of rank-breaking Achilles,
for in Troy he had first made promise and nodded agreement
giving the girl, and for them now the gods were achieving the marriage.
Her therefore with the horses and chariots now he was sending
forth to the far-famed town of the Mýrmidons, ruled by her husband.
10 But for his son he was bringing Alektor's daughter from Sparta;
this son, strong Megapénthes, was born when his father was far off,
out of a slave, for the gods sent no more children to Helen
once she had born a first child, Hermíonè, who was a charming
girl endowed with the beauty of Aphrodítè the golden.
15   Thus they were banqueting there in the spacious and high-roofed palace,
kinsmen, neighbors, and friends of the glorious lord Meneláos,
taking delight, and among them was singing a godlike singer,
playing the lyre; and as well two tumblers were dancing about them—
they had begun with the song and were whirling around in the middle.
20   Then in the gateway court of the house those two and their horses—
valiant Telémachos and the illustrious scion of Nestor—
halted and stood. As he came forth, strong Eteóneus saw them,
ready and nimble attendant of glorious Lord Meneláos.
Taking the message, he went through the house to the shepherd of people;
25 there then, standing beside him, in these winged words he addressed him:
"Here have arrived some strangers, belovèd of Zeus Meneláos,
two men who in appearance are like great Zeus's descendants.
Tell me whether we should unharness their swift-footed horses
or instead send them away to another who would entertain them?"
30   Sorely displeased, thus spoke to him then light-haired Meneláos:

"No mere fool have you been, Boëthoös' son Eteóneus,
never before, yet now like a child you are uttering folly.
Certainly Helen and I ate many hospitable dinners
others provided for us as we came here, hoping that Zeus would
35　sometime soon put an end to our grief. Unharness the strangers'
horses, and bring the men into the hall to partake of the feasting."
　　So he spoke, and the man sped off through the hall, calling other
ready and nimble attendants to follow along on the service.
First unhitching the sweat-drenched horses from under the harness,
40　they then fastened the ropes to the crib where the horses were foddered,
threw them wheat in the manger and mingled with it white barley;
leaning the chariot then on the shimmering wall of the gateway,
into the sacred abode they led them; and when they beheld it,
they at the house of the ruler belovèd of Zeus were astonished,
45　such was the radiant splendor, as if of the sun or the full moon,
there in the high-roofed house of the glorious lord Meneláos.
When by looking at it with their eyes they had taken their pleasure,
they stepped into the well-polished tubs and were given a washing.
When maidservants had bathed them and rubbed them with oil of the olive,
50　they threw garments about the two men, wool mantles and tunics;
then they sat on the chairs near Atreus' son Meneláos.
Hand-washing water a maid then carried to them in a lovely
gold-wrought pitcher, and over a basin of silver she poured it,
so they could wash; nearby she set out a well-polished table.
55　Carrying food, the revered housekeeper approached them and set it
close to them, many a dish she gladly supplied from her storage.
Platters of meat an attendant lifted and set there beside them,
every sort, then close to their hands placed gold drinking goblets.
Nodding a welcome to them spoke forth light-haired Meneláos:
60　　"Help yourselves to the food and enjoy it; and when you have finished
eating your fill of the meal, we will ask you who among mankind
both of you are; for in you not lost is the race of your parents—
no, your race is of men who are rulers belovèd of great Zeus,
scepter-endowed, since never could base men beget such children."
65　　So he spoke; and the plump roast chine of an ox in his hands then
taking, he set it for them—as his own share it had been placed there.
They put forth eager hands to partake of the food lying ready.
When they had quite satisfied their appetites, drinking and eating,
then did Telémachos speak these words to the scion of Nestor,
70　keeping his head near his, so as not to be heard by the others:

123

"Scion of Nestor, in whom my spirit delights, take notice
here in the echoing house, of the radiant gleam of the bronzes,
and of the gold and the amber and ivory, and of the silver.
So I suppose are the courts of Olympian Zeus on the inside—
75   such inexpressible wealth: I am held in wonder observing."

So as he said these words, light-haired Meneláos was hearing;
raising his voice he spoke, and in these winged words he addressed them:
"Dear youths, none among mortals with Zeus could ever be rival:
his is a house undying, and deathless the treasures within it;
80   some man might be a rival to me in his goods—or perhaps not
anyone is: when much I had suffered and far I had wandered,
I brought these in my ships, in the eighth year came to my country.
First I wandered to Cyprus, Phoenicia, and to the Egyptians,
reached Ethiopians too and Sidonian folk and Erémboi,
85   Libya too, where the lambs sprout horns already at lambing.
Thrice do the sheep bear young in a year's full circle of seasons;
in that land neither master nor shepherd is lacking of any
cheeses from goats nor of savory meat, nor is sweet milk wanting;
ever the flocks give forth an abundance of milk for the sucklings.
90   As around those parts I kept roaming, collecting an ample
store of provisions, another man meanwhile slaughtered my brother,
stealthily, all unawares, by the guile of a murderous bedmate;
so no joy do I have as the lord of these many possessions.
Even from your own fathers, whoever they are, of these matters
95   you will have heard, since much I suffered and ruined a household
pleasant to dwell in, containing my goods so many and noble.
Would that I had but a scant third portion of them for my living
here in the house and the men were safe who in those days perished
there in the broad Troäd, faraway from horse-nourishing Argos.
100   Nevertheless, over all of the dead though mourning and weeping
many and many a day while sitting at home in our palace—
sometimes I will content my mind with lamenting and other
times leave off, for the chill of lament soon comes to a surfeit—
though I lament for them all, I mourn over none of the others
105   as for the one who makes me detest both eating and sleeping
when I remember him, since no other Achaian endured so
much as Odysseus endured and accomplished; and yet for himself was
sorrow to be his portion, for me grief never forgotten
over him—he has been gone so long a time, nor do we yet know
110   whether he lives or has perished. For him they surely are mourning,

old Laërtes his father, Penelope thoughtful and constant,
also Telémachos, whom he left newborn in the palace."
    So he spoke and in him roused longing to mourn for his father;
hearing of him, he cast tears down to the ground from his eyelids,
115 lifted his mantle of purple in front of his eyes to conceal them,
held it in both of his hands. Meneláos observed as he did it,
then he began to revolve his thoughts in his mind and his spirit,
whether to leave it to him to begin some talk of his father
or to inquire of him first and to test him on each of the details.
120   As he was pondering over these things in his mind and his spirit,
Helen herself came out of her high-roofed fragrant apartment—
she in appearance was much like Artemis of the gold distaff.
Following her was Adréstè, who set her a well-made armchair;
then Alkíppè was bringing a coverlet woven of soft wool;
125 Phylo was bringing a basket of silver, the one that Alkándrè,
consort of Pólybos, once gave Helen. He lived in Egyptian
Thebes, where most of the riches of men lie stored in their houses;
two silver basins for bathing he gave to the lord Meneláos,
gave him as well two tripods and ten gold talents of bullion.
130 Then on her own his wife made Helen magnificent presents,
gave her a gold-wrought distaff as well as a basket of silver
mounted on wheels, and with gold were the rims on it skillfully finished.
This now the handmaid Phylo was bringing; she set it beside her,
stuffed with a yarn finespun for the weaving; the distaff was lying
135 over it, holding a wool of a dark blue-violet color.
There in her chair she sat, and beneath for her feet was a footstool.
Straightway about each thing in her words she questioned her husband:
    "Do we know, Meneláos belovèd of Zeus, about these men,
who they claim that they are who have made this trip to our palace?
140 Shall I dissemble or utter the truth? For my spirit commands me.
Never, I think, has anyone seemed so like to another,
neither a woman nor man—I am held in wonder observing—
as now this one resembles the son of greathearted Odysseus,
even Telémachos, whom he left newborn in the palace,
145 that man, when on account of my bitch-eyed self you Achaians
went beneath Troy, meditating a fierce unwearying warfare."
    Answering her in return spoke forth light-haired Meneláos:
"Now I too am aware of the likeness that you have detected:
such were the feet of the man, such also the hands in appearance;
150 such was the glance of his eyes and his head and the tresses upon it.

Just now, having recalled to my memory thoughts of Odysseus,
I was conversing of him and of what great sorrows for me he
suffered; and bitter the tear he was shedding from under his eyebrows,
lifting his mantle of purple in front of his eyes to conceal them."

155   Answering him, thus spoke Peisístratos, scion of Nestor:
"Atreus' son Meneláos, the Zeus-loved lord of the people,
certainly this is the son of that man, as indeed you are saying;
nevertheless he is modest and thinks it shame in his spirit,
thus for the first time coming, to show ineptness in speaking

160   here before you, whose voice like that of a god we rejoice in.
Me also, as an escort, the horseman Gerenian Nestor
sent to accompany him, since he was desiring to see you,
so that you might give counsel to him, some word or some action.
Many the pains he endures, that child whose father is absent,

165   there in his palace, to whom no others are giving assistance;
so with Telémachos now—his father is gone, and no other
people are there in his country who might guard him from disaster."

        Answering him in return spoke forth light-haired Meneláos:
"What great joy, that the son of a man so dearly belovèd,

170   who for my sake endured many trials, has come to my palace!
When he arrived, I thought, I would welcome him more than the other
Argives, if wide-thundering Zeus the Olympian granted
us a return to our homes in our swift ships over the sea-brine.
I would have settled a city for him, built dwellings in Argos,

175   brought him from Ithaka hither, along with his son and possessions,
also all of his people, and cleared out one of the cities
settled around me, among those which I govern as ruler.
Then we would meet here often together, and nothing would ever
separate us, entertaining each other in pleasure and friendship—

180   never until the dark cloud of our death wrapped round and concealed us.
It was the god himself who in some way must have been jealous;
he caused him to be wretched, the one man not to return home."

        So he spoke; in them all he aroused a desire for lamenting.
Argive Helen the offspring of Zeus began weeping in sorrow;

185   so did Telémachos weep, so Atreus' son Meneláos;
neither indeed did the scion of Nestor have eyes that were tearless,
for in his heart he thought of Antílochos, handsome and valiant—
Memnon, the glorious son of resplendent Morning, had killed him.
Thus of his brother he thought as in these winged words he addressed him:

190   "Atreus' son, old Nestor was always saying that you are

thoughtful above all men, whenever we called you to mention
there as we sat in the palace and asked each other about you.
Now therefore if you can, take heed of my words, for I get no
pleasure from making lament with my dinner; and soon will the Morning
195 come, born early at dawn—though I do not blame anyone for
mourning whoever of mortals has died and encountered his doomsday.
This one honor alone we bestow on miserable mortals,
cutting our hair off, casting the tears from our cheeks to lament them.
Yes, I too have a brother who perished, and he was by no means
200 worst of the Argives—you would have known him; for I never either
met him or looked upon him; they say Antílochos was far
better than others in swiftness of running as well as in fighting."
      Answering him in return spoke forth light-haired Meneláos:
"Friend, since you have been saying exactly the things that a thoughtful
205 man would be saying or doing, and one yet older than you are—
such is the father you have, you too speak words that are thoughtful.
That man's offspring is easily known for whom Zeus son of Kronos
spins out luck as his portion at birth and the day of his marriage;
such he bestowed on Nestor, for all of his days without ceasing,
210 first, for himself to grow old in his halls in prosperous comfort,
then for his sons to be prudent as well as excellent spearmen—
let us give over the weeping that just now fell on our spirits,
then once more be mindful of dinner and pour out the water
over our hands. And indeed, in the morning as well, there will be more
215 stories for me and Telémachos both to relate to each other."
      So he spoke; on his hands Asphálion poured out the water,
ready and nimble attendant of glorious Lord Meneláos.
They put forth eager hands to partake of the food lying ready.
      Then other things were devised by Helen the daughter of great Zeus:
220 straightway into the wine they were drinking she cast an elixir
banishing sorrow and anger and ridding the mind of all evils.
He who swallowed the potion when it had been mixed in the wine bowl
would not shed any tears from his cheeks for the day that he drank it,
even although his mother and father had both of them perished,
225 even although his brother or much loved son in his presence
were to be killed with a sword, while he with his eyes was observing.
Such were the subtle and excellent drugs that the daughter of Zeus had,
which Thon's wife Polydámna had given her—she was of Egypt,
where there are many medicinal herbs that the grain-giving plowlands
230 bring forth; many are good in a mixture, and many are baneful.

Every man is an expert doctor, beyond any other
people in skill, since theirs is the race of the healer Paiéon.
When she had put this in and had ordered the wine to be poured out,
once more starting the talk, she spoke these words as an answer:
235 "Atreus' son Meneláos, belovèd of Zeus, and as well you
children of men most noble, to one now, then to another,
Zeus the great god gives blessing and bane, since he can do all things.
Go on now with your meal, while sitting at ease in the palace,
taking delight in stories, for I will tell one that is fitting.
240 Though of them all I will not now speak to you, nor will I name them,
so very many the trials of steadfast-hearted Odysseus,
yet what a deed this was that the strong man dared and accomplished
when in the land of the Trojans Achaians were suffering sorrows!
After subjecting himself to a wretched and pitiless scourging,
245 over his shoulders he threw a poor covering, then like a servant
entered the wide-wayed city of men by whom he was hated;
taking disguise, he made himself like another, a beggar
whom he had never resembled beside the Achaians' vessels.
Thus like him he entered the town of the Trojans, and they all
250 failed to suspect him: no one but me knew him as he then was;
I kept questioning him, but he subtly avoided replying.
But then, when I had bathed him and rubbed him with oil of the olive,
I threw garments about him and swore him an oath of the strongest
not to reveal that Odysseus had been in the midst of the Trojans,
255 not, at least, until he had returned to the tents and the swift ships;
then in turn he informed me of all the Achaians' intentions.
When with his long-edged blade he had slaughtered a number of Trojans,
he went carrying much intelligence back to the Argives;
others were shrilly lamenting, the women of Troy, but my own soul
260 only rejoiced; for already my heart had been turned toward going
back to my home, and I groaned for the madness that Aphrodítè
gave when she led me there from the much loved land of my fathers,
leaving behind my child and my marriage chamber and husband,
who lacked nothing at all in either his mind or his beauty."
265 Answering her in return spoke forth light-haired Meneláos:
"Certainly all this, wife, you speak as is fitting and proper.
Now for some time I have learned of the minds and the counsels of many
men who were heroes, and much of the earth I have covered in journeys;
yet not once have I looked with my eyes on another his equal,
270 such was the strength and the spirit of steadfast-hearted Odysseus.

Such also was this deed that the strong man dared and accomplished
inside the well-hewn horse, when all of the Argive chiefs were
sitting within it and bringing destruction and doom to the Trojans.
You came then to the place—it must have been one of the gods who
275   bade you to do it, who wished to bestow more fame on the Trojans.
Godlike Deïphobos also followed along at your coming.
Thrice you circled the hollow ambush, feeling the surface,
calling out loudly and naming the names of the Dánaän nobles,
making your voice like those of the bedmates of all of the Argives;
280   I meanwhile with the scion of Tydeus and noble Odysseus,
sitting amidst those men in the horse, heard how you were calling.
Both Diomédes and I then wanted to spring up and either
go outside or at least give answer at once from the inside;
yet in spite of our longing, Odysseus prevented and checked us.
285   There then all of the rest of those sons of Achaians were silent;
Ántiklos only among them was wanting to utter a speech in
answer to you; but Odysseus continued pressing his strong hand
firmly across his mouth, and he thus saved all the Achaians,
held him until you were taken away by Pallas Athena."

290   Thoughtful Telémachos then spoke out to him, giving an answer:
"Atreus' son Meneláos, the Zeus-loved lord of the people,
greater the woe: none of those things kept him from wretched destruction
nor would have done even if his heart were of iron within him.
But come, send us away to our beds, so that speedily we may
295   take our pleasure in lying at rest there, under a sweet sleep."

        So did he say; then, calling the housemaids, Argive Helen
bade them to put beds out in the portico, throwing upon them
rugs of a beautiful purple, upon those spread out the covers,
then bring mantles of wool to be drawn up over the sleepers.
300   Out of the hall they went, in their hands all carrying torches,
then spread covers for bedding; the guests were led out by a herald.
Those two lay down to sleep in the gateway court of the palace,
valiant Telémachos and the illustrious scion of Nestor;
Atreus' son took sleep in a room inside the high palace;
305   there at his side lay long-robed Helen, the splendor of women.

        Soon as the Dawn shone forth rose-fingered at earliest daybreak,
out of his bed then rose the great crier of war Meneláos,
put on his clothing, and hung his keen-edged sword on his shoulder;
under his glistening feet he fastened his beautiful sandals,
310   then went out of the chamber resembling a god in appearance,

there by Telémachos sat, and said these words, calling upon him:
"Hero Telémachos, what is the need that has brought you hither
into divine Lakedaímon across the broad back of the deep sea?
Is it public or private? Now tell me the truth of the matter."

315   Thoughtful Telémachos then spoke out to him, giving an answer:
"Atreus' son Meneláos, the Zeus-loved lord of the people,
I come hoping that you might tell me some news of my father.
My household is devoured, and my fertile fields have been ruined;
yes, my palace is full of my enemies, men who are always

320   killing my thick-thronged sheep and my swing-paced crooked-horned cattle,
suitors who seek my mother, of such overbearing presumption.
Therefore have I come here to your knees now, thinking you might be
willing to tell of his wretched destruction, in case you perhaps have
seen it with your own eyes or have heard the report of another

325   wandering man; for his mother indeed bore him to be woeful.
Spare me nothing, extenuate nothing, nor show any pity;
tell me all to the end, however it came to your notice.
Here I implore you, if ever my father, the noble Odysseus,
brought to fulfillment in word or in work anything he had promised

330   when in the land of the Trojans Achaians were suffering sorrows,
now call them to remembrance and tell me the truth of the matter."
        Mightily vexed, thus spoke to him then light-haired Meneláos:
"Shameful to think what strong-hearted man is the one whose bed they
want to be bedded in, they themselves being spiritless cowards!

335   So when a doe having fawns newborn, still sucking her sweet milk,
lulls them to sleep in a thicket, the lair of a powerful lion,
then goes off to the grassy ravines and the spurs of the mountain,
seeking her forage, and then, when he comes back into his covert,
both on the brood and the mother he visits a hideous doomsday,

340   so upon those men Odysseus will visit a hideous doomsday.
Oh Zeus, father of all, and Athena as well and Apollo,
would that he might be such as he was when in well-built Lesbos
he stood up in a contest and wrestled with Phílomeleídes—
strongly he gave him a fall, so that all the Achaians exulted.

345   Would that Odysseus in such a condition could mix with the suitors!
Then they all would become quick-dying and bitterly married!
As for the things you inquire and entreat of me, never would I say
anything swerving away from the truth nor ever deceive you,
but whatever the facts the unerring old man of the sea said,

350   not one word of it all will I hide from you now or conceal it.

"At that time, I was still in Egypt, though eager to go home,
held by the gods for not offering hecatombs full and effective—
always the gods want mortals to keep in mind their commandments.
Now then, there is an isle in the seaway surging and dashing,
355   lying in front of the Nile and of Egypt, that men call Pharos,
just such distance away as a hollow galley traverses
one whole day if a whistling wind blows freshly behind her.
Therein a harbor affords good mooring, from which men launch their
balanced ships on the sea, first drawing a store of dark water.
360   Twenty whole days I was held by the gods then, nor were there ever
winds that appeared blowing out to the sea-brine, those of the sort which
furnish conveyance to galleys across the broad back of the deep sea.
Now the supplies and the strength of the men would have all been depleted
had not one of the gods felt pity for me and preserved me—
365   of the old man of the sea, strong Proteus, she was the daughter,
Eídothéa, for hers was the heart I especially roused up.
She encountered me straying alone and apart from my comrades—
since they always were wandering over the island and fishing,
using their bent fishhooks, because hunger afflicted their stomachs.
370   Standing beside me then, she spoke these words and addressed me:
'Are you so childish a fool now, stranger, so feeble of spirit,
or do you willingly yield and delight in suffering sorrows?
Thus you are kept a long time on the island, and you are unable
ever to find a way out, and the hearts of your comrades are dwindling.'
375   "So she spoke, and in turn I addressed her, giving an answer:
'I will indeed speak plainly, whoever you are, though a goddess,
how I am held here quite unwilling; but surely I must have
done some trespass against the immortals who hold the broad heaven.
But now tell me yourself, for the gods have all in their knowledge,
380   which of the deathless gods impedes me and hampers my journey—
and of my homecoming, how on the fish-thronged sea I will travel.'
    "So I spoke, and at once that splendor of goddesses answered:
'These things, stranger and friend, I will tell you exactly and fully.
Often to this place comes the unerring old man of the sea-brine
385   Proteus, a deathless Egyptian, the god who knows all the deepest
chasms in every sea, and Poseidon's underlieutenant;
he they say is my father, and he it was who begot me.
If somehow you were able to wait in an ambush and seize him,
he would inform you about your road and the length of your journey—
390   and of your homecoming, how on the fish-thronged sea you will travel.

Then too he would inform you, belovèd of Zeus, if you wish it,
what has been done in your palace, the evil as well as the good things,
while you have thus been making a lengthy and arduous journey.'
   "So she spoke, and in turn I addressed her, giving an answer:
395 'For the divine old man, you yourself now show me an ambush,
lest somehow in advance he see me and know to avoid me,
since it is hard for a god to be quelled by a man who is mortal.'
   "So I spoke, and at once that splendor of goddesses answered:
'These things I will indeed now tell you exactly and fully.
400 Soon as the sun as it courses the sky stands high in midheaven,
then the unerring old man of the sea goes out of the sea-brine
under the west wind's breath, concealed in a darkening ripple;
when he emerges, he takes his rest under hollow caverns;
then do the seals, the offspring of the salt sea's beautiful daughter,
405 rise from the silvery sea-brine and sleep in a huddle around him,
breathing the sharp sour smell of the sea with its many abysses.
There will I lead you as soon as the morning has made its appearance,
and in a row I will lay you, so you choose well from your comrades
three of the best who are going with you in the well-benched galleys.
410 I will inform you of all of the old man's crafty devices.
First then he will go over the seals and be sure of the number;
when he has counted them off by fives and has fully reviewed them,
there in the midst he will lie, as a herdsman lies with his sheep flocks.
Just at the time when first you observe him lying in slumber,
415 straightway then be prepared to exert your strength and your vigor,
holding him there in spite of his desperate struggle to flee you.
He will attempt flight, making himself into every creature
living and moving on earth, into water and furious wildfire;
you maintain irresistible grips, press harder and harder.
420 But when at last as himself he speaks to you, asking a question,
such as he was when first you observed him lying in slumber,
finally then give over your violence, freeing the old man,
hero, and ask which one of the gods in a rage persecutes you—
and of your homecoming, how on the fish-thronged sea you will travel.'
425   "So having spoken, she plunged down under the billowing seaway.
Straightway then to the galleys, to where on the sand they were standing,
I set forth; and in me as I went was the heart much troubled.
But when I had arrived back there at the sea and the galleys,
we made ready the meal, and ambrosial night came upon us;
430 then we lay down to sleep on the tide-heaped sand of the seashore.

Soon as the Dawn shone forth rose-fingered at earliest daybreak,
just at that time I walked by the shore of the sea of the wide ways,
uttering many a prayer to the gods, and along with me took three
comrades, those that I trusted the most in every venture.

435   "Meanwhile she, having plunged down under the sea's broad bosom,
came back bringing with her four sealskins out of the seaway,
all of them recently flayed: she was planning a snare for her father.
When she had scooped out beds for us all in the sand of the seashore,
she sat waiting for us, and as we came right up beside her,

440 laid us there in a row, over each man throwing a sealskin.
Then would the ambush have been most horrible, such was the baneful
odor that horridly rose from the sea-bred seals to afflict us.
What man ever would lie in a bed with a deep-sea monster?
But she saved us herself and devised a great cure for the nuisance:

445 bringing ambrosial unguent sweet in the breathing, she put it
under the nostrils of each, thus killing the smell of the monster.
So we remained for the whole of the morning with resolute spirits.
Soon as the seals came out of the sea-brine, huddled together,
they lay down in a row on the tide-heaped sand of the seashore.

450 Out of the sea at midday did the old man come, and he found his
well-fed seals, and he went through them all, and he counted the number,
counted us first among all of his seabeasts, nor in his spirit
noticed that it was a trick; then he too laid himself down there.
Shouting and screaming, we launched an assault on him, casting about him

455 arm-holds; nor did the old man forget his craft or his cunning
but to begin transformed himself to a long-bearded lion,
then to a serpent and next to a panther and then to a huge boar;
then he became running water, a tree next, lofty and leafy.
We maintained irresistible grips with a resolute spirit.

460 But when at last the old man of the crafty devices was weary,
finally then he addressed me in these words, asking a question:
'Which of the gods now, Atreus' scion, has shared in your counsels,
so you could ambush and take me unwilling? And what do you need here?'

    "So he spoke, and at once I addressed him, giving an answer:
465 'You know, old man—why do you say these things to evade me?—
how I am kept a long time on the island, and I am unable
ever to find a way out, and the heart inside me is dwindling.
Now you instead tell me, as the gods have all in their knowledge,
which of the deathless gods impedes me and hampers my journey—

470 and of my homecoming, how on the fish-thronged sea I will travel.'

"So I spoke, and at once he addressed me, giving an answer:
'Certainly, you should have gone on board only after devoting
excellent victims to Zeus and the rest of the gods, so that swiftly
you might sail on the wine-dark sea and arrive in your homeland.

475 For it is not your fate to behold your friends and to go back
there to your well-built house, back there to the land of your fathers,
ever before once more in the flood of the river of Egypt
fallen from Zeus you enter and offer up sacred oblations
there to the deathless gods, the immortals who hold the broad heaven;

480 then will the gods grant you that journey for which you are eager.'
"So he spoke, and the heart inside me was utterly shattered,
since he had bade me to go on the seaway misty and murky
back once more into Egypt, a lengthy and arduous journey.
Nevertheless I addressed him in these words, giving an answer:

485 'These things I will perform, old man, in the way you have ordered.
But come now, tell me this and recount it exactly and fully,
whether unharmed the Achaians have all gone home in their galleys,
those whom Nestor and I left there when we sailed from the Troäd,
or whether anyone died by a harsh death while on his galley

490 or in the arms of his friends after he had wound up the warfare.'
"So I spoke, and at once he addressed me, giving an answer:
'Atreus' son, why ask me about this? You do not need it,
either to know it or learn what I think, and I do not imagine
you will be long without tears, once you have heard all of the story.

495 Many of them, indeed, were destroyed, while many are left still;
yet two only among those chiefs of the bronze-clad Achaians
died on the way back home—you were present yourself at the fighting;
one I suppose still lives and is held in the midst of the broad sea.
Ajax among his long-oared galleys was brought to destruction.

500 First however Poseidon had brought him near the enormous
rocks of the headland of Gyrai, and there from the sea he had saved him;
now he had fled from his doom, in spite of the hate of Athena,
if he had not hurled arrogant words, quite stricken to madness,
saying he fled from the sea's great gulfs though the gods were unwilling.

505 As he was uttering these loud vaunts, he was heard by Poseidon;
straightway then in his powerful hands he lifted his trident;
striking a rock on the headland of Gyrai, he split it asunder;
one part stayed there, and one broke off, fell into the seaway—
Ajax was sitting on it when first he was stricken to madness—

510 carrying him down into the sea unbounded and surging.

So it was there that he died when he drank of the salt seawater.
Then for a time your brother avoided the Fates and escaped them,
while in his hollow galleys, for sovereign Hera preserved him.
But when he was about to arrive at the steep high mountain
515   jutting at Máleia, then did a stormwind, seizing upon him,
carry him over the fish-thronged seaway, heavily groaning,
off to the bounds of the land in which Thyéstes before had
dwelt, but inhabited then by Aigísthos, the son of Thyéstes.
But when also from there the way seemed quite safe for returning,
520   then gods shifted the wind once more, and they came to their homeland;
there he rejoiced as he stepped out onto the land of his fathers,
and as he touched his country, he kissed it; and many a hot tear
poured down out of his eyes when gladly he looked on his own land.
But from a lookout a watchman observed him, one whom Aigísthos,
525   guileful of mind, had guided and set there, promising payment,
two gold talents; he watched for a whole year, lest Agamemnon,
passing him by unseen, should recall his impetuous valor.
Taking the message, he went to the house of the shepherd of people.
Then Aigísthos at once took thought of a crafty contrivance:
530   choosing from out of the town twenty men of the best, in an ambush
he set them, on the other side ordered a meal made ready,
then went down with his horses and chariots, pondering shameful
deeds, to invite to the feast Agamemnon, shepherd of people.
He led him to his house unaware of his ruin and killed him
535   while he was dining, the way one slaughters an ox at the manger.
None of the comrades was left who had come with Atreus' scion,
none of Aigísthos' either, but they were all killed in the palace.'

     "So he spoke, and the heart inside me was utterly shattered;
there in the sand I sat down sorrowing, nor did my spirit
540   wish any longer to live and to look upon Helios' sunlight.
When I had sated myself with groveling, weeping, and groaning,
then the unerring old man of the sea spoke out and addressed me:
'No more, Atreus' son, incessantly weep such a long time,
since we will never accomplish a thing that way; but in swiftness
545   try to discover a means to return to the land of your fathers.
Either alive you will find Aigísthos, or else that Orestes,
coming before you, has killed him, and you will take part in the grave rites.'

     "So he spoke, and at once my heart and my valorous spirit
deep in my breast took comfort again, in spite of my sorrow.
550   Raising my voice I spoke, and in these winged words I addressed him:

'Now of these men I know; but inform me as well of the third man—
him who still is alive and is held in the midst of the broad sea,
or he is dead. I would like in spite of my sorrow to hear it.'

    "So I spoke, and at once he addressed me, giving an answer:
555 'He is the son of Laërtes, in Ithaka keeping his dwelling.
I saw him on an island; he shed great tears in abundance
there in the halls of Kalýpso, a nymph who keeps him beside her
forcibly. He is unable to leave for the land of his fathers,
since neither well-oared ships does he have near at hand nor companions
560 who might serve to convey him across the broad back of the deep sea.
Nor is it fated for you, Meneláos beloved of great Zeus,
in horse-pasturing Argos to die and encounter your doomsday,
but to the plain of Elysium then the immortals will send you
and to the end of the earth, where dwells light-haired Rhadamánthys.
565 That is the place where men have a life most easy and pleasant:
there is no snow or tempestuous winter, and never does rain fall;
always instead clear freshening breezes of Zephyr are breathing,
sent to the land by the Ocean to blow upon men and refresh them.
You have Helen, and so Zeus' son-in-law you are reckoned.'

570   "So he spoke, and he plunged down under the billowing seaway.
Straightway then to the galleys, along with the godlike comrades,
I set forth; and in me as I went was the heart much troubled.
But when we had arrived back there at the sea and the galleys,
we made ready the meal, and ambrosial night came upon us;
575 then we lay down to sleep on the tide-heaped sand of the seashore.

    "Soon as the Dawn shone forth rose-fingered at earliest daybreak,
first we dragged our ships out into the luminous sea-brine,
set up the mast poles, and hoisted the sails in the balanced galleys;
going aboard themselves, the men took their seats at the oarlocks;
580 sitting in rows, they beat their oars on the silvery sea-brine.
Back once more in the river of Egypt fallen from Zeus we
beached our galleys and offered our hecatombs full and effective.
I then, after appeasing the wrath of the gods who live always,
piled Agamemnon a mound, that his fame might not be extinguished.
585 These things finished, I started for home; the immortals provided
winds that were fair; to my own dear fatherland swiftly they brought me.

    "But come now, stay here with me yet for a while in the palace;
visit until some time has elapsed, the eleventh or twelfth day;
then I will send you off well: I will give you glorious presents,
590 three fine horses, a well-carved chariot; I will present you

also a beautiful cup, so that all of your days, as you pour out
offerings for the immortals, you call me back to remembrance."
    Thoughtful Telémachos then spoke out to him, giving an answer:
"Atreus' son, do not try to detain me here for a long time.
595 I could indeed stay close to your side for the space of a whole year,
sitting at ease; no longing for home or for parents would seize me,
for a most wondrous delight I take as I listen to all your
speeches and tales; but in sacred Pylos the comrades are growing
weary for me already; for some time now you have kept me.
600 As for a gift, whatever you give, let it be some treasure,
since I will not take horses to Ithaka, rather will leave them
here to be glories for you, since you are the lord of a spacious
plain upon which much clover abounds and the grass of the marshes,
plentiful wheat, much rye, and as well broad ears of white barley.
605 There are in Ithaka no wide courses nor meadow for grazing;
goats breed there—more pleasing it is than a land that breeds horses.
None of the islands that slope to the sea is well suited for riding
horses or has fine meadows, and Ithaka less than all others."
    So he spoke; with a smile, the great crier of war Meneláos
610 gave him a pat with his hand and said these words, calling upon him:
"You are of excellent blood, dear child, so well you are speaking;
therefore I will exchange these things for you, since I can do so.
I will present you, of all of the gifts which lie in my palace,
treasures of mine, that one which is finest and far the most honored:
615 I will present you a well-made wine bowl which is entirely
fashioned of silver; with gold are the rims on it skillfully finished;
it is a work of Hephaistos that valorous Phaídimos gave me—
he the Sidonians' king, whose palace provided me shelter
when I visited there: I wish to bestow it on you now."
620   Such things then they spoke and addressed each one to the other;
then to the house of the godlike king came guests for a banquet;
sheep they were driving, and wine, beneficial to men, they were bringing;
food was conveyed there too by the wives in beautiful head scarves.
    So it was that they busied themselves in the halls with a dinner.
625 Meanwhile all of the suitors, in front of the house of Odysseus,
were entertaining themselves in hurling the disk and the goat-spear,
just as before, on the well-smoothed grounds, in shameless presumption.
There was Antínoös sitting and godlike Eurýmachos also;
they were the chiefs of the suitors and best by far in their prowess.
630 Phronios' son Noëmon approached them; standing beside them

then, he addressed Antínoös these words, asking a question:
"Do we or do we not, Antínoös, know in our spirits
what day Telémachos comes back homeward from sandy-soiled Pylos?
He left taking a galley of mine that I now am in need of—

635   over to Elis of spacious domains I would go, to a place twelve
horses of mine are, mares, at their teats hard-laboring mule-colts,
not yet broken; of these I would now drive one off to break him."
So did he say; they wondered at heart, not having suspected
he had departed for Neleian Pylos, but thought he had stayed there,

640   out on the land somewhere with the flocks or perhaps with the swineherd.
Then spoke answering him Antínoös son of Eupeíthes:
"Tell me the truth: what day did he leave here? Which of the young men
went in his company? Chosen from Ithaka were they, or rather
hirelings and slaves of his own? He could also have done it in this way.

645   Truthfully speak to me now about these things, so that I know well
whether against your will, by force, you were robbed of your black ship,
or if you willingly gave it because he requested to take it."
Phronios' son Noëmon addressed him, giving an answer:
"I quite willingly gave it—and what would anyone else do

650   when the request was made by a man like him, whose afflictions
weighed on his heart? It would be most harsh to refuse him the present.
Those who accompanied him were the best young men in the country
after ourselves; and of them I recognized one as the leader,
Mentor—or else some god who was like him in every feature.

655   Nevertheless I wonder, for I saw glorious Mentor
yesterday morning; before, he was boarding the galley for Pylos."
So having spoken to them, he returned to the house of his father;
then in both of the chiefs the audacious hearts were indignant;
they put a stop to the contests and seated the suitors together.

660   Then among them thus spoke Antínoös son of Eupeíthes,
grievously pained, with a heart grown utterly black in its anger,
filled to the brim; and his eyes shone forth like radiant blazes:
"Well then, what a great exploit Telémachos now has accomplished
insolently, this journey! We thought he would never achieve it.

665   This young boy has eluded so many, defying our wishes,
dragging a ship to the sea and selecting the best in the country.
He will begin to be yet more trouble—but soon on his strength may
Zeus bring ruin, before he arrives at the measure of manhood!
But come, give to me now a swift galley and twenty companions,

670   so I can ambush him when he comes, keeping watch in the channel

which from the Ithakan isle divides Samè, rugged and rocky;
thus most grievously he will have sailed in search of his father."
    So did he say; they all then assented and bade that it be so;
straightway arising, they went back into the house of Odysseus.
675   No very long time now did Penelope go without knowing
what plans deep in their hearts those suitors were secretly plotting;
Medon the herald reported to her what he heard of their counsels
standing outside of the court in which they were weaving their intrigue.
He set forth through the house to Penelope, bearing the message;
680   as he was crossing the threshold, Penelope spoke and addressed him:
    "Herald, what is the cause the illustrious suitors have sent you?
Was it to let us know that the housemaids of godlike Odysseus
now are to cease their labors and make them ready a banquet?
May they never again come courting or gather together—
685   may they feast for the final, the last time now in the palace—
you who often assemble to lay waste much of the living,
goods of ingenious-minded Telémachos. Not in the least you
listened to what your fathers before you, when you were children,
said, what manner of man was Odysseus among your own parents:
690   neither in acting or speaking he did anyone injustice
here in his land, of the sort that divine kings use as a custom—
one of his people a ruler will hate, while loving another.
Never against any man he at all wrought reckless abuses.
But this spirit of yours is apparent, and so are your shameful
695   exploits: for deeds well done, there never is gratitude later."
    Then in answer to her spoke Medon, sagacious and knowing:
"Would that ingratitude, Queen, were the total account of the evil!
But far greater another, and far more grievous, that now these
suitors devise: may it not be achieved by the scion of Kronos!
700   They are intending to slaughter Telémachos soon with a keen bronze
blade as he comes back home, for he left to seek news of his father,
going to sacred Pylos and then to divine Lakedaímon."
    So he spoke, and her limbs and the heart inside her were loosened;
speechlessness for a long time gripped her, and both of her eyes were
705   filled with the tears she shed, and her rich full voice was arrested.
Finally then she addressed him in these words, giving an answer:
"Why has my child gone away from me, herald? No need was upon him
that he should go on board swift-voyaging galleys that serve for
men as the steeds of the sea to cross over the great wide waters.
710   Was it that even his name might be among men no longer?"

Answering her in return spoke Medon, sagacious and knowing:
"I do not know whether some god roused him or whether his own heart
stirred him up to the voyage to Pylos in order to find out
either about his father's return or the doom he encountered."

715 So having spoken, he went back down through the house of Odysseus.
Sorrow that crushes the heart poured round her, and she could no longer
bear to sit down on a chair, of the many there were in the dwelling;
rather she sat on her rich and elaborate bedroom's threshold,
raising a piteous moan, and around her all of the housemaids

720 whimpered, as many as dwelt in the house, both younger and older.
Thus then, constantly weeping, Penelope spoke and addressed them:
"Friends, hear this; for to me the Olympian gives a surpassing
sorrow, beyond all women in my time reared or begotten,
I who had long since lost my noble and lion-souled husband,

725 who of the Dánaäns was outstanding in every virtue,
whose noble fame through Hellas has spread and the middle of Argos.
Now has my much loved son been carried away by the stormwinds,
swept from the halls unnoticed, nor did I hear of his parting—
wretches, for not even one of you took it in mind to arouse me

730 out of my bed, although in your hearts you knew very clearly
when that boy went away in the hollow and dark-hued galley!
For if I ever had learned of this journey that he was intending,
either he would have remained, however desirous of parting,
or else he would have left me dead back here in the palace.

735 But one of you go quickly and summon my old manservant
Dolios, whom my father bestowed on me when I came here,
who of my well-wooded garden is keeper, that speedily he may
visit and sit by Laërtes and tell him of all that has happened,
so that perhaps the old master can weave some scheme in his spirit,

740 then go out and complain to the people that they are intent on
doing away with his offspring and that of the godlike Odysseus."
Speaking to her then answered the nurse much-loved Eurykleía:
"Dear girl, either now kill me at once with the pitiless bronze or
let me remain in the house; but the story shall not be a secret.

745 I knew all the affair; I gave him whatever he ordered,
furnished the bread and sweet wine; and of me a great oath he exacted,
not to inform you before some time had elapsed, on the twelfth day,
or until you yourself should have missed him and heard of his leaving,
so that you might not injure your beautiful skin with your weeping.

750 But now, when you have bathed and have put clean clothes on your body,

going upstairs to your chamber along with your women attendants,
pray to Athena the daughter of Zeus who carries the aegis,
for it is possible then she would save him even from dying.
Do not distress a distressed old man, for I cannot imagine
755   that by the fortunate gods the descent of Arkeísios' son is
utterly hated, but there will be someone yet who will keep this
high-roofed house, I am sure, and the fertile fields in the distance."
    She spoke, lulling her anguish and stopping her eyes from their weeping.
After Penelope bathed and had put clean clothes on her body,
760   she went up to her chamber along with her women attendants,
poured in a basket the barley for sprinkling, and prayed to Athena:
"Hear me, offspring of Zeus of the aegis, unwearying goddess:
if in his palace Odysseus of many devices has ever
burnt in your honor the fat thigh pieces of sheep or of heifers,
765   now, I pray, call them to remembrance and rescue my dear son;
guard and defend him from those overbearing and arrogant suitors."
    So she spoke, ululating; her prayer was heard by the goddess.
There in the shadowy hall were the suitors arousing an uproar;
such are the words which one of the arrogant youths would have spoken:
770   "Surely the much wooed queen is preparing to give us a marriage
banquet and does not know that a death for her son is determined."
    So would he say, but they knew not how these things were determined.
Then Antínoös spoke and addressed them, giving them counsel:
"Foolhardy friends, keep guard against words too bold and offensive,
775   all of that sort, lest even within, someone should report them.
But come, let us arise from our seats and in silence accomplish
what we have said, in the way that to all of our minds seemed fitting."
    So he spoke, and he chose out twenty good men as companions;
they set forth to the swift-sailing ship and the shore of the deep sea.
780   First they dragged their ship out into the depths of the sea-brine,
set up the mast pole, and hoisted the sails in the dark-hued galley;
next they fastened the oars in the oxhide thongs of the oarlocks,
all in an orderly fashion; above they spread out the white sails;
weapons were carried aboard by valorous-hearted attendants.
785   Out from the beach in the water they anchored her, then, disembarking,
there on the shore took supper and waited the evening's onset.
    Prudent Penelope meanwhile, remaining above in her chamber,
lay without eating and not partaking of drink or of victuals,
wondering whether her faultless son would escape from the slaughter
790   or if he might be quelled by the haughty and arrogant suitors.

Just as a lion amidst an assemblage of huntsmen ponders
fearfully when they draw their treacherous circle about him—
over her pondering thus there came a delectable slumber;
soon, sinking back, she was sleeping, and all of her limbs were unloosened.

795   Then other things were devised by the goddess bright-eyed Athena.
First she created a phantom and likened its form to a woman,
Íphthimè, who also was greathearted Ikários' daughter;
she had been taken to wife by Eúmelos, dwelling in Phérai.
Then she dispatched this shape to the palace of godlike Odysseus,

800 so as Penelope lay there woefully mourning and wailing,
it might cause her to cease from her wailing and tearful lamenting.
Into the chamber it went, by the oxhide thong of the door latch;
standing above her head, it spoke these words and addressed her:
      "Are you sleeping, Penelope, sorrowing so in your spirit?

805 Not in the least will the gods who live in comfort allow you
either to mourn or to trouble yourself, since he is yet able,
your dear child, to return: to the gods he is no transgressor."
      Prudent Penelope then spoke out to her, giving an answer,
while at the dream gates she kept slumbering deeply and sweetly:

810 "Why have you come to me here, dear sister? For never before now
have you paid me a visit, as you dwell far at a distance.
Then moreover you bid me to cease from my woes and afflictions,
all of the many that worry and vex me in mind and in spirit,
I who had long since lost my noble and lion-souled husband,

815 who of the Dánaäns was outstanding in every virtue,
whose noble fame through Hellas has spread and the middle of Argos.
Now has my much loved son gone away on a hollow galley
foolishly—neither in deeds nor in words is he yet very skillful.
It is for him that I now feel grief, even more than the other,

820 yes, and for him that I tremble and fear, lest something befall him,
whether from those to whose land he journeys or out on the seaway—
numerous foes he has who scheme and maneuver against him,
hoping to kill him before he returns to the land of his fathers."
      Answering her in return spoke forth that dim apparition:

825 "Take heart, and be not at all too fearful for him in your spirit,
such a great escort is she who goes with him—other men also
pray her to stand by them with assistance, for she has the power—
Pallas Athena; and she takes pity on you in your sorrow;
she is the one who has sent me now to inform you of these things."

830   Prudent Penelope then spoke answering words and addressed her:

142

"If you are truly divine and have heard these words of a goddess,
come, I beseech you, tell me about that man so afflicted,
whether perhaps he lives, still looks upon Helios' sunlight,
or he has died already and dwells in the palace of Hades."

835   Answering her in return spoke forth that dim apparition:
"No, as to that man now, I will not tell all of the story,
whether he lives or has died; for to speak vain words is an evil."

So did it say, then parted from her by the latch on the doorpost
into the breath of the winds; and Ikários' daughter awakened

840   out of her sleep, and her heart grew warm in cheerful assurance,
so distinctly the dream in the dead of the night sped upon her.

Boarding, the suitors at once sailed out on the watery pathway,
pondering in their minds for Telémachos pitiless murder.
There is a rock-strewn isle in the midst of the sea that is halfway

845   off of the Ithakan coast toward Samè, rugged and rocky,
Ásteris, not very big, having two ship-sheltering harbors;
there for Telémachos now the Achaians awaited in ambush.

BOOK 5

Dawn rose out of her bed, from beside resplendent Tithónos,
so that she might bring light to the deathless gods and to mortals.
Straightway the gods sat down in a session together, among them
Zeus who thunders above, whose sovereign power is greatest.
5　Then did Athena, recalling the manifold woes of Odysseus,
speak to them, for it concerned her that he was still in the nymph's house:
　"Oh Father Zeus and the rest of the fortunate gods, ever-living,
let no king with a scepter be kindly of heart any longer,
never compassionate, nor of a mind that is skillful in justice;
10　let him instead be ever malignant and do what is not just,
since not one of the people is mindful of godlike Odysseus,
even among those people he ruled, like a father in mildness.
But on an island he lies and is suffering terrible sorrows
there in the halls of Kalýpso, a nymph who keeps him beside her
15　forcibly. He is unable to leave for the land of his fathers,
since neither well-oared ships does he have near at hand nor companions
who might serve to convey him across the broad back of the deep sea.
Now moreover the suitors are scheming to slaughter his much loved
son as he goes back home, for he left to seek news of his father,
20　going to sacred Pylos and then to divine Lakedaímon."
　Answering her in return spoke forth the cloud-gathering god Zeus:
"Oh my child, what a word has escaped from the fence of your teeth now!
Was this not the design which you yourself recommended,
so when Odysseus returns he can pay them back for their evils?
25　As for Telémachos, skillfully guide him, for you have the power,
so that he quite unharmed may arrive in the land of his fathers,
while on their galley the suitors may sail back homeward in failure."
　So he spoke, then addressed these words to his dear son Hermes:
"Since in our other affairs you serve as the messenger, Hermes,
30　say our certain decree to the nymph with the beautiful tresses:

send home steadfast-hearted Odysseus, that he may return now,
having as escort none of the gods nor of men who are mortal;
but on a makeshift rope-tied raft, after suffering sorrows,
let him arrive on the twentieth day in Scheria's fertile
35 land where dwell the Phaiákian people, the gods' near kindred.
As to a god, they will show him honor with hearts unstinting,
send him away on a ship to the much loved land of his fathers,
giving him treasures of bronze and of gold in abundance and garments,
much—so much that Odysseus from Troy could never have brought it
40 if he had come unharmed with his own fair share of the booty.
For it is thus his fate to behold his friends and to go back
there to his high-roofed house, back there to the land of his fathers."
        He spoke, nor was ignored by the messenger, slayer of Argos.
Straightway under his feet he fastened his beautiful sandals,
45 golden, undying, divine, which carry him over the water,
over the measureless surface of earth with the breath of the stormwind,
took up the wand he uses for charming the eyes of whatever
man he wishes, and others again he arouses from slumber.
This he held in his hand as he flew, the strong slayer of Argos.
50 Passing Piéria, onto the sea he plunged from the ether,
then kept speeding ahead on the wave, like a ravenous seabird
which while hunting for fish in the terrible troughs of the barren
deep sea, drenches its thick-feathered wings in the salt seawater;
like that bird, over many a wave now Hermes was riding.
55 But when finally he had arrived at the faraway island,
there he stepped from the violet seaway and into the land went
onward until he arrived at the great deep cavern in which was
dwelling the nymph with the beautiful tresses; he found her inside it.
There was a great fire burning upon her hearth, and the fragrance
60 made by the blaze of the easily split cedarwood and the citron
spread far over the isle; inside, in her beautiful voice she
sang as she wove with a shuttle of gold to and fro on a fabric.
On all sides of the cavern a flourishing woodland was growing,
trees like alder and poplar and cypress, agreeably scented;
65 there in the grove were the long-winged birds now settled and roosting,
tree owls, falcons and hawks, and the long-tongued crows of the sea-brine,
cormorants, birds that depend on working the sea for their living.
Right there next to the hollow cavern extended a garden
vine in the prime of its growth, with clusters of grapes in abundance.
70 There four springs in a row poured out pure shimmering water

close to each other, and then each turned in a different direction.
Grassy and soft was the meadow around and with violets blooming,
celery too, so that anyone coming there, though an immortal,
looking upon it would marvel and feel great joy in his spirit.

75   There now marveling stood that messenger, slayer of Argos.
But then, when in his heart he had marveled at all he was seeing,
straightway he entered the spacious cavern, and when she beheld him
face her, Kalýpso the glorious goddess did not fail to know him,
since not wanting in knowledge, each one of the others, the deathless

80 gods are, even if some maintain their abodes at a distance.
There in the cavern he did not find greathearted Odysseus,
but on the shore he sat, as before he had done, and lamented,
breaking his heart with his tears and his moans and insatiable sorrows;
over the desolate sea he would gaze while letting his tears flow.

85 Questioning Hermes, Kalýpso the glorious goddess addressed him,
when she had bade him sit in a gorgeous and glittering armchair:
    "God of the gold wand, Hermes, and why, pray tell, have you come here,
honored and welcome? For you have not visited often before now.
Speak what you have in your mind, for my heart bids me to achieve it

90 if I am able to do it and if it can well be accomplished.
But first follow, so I may provide you fit entertainment."
    So having spoken, and placing a table beside him, the goddess
filled it full of ambrosial victuals and mixed red nectar.
He began drinking and eating, the messenger, slayer of Argos.

95 When he had finished the meal and had pleased his heart with the victuals,
finally then he addressed her in these words, giving an answer:
    "You ask me of my coming—a god by a goddess is questioned;
truthfully now I will tell you the story, for so you have bidden.
Zeus gave order that I come hither, though I did not wish to—

100 who of his own will ever would run over such vast briny
seawater? Nowhere near is a city of mortals in which they
celebrate rites for the gods or devote them choicest oblations.
But no possible way is another god able to transgress
or to make vain the intention of Zeus who carries the aegis.

105 They say there is a man with you here, the most woeful of all those
men who around the great city of Priam were fighting their battles
nine years; then in the tenth, ransacking the city, they started
homeward; but while they were journeying back they offended Athena,
so against them she roused a bad windstorm and towering billows.

110 Thereupon all of the rest were destroyed, his noble companions;

him however the wind and the waves bore, bringing him hither.
Now you are bidden to send him away in all possible swiftness;
for it is not his fate to be lost here, far from his loved ones;
but his portion is yet to behold his friends and to go back
115   there to his high-roofed house, back there to the land of his fathers."
      So he spoke, and Kalýpso the glorious goddess was shaken;
raising her voice she spoke, and in these winged words she addressed him:
"Gods, you are cruel and harsh and beyond all others are jealous,
who are resentful and grudging when goddesses lie beside mortals
120   openly, should one of us take a man as her own dear bedmate.
Thus it was when Oríon was taken by Dawn the rose-fingered;
so much time did the gods who abide in comfort begrudge it,
till in Ortýgia once chaste Artemis, she of the gold throne,
killed him, visiting him with her mild and benevolent missiles.
125   Thus it was when Deméter, the goddess with beautiful tresses,
yielding her heart to Iásion, joined him in bed and affection
out in a thrice-plowed fallow; but not very long unaware was
Zeus, who killed him by hurling a scintillant bolt of his lightning.
Thus now, gods, you begrudge me to be with a man who is mortal,
130   whom I rescued as he was alone and astride of a keel beam
when Zeus struck the swift ship with a scintillant bolt of his lightning
so in the midst of the wine-dark sea she would shatter to pieces.
Thereupon all of the rest were destroyed, his noble companions;
he however was borne by the wind and the waves and brought hither.
135   He is the man I have loved and have cherished beside me and promised
I would make him immortal and ageless forever and ever.
But as no possible way is another god able to transgress
or to make vain the intention of Zeus who carries the aegis,
let him go, if indeed that god now bids and commands it,
140   over the desolate sea. But to no place I will convey him,
since neither well-oared ships do I have near at hand nor companions
who might serve to convey him across the broad back of the deep sea.
Yet with a good will I will advise him and keep no secrets,
so that he might go back unharmed to the land of his fathers."
145   Speaking to her then answered the messenger, slayer of Argos:
"Thus now send him away, submitting to Zeus and his anger,
lest he perhaps hereafter begrudge it and wrathfully spurn you."
      So having spoken departed from her the strong slayer of Argos.
Then did the lady and nymph go seek greathearted Odysseus,
150   since she in fact took heed of the message that Zeus had dispatched her.

Sitting away on the shore she discovered him: never his eyes were
dry from the tears that he wept; out of him was the sweet life flowing
as for returning he yearned, for the nymph no longer was pleasing.
Yet of necessity he kept passing the nights in the spacious
155　cavern beside her, the man unwilling with her who willed it;
then each day he would sit down there by the rocks and the seashore,
breaking his heart with his tears and his moans and insatiable sorrows;
over the desolate sea he gazed while letting his tears flow.
Standing beside him then, that glorious goddess addressed him:
160　　"Miserable man, do not mourn any longer beside me, nor let your
life be wasted; for now I will send you away with a good will.
But come, cut long beams with an ax, then join them together
into a broad raft-boat; and upon it fasten the half decks
high up, to carry you over the seaway misty and murky.
165　Then for my part I will put in the boat heart-pleasing provisions,
victuals and water and sweet red wine to protect you from hunger,
clothe you in garments as well and dispatch you favoring breezes,
so that you quite unharmed may arrive in the land of your fathers,
if in fact it is willed by the gods who hold the broad heaven,
170　those who are stronger than I in devising as well as achieving."
　　　So as she spoke he shuddered, much-suffering noble Odysseus;
raising his voice he spoke, and in these winged words he addressed her:
"Some other thing you plan for me, goddess, and not a conveyance,
you who bid me to cross on a raft the great gulf of the deep sea,
175　dreadful and hard to traverse: not even the balanced galleys,
swift in sailing, can cross it, exulting in Zeus-sent breezes.
Never will I go onto a raft while you are unwilling,
if you will not deign, goddess, to swear me an oath of the strongest
you are not plotting for me some other infliction of evil."
180　　So he spoke; with a smile, that glorious goddess Kalýpso
gave him a pat with her hand and said these words, calling upon him:
"What an accomplished rogue you are, not clever for nothing,
such is the word you cunningly thought to return as an answer.
Now earth witness to this, and the wide sky stretching above us,
185　so too the water of Styx, down-flowing, for this is the greatest
oath and the oath most dreadful among us blessèd immortals:
I am not plotting for you some other infliction of evil.
Rather, I think those things and devise plans just of the sort which
I would contrive for myself should ever the need come upon me.
190　For it is true that my mind is a just one, nor is an iron

heart in this bosom of mine, but a heart instinct with compassion."
　　So having spoken to him, then swiftly the glorious goddess
led him forward, and he came on in the goddess's footsteps.
Soon both goddess and man had arrived at the spacious cavern;
195　there he took his seat in an armchair, that very one whence
Hermes had risen; the nymph placed every manner of food which
men who are mortal consume near him for his eating and drinking.
She herself sat down there just opposite godlike Odysseus;
near her the handmaids placed ambrosial viands and nectar.
200　They put forth eager hands to partake of the food lying ready.
When they had quite satisfied their appetites, drinking and eating,
speaking among them opened Kalýpso, the glorious goddess:
　　"Zeus-sprung son of Laërtes, Odysseus of many devices,
so is it true to your home, to the much loved land of your fathers,
205　you now want straightway to depart? Even so, may you prosper!
Nevertheless, if you knew in your mind how many afflictions
fate will allot you before you arrive in the land of your fathers,
you would remain with me here and would keep watch over the household;
then you would be an immortal, in spite of your yearning to see your
210　bedmate, her for whom always, all of your days, you are longing.
Not indeed that I call myself less noble than she is
either in form or in beauty, because no way is it fitting
for mere mortals to rival immortals in form or appearance."
　　Speaking to her then answered Odysseus of many devices:
215　"Lady and goddess, do not be angry with me over this, for I know these
things very well: much slighter than you to behold face-to-face is
prudent Penelope, in her appearance as well as in stature,
seeing that she is a mortal and you are immortal and ageless.
But even so I desire—yes, all of my days I am longing—
220　yet to arrive back home and to look on the day of returning.
If on the wine-dark sea some god might bring me to shipwreck,
I will endure, for I have in my breast a heart patient in sorrows,
I who have suffered so much already and labored so greatly,
both on the waves and in war: let this be added upon them."
225　　So did he say; and the sun went down, and the dusk came upon them.
Entering into a nook of the spacious cavern, the two then
took their pleasure in love and remained there close to each other.
　　Soon as the Dawn shone forth rose-fingered at earliest daybreak,
straightway Odysseus attired himself in a mantle and tunic;
230　so too the nymph put on a capacious and shimmering mantle,

graceful and delicate; fastened around her waist was a lovely
girdle of gold, and above on her head she was wearing a head scarf.
Then she began to devise greathearted Odysseus' conveyance.
First she gave him an ax of a huge size, fitted for gripping,

235   fashioned of bronze and on both sides sharpened; and there was a splendid
handle upon it, made out of olive wood, solidly fitted.
Then she provided an adze, well-polished, and led him the way far
off to the edge of the isle, to a place where trees grew the tallest—
trees like alders and poplars, and firs too, towering skyward,

240   long since sapless and dry, so that they would be light in the floating.
Straightway, when she had shown him the place where trees grew the tallest,
then did Kalýpso the glorious goddess return to her dwelling;
he began cutting the timber and rapidly finished the labor,
threw down twenty in all, with the bronze ax carefully trimmed them,

245   skillfully planed them, and made them straight by stretching a chalk line.
Meanwhile Kalýpso the glorious goddess had brought him a gimlet;
he bored holes through all of the beams, fitted each to the others;
then with the bolts and the fastening clamps he solidly joined them.
Just as a man might lay out the hold of a ship, a capacious

250   vessel to transport goods—some carpenter skilled as a joiner—
such was the measure of this broad raft that Odysseus constructed.
Building a deck, he fitted and fixed it above to the close-set
ribs, then fastened the long side beams to the hull to complete it,
set up a mast inside, with a yardarm fitted upon it;

255   then in addition he fashioned a tiller, so he could direct her.
Then all around her sides he fastened the bulwarks of plaited
mats as defense from the waves; and he piled in masses of brushwood.
Meanwhile Kalýpso the glorious goddess had carried him fabric,
so he could make him a sail; this too he skillfully fashioned.

260   After he tied in position the braces, the sheets, and the halyards,
then with his levers he dragged her down to the luminous sea-brine.
    It was the fourth day now when all of the work was completed;
then on the fifth he was sent from the island by noble Kalýpso,
when she had made him dress in fragrant attire and had bathed him.

265   Into the vessel a skin full of dark wine then did the goddess
load and another one, larger, of water, a sack of provisions
too, and she put in meat, many morsels to quicken the spirit;
then she sent him a favoring wind, unharmful and gentle.
Noble Odysseus rejoiced at the wind while spreading the sails out;

270   using the tiller to steer, he skillfully guided the vessel

straight as he sat in the stern; no sleep ever fell on his eyelids
while he was watching the Pleíades and late-setting Boötes
and the Great Bear—men call it another name also, the Wagon—
which turns round in position and keeps its eye on Oríon
275   and is alone in not having a share in the baths of the Ocean—
for it was this that Kalýpso the glorious goddess had bidden
him to maintain on his left while he was traversing the seaway.
So then crossing the seaway, for seventeen days he was sailing;
then on the eighteenth appeared to his vision the shadowy mountains
280   in the Phaiákians' country, the part that to him was the nearest:
like some shield it appeared on the seaway misty and murky.

Journeying from the Ethiopians then, the strong shaker of earth saw
him far off from the peaks of the Sólymoi, for he observed him
sailing along on the sea; in his heart was the god most wrathful;
285   angrily shaking his head, he said to himself in his spirit:
"Oh what shame, that concerning Odysseus the gods have entirely
changed their minds while I was among the Ethiopian people!
Now he is near the Phaiákians' country; for him it is fated
there to escape the calamitous end of the woe that has dogged him.
290   But I think I will yet drive him into quite enough evil."

So he spoke, and he gathered the storm clouds, stirred up the seaway,
wielding his trident in both of his hands; and of all of the winds he
roused up all of the blustering gusts, and the sea and the mainland
covered and hid in the clouds, while night rushed down from the heaven.
295   East wind, south wind, and bane-blowing west wind, clashing together,
rose, and the north wind, getter of clear skies, rolling a huge wave.
Then in Odysseus the limbs and the heart inside him were loosened;
thus in his anguish he spoke to his own magnanimous spirit:
"Oh how wretched I am! Now finally what will befall me?
300   I much fear that the goddess declared all this without erring,
when she said that at sea, before reaching the land of my fathers,
I would be full of distress: now this is all being accomplished.
Such are the clouds with which Zeus covers the breadth of the heaven
over and stirs up the sea; and in storm gusts all of the winds are
305   savagely blowing, and now I am certain of sheer destruction.
Thrice were the Dánaäns blessèd and four times, those who were slaughtered
there in the broad Troäd, bearing succor to Atreus' scions.
So it were better for me to have died and encountered my doomsday
on that day when a host of the Trojans were hurling at me their
310   bronze-tipped spears over Peleus' son, as he lay there dying.

I would have had death rites; my fame the Achaians would cherish;
now instead it is doomed that a death most wretched should take me."
    As he was uttering this, from above an enormous and dreadful
wave drove, crashing upon him and spinning the raft in a circle.
315 He was himself thrown far from the raft in the water; the tiller
he let fly from his hands, while a terrible gust of the jostling
stormwinds came on the vessel and shattered the mast in the middle;
far to a distance the sail and the yard fell into the seaway.
Under the water it put him a long time, nor was he able
320 quickly to come up out of the furious rush of the huge wave,
weighed down so by the clothing that noble Kalýpso had furnished.
Finally, when to the surface he rose, he was spitting the bitter
sea-brine out of his mouth as it ran from his head in torrents.
Yet he did not lose thought of the raft, though he was exhausted;
325 but in the waves he struggled to reach it and held to it firmly,
then crouched down in the middle, avoiding a fatal conclusion.
Over the flood it was borne by a huge wave hither and thither.
As when the north wind pushes the tumbleweeds, late in the summer,
over the plain—they gather in dense balls, one to another—
330 so winds carried the raft on the high sea, hither and thither.
It would be thrown by the south to the north wind, so he could bear it,
then yielded up by the east to the west wind, so he could drive it.
    Then did Ino of beautiful ankles, the daughter of Kadmos,
notice him—that Leukothéa who formerly spoke as a mortal
335 but in the depths of the sea now shared in the honors of godhood.
Pity she felt for Odysseus the wanderer suffering sorrows;
out of the sea she rose like a shearwater spreading its wings out,
sat down there on the raft, and a word like this she addressed him:
    "Miserable man, why yet does the great earth-shaker Poseidon
340 feel such vehement wrath as to cause these many afflictions?
He will in fact not ruin you wholly, as much as he wants to.
But do just as I say, for you do not seem to be witless:
strip off all those clothes and abandon the raft to be carried
on by the winds, then swim with your hands as you strive for a landing
345 on the Phaiákians' shore: it is there your lot to be rescued.
Come now, fasten around your breast this scarf, an immortal
one, and do not fear either to suffer affliction or perish.
But when you with your hands have at last laid hold of the mainland,
then untie it and throw it again in the wine-dark seaway,
350 far from the mainland, and turn yourself in the other direction."

So these words having spoken the goddess gave him the head scarf;
she herself, in the guise of a shearwater still, sank back down
into the billowing sea; black waves closed round and concealed her.
He then pondered the matter, much-suffering noble Odysseus;
355   thus in his anguish he spoke to his own magnanimous spirit:
    "Wretch that I am! Against me, I fear, some immortal is weaving
treachery, seeing that she bids me to abandon the raft-boat.
Nevertheless, I will not yet heed her, because with my eyes I
saw that land still distant in which, she said, is my refuge.
360   But instead I will do what seems to me better and safer:
while these beams of the raft are together and firm in the joinings,
just so long I will stay and endure, though suffering hardships;
but when a wave does shatter the raft into pieces beneath me,
then I will swim, since nothing that I can devise would be better."
365   As he was pondering over these things in his mind and his spirit,
quickly Poseidon the shaker of earth stirred up a huge billow,
terrible, dangerous, arching aloft, then drove it against him.
As when a blustering wind so blows the dry chaff of a harvest
piled in a heap as to scatter it out in every direction,
370   so now the boat's great timbers were scattered about; but Odysseus,
sitting astride one beam, went on as if riding on horseback,
stripping himself of the garments that noble Kalýpso had furnished.
Quickly he fastened around his breast that scarf of the goddess,
then plunged headfirst into the sea-brine, spreading his arms out,
375   ready and eager to swim. And the strong earth-shaker observed him;
angrily shaking his head, he said to himself in his spirit:
    "Thus now wander the sea, while suffering many afflictions,
till such time as you mingle with people belovèd of heaven.
Not even then, I imagine, will you make light of your troubles."
380   So having spoken of him, he lashed up his fair-maned horses;
straightway to Aigai he came, where he has his glorious palace.
    Then other things were devised by Athena the daughter of great Zeus:
first, each wind of the others she bound from the ways it was blowing,
laid her commands on them all to be quiet and rest in silence;
385   then she aroused the swift north wind and broke up the billows before him,
so that among the Phaiákians, lovers of rowing, would mingle
Zeus-descended Odysseus, avoiding his death and destruction.
Thus two nights and two days he was wandering over the swollen
billows, and many a time was his spirit expecting his ruin;
390   but when the fair-haired Morning had brought full light on the third day,

finally then did the wind stop blowing, and straightway a windless
calm fell over the sea; and he saw with a sharp glance forward,
as on a great wave-swell he rose, he was close to the mainland.
As most welcome appears to his children the life of a father

395   who has been lying in sickness and suffering mighty afflictions,
wasting away a long time—a malevolent spirit attacked him;
then, an event most welcome, the gods free him from his evil—
so most welcome the land and the woods now appeared to Odysseus;
he swam eagerly onward to set his feet on the dry land.

400   But when he was as far from the land as a man's shout carries,
then he could hear the loud roar of the sea on the rocks and the sand bars,
for the enormous breakers were crashing against the dry mainland,
fearfully spewing, and it was all covered with foam from the sea-brine.
Here were no harbors to keep ships safe, no sheltering roadsteads,

405   but there were headlands jutting and crags and immovable boulders.
Then in Odysseus the limbs and the heart inside him were loosened;
thus in his anguish he spoke to his own magnanimous spirit:
      "Wretch that I am! Since Zeus has accorded to me to behold this
land unhoped for, and I by cleaving the gulf have attained it,

410   but now nowhere appears a way out of the silvery sea-brine,
since here, off of the shore, there are sharp reefs; over them roaring
billows are crashing and breaking; a smooth cliff rises beyond them;
close to the shore is the sea too deep; I will never be able
even to stand on both of my feet and escape from these evils;

415   leaving the water, I might be picked up and dashed by a mighty
wave on a rock's rough edges, and then my attempt will be useless.
Yet if I swim still farther along till perhaps I discover
beaches that slant out into the breakers or safe sea havens,
I am afraid that again may a storm wind, seizing upon me,

420   carry me out on the fish-thronged seaway, heavily groaning,
or that a god may arouse an enormous monster against me
out of the sea, where many are reared by renowned Amphitrítè,
since I know I am odious to the renowned earth-shaker."
      As he was pondering over these things in his mind and his spirit,

425   onto a headland jagged and rocky a great wave bore him.
There his skin would have been stripped off, his bones have been shattered,
had no thought been put in his mind by bright-eyed Athena;
quickly with both of his hands he clutched at a rock as he rushed by;
groaning, he held it until the enormous breaker had passed him.

430   So he escaped that danger; but then, back-flowing, the billow

struck him as it rushed outward and hurled him afar in the seaway.
As when a sea polypus gets dragged up out of its chamber,
many small pebbles and sand stay clinging to each of its suckers,
in like manner, as he was dragged from the rock, was the skin stripped
435   off of his powerful hands; and the great wave covered and hid him.
Then against fate unhappy Odysseus had come to destruction
had not cunning been given to him by bright-eyed Athena.
He got clear of the surf that was spewing up onto the mainland;
swimming along outside, he looked toward land to discover
440   beaches that slanted out into the breakers or safe sea havens.
But when at last as he swam he came to the mouth of a river
fair in its flowing, it seemed to him then that place was the best one,
smooth, unbroken by rocks, and protected as well from the storm winds.
Then as he felt it flowing, he uttered a prayer in his spirit:
445   "Hear me, Lord, whoever you are, for with many entreaties
out of the sea I reach you, escaping the threats of Poseidon,
since anyone among men who comes as a wanderer merits
reverence even from gods, the immortals, as I have indeed now
come to your stream and your knees to beseech you, for much have I suffered.
450   But now, Lord, show mercy, for I as a suppliant claim it."
        So he spoke, and the god then at once stopped flowing and held his
waves back, making it smooth in front of him; quickly he brought him
safe to the mouth of the river; and he bent both of his knees down,
letting his strong hands fall, for his heart was subdued by the sea-brine.
455   His whole body was swollen, and out of his mouth and his nostrils
much seawater was gushing; and there, both breathless and voiceless,
he lay weak and unmoving: a terrible weariness held him.
When he recovered his breath and the strength came back to his spirit,
finally then he untied from his body the scarf of the goddess;
460   into the river that flowed with the salt seawater he threw it.
Back it was borne on the stream by a great wave; hastily Ino
took it into her hands; then turning away from the river,
he sank down in the reeds and the grain-giving earth began kissing.
Thus in his anguish he spoke to his own magnanimous spirit:
465   "Oh, what is this I suffer? What finally now will befall me?
If for a miserable night I keep watch here by the river,
surely the baneful frost and the nourishing dew may together
quite overwhelm me, weak as I am, my spirit exhausted;
then also, toward morning a cold breeze blows from the river.
470   But if I climb farther up this slope to the shadowy woodland,

then lie down in the dense-growing shrubbery, even if I am
spared by cold and exhaustion, and sweet sleep does come upon me,
I much fear that I might be a victim and prey for the wild beasts."
    So as he pondered the matter, the best course seemed to be this one:
475 he set forth for the woodland and found it close to the water
by a conspicuous clearing and there came upon two bushes,
both from the same stock growing, a wild olive tree and a tame one.
These no watery breath of the blustering winds ever blew through,
nor with its beams did the radiant sun ever strike to the bottom,
480 nor did the rain penetrate them all of the way, for they were so
thick, each twining its limbs with the other; beneath them Odysseus
crept, and at once with his hands he gathered together an ample
pallet, for there an enormous abundance of leaves had collected,
such as would furnish protection for two, nay even for three men,
485 in some season of storms, though harshly the weather was raging.
Looking at it he rejoiced, much-suffering noble Odysseus;
he lay down in the middle and heaped up leaves all around him.
As when somebody covers a brand in the black dying embers,
far at the bounds of the fields—no other men, neighbors, are near him—
490 saving the seed of the fire so he need not light it from elsewhere,
so was Odysseus concealed in the foliage; thereon Athena
poured sleep down on his eyes, so that it might quickly relieve him
from the exhaustion of labor, and covered his eyelids over.

BOOK 6

Thus he lay there and slept, much-suffering noble Odysseus,
quite overcome by fatigue and exhaustion; and meanwhile Athena
went to the city and land where dwell the Phaiákian people.
They had at one time lived in a spacious domain, Hypereía;
5   neighbors of theirs, the Cyklópes, a haughty and arrogant people,
kept invading and harrying them, for in strength they were greater.
Godlike Naúsithoös roused them from there, led a migration,
settled in Scheria then, far distant from grain-eating mortals,
raised great walls to encircle the city and built many houses,
10   also established the shrines of the gods and divided the plowlands.
But he had now been quelled by his doom and departed for Hades,
so that Alkínoös ruled—from the gods were his knowledge and wisdom.
Now to his palace proceeded the goddess bright-eyed Athena,
pondering plans for the homeward return of greathearted Odysseus.
15   There she entered and went to the elegant chamber in which lay
sleeping a girl who was like the immortals in form and appearance,
Naúsikaä, and who was greathearted Alkínoös' daughter.
Near her were two handmaids whose beauty the Graces had given,
one by each of the doorposts; the lustrous doors had been fastened.
20   She like the breath of a wind rushed down to the bed of the maiden;
standing above her head, she spoke these words and addressed her,
closely resembling the daughter of Dymas, renowned for his galleys,
who was a girl of her age and in whom her spirit delighted.
Making herself like her now spoke forth bright-eyed Athena:
25   "Naúsikaä, how then could your mother have borne you so heedless?
All of your shimmering garments are lying away uncared for,
though your marriage is surely approaching, the day you must put on
beautiful clothing and furnish the garments for those who escort you.
For it is from these things that among men noble opinion
30   spreads, and your father as well as the lady your mother are gladdened.

Come now, let us go washing at daybreak's earliest glimmer;
I will accompany you as a work mate, so that you quickly
ready yourself, since not much longer will you be a virgin;
for already the noblest of all the Phaiákians living
35 here in the country, of your own lineage, seek you in marriage.
But come now, in the morning arouse your glorious father;
get him to furnish you mules and a wagon to carry the clothing,
girdles and mantles and gowns, and the covers of shimmering fabric.
Then for yourself also it will be much better than if you
40 went on foot, for the wash troughs lie far away from the city."
      So having spoken departed the goddess bright-eyed Athena
up to Olympos, on which they say that the seat of the gods is
always secure, not shaken by winds, nor ever by rainfall
moistened, nor does any snow come near, but a clear sky stretches
45 cloudless above, and resplendent radiance dances upon it;
all of their days in that place do the fortunate gods take pleasure.
Thither departed the bright-eyed one, having talked to the maiden.
      Straightway the fair-throned Dawn then arrived and from slumber awakened
Naúsikaä of the beautiful robes; at her vision she marveled,
50 then set off through the house to report these things to her parents,
her dear father and mother, and still inside it she found them.
Close to the hearth with the women attendants her mother was sitting,
spinning the sea-purple yarn from a distaff; there at the door she
met her father as he set out for the council of famous
55 princes, to which by the noble Phaiákians he had been summoned.
Standing beside her much loved father, she spoke and addressed him:
      "Daddy dear, will you not make ready a lofty and well-wheeled
wagon for me, so that I might carry the glorious garments
down to the river for washing, the ones I have lying dirty?
60 Then moreover for you it is seemly, when you with the foremost
councilors ponder your counsels, to have clean clothes on your body.
As for the five dear sons who were born to you here in the palace,
two of them married already and three unmarried and thriving,
they want always to dress in clothes that are recently laundered
65 when they go to a dance; these things all trouble my spirit."
      So she spoke; she was bashful to mention to her dear father
flourishing marriage; but he saw all and returned her an answer:
"Neither the mules, my child, nor anything else I begrudge you.
Go then; some of the servants will ready a lofty and well-wheeled
70 wagon for you, one fitted above with a carrier-basket."

So having said, he called to the servants, who heeded his orders.
First, outside of the house they readied a well-wheeled mule-drawn
cart; then, bringing the mules, they hitched them up to the wagon.
Out of her chamber his daughter now carried the shimmering clothing;
75   then she stowed it away inside of the well-polished wagon.
Into a chest her mother put food which pleases the spirit,
every sort, and she put in meat; then into a goatskin
vessel she poured sweet wine; as the girl climbed onto the wagon,
she gave her in a gold-wrought flask soft oil of the olive,
80   which she would use for anointing herself and her women attendants.
She took hold of the whip and the shimmering reins of the mule team,
whipped them to drive them ahead, and the two mules, clattering loudly,
strained forth then without stinting and carried the clothes and the maiden,
not by herself, but together with her went others, her handmaids.
85   When they finally came to the beautiful streams of the river,
where there were permanent laundering places—the plentiful lovely
water was flowing around them, for cleansing the dirtiest clothing—
then their mules they unharnessed and turned them loose from the wagon,
set them running along to the banks of the eddying river
90   so they could feed on the honey-sweet field grass; lifting the garments
out of the cart with their arms, they carried them to the dark water;
briskly they trampled on them in the troughs and competed in labor.
When they had laundered the clothing, and all of the dirt they had washed out,
then they spread it in rows on the seashore, down where the sea when
95   pounding the land came over the pebbles and washed them the cleanest.
When they had bathed and had rubbed themselves with the oil of the olive,
then they readied and ate their meal by the banks of the river,
waiting a time for the clothes to be dried in the heat of the sunshine.
After the girl and her servants had had their fill of the victuals,
100   then they started to play with a ball, throwing off their head scarves;
white-armed Naúsikaä was the leader in singing among them.
As when Artemis shooter of arrows goes over the mountains,
either the towering peak Taygétos or high Erymánthos,
taking delight in the hunt, in pursuing the boars and the swift deer,
105   there at her side play daughters of Zeus who carries the aegis,
nymphs who inhabit the fields; in her heart then Leto rejoices—
over them all her daughter is holding her head and her forehead;
easily she is discerned, though all the companions are lovely;
so was the unwed girl outstanding among her attendants.
110   But when she was about to return once more to the palace,

159

after the mules had been yoked and the beautiful garments were folded,
then other things were devised by the goddess bright-eyed Athena,
so that Odysseus would waken and see that girl with the fair face,
who might lead him the way to the town of Phaiákian people.
115 Just as the princess was throwing the ball toward one of her handmaids,
missing the handmaid, into the depths of an eddy she threw it;
far their voices resounded, and noble Odysseus awakened;
he sat up and considered the matter in mind and in spirit:
"Ah me, what are the people whose land this time I have come to?
120 Are they bold and offensive and violent, lacking in justice,
or are they kindly to strangers, endowed with a god-fearing conscience?
Such is the womanish clamor of girls now sounding around me,
as of the nymphs who inhabit the steep-sloped heads of the mountains,
also the springs of the rivers and grassy and watery meadows.
125 Or am I now, perhaps, near people whose voices are human?
But come, let me myself make trial and see what the truth is."
So having spoken, from under the shrubs crept noble Odysseus,
then with his strong hand tore from the thick-grown coppice a leafy
branch, so that he might cover his body, concealing his privates.
130 Then he went like a mountain-bred lion, who trusting his prowess
sets forth, windblown, drenched by the rain, with the eyes in his muzzle
brightly ablaze, and he straightway goes among cattle or sheep flocks
or else after the deer of the wilds; for his belly commands him
even to try for the flocks by approaching a strong-built homestead;
135 so was Odysseus among those maidens with beautiful tresses
going to mingle, although he was nude, for the need was upon him.
Dreadful he seemed to their eyes, made filthy and foul by the sea-foam;
they took flight on the spits of the seashore, hither and thither.
Only Alkínoös' daughter remained in the place; for Athena
140 into her heart put courage and out of her limbs took terror.
She stood facing him firmly; Odysseus considered the matter,
whether to cling to the knees of the fair-faced girl and beseech her
or as he was, while standing apart, with the mildest of speeches
pray her that she might show him the city and give him a garment.
145 So as he pondered the matter, the best course seemed to be this one:
he would entreat her, standing apart, with the mildest of speeches,
lest if he cling to her knees, in her spirit the girl would be angry.
Then straightway he addressed her a speech both gentle and cunning:
"Here at your knees am I, Lady: are you some god or a mortal?
150 If indeed you are one of the gods who hold the broad heaven,

Artemis, daughter of powerful Zeus, is the goddess to whom I
liken you nearest of all in beauty and size and appearance.
If instead you are one of the mortals who dwell on the earth now,
blessèd for you thrice-told are your father and reverend mother,
155   thrice your brothers are blessèd: the hearts inside them are surely
always brightly aglow with benevolent gladness for your sake,
when they behold so budding a branch take part in the dancing.
He is indeed most blessèd in heart, above others distinguished,
who will prevail with his courtship presents and lead you homeward,
160   since with my eyes I never have seen such another as you are,
neither a woman nor man: I am held in wonder observing.
Yet one time, by Apollo's altar in Delos, I witnessed
something as lovely, the fresh young stem of a date palm growing,
for I had gone there, too; and a numerous company followed
165   me on the journey, on which I would have many evil afflictions.
So in the same way, looking at that I marveled in spirit
long, since never had grown from the earth any shaft of such beauty.
So I admire you, Lady, and marvel, and feel dread terror
even to touch your knees, though harsh is the sorrow upon me,
170   since from the wine-dark sea I escaped on the twentieth day just
yesterday; ever the waves and the violent tempests were driving
me from the isle of Ogygia; and here some god has now cast me,
so that perhaps here too I can suffer affliction: I do not
think it will cease, but the gods will achieve yet more before that comes.
175   But now pity me, Lady; for suffering many afflictions
I first come to you here, and I do not know any other
person among all those who possess this city and country.
Show me the city and give me a rag to be fastened about me,
if, coming here, you brought some wrapper, perhaps, for the clothing.
180   Then may the gods grant you what you in your spirit are wishing;
may they endow you with blessings, a husband and house, and a noble
concord of mind: for than this there is no gift better or greater,
when both husband and wife in concord of mind and of counsel
peacefully dwell in a house—to their enemies greatest affliction,
185   joy to benevolent friends, but especially known to their own hearts."
　　White-armed Naúsikaä then spoke these words as an answer:
"Stranger—because you seem neither base nor without understanding—
Zeus himself, the Olympian, gives out fortune to mankind,
both to the base and the noble, to each one just as he wishes;
190   so he has given you this, yet nevertheless you must bear it.

Now, however, since you have arrived at our city and country,
certainly neither of clothes nor of other things you shall be lacking
such as befit a long-suffering supplicant when he approaches.
I will now show you the city and tell you the name of the people:
195 they are Phaiákians, those who possess this city and country;
I am myself greathearted Alkínoös' daughter; upon him
all of the vigor and force the Phaiákians have are dependent."
    So did she say, then called to her handmaids with beautiful tresses:
"Handmaids, stand by me here; where, seeing the man, do you run to?
200 Surely you did not think him a man with hostile intentions?
There is not now any mortal, nor one to be born, of such vigor
that he would come to the land the Phaiákian people inhabit
bringing hostilities here, so much the immortals esteem us.
Off at a distance we dwell, in the deep sea surging and dashing,
205 farthest of all; no other men have any dealings among us.
No, this man is a luckless wanderer who has arrived here;
we must now give him succor, for every stranger and beggar
has the protection of Zeus, and a gift though little is welcome.
But come, handmaids, and give both victuals and drink to the stranger;
210 wash him off in the river where there is a shelter from breezes."
    So did she say; they came up and stood, each urging the others;
then to a place with shelter they guided Odysseus, as ordered
Naúsikaä, greathearted Alkínoös' much loved daughter.
Near him they laid out pieces of clothing, a mantle and tunic,
215 gave him as well, in the gold-wrought flask, soft oil of the olive;
then they bade him to wash himself in the streams of the river.
Noble Odysseus instead spoke thus to the women attendants:
    "Handmaids, stand as you are at a distance, that I of myself may
wash from my shoulders the sea-foam and then may rub on my skin this
220 oil of the olive, for it has a long time wanted anointing.
Not in your sight will I bathe myself—I am far too bashful
thus to go utterly nude among handmaids with beautiful tresses."
    So did he say; they went to a distance and talked to the maiden.
Then with the water he dipped from the river the noble Odysseus
225 cleansed his skin of the foam which covered his back and broad shoulders,
also wiped from his head the salt scurf of the desolate sea-brine.
When he had washed off every part and anointed his skin, he
clothed himself in the garments the unwed maiden had furnished;
straightway Athena the offspring of Zeus transformed him and made him
230 taller to see than before, more mighty; the hair on his head she

made flow down in thick curls that resembled a hyacinth flower.
As when a man well-skilled at the task lays gold over silver—
one who was taught his craft by Hephaistos and Pallas Athena,
every sort of technique—and the work he achieves is delightful,
235 so upon him did she now pour grace, on his head and his shoulders.
Going away from the others, he sat on the shore of the deep sea,
brightly agleam in his beauty and grace; and the girl was astonished.
Finally then she spoke to the maids with the beautiful tresses:
    "Listen to me now, white-armed handmaids, and hear what I tell you.
240 Not unwilled by all of the gods who inhabit Olympos
is this man to encounter the godlike Phaiákian people,
seeing that whereas before he seemed to me ugly and wretched,
now he resembles the gods, the immortals who hold the broad heaven.
How I wish that a man like him could be called my husband,
245 making the land his home, and that it might please him to stay here!
But come, handmaids, and give both victuals and drink to the stranger."
    So she spoke, and the others at once both heard and obeyed her,
so that they placed both victuals and drink by the side of Odysseus.
He began drinking and eating, much-suffering noble Odysseus,
250 greedily, since he had long been fasting and taken no victuals.
    Then other things were devised by Naúsikaä of the white arms:
folding the clothes, she loaded them onto the beautiful wagon,
harnessed the mules with the powerful hooves; then she herself mounted.
Urging Odysseus, she spoke to him these words, calling upon him:
255   "Get up, stranger, to go to the city, that I may convey you
now to the house of my provident father, and there, I am certain,
you will discover the best among all the Phaiákian people.
But do just as I say, for you do not seem to be witless:
while we are passing among these fields and the farms of the people,
260 so long you, with the maids in attendance, will rapidly follow
after the mules and the wagon; and I will be guide on the journey.
But then, when we arrive in the city—around it are lofty
walls, and a beautiful harbor is on each side of the city,
making a narrow entrance; the tractable galleys are drawn up
265 right to the road, and for every one of them all is a slipway.
There by the beautiful shrine of Poseidon a place of assembly
stands, strong-built out of stones dragged thither and deeply embedded.
There men busy themselves with their dark ships' rigging and tackle,
mending the sails and the cables, and put smooth points on the oar blades.
270 For the Phaiákians care no whit for the bow or the quiver

but for the masts and the sails of their ships and the balanced vessels
which they delight to employ in crossing the silvery sea-brine.
I would avoid their slanderous words, lest somebody later
make a reproach: in the country are some very arrogant people,

275 thus might say one of those inferior men when he met me:
'Who is it following Naúsikaä there, handsome and tall, that
stranger, and where did she find him? No doubt he will make her a husband!
Either she came to the aid of a wanderer thrown from his galley—
one who dwells far away, since nobody lives very near us—

280 or else he is a god she has much entreated, who comes down,
heeding her prayer, out of heaven, and all of her days he will keep her.
Better if she herself went traveling, finding a husband
elsewhere, seeing that these Phaiákians she has dishonored
here in the land, those many and excellent suitors who court her.'

285 So will they say, and to me these things will be bitter reproaches.
I myself would reprove any other who acted in that way—
while her dear father and mother were living, against their wishes
mingled with men as a friend before openly joining in marriage.
Stranger, at once pay heed to my words, so that you very quickly

290 get a conveyance, a way to return back home, from my father.
Close to the road you will find a magnificent grove of Athena,
poplars; within it a spring wells forth, and a meadow surrounds it.
There is my father's estate, his fruitful and flourishing orchard,
out of the city the distance away that a man's shout carries.

295 Sit down there in the grove and remain some time, until we have
made our way through the city and come to the house of my father.
But when at last you are certain that we have arrived at the palace,
then go into the town of Phaiákians, making inquiry
where you can find my father greathearted Alkínoös' palace.

300 It is most easily known, though you should inquire of a backward
child, since not in the least are the other Phaiákians' houses
built so well as to equal the hero Alkínoös' palace.
But then, soon as the house encloses you there, and the courtyard,
pass very quickly along through the main hall, till you have come to

305 my dear mother, who sits in the light of the fire by the fireplace,
spinning the sea-purple yarn from a distaff, a marvel to witness,
leaning her chair on a pillar; her women are sitting behind her.
There also is the chair of my father, supported against it,
where he sits as he drinks his wine, much like an immortal.

310 When you have gone past him, then onto the knees of my mother

throw your hands in entreaty, that you might joyfully, quickly
see your day of return, no matter how far you have come from.
If my mother is kindly disposed toward you in her spirit,
then good hope may you have to behold your friends and to go back
315 there to your well-built house, back there to the land of your fathers."
   When she had said these words, she goaded the mules with her shining
whip-rod; rapidly they went away from the streams of the river.
Well they trotted along, with their feet wide-straddled and prancing.
She kept hold of the reins so the others on foot might follow,
320 both handmaids and Odysseus; and wisely she wielded the whip-rod.
Then as the sun went down they came to the famous and holy
grove of Athena, within which sat down noble Odysseus.
Straightway he to the daughter of powerful Zeus began praying:
   "Hear me, offspring of Zeus of the aegis, unwearying goddess,
325 now at last listen to me, since earlier you did not listen
when I was stricken, as then the renowned earth-shaker had struck me;
make the Phaiákians pity and love me as I go among them."
   So he spoke as he prayed; he was heard by Pallas Athena.
Not yet did she appear to him openly, since for her father's
330 brother she felt due respect: he was swelling with violent wrath at
godlike Odysseus until he arrived at last in his country.

BOOK 7

Thus prayed there in the grove much-suffering noble Odysseus,
while to the city the strength of the mule team carried the maiden.
Finally, when she arrived at the glorious house of her father,
she stopped them in the courtyard gate, and her brothers around her
5 stood there like the immortals; and quickly from under the wagon
they unharnessed the mules, and the clothes they took in the palace.
She herself then went into her room, and an old Apeiraían
woman ignited the fire, her chambermaid Eúrymedoúsa,
whom once tractable galleys had carried away from Apeírè;
10 she had been picked as a prize for Alkínoös, since he commanded
all the Phaiákians: like some god did the people obey him.
She took care of the white-armed Naúsikaä in the palace;
she now kindled a fire, in the room made ready her supper.
   Then too Odysseus arose to go into the city; Athena
15 poured thick mist, in her loving benevolence, over Odysseus,
lest some man, a greathearted Phaiákian, coming across him,
speak in words of derision to mock him or ask who he might be.
But as he just was about to go in the agreeable city,
there at the gate he was met by the goddess bright-eyed Athena,
20 who now appeared in the guise of a young girl holding a pitcher.
She stood near him, and noble Odysseus addressed her a question:
   "Child, will you please now lead me the way to the house of a certain
man, Alkínoös, who is the ruler among these people?
For as a poor long-suffering stranger I have arrived here,
25 come from a land far off at a distance; and therefore I do not
know any man among those who possess these fields and the city."
   Speaking to him then answered the goddess bright-eyed Athena:
"Certainly, stranger and father, the house which you have inquired of
I will point out, for it lies near that of my excellent father.
30 But come silently now—I will be your guide on the journey—

casting your eyes on none of the people nor asking them questions,
for in fact they do not much tolerate men who are strangers,
nor to a person who comes from abroad are they friendly or gracious.
They put confidence rather in swift ships, rapidly sailing
35 over the vast sea gulfs, as the great earth-shaker has granted:
swift as a wing in flight or the motion of thought are their galleys."
      So having spoken to him, then speedily Pallas Athena
led him forward, and he came on in the goddess's footsteps.
But the Phaiákians, famed for their fine ships, never observed him
40 as among them he passed through the city; for fair-haired Athena
did not allow it, the august goddess; a marvelous mist she
poured in her heartfelt loving benevolence over his body.
Much did Odysseus admire their balanced ships and the harbors,
also the places the heroes would meet and the lengthy and lofty
45 walls with their sharp stakes fastened above—to behold a great wonder.
But when they had arrived at the glorious house of the ruler,
speaking among them opened the goddess bright-eyed Athena:
      "This then, stranger and father, is that very house that you bade me
show you; and you will discover the princes belovèd of heaven
50 eating a dinner within; now enter—do not in your spirit
feel any fear, for in every effort, the man who is boldest
finishes best, even if he comes from a faraway country.
There you will first encounter the queen as you enter the chambers,
called by the name of Arétè, 'to whom one prays,' and she springs from
55 those ancestors that brought forth King Alkínoös also.
Naúsithoös to begin did the great earth-shaker Poseidon
father upon Periboía, the noblest of women for beauty;
she was the lastborn girl of Eurýmedon, mighty in spirit,
who once reigned as the king of the haughty and arrogant Giants.
60 But he ruined his reckless people and was himself ruined.
Mingling with her in love had Poseidon fathered an offspring,
great-souled Naúsithoös, who ruled the Phaiákian people.
Naúsithoös Rhexénor and this Alkínoös fathered;
sonless the first one was when Apollo whose bow is of silver
65 struck him, a bridegroom still, but he left in the palace a single
daughter, Arétè, and then Alkínoös made her his consort;
such was the honor he showed her as no other women alive on
earth now ever are honored who keep house under their husbands.
So entirely has she in their hearts been honored, and still is,
70 first by her own dear children and by Alkínoös also,

then by the people themselves, who like some goddess regard her,
welcoming her with their speeches whenever she goes in the city,
since no whit is she wanting in excellent judgment and wisdom,
so that for those, even men, she favors, she settles their quarrels.

75   If that lady is kindly disposed toward you in her spirit,
then good hope may you have to behold your friends and to go back
there to your high-roofed house, back there to the land of your fathers."
        So having spoken departed the goddess bright-eyed Athena
over the desolate sea, and agreeable Scheria leaving,

80   quickly to Marathon came and to Athens, the city of broad ways,
entered the strong-built house of Eréchtheus. Meanwhile Odysseus
went to the glorious house of Alkínoös; much did his spirit
ponder as he stood there before stepping across the bronze threshold,
such was the radiant splendor, as if of the sun or the full moon,

85   there in the high-roofed house of Alkínoös, mighty in spirit.
Bronze were the walls that had been built out both ways from the threshold
back to the inmost chamber; a dark blue frieze ran around them;
gold were the doors which shut in the strong-built house on the inside,
silver the posts of the doors which stood on the bronze-clad threshold;

90   silver as well was the lintel above, but of gold was the door hook.
Silver and gold were the dogs which sat at the sides of the doorway;
these had Hephaistos made with ingenious craft and adroitness
so as to guard that house of Alkínoös, mighty in spirit,
always, for they were immortal and ageless forever and ever.

95   There inside by the walls, one side and the other, were armchairs
set all the way to the inmost room from the threshold; upon them
covers were spread, fine-woven and elegant work of the women.
On these chairs the Phaiákian lords were accustomed to take their
seats when drinking and eating; for theirs was unfailing abundance.

100   Young men fashioned of gold, upon well-built pedestals mounted,
stood there holding aloft in their hands bright fiery torches,
making the nighttime light in the palace for those who were feasting.
Then, of the slaves in the palace, the housemaids, fifty in number,
some are at handmills grinding the grain, of the color of apples;

105   some stand weaving on looms, while others are seated and spinning
yarn on the distaff, quick as the leaves of a tall slim poplar;
soft oil pressed from the wool drips off of the close-woven fabric.
Just as above all men the Phaiákian sailors are skilled in
driving a swift ship over the seaway, so are the women

110   skilled in managing looms, for Athena to them beyond others

granted a knowledge of beautiful work and an excellent judgment.
Outside the courtyard next to the door is an orchard of four broad
measures of land, with a wall built round it in either direction,
where there are tall trees growing, with great luxuriant blossoms—
115 pear trees, fine pomegranate trees, apple trees, glorious-fruited;
fig trees laden with sweetness, and olives of flourishing fullness.
Nor are the fruits these bear ever ruined or lost, but instead they
last all year, both winter and summer, and always the west wind,
Zephyr, is blowing to make some grow, bring others to ripeness.
120 Pear upon pear grows older, and apple is added to apple,
cluster to cluster of grapes, new figs to the figs that have ripened.
There moreover his vineyard is planted in fruitful abundance:
one of its parts is a level and warm plateau, where the grapes are
dried in the heat of the sun, while workers are harvesting others;
125 others they tread in the press; in front are the grapes that are not yet
ripe now casting their blossoms, and some turn slowly to darkness.
Close to the nethermost row in ordered plantations are growing
vegetables of all sorts, bright-gleaming in ceaseless abundance.
Therein rise two springs, one spreading abroad through the whole great
130 garden, and under the courtyard threshold the other is flowing
right to the high-built house—from it water is drawn by the townsmen.
Such were the glorious gifts of the gods to Alkínoös' household.
     There now marveling stood much-suffering noble Odysseus.
But then, when in his heart he had marveled at all he was seeing,
135 quickly he went on over the threshold, into the palace.
He found there inside the Phaiákian leaders and princes
pouring the wine from their cups to the keen-eyed slayer of Argos;
his was the last libation, when they took thought about sleeping.
On in the house then went much-suffering noble Odysseus,
140 keeping the thick mist yet that Athena had poured all around him,
till he came to Arétè and King Alkínoös. Quickly
throwing his hands on the knees of Arétè, Odysseus embraced them;
finally then the miraculous mist poured back from his body.
They fell silent as soon as they saw that man in the palace,
145 wondering much as they looked; but Odysseus began his entreaty:
     "Lady Arétè, the daughter of godlike noble Rhexénor,
suffering much I have come to your knees and as well to your husband,
also to these who are dining, to whom may the gods grant blessings—
prosperous lives, and may each in his time bequeath to his children
150 treasures of worth in his house and the prizes the people have given.

But now raise a conveyance for me, so I come to my country
quickly, for far from my friends I have long been suffering sorrows."
    So he spoke, and he took his seat by the hearth in the ashes
close to the fire; they all fell quiet and sat in silence.
155 Finally then spoke out Echenéos, the elderly hero
who among all the Phaiákian men was of earliest birth date,
so he excelled in speaking and knew much lore of the ancients;
he with benevolent wisdom addressed them, giving them counsel:
    "Lord Alkínoös, it is not good nor in any way fitting
160 thus for a stranger to sit on the ground by the hearth in the ashes;
all these others, awaiting your word, hold back in silence.
Come now, go to our guest; on an armchair studded with silver
seat him, raising him up; then order the herald to mix more
water and wine, that to Zeus the great hurler of thunderbolts we may
165 pour a libation: of reverend suppliants he is protector.
Let a housekeeper provide our guest with a meal from her storage."
    When he had heard these things, Alkínoös, sacred in power,
taking the hand of ingenious various-minded Odysseus,
raised him up from the hearth; on a splendid armchair he placed him,
170 making his son stand up, Laódamas gentle and valiant,
who sat nearest to him, for indeed he especially loved him.
Hand-washing water a maid then carried to him in a lovely
gold-wrought pitcher, and over a basin of silver she poured it,
so he could wash; nearby she set out a well-polished table.
175 Carrying food, the revered housekeeper approached him and set it
close to him, many a dish she gladly supplied from her storage.
He began drinking and eating, much-suffering noble Odysseus.
Finally then did mighty Alkínoös speak to the herald:
    "Mix wine now in the bowl, Pontónoös, then pour it out for
180 all in the hall, that to Zeus the great hurler of thunderbolts we may
pour a libation: of reverend suppliants he is protector."
    So did he say; Pontónoös, mixing the wine, honey-hearted,
poured it out into all of the cups to begin the observance.
When they had made libations and drunk whatever their hearts wished,
185 then Alkínoös spoke, and in words like these he addressed them:
    "Listen to me as I speak, Phaiákian leaders and princes,
so I can say such things as the heart in my breast is demanding.
Now you have eaten the meal, go back to your homes for the night's rest;
early at dawn we will call to the house yet more of the elders,
190 then entertain this stranger within our chambers and offer

beautiful gifts to the gods, and about a conveyance we then will
take thought, so that the stranger without more labor or trouble,
with the conveyance we give, may arrive in the land of his fathers
swiftly, rejoicing in spirit, though it lie far at a distance;
195   may he not in the passage endure more evil and sorrow
till he arrives and alights in his country; but then he will surely
suffer whatever the Fates and the dismal Spinners had spun out
with their thread as his portion when he was born to his mother.
If however he be an immortal descended from heaven,
200   this indeed is a thing quite new that the gods are contriving,
seeing that always before have the gods been manifest clearly
here among us, when glorious hecatombs ever we offer;
seated beside us, right where we are, they have taken their dinner.
Nor from a traveler who was alone, if he met with immortals,
205   never a thing would they hide, since we in fact are a race as
near to them as the Cyklópes or ravening tribes of the Giants."
      Speaking to him then answered Odysseus of many devices:
"Otherwise trouble your mind, Alkínoös, since I am surely
not like any immortal of those who hold the broad heaven,
210   either in form or in stature, but like mere men who are mortal.
Those you know among men who have had most grief to contend with,
it is to them I would liken myself in pains and distresses.
Yet even more could I tell you about those plentiful evils,
such great numbers of which by the will of the gods I have suffered.
215   But instead let me eat my dinner in spite of my grieving;
since there is not one thing more shameless or gross than the hateful
belly, which orders a man to remember it by a compulsion,
even if he is exhausted and feels in his heart great sorrow.
So even though I have great sorrow at heart, it is always
220   ordering me to devour and to drink, and of all those woes which
I have endured it makes me forgetful and bids me to fill up.
You however arouse yourselves at the morning's appearance,
so as to carry and set me, the wretch that I am, in my country,
though I have suffered so much; may the life then leave me when I have
225   seen my possessions and servants and my great high-roofed palace."
      So did he say; they all then assented and urged that it be so,
granting the stranger conveyance, for properly he had addressed them.
When they had poured libations and drunk whatever their hearts wished,
then they departed to rest for the night, each one to his own house.
230   Meanwhile noble Odysseus remained in the hall for a while yet;

there at his side were Arétè and godlike Alkínoös sitting;
servants were putting in order the furniture used for the dinner.
Speaking in these words, white-armed Arétè began to address them,
for as she looked, she observed that his tunic and mantle were handsome
235 garments that she herself and her women attendants had fashioned.
Raising her voice she spoke, and in these winged words she addressed him:
    "Stranger, to start with I will myself now ask you a question:
Who are you? Whence do you come? Who gave you the clothes you are wearing?
Did you not say you had come here wandering over the seaway?"
240   Speaking to her then answered Odysseus of many devices:
"It would be difficult, Queen, to recite in every detail
all my woes, for the gods in heaven have given me many;
this I will say about what you are asking and making inquiry:
There is an island, Ogygia, that lies faraway in the sea-brine,
245 wherein the daughter of Atlas, Kalýpso of beautiful tresses,
dwells, a most cunning and terrible goddess. Nobody ever
mingles with her, not one of the gods nor of men who are mortal.
Only myself in my misery some god led to her hearthside,
when Zeus struck the swift ship with a scintillant bolt of his lightning
250 so in the midst of the wine-dark sea it would shatter to pieces.
All of the others with me were destroyed, my noble companions,
while I, taking the keel of the tractable ship in my arms, was
carried ahead nine days; on the tenth, in the darkness of nighttime,
to the Ogygian island the gods brought me, where Kalýpso
255 dwells, of the beautiful hair, dread goddess; and there she received me
kindly: and me she has loved and has cherished beside her and promised
she would make me immortal and ageless forever and ever;
nevertheless she never persuaded the heart in my bosom.
There I remained seven years unceasingly, ever bedrenching
260 with my tears the ambrosial garments Kalýpso provided.
But when the eighth year came, in the course of the seasons' revolving,
finally then she roused me and gave me orders to leave her,
either because of a message from Zeus or because her own mind changed.
She sent me on a well-bound raft and abundant provisions
265 gave me, bread and sweet wine; in ambrosial garments she dressed me;
then she sent me a favoring wind, unharmful and gentle.
Thus I sailed a full seventeen days far over the seaway;
then on the eighteenth appeared to my vision the shadowy mountains
which rise up in your land; and my heart grew happy within me,
270 luckless wretch! I was destined to meet yet more of the many

troubles Poseidon the shaker of earth kept sending against me.
So by rousing the winds against me he hindered my voyage,
also raised up a sea unspeakable: nor would the billows
let me stay on the raft to be borne on, heavily groaning—
275 powerful stormwinds shattered and scattered it. Nevertheless by
cleaving the gulf of the sea I swam, and the wind and the water
carried me ever ahead till they brought me close to your country.
There as I went from the water a wave would have driven me crashing
onto the land, on a great rock thrown me, a place that was cheerless;
280 drawing away, however, I swam back outward until I
came to the river; it seemed to me then that place was the best one,
smooth, unbroken by rocks, and protected as well from the stormwinds.
Struggling for life, I dropped from the waves; the ambrosial night came
down over me; then out of the river descended from heaven
285 when I had gone, I slept in the bushes, collecting around me
leaves in a heap; and upon me a god poured measureless slumber.
There in the leaves I slept, exhausted and troubled in spirit,
all night long, then into the morning and up until midday;
but as the sun was declining, the sweet sleep finally freed me.
290 There on the beach by the sea I saw the handmaids of your daughter
playing, and she herself was among them, resembling a goddess.
Her I beseeched; in her noble intelligence she was unerring—
as you would hardly expect, on meeting a person so youthful,
she would behave so well, since always the younger are thoughtless.
295 Then she gave me of bread and of glistening wine an abundance,
made me bathe in the river, and gave me the clothes I am wearing.
These things I have related exactly, in spite of my sorrow."
    Answering him in return, Alkínoös spoke and addressed him:
"Stranger, at least about this, my child was deficient in proper
300 thought, that she did not lead you along with her women attendants
here to our palace, for she was the one you first supplicated."
    Speaking to him then answered Odysseus of many devices:
"Hero, do not for my sake find fault with your blameless daughter,
since in fact she bade me to follow along with her handmaids;
305 I did not want to, however, for I was afraid and embarrassed,
lest your heart, when you saw, might possibly find it offensive,
since we races of men on earth are extremely suspicious."
    Answering him in return, Alkínoös spoke and addressed him:
"Stranger, at least in me is the heart in my breast not such as
310 fruitlessly falls into anger: in all things, measure is better.

Oh Zeus, father of all, and Athena as well and Apollo,
would that you might, being such as you now are, thinking as I think,
have my child as your wife and remain here still to be called my
son-in-law; I would give you a house and possessions if you were
315 willing to stay, since no Phaiákian ever will keep you
here unwilling: for that may Zeus our father not favor!
For your conveyance, a day I appoint to it, so as to make you
certain about it—tomorrow; and while you are lying subdued by
sleep, they will drive through the calm of the sea, in order that you may
320 reach your country and house and whatever to you is belovèd,
even if it be much more distant from here than Euboía,
which is the farthest land of them all, say some of our people
who once saw it, the time they took fair-haired Rhadamánthys
there on a voyage to visit with Títyos, offspring of Gaia.
325 They went there and without getting weary accomplished the mission,
then on the same day came back home and completed the journey.
You will observe for yourself in your mind what excellent ships I
have, how noble the youths who toss up the sea with their oar blades."
  So he spoke; he rejoiced, much-suffering noble Odysseus,
330 prayed to the father of all, and said these words, calling upon him:
"Oh father Zeus, may it be that Alkínoös brings to fulfillment
all that he speaks! And upon this grain-giving earth may he ever
have unquenchable fame! And may I go back to my homeland!"
  Such things then they spoke and addressed each one to the other;
335 then to her handmaids white-armed Arétè directed her orders,
bade them to put beds out in the portico, throwing upon them
rugs of a beautiful purple, upon these spread out the covers,
then bring mantles of wool to be drawn up over the sleeper.
Out of the hall they went, in their hands all carrying torches;
340 when they had spread out thick soft bedding with speed and adroitness,
coming to stand by Odysseus they spoke these words and aroused him:
"Get up, stranger, and come, for a bed has been made for your comfort."
So they spoke, and to him it seemed most pleasant to lie down.
  Thus he lay there and slept, much-suffering noble Odysseus,
345 while Alkínoös slept in a room inside the high palace;
there did the lady his wife make ready the bedding and share it.

BOOK 8

Soon as the Dawn shone forth rose-fingered at earliest daybreak,
out of his bed Alkínoös sacred in power bestirred him;
then rose also the Zeus-sprung sacker of cities Odysseus.
Leading the way, Alkínoös sacred in power proceeded
5   to the Phaiákians' gathering place, built close to the galleys.
Having arrived, they took their seats on smooth-polished bench-stones
close to each other; but through the whole town went Pallas Athena,
making herself to resemble sagacious Alkínoös' herald,
pondering plans for the homeward return of greathearted Odysseus.
10 Standing beside each man, she spoke these words and addressed them:
    "Come now, bestir yourselves, Phaiákian leaders and princes;
go straightway to assembly, that you might hear of the stranger
who just recently came to sagacious Alkínoös' palace,
wandering over the seaway, in form most like the immortals."
15   So she spoke and in each man stirred up valor and spirit.
Speedily then were the place of assembly and all of the benches
filled with the men who gathered, and many there were who wondered
when they beheld the ingenious son of Laërtes: Athena
poured down marvelous grace over him, on his head and his shoulders,
20 made him taller than he had been, more mighty to look at,
so he would be most cherished by all the Phaiákian people,
feared and respected among them, and he could accomplish the many
trials by which the Phaiákians tested the worth of Odysseus.
Then when they had collected and all were gathered together,
25 first Alkínoös spoke and addressed them, giving them counsel:
    "Listen to me as I speak, Phaiákian leaders and princes,
so I can say such things as the heart in my breast is demanding.
Here has a stranger—I know not who he is—come to my palace
wandering, whether from men of the dawn or from those of the sunset;
30 he asks us for conveyance, beseeches that it be assured him.

Let us then, as in earlier times, make haste with a convoy,
seeing that never has anyone else who came to my palace
stayed long here in the country lamenting about a conveyance.
But come now, let us drag a black ship to the luminous sea-brine,
35 one now making the first of her voyages, then from the city
choose fifty-two young men who have earlier proven the bravest.
Straightway, when you have carefully fastened the oars in the oarlocks,
disembark, and at once get busy preparing a speedy
dinner, returning to us; an abundance for all I will furnish.
40 These are the orders I lay on the young men; as for the others,
princes endowed with scepters, do you to my beautiful palace
come, so that we in the halls may extend this stranger a welcome;
let nobody refuse this bidding. And summon the godlike
singer Demódokos hither; for he is endowed by a god with
45 song which pleases, however his heart exhorts him to sing it."
    So having spoken to them, he started ahead, and they followed,
those with the scepters; the herald went after the godlike singer.
Then those fifty-two youths chosen out for the convoy set forth
as he had bidden, to go to the shore of the desolate sea-brine.
50 But when they had arrived down there at the sea and the galley,
then they dragged the dark ship out into the depths of the sea-brine,
set up the mast pole, and hoisted the sails in the dark-hued galley;
next they fastened the oars in the oxhide thongs of the oarlocks,
all in an orderly fashion; above they spread out the white sails.
55 Out from the beach on the water they anchored her, then they at once set
forth to return to sagacious Alkínoös' massive palace.
Every portico, courtyard, room in the building was filled with
men who had gathered; and many there were, both younger and older.
There among them Alkínoös offered a sacrifice: twelve sheep,
60 eight of his white-tusked pigs, and as well two swing-pacing oxen.
These they flayed and prepared, and arranged an agreeable banquet.
    Soon did the herald approach, conducting the trustworthy singer;
dearly the Muse loved him, and she gave him a good and an evil,
taking the sight from his eyes while giving the art of sweet singing.
65 Then Pontónoös placed him an armchair, studded with silver,
right in the midst of the diners and leaned it against a tall pillar.
After the herald had hung up the clear-toned lyre on its peg there
over his head, he showed him how in his hands he could take it,
set a food basket and beautiful table beside him, and set him
70 wine in a goblet to drink whenever his spirit commanded.

They put forth eager hands to partake of the food lying ready.
When they had quite satisfied their appetites, drinking and eating,
straightway the Muse incited the singer to sing of men's famous
deeds, from the lay whose fame at the time reached up to wide heaven,
75 even the strife of Odysseus and Peleus' scion Achilles—
how one time at a bountiful feast of the gods they had quarreled
with most violent words; and the leader of men Agamemnon
felt great joy in his mind that the noblest Achaians were fighting,
for in a prophecy thus he was told by Phoibos Apollo
80 once in Pytho the holy, the time he crossed the stone threshold
seeking advice, for the onset of evil was billowing over
Trojans and Dánaäns both, by the counsels of Zeus Almighty.
      This the illustrious singer was singing to them, and Odysseus
took in his stalwart hands the voluminous mantle of purple,
85 drawing it over his head, concealing his beautiful features;
he felt shame to shed tears from his eyes with Phaiákians looking.
But whenever the godlike singer would pause in his singing,
wiping away his tears, from his head he took off the mantle;
taking a two-handled cup, to the gods he poured a libation.
90 But as again he started to sing, the Phaiákian nobles
urging him on to his song, for they took great joy in the story,
then once more would Odysseus, concealing his head, begin weeping.
There he was shedding his tears unobserved by all of the others;
only Alkínoös noticed and took good mind of the man who
95 sat there close to his side; and he heard him heavily groaning.
Straightway then he addressed the Phaiákians, lovers of rowing:
      "Listen to me as I speak, Phaiákian leaders and princes;
now in our hearts we are quite satisfied with the well-shared banquet,
as with the lyre, which makes a companion to plentiful feasting.
100 Therefore now let us go outside and make trial in contests,
every sort, that the stranger may say to his friends in his country,
when he returns to his home, how easily we surpass others,
whether in boxing or wrestling, in swiftness of foot or in jumping."
      So having spoken to them, he started ahead, and they followed.
105 After the herald had hung up the clear-toned lyre on its peg there,
taking Demódokos' hand, he led him out of the chamber,
guiding him forward on that same pathway the others had followed,
all of the noblest Phaiákian men who would witness the contests.
They all went to the place of assembly, along with a countless
110 multitude; many and excellent youths stood up for the contests:

noble Akróneos rose, Okýalos also, Elátreus,
Nauteus, Prymneus too, Anchíalos also, Erétmeus,
Ponteus, Proreus too, Anabésineós, and then Thóön,
then Amphíalos, scion of Tekton's son Polynéos.

115 Also Eurýalos rose, to man-slaughtering Ares an equal,
Naúbolos' son, who was best among all the Phaiákian nobles
after the noble Laódamas, both in build and in beauty.
Also the three offspring of the noble Alkínoös stood up—
first Laódamas, Halios then, and godlike Klytonéos.

120 These men first made trial of speed by running a footrace.
Stretching away from the post was the course they ran; and together
swiftly they all flew along, stirring up much dust from the meadow.
Easily best of the men in running was brave Klytonéos;
just so far as the range in a fallow field of a mule team,

125 so far ahead, outstripping the others, he ran to the people.
Next they started a trial of strength in arduous wrestling;
best in this was Eurýalos, vanquishing all of the nobles.
Over them all in the jump Amphíalos proved outstanding;
easily strongest of all was Elátreus, throwing the discus;

130 boxing Laódamas won, Alkínoös' excellent scion.
Finally, when they all had delighted their minds with the contests,
then among them Laódamas spoke, Alkínoös' scion:
    "Come, friends, let us inquire of our guest if he knows and is skilled in
any of these competitions—he is not weak in his body,

135 either in thighs or in calves or above in the arms on his shoulders;
stout is his neck and enormous his strength; not lacking in youthful
vigor is he, but he has been broken by many afflictions.
For in fact I believe there is nothing else worse than the sea in
pounding a man to destruction, though he be rugged and stalwart."

140 Answering him in return Eurýalos spoke and addressed him:
"Surely, Laódamas, you have said words most fitting and proper.
Now go challenge the man yourself in the words you address him."
    When he had heard these things, Alkínoös' excellent scion
went to the middle and stood and addressed these words to Odysseus:

145 "You too, father and guest, come give it a try in the contests,
if you are skilled in any—to know athletics befits you,
since for a man while he is alive, no glory is greater
than such honors as he with his feet or his hands can accomplish.
Come now, give it a trial and scatter the cares from your spirit;

150 not much longer will you be kept from the journey—already

178

there is a ship dragged down to the sea, and the comrades are ready."
      Speaking to him then answered Odysseus of many devices:
"Why do you bid me thus, Laódamas, all of you, taunting?
Cares indeed I have in my heart much greater than contests,
155   I who have suffered so much already and labored so greatly;
now I sit among you in assembly and long for the day I
go back home, entreating the ruler and all of the people."
      Then Eurýalos spoke and replied—to his face he reproached him:
"Certainly, stranger, I do not think you are like any man who
160   knows athletics, of all those many that men can engage in,
but one much occupied with a galley of numerous oarlocks,
who is a captain of sailors who also serve as his merchants,
minding the cargo for sale, then trafficking over the homeward
lading, and eager for profit—you do not seem like an athlete."
165   Looking from lowering brows said Odysseus of many devices:
"Friend, you do not speak well; you are like one recklessly foolish.
So have the gods not given to all men pleasing endowments
equally, strength of the body or shrewdness or eloquent speaking;
for one man is without distinction or beauty of features,
170   but on his speeches a god puts grace as a crown, so that others
look upon him and rejoice; unfalteringly he can speak with
pleasing and modest demeanor and shine among men in assembly;
like some god they regard him whenever he goes in the city.
Somebody else, however, is like the immortals in beauty,
175   but no grace does he have to be set as a crown on his speeches.
So with yourself: outstanding in form—not even a god would
make you otherwise—yet for intelligence empty and fruitless.
Deep in my breast you have stirred up indignation within me,
so out of order you speak. I am not unskilled in athletics,
180   as in your words you assert, but I think I have been among those who
came first, when in my hands and my youthful vigor I trusted.
Now I am gripped by affliction and sorrow, for much have I suffered,
cleaving a way through battles of men and the troublesome billows.
Yet even though I have borne much woe, I will try these contests,
185   since your word bites into my heart; your speaking has roused me."
      So he said; still in his cloak he sprang up, seizing a discus,
bigger, of heavier weight, more massive—and not by a little—
than the Phaiákians used to compete with each other in throwing.
Whirling around in place, he hurled it forth from his massive
190   hand, and the stone hummed loudly, and down to the earth they cowered—

those men famed for their ships, the Phaiákians, long-oar wielders—
under the rush of the stone, which flew past all of the others'
marks as it sped from his hand; and Athena established the distance,
making herself like a man, and said these words, calling upon him:

195   "Even a blind man, stranger, could clearly distinguish your marker,
just by feeling around, for it is not mixed with the many
but is the first by far. So be of good heart for this contest;
no Phaiákian hurler will reach this mark or surpass it."
        So she spoke; he rejoiced, much-suffering noble Odysseus,

200   happy to see an agreeable comrade there at the contest.
To the Phaiákians then he spoke with an easier spirit:
"Now you younger men, reach this marker; for maybe another
later will throw that far—I suppose may throw even farther.
Then of the others, whatever his heart and his spirit command him,

205   let him come here and try it—for you have angered me greatly—
boxing or wrestling or even a footrace: nothing I grudge you;
all the Phaiákians save for Laódamas I will contend with,
seeing that he is my host—who would fight with the friend who received him?
That man surely is mindless, a nobody blind to all value,

210   who in an alien country would challenge his host to contentious
trials, for by so doing he cuts off all of his profit.
But of the rest, indeed, I refuse no man nor despise him;
I want rather to know and compete with him, person to person.
Not in all of the contests in which men meet am I worthless;

215   well do I know how to handle a well-trimmed bow and to use it;
I would be first in hitting a man when shooting my arrows
into the enemy troops, even if there were many companions
standing beside me and firing their bows at the men who opposed them.
Philoktétes alone in wielding a bow could surpass me

220   when in the land of the Trojans Achaians were shooting their arrows.
But of the others, I reckon that I am the best by a long way,
many as are those eaters of food who live on the earth now.
I would not wish to contend with the men who were living before us,
not against Herakles nor Oichálian Eúrytos either,

225   who used even to strive in archery with the immortals.
That was the cause great Eúrytos suddenly died, and he did not
reach old age in his house; for Apollo, provoked into anger,
killed him because he challenged the god to an archery contest.—
I can throw spears too, farther than anyone else can shoot arrows.

230   Only on foot I fear that among the Phaiákians one might

pass me in speed; for in many a wave I was quite overpowered
most disgracefully, since the provisions I had on the ship were
insufficient to last me; and so my joints were all loosened."
    So did he say; then all of the people were hushed into silence;
235   only Alkínoös spoke, and in these words gave him an answer:
"Stranger, because you are not ungraceful in telling us these things
but are desiring to show us the excellence you are possessed of,
angry because that man insulted you, standing beside you
in the assembly—as never a man who knew in his mind what
240   sensibly might be spoken would censure your excellent prowess—
but come now, pay heed to my word, so that you to another
hero may tell it later, when you, back home in your palace,
sitting beside your wife and your children, are eating your dinner,
summoning into your mind our excellence, all the achievements
245   Zeus grants also to us, as he has from the time of our fathers,
for we are not outstanding in fistfights, neither as wrestlers;
but on our feet we run very fast, in our ships we are skillful.
Always our dinners we hold most dear, and our lyres and our dances,
changes of clothing and warm baths too, and our beds we delight in.
250   But come, those who are best among all the Phaiákian dancers,
frolic and dance, so the stranger can say to his friends in his country,
when he returns to his home, how easily we surpass others,
whether in sailing or swiftness of foot, in dancing or singing.
Somebody now go bring to Demódokos quickly the clear-toned
255   lyre which still, I suppose, lies somewhere back in our palace."
    So godlike Alkínoös spoke; then quickly the herald
set out to carry the hollow lyre from the house of the ruler.
Then those chosen as stewards arose—in all there were nine men,
public officials who ably arranged the details for the contest.
260   These now, smoothing the ground, laid out a fine space for the dancing.
Soon did the herald return and approach them, bringing the clear-toned
lyre to Demódokos, who went into the middle; around him
youths in their first bloom stood, well trained in the movements of dancing;
then they pounded the ritual floor with their feet; as Odysseus
265   gazed at the flickering speed of the feet, he marveled in spirit.
    Then the bard struck up a beautiful song by playing a prelude,
telling the love between Ares and beautiful-wreathed Aphrodítè,
how at first they had mingled in love in the house of Hephaistos
secretly; numerous gifts he had given to her and the marriage
270   bed of Hephaistos her lord dishonored; but Helios quickly

181

carried the message to him: he had seen them mingling in love play.
Then did Hephaistos, as soon as he heard the heart-anguishing story,
set forth out to his forge; in his heart he was plotting them evils.
There on the block he placed the huge anvil, and bands that could not be
275 broken or loosened he hammered, so they would remain without moving.
Then when he had contrived this trap, in his anger at Ares,
he went into the room where lay his bed so belovèd;
there he spread out the bands all over, surrounding the bedposts;
many of them, moreover, he hung overhead from the roof beam,
280 like fine webs of a spider, that nobody ever would notice,
even a fortunate god—so treacherously he contrived it.
Finally, when he had fastened the whole trap there on the bedstead,
he made semblance of going to Lemnos, the well-built city,
which among all of the lands on earth is to him far dearest.
285 Nor was a blind watch kept by Ares the god of the gold reins,
when he observed that Hephaistos renowned for his art was departing;
he set off to the house of the noble and famous Hephaistos,
craving the loving embraces of beautiful-wreathed Kythereía.
She, who had recently come from the house of her father, the mighty
290 scion of Kronos, had taken a seat; he entered the palace,
took her hand in his own, and said these words, calling upon her:
    "Come here, darling, to bed; let us lie in it taking our pleasure,
seeing Hephaistos is not in the house—he has surely already
parted for Lemnos to visit the Sintians, savage in speaking."
295   So he spoke, and to her it seemed most pleasant to lie down.
Going to bed they soon fell asleep, and the bands all around them,
wrought by various-minded Hephaistos, were gathered and tightened;
not one inch were they able to move their limbs or to raise them.
Then they knew that no longer was there any way of escaping.
300 Quickly the glorious twice-lame cripple arrived and approached them;
he had retraced his steps before reaching the country of Lemnos—
Helios, who had been keeping a lookout, had told him the story.
He went back to his house, much troubled and heavy in spirit;
there he stood in the entrance, and fierce was the anger that seized him;
305 vehemently he shouted, to all of the gods made his outcry:
    "Oh Father Zeus and the rest of the fortunate gods, ever-living,
come here, see a ridiculous deed, one not to put up with:
how since I am a cripple the daughter of Zeus Aphrodítè
ever dishonors and scorns me and loves all-ravaging Ares,
310 since indeed he is handsome and sure on his feet, whereas I was

born misshapen and lame; and for that no one is to blame but
my own mother and father—I wish they never had had me!
Look now, see where the two lie sleeping in loving embraces,
having retired to my bed—I am stricken with grief as I see it!
315 But I suppose they would not lie thus any more, not a moment,
much as they love each other, and not very soon will the two be
wanting to sleep, but instead this trap and these bands will restrain them,
till such time as our father returns to me all of the presents
which for the sake of the bitch-eyed girl I gave as a bride price,
320 since his daughter is lovely but uncontrollably lustful."
        So he spoke; to the bronze-floored chamber the gods came thronging:
earth-upholding Poseidon arrived, and the powerful runner
Hermes arrived, and the lord who works from a distance, Apollo.
Each of the goddesses kept to her house in modest decorum.
325 Meanwhile the gods, those givers of benefits, stood in the forecourt;
then in the fortunate gods rose up unquenchable laughter
when they saw the devices of various-minded Hephaistos.
Thus would one of them say as he looked at another beside him:
        "Bad deeds never succeed, for the slow man catches the swift one,
330 as now, slow and a cripple, Hephaistos, employing his skill, has
overcome Ares, the fleetest of gods who inhabit Olympos;
therefore Ares must pay the adulterer's fine to Hephaistos."
        Such things then they spoke and addressed each one to the other;
then did Apollo the lord, son of Zeus, speak, questioning Hermes:
335 "Hermes the scion of Zeus, great messenger, benefit-giver,
how would you like to be captured and held in the powerful bindings,
if in bed you were sleeping beside Aphrodítè the golden?"
        Speaking to him then answered the messenger, slayer of Argos:
"Would it were so now, lord who shoot from a distance, Apollo,
340 would there were thrice this number of measureless bindings about us,
all you gods and the goddesses also were gazing upon us—
even so I would be sleeping beside Aphrodítè the golden!"
        So he answered and stirred up laughter among the immortals;
laughter did not take hold of Poseidon, but always he kept on
345 praying Hephaistos, acclaimed for his labor, to liberate Ares;
raising his voice he spoke, and in these winged words he addressed him:
"Set him free, and I promise for him whatever you order;
he shall requite you all that is fitting among the immortals."
        Speaking to him then answered the glorious twice-lame cripple:
350 "Earth-upholding Poseidon, do not enjoin me to do this:

worthless it is to be pledged with the pledge of a man who is worthless.
How could I hold you bound to your promise among the immortals
if now Ares departs and evades his debt and his bindings?"
    Speaking to him then answered the great earth-shaker Poseidon:
355 "Surely, Hephaistos, if Ares, evading the debt that he owes you,
leaves to escape it, I will myself then make you the payment."
    Then spoke giving an answer the glorious twice-lame cripple:
"Now to deny your word is not possible, nor is it seemly."
    So having spoken, the mighty Hephaistos loosened the bindings.
360 Those two, when they were freed from the trap in spite of its stoutness,
straightway rushed from the chamber; to Thrace he quickly departed,
while in Cyprus arrived Aphrodítè the lover of laughter,
coming to Paphos, in which are her precincts and sweet-smelling altar.
After the Graces had bathed her and rubbed her with oil of the olive
365 of the ambrosial kind used only for gods who live always,
then they dressed her in charming array, a great marvel to look at.
    This the illustrious singer was singing to them, and Odysseus
felt great joy in his mind as he listened, and so did the others,
those men famed for their ships, the Phaiákians, long-oar wielders.
370   Halios then and Laódamas Lord Alkínoös bade to
dance by themselves, since they were the ones nobody could rival.
When they had taken up into their hands a most beautiful purple
ball, one made for their dance by Pólybos, cunning and skillful,
one of the dancers would bend himself well backward and hurl it
375 up to the shadowy clouds; and the other would leap from the earth and
easily catch it before his feet to the ground had descended.
When they had proven themselves in throwing the ball straight upward,
then they started to dance on the earth so abounding in nurture,
rapidly changing positions; around the arena the other
380 youths stood beating the time; and the din rose louder and louder.
    Finally then to Alkínoös thus spoke noble Odysseus:
"Lord Alkínoös, most distinguished among all the people,
as in your words you boasted that yours were the finest of dancers,
so is it shown in effect. I am held in wonder, observing."
385   So as he spoke, Alkínoös sacred in power was gladdened;
straightway then he addressed the Phaiákians, lovers of rowing:
"Listen to me as I speak, Phaiákian leaders and princes;
this our guest is a man, I think, most thoughtful and prudent.
But come now, let us give him a guest-gift, as is befitting.
390 For there are twelve men here distinguished as kings in the country,

leaders who govern the people; and I myself am the thirteenth.
Let each one of you princes contribute a robe that is freshly
washed, and a tunic, and much-prized gold to the weight of a talent.
Let us at once bring these all together now, so that our guest may
395   go to his dinner with them in hand and rejoicing in spirit.
But with words and a present Eurýalos now must approach him,
making amends; for he said to him words not fitting or proper."
    So did he say; they all then assented and bade that it be so;
each one sent out a herald to bring gifts back to the palace.
400   Answering him in return Eurýalos spoke and addressed him:
"Lord Alkínoös, most distinguished among all the people,
I will indeed make fitting amends to our guest, as you bid me.
I will present to him now this sword, all bronze, with a silver
hilt, and the scabbard as well I will give to him, fashioned of new-sawn
405   ivory circling the blade; it will be worth much to its owner."
    So as he said, he placed in his hands the sword studded with silver;
raising his voice he spoke, and in these winged words he addressed him:
"Farewell, father and stranger, and if some troublesome word has
been said here, may the stormwinds rapidly seize and disperse it!
410   Then may the gods grant you to behold your wife and to go back
home, since far from your friends you have long been suffering sorrows."
    Speaking to him then answered Odysseus of many devices:
"Farewell to you too, friend, and to you may the gods grant blessings;
may you never hereafter have cause to regret or to miss this
415   sword which now in making amends with your words you present me."
    Thus, and around his shoulders he hung the sword studded with silver.
Then did the sun go down, and the glorious presents were brought there,
and to Alkínoös' house they were carried by excellent heralds.
Straightway the children of noble Alkínoös took in their hands those
420   beautiful presents and placed them beside their virtuous mother.
Leading the way, Alkínoös sacred in power proceeded;
having arrived, they took their seats on the high-raised armchairs.
Finally then did mighty Alkínoös speak to Arétè:
    "Bring here, wife, a magnificent coffer, the one that is finest;
425   put inside it yourself both a well-washed robe and a tunic.
Over the fire warm up a bronze cauldron for heating the water,
so that our guest, having bathed and beheld here, lying in order,
all these presents the noble Phaiákians now have provided,
may take pleasure in dining and hearing the hymn of the singer.
430   I myself will present him with my own beautiful goblet

fashioned of gold, so that all of his days he keeps me in mind when
pouring libations to Zeus and the other gods, there in his palace."
    So did he say; and Arétè addressed her women attendants,
bade them quickly to place a great tripod over the fireplace.
435 Then in the blaze of the fire first setting a bathwater cauldron,
into it they poured water, and put wood under, and lit it.
Over the cauldron's belly the fire spread, heating the water.
Meanwhile, out of her room, a most beautiful coffer Arétè
brought to the guest, and she put into it the magnificent presents,
440 all of the garments and gold the Phaiákian princes had given,
placed inside it herself both a robe and a beautiful tunic.
Raising her voice she spoke, and in these winged words she addressed him:
    "You now see to the cover and speedily fasten the binding,
lest someone on the journey should damage it during the times when
445 you rest sweetly asleep as you go in the dark-hued galley."
    When he had heard these words, much-suffering noble Odysseus
straightway fitted the cover and speedily fastened the binding,
subtle and intricate, which Lady Circè had taught to his mind once.
Then, not waiting a moment, the housekeeper bade him to enter
450 into the tub to be bathed; he looked at the warm bathwater
glad in his heart, since he had not known such careful attendance
since he had left the abode of Kalýpso of beautiful tresses;
during that time, like a god's was the care unfailingly shown him.
When maidservants had washed him and rubbed him with oil of the olive,
455 they threw garments about him, a beautiful cloak and a tunic;
he stepped out of the bathtub and went to the men who were drinking
wine there. Naúsikaä, endowed by the gods with her beauty,
stood by the pillar supporting the roof beams, stoutly constructed;
much she marveled as she with her eyes caught sight of Odysseus.
460 Raising her voice she spoke, and in these winged words she addressed him:
    "Farewell, stranger; and even at home in your country, remember
me sometimes, that to me you are first in debt for survival."
    Speaking to her then answered Odysseus of many devices:
"Naúsikaä, greathearted Alkínoös' much loved daughter,
465 thus Zeus bring it to pass, the loud-thundering husband of Hera,
make me to go back home and to look on the day of returning!
So even when I am there I will pray to you as to a goddess,
always, all of my days, for my life you gave to me, maiden."
    Thus, and he sat by King Alkínoös there in an armchair.
470 Now they passed out portions and mingled the wine and the water.

Soon did the herald approach, conducting the trustworthy singer
honored among that people, Demódokos; placing an armchair
right in the midst of the diners, he leaned it against a tall pillar.
Thus then spoke to the herald Odysseus of many devices,
475   cutting a slice of the meat—though even at that there was more left—
off of the back of the white-tusked boar, rich fat all around it:
     "Come then, herald, and take this meat to Demódokos so that
he may eat, and in spite of my sorrowing, I will embrace him.
For among all men living on earth have singers a rightful
480   portion of honor and loving esteem, since they have been taught their
lays by the Muse, who holds in affection the company of singers."
     So he spoke; to the hero Demódokos then did the herald
carry and give it; the singer received it, rejoicing in spirit.
They put forth eager hands to partake of the food lying ready.
485   When they had quite satisfied their appetites, drinking and eating,
then to Demódokos spoke Odysseus of many devices:
     "You I honor with praises, Demódokos, over all mortals;
it was the Muse, Zeus' daughter, who taught you, or even Apollo.
For indeed in due order you sing the Achaians' adventures—
490   what the Achaians achieved, what suffered, and what were their labors—
as if you had yourself been there or had heard from another.
But come, passing the rest, now sing the device of the wooden
horse that Epeíos constructed with aid from the goddess Athena,
which was the stratagem noble Odysseus led to the upper
495   citadel, filled with the men who to Ilion carried destruction.
If now these things you can relate to me fitly and truly,
I will at once then spread the report among every people
how the benevolent god endowed you with marvelous singing."
     He spoke; moved by the goddess, he started his song and revealed it,
500   taking it up where some of the Argives, boarding the well-benched
galleys, were sailing away, having thrown fire into their cabins.
Meanwhile others were sitting about celebrated Odysseus,
hidden inside of the horse in the Trojans' place of assembly,
for to the uppermost city the Trojans themselves had dragged it.
505   Thus it stood in the place, and the men there seated around it
talked interminably; three plans found favor among them:
whether for smashing the hollow of timber with pitiless bronzes;
dragging it up to the brink of a cliff, then toppling it over;
or just leaving it there for the gods, a great charm and appeasement.
510   This last way was the one that was going to come to fulfillment,

for it was fate that the city be lost, since it had received that
great wooden horse in its midst, inside which all of the noblest
Argives sat who were bringing destruction and doom to the Trojans.
He sang too how the city was sacked when the sons of Achaians
515 streamed forth out of the horse and abandoned the hollow ambush,
how, some here and some there, he sang, they ravaged the high-built
city; Odysseus himself went straight to Deíphobos' palace,
much like Ares in form, and with him godlike Meneláos.
There, as the singer related, he dared the most terrible fighting,
520 then he triumphed at last by the aid of greathearted Athena.
      This the illustrious singer was singing to them, and Odysseus
melted: the salt tears drenching his cheeks flowed down from his eyelids.
Just as a wife might weep as she falls on her own dear husband
who has himself just fallen in front of his city and people,
525 warding away from the town and his children a pitiless doomsday—
she then, as she beholds him dying and gasping his breath out,
throwing herself on him, cries shrilly; behind her the foemen,
striking at her with their spears, all over her back and her shoulders,
carry her off to enslavement, to have hard toil and affliction;
530 with a most piteous sorrow the cheeks of the weeper are wasted—
such was the piteous tear that Odysseus poured from his eyebrows.
There he was shedding his tears unobserved by all of the others;
only Alkínoös noticed and took good mind of the man who
sat there close to his side; and he heard him heavily groaning.
535 Straightway then he addressed the Phaiákians, lovers of rowing:
      "Listen to me as I speak, Phaiákian leaders and princes:
now let Demódokos leave off playing the lyre with the clear tone,
for as he sings these things, not all, it appears, is he pleasing.
Since we started the meal and the godlike singer began his
540 song, never since that time has the stranger desisted from woeful
sorrowing; surely a terrible grief came over his spirit.
But come, let him leave off, so that all take pleasure together,
guest-entertainers and guest, since that way will be much better,
seeing that these things all have been done for the stranger we honor—
545 furnishing convoy, giving affectionate presents in friendship.
Good as a brother the guest and the suppliant is to the man who
touches upon sound sense, if only the least, in his spirit.
Therefore now no longer conceal with a guileful intention
what I am going to ask: it is better for you to reveal it.
550 Tell me the name by which your father and mother and others

called you there in your city, as well as those living around it.
For among all mankind no person is utterly nameless,
neither the base nor the noble, when once he is brought into being,
but to them all some name is assigned by the parents who bear them.
555 Speak to me also about your land, your people and city,
so that our ships, by their own minds guided, may carry you thither.
For no steersmen are there upon any Phaiákian vessels
nor any steering device of the sort which other ships carry;
but of themselves they know men's thoughts and perceive their intentions;
560 they know also the cities of all mankind and the fertile
farmlands; and rapidly they cross over abysses of sea-brine
shrouded about by the mist and the clouds, nor ever is any
fear that they might incur some damage or come to destruction.
Nevertheless, I heard my father Naúsithoös say
565 this on a time, predicting to me that Poseidon would one day
grudge it of us that for every man we provide safe convoy—
said that a well-made ship of Phaiákian men on the way back
home from a convoy once on the seaway misty and murky
he would smash and would hide our city behind a huge mountain.
570 So did the old man say; these things that god may accomplish
or else leave unachieved, whichever his heart finds pleasing.
But come now, tell me this and recount it exactly and fully,
where off-course you were driven, and what were the countries of men you
came to, and then of the men themselves and their well-settled cities—
575 such as are cruel and savage and violent, lacking in justice,
those who are kindly to strangers, possessed of a god-fearing conscience.
Tell me why you are weeping and sorrowing deep in your spirit,
hearing the Argives' and Dánaäns' fate and of Ilion's ruin.
This have the gods brought forth: they have spun the destruction of peoples,
580 so that it might be a song for the men who live in the future.
Did some kinsman by marriage, a brave one, come to destruction
there before Ilion, brother- or father-in-law, the relations
nearest a man just after his own blood kin and his clansmen?
Or was he rather a comrade, a man of congenial spirit,
585 noble and brave? Since no less worthy or dear than a brother
ever is proven a comrade who knows discretion and prudence."

BOOK 9

Speaking to him then answered Odysseus of many devices:
"Lord Alkínoös, most distinguished among all the people,
it is indeed both good and agreeable hearing a singer
noble as this one is, most like to the gods in his singing.
5 For I think there is nothing of greater perfection or pleasure
than at a time when festive delight holds all of the people;
in their houses the feasters are listening well to a singer,
sitting in orderly rows; and beside them tables are filled with
victuals and meat; and the wine server draws wine out of the mixing
10 bowl, then takes it around, and he fills up each of the goblets.
This is to my own thinking a time most lovely and pleasant.
Now is the heart inside you determined to ask of my grievous
sufferings, so that I groan yet longer in sorrow and anguish.
What is the first thing then, what later, that I shall recite of
15 all my woes? For the gods in heaven have given me many.
Now to begin, my name I will tell you, in order that you may
know it, and then, when I have escaped from the pitiless doomsday,
I may remain your friend, though my home be far at a distance.
"I am Odysseus the son of Laërtes, who am among all men
20 noted for crafty designs, and to heaven my fame has ascended.
Ithaka, bright in the sun, is my home; thereon is the peak of
Nériton, trembling with leaves, most eminent; numerous islands
lie in the sea there around, each one of them close to another—
they are Doulíchion, Samè, and also wooded Zakýnthos.
25 It lies low in the sea and the farthest of all of the islands
out toward dusk—in the distance, the rest face dawn and the sunshine—
rugged, but fine in the youths that it nourishes; nor is there ever
anything else I can see that is sweeter to me than my country.
"Now it is true, I was held by Kalýpso the glorious goddess
30 there in her spacious cavern; she wanted to make me her husband;

so in the same way Circè the guileful nymph of Aiaía
held me there in her palace and wanted to make me her husband.
Nevertheless she never persuaded the heart in my bosom.
Nothing is sweeter, it seems, than a man's own country and parents,
35 even for one who settles abroad on a bountiful homestead
somewhere distant, in foreign domains and apart from his parents.
Now then, let me relate my return, with the many afflictions
which at the time I parted from Troy Zeus loaded upon me.
    "To the Kikonians drove me the wind that from Ilion bore me,
40 Ísmaros, where I ravaged the city and ruined the people.
Out of the city we took their wives and their many possessions,
sharing them so as we left no man was deprived of his portion.
There, although I commanded that we should at once on our nimble
feet take flight, they—childish in folly—would not be persuaded.
45 There much wine they were drinking, and great was the number of sheep they
killed on the shore of the sea, and of swing-paced crooked-horned cattle.
Meanwhile, fleeing Kikonians summoned Kikonian tribesmen
who were their neighbors, at once more warlike and stronger in numbers,
living upcountry, and highly accomplished in fighting with men on
50 horseback—well skilled too in fighting on foot when the need rose.
They came soon, in the manner of flowers or leaves in their season,
early at dawn; then truly a doom most evil from Zeus we
had—we were so ill fated that manifold woes we would suffer.
All of the warriors stood by the swift ships fighting the battle;
55 throwing their bronze-tipped spears, each side kept striking the other.
While it was morning as yet and the sacred daylight was waxing,
we stood holding them off, though they were much stronger in numbers.
But as the sun turned downward, the time when oxen are unyoked,
then the Kikonians carried the battle and beat the Achaians.
60 So out of each of the galleys were six of my well-greaved comrades
slaughtered; the rest of us fled, escaping from death and destruction.
    "Farther along we sailed from the place; in our hearts we lamented—
glad to flee death as we were—the destruction of our dear comrades.
Nor would I let my tractable ships go forward before some
65 crewman had called three times on each of the wretched companions
who died there in the plain, brought down by Kikonian spearmen.
Then at the ships cloud-gathering Zeus set Boreas' stormwinds
raging in furious tempest; the earth and the seaway alike he
hid in a thick cloud cover, and night rushed down from the heavens.
70 Plunging their bows in the water, the galleys were driven; the sails were

shredded to tatters, to three or four rags, by the force of the stormwinds;
all these, fearing destruction, we lowered and stored in the galleys.
Eagerly then we rowed on forward and into the mainland.
There two nights and as well two days, unbroken, incessant,
75 we lay eating our hearts in weariness mingled with sorrow.
But when the fair-haired Morning had brought full light on the third day,
setting the masts upright and the white sails hoisting upon them,
we sat down, and the wind and the steersmen guided us forward.
Now I would have arrived unscathed in the land of my fathers,
80 but as I rounded the Máleian headland, the wave and the current—
Boreas too—beat me from my course, past Kýthera drove me.

"Nine days then I was carried from there by the ruinous stormwinds
over the fish-thronged sea; on the tenth to the Lotus-eaters'
country we finally came, where people eat flowery victuals.
85 There we went out onto the land and drew up fresh water;
quickly the comrades took their supper beside the swift galleys.
But then, when of the food and the drink we all had partaken,
some of the comrades I sent forth to explore and discover
what sort of men, what eaters of food, might live in the country;
90 two of the men I chose, and a third I sent as a herald.
Quickly departing, the men met up with the Lotus-eaters.
For these comrades of ours, those Lotus-eaters devised no
loss or destruction but gave them flowers of lotus to feed on.
Any of them who ate of the honey-sweet fruit of the lotus
95 wished no more to return us a message or take his departure;
rather, they wanted to stay right there with the lotus-eating
people to feed on lotus and always forget their returning.
These men weeping I led by force to the galleys and dragged them
onto the hollow ships, where I bound them under the benches.
100 Then straightway I ordered the rest of the trustworthy comrades
quickly, without lost time, to embark on the swift-sailing galleys,
lest some eat of the lotus and wholly forget their returning.
Hastily then they boarded and took their seats at the oarlocks;
sitting in rows they beat their oars on the silvery sea-brine.
105   "Farther along we sailed from the place; in our hearts we lamented.
After a time, we came to the land of an arrogant, lawless
race, the Cyklópes, who put their trust in the gods undying,
so that they plant no plants with their hands, neither do any plowing;
rather, the crops all grow unsown and without cultivation,
110 grains like barley and wheat and the vines which yield them a full rich

wine from the grapes; and the rainfall of Zeus grows them to perfection.
These men have no meetings for counsel nor customs of justice,
but they keep their abodes on the peaks of the loftiest mountains,
where in the hollow caves each one of them governs as master
115 over his children and wives, and they take no care of each other.
    "There is a fertile island that spreads outside of the harbor,
not very near the Cyklópes' domain nor again very distant,
covered with woods; and upon it are wild goats, countless in number,
since no coming and going of people prevents them from roaming;
120 neither do hunters with dogs ever land there, men who in forests
suffer afflictions as they hunt game in the peaks of the mountains.
Nor is it occupied by sheep flocks grazing or plowlands,
but it remains through all of its days unplowed and unplanted,
utterly empty of men, and to bleating wild goats gives pasture.
125 For the Cyklópes possess no galleys with cheeks of vermilion,
nor are there shipwrights found among them, such men as would make them
well-benched galleys; and these might carry them forth to arrive at
each of the various cities of men, in the manner that often
men sail over the sea in vessels to visit each other—
130 they would have made this island a settlement pleasant and useful.
For it is not at all bad but would bear all things in their seasons,
since there are meadows on it by the shores of the silvery sea-brine,
soft and sufficiently watered; the grapevines never would perish.
There also are smooth arable lands; deep grain they would harvest
135 always, in season, for under the surface the soil is most fertile.
There is a port, good moorage, in which no hawser is needed,
nor need anchors be cast nor the stern be tied by its cables;
but having beached their vessels, the sailors could stay till the time their
hearts roused them to depart and the breezes were blowing upon them.
140 Then at the head of the harbor is flowing a stream of bright water,
rising from under a rock; black poplars are growing around it.
There we sailed to the shore; some god it was who was guiding
us through the murk of the night, since nothing was clear to our vision;
for our ship was engulfed in a deep mist, nor did the moon shine
145 down on us out of heaven, but by the thick clouds it was hidden.
There with our eyes nobody could catch any sight of the island,
nor indeed did we even observe the long waves that were rolling
into the shore, not until we were beaching the well-benched galleys.
After the galleys were beached, we next took all of the sails down,
150 then ourselves disembarked on the tide-heaped sand of the seashore;

there on the beach we slept and awaited the glorious morning.
    "Soon as the Dawn shone forth rose-fingered at earliest daybreak,
then all over the island we wandered, and marveled to see it.
Briskly the nymphs, those daughters of Zeus who carries the aegis,
155 roused up mountain goats, so that the comrades might have dinner.
Quickly the well-curved bows and as well the long-socketed goat spears
we took out of the ships, and dividing ourselves into three groups
started to shoot; and a god soon granted us game in abundance.
Now there were twelve ships then in my company; they were allotted,
160 each one, nine of the goats, while I chose ten as my own share.
So it was that for that whole day till the hour of the sunset,
we sat banqueting there on meat unstinted and sweet wine.
For the red wine in the galleys had not yet all been depleted;
some yet remained, since all of us drew off much in our storage
165 jars at the time we seized the Kikonians' sacred city.
At the Cyklópes' domain we gazed—nearby were the people—
noticed the smoke of their fires and the bleating of goats and of sheep flocks.
Soon as the sun went down and the shadows of night came upon us,
then we lay down to sleep on the tide-heaped sand of the seashore.
170   "Soon as the Dawn shone forth rose-fingered at earliest daybreak,
then I called an assembly and spoke among all the companions:
'All you others remain here now, my trustworthy comrades;
meanwhile, going ahead with my galley as well as my comrades,
I will learn something about these men, whoever they might be,
175 if they are bold and offensive and violent, lacking in justice,
or hospitable rather, possessed of a god-fearing conscience.'
    "So I spoke, and I boarded the galley and bade the companions
get themselves on board and at once cast off the stern cables.
Hastily then they boarded and took their seats at the oarlocks;
180 sitting in rows, they beat their oars on the silvery sea-brine.
But then, when we arrived at the place that was nearest the island,
there we observed, at the edge of the land by the sea, was a lofty
cavern, with bay trees hanging above it; within were abounding
flocks both of sheep and of goats kept stabled; around it a courtyard
185 lay, with a high wall built out of stones dragged up from a quarry
and out of long pine timbers and oak trees, lofty and leafy.
Inside a monstrous man was accustomed to sleep: he would herd his
sheep flocks a long way off, and he never consorted with others;
but he was living aloof, by himself; in his mind he was lawless.
190 He was indeed most wondrously monstrous and not like a mortal

man, a consumer of food, but a forested peak of the lofty
mountains, a pinnacle seen by itself and apart from the others.

"Straightway then I ordered the rest of the trustworthy comrades
there by the galley to stay and to keep watch over the galley;
195   I then, choosing among my comrades twelve of the bravest,
started away, and I carried along dark wine in a goatskin,
sweet wine given to me by Maron, the son of Euánthes,
priest of Apollo who strides around Ísmaros guiding and guarding,
since we guarded and saved him, along with his wife and his children,
200   honoring him, for he made his home in the forested grove of
Phoibos Apollo; and so he gave me glorious presents;
gold well-wrought and refined he presented to me, seven talents;
also a wine bowl wholly of silver he gave me, and then he
poured out wine in addition, in all twelve jars, double-handled—
205   sweet unmixed wine, drink for a deity. Nor was there any
servant or any attendant who knew of it, there in his household—
save for himself and his own dear wife, one housekeeper only.
When on any occasion he drank this honey-sweet ruddy
wine, he would fill one cup and with it pour water of twenty
210   measures; and sweet was the fragrance that rose up out of the wine bowl,
fit for a god: there would be no pleasure at all in abstaining.
So of this wine I filled a large goatskin, carrying also
food in a bag; for the valorous spirit in me was assured that
soon I would meet with a man endued with the mightiest prowess,
215   savage, with no true knowledge of justice or civilized customs.

"Speedily we went up to the cave, but we did not find him
there inside; he was grazing his fat flocks out in the pasture.
We went into the cave and observed each thing with amazement:
baskets were heavily laden with cheeses; the lambs and the kids were
220   crowded together in folds and divided according to ages,
penned up separately: one pen held firstlings, another
middlings, a third one younglings; with whey were all of the well-wrought
vessels, the buckets and pans into which he milked, overflowing.
Thereupon, my companions at once spoke up and implored me
225   first to take some of the cheeses and go back, then on returning
quickly to drive off the lambs and the kids from the pens and to take them
onto the swift-sailing galley and sail out into the sea-brine.
I however would not be persuaded—it would have been better!—
not till I saw him and found whether he might give me some guest-gifts.
230   When he appeared he would not be pleasing at all to my comrades.

"Kindling a fire, we first made offerings, then for ourselves took
some of the cheeses and ate us a meal; there sitting within we
waited until he came from his herding; a ponderous load of
dried-out wood he was bringing, to use in preparing his supper.

235 Once inside of the cave, he threw it down, making a clatter;
fearfully we all scurried away to the depths of the cavern.
Into the spacious cavern he next drove all of the fattened
flock he was going to milk, but the males he left in the high-walled
yard outside, both the rams and the billy goats, close to the doorway.

240 Then an enormous rock he lifted and placed as a doorstone—
it was a ponderous mass which twenty-two excellent four-wheeled
wagons could never have raised from the ground, all straining together,
such was the towering clifflike rock that he set in the doorway.
Taking a seat, he milked his sheep and his goats, loud-bleating,

245 all of them, each in turn, then set a lamb under each mother.
Straightway, half of the fresh white milk he curdled with fig juice,
then in wickerwork baskets he gathered the curds to make cheeses;
half however he left in the milk pails, so that it might be
there when he wanted to drink it and might make part of his supper.

250 But when finally, working with speed, he had finished his labors,
then he kindled the fire; and he saw us and asked us a question:
"'Strangers, who are you, and whence do you sail on the watery pathways?
Have you affairs in trading, or do you fruitlessly wander
over the sea in the manner of pirates who wander at random,

255 putting their lives in danger and visiting evil on strangers?'
"So he spoke, and the hearts inside us were utterly shattered,
terrified so at the loud deep voice and the monstrous person.
Nevertheless I addressed him in these words, giving an answer:
'We are Achaians returning from Troy who were driven astray by

260 all of the violent winds on the great vast gulfs of the deep sea;
seeking our homes by a different route, by different ways than
others we came; it was thus, I suppose, Zeus wished to contrive it.
It is our boast to be soldiers of Atreus' son Agamemnon,
whose fame now is the greatest of anyone under the heavens,

265 since so splendid a city he sacked, so many the men he
brought to destruction; and we have arrived here, come to your very
knees in the hope you will grant us a guest-gift or in another
manner present us a present, for such is the custom with strangers.
Come now, honor the gods, good man; we are suppliants asking.

270 Zeus himself, the protector of suppliants, keeper of strangers,

god of encounters, accompanies strangers to honor and guard them.'

"So did I say; straightway he answered in pitiless spirit:
'You are a simpleton, stranger, or else from afar you have come here,
you who bid me to shrink from offending the gods or to fear them.
275 For the Cyklópes are not much troubled with Zeus of the aegis
nor with the rest of the fortunate gods, since we are far stronger.
Nor for the sake of avoiding the anger of Zeus would I ever
spare either you or your comrades unless my spirit commanded.
But come, tell me the place in which on arriving you left your
280 well-made ship, far away or nearby, so that I may know it.'

"He spoke, trying me out, but I knew too much and was not tricked;
rather, in turn I addressed him an answer deceptive and crafty:
'It was Poseidon the shaker of earth who shattered my galley,
throwing her onto the rocks on the boundary coast of your country,
285 bringing her close to a cape when the wind drove her from the seaway.
I however with these have escaped from a sheer destruction.'

"So I spoke; he returned no answer, in pitiless spirit;
springing instead to his feet, he stretched his hands to my comrades;
two he snatched up together and dashed them down on the ground like
290 puppies; the brains ran out all over the floor and bedrenched it.
Butchering these up, limb by limb, he readied his supper;
then he ate like a mountain-bred lion and left out nothing—
innards as well as the flesh and the bones with the succulent marrow.
Uttering loud lamentations, to Zeus we lifted our hands up,
295 seeing the pitiless deed, our impotence gripping our spirits.
But then, soon as the Cyklops had filled his enormous stomach,
eating the flesh of the men, then drinking the milk unmingled,
he lay down in the cave, through the sheep flock stretching his body.
Then I pondered the matter in my magnanimous spirit:
300 I would go nearer, and drawing the keen-edged sword from the thigh sheath,
square in the chest I would stab, where the midriff holds in the liver,
feeling for it with my hand; but a new thought kept me from striking,
since right there we too would have perished in sheer destruction,
seeing that never would we have been able to thrust from the lofty
305 door with the strength of our hands that ponderous rock he had put there.
So then, making lament, we awaited the glorious morning.

"Soon as the Dawn shone forth rose-fingered at earliest daybreak,
first he kindled a fire, then milked the magnificent sheep flock,
all of them, each in turn, then set a lamb under each mother.
310 But when finally, working with speed, he had finished his labors,

two more men he snatched up together and readied his breakfast.
After he ate, he herded the fat flock out of the cavern,
easily lifting the huge doorstone from its place, but at once he
put it back, like somebody putting a lid on a quiver.

315   Then with a loud shrill whistle, the Cyklops guided the fat flock
into the mountains; but I was left inside pondering evils—
if I could pay him back and Athena would grant me the glory.
This is the plan which seemed to me then in my spirit the best one.
For a huge club of the Cyklops was lying alongside the sheepfold,

320   olive wood, not yet cured; he had cut it down so that he could
carry it once it was dry; and as we observed it, we thought it
equal in size to the mast of a broad black galley of twenty
oars, one carrying cargo and crossing the vast sea chasms—
such it was in its length, such too in thickness, to look at.

325   Standing beside this, I hewed off it the length of a fathom,
then I handed the stake to the comrades and told them to scrape it.
So they made it all smooth, while I stood near them and sharpened
it to a point; in the flame of the fire I put it to harden.
Then I took it away and concealed it under the ordure

330   which in enormous abundance was strewn all over the cavern.
Next I ordered the others to cast their lots to determine
which of the men must venture with me in lifting the stake and
twisting it into his eye when upon him came a sweet slumber.
Those who drew it were men whom I myself wanted chosen,

335   four of the best; I reckoned myself as the fifth one among them.
Then in the evening he came driving his fine-fleeced sheep home;
straightway into the spacious cavern he herded the fat flock,
all of them; none did he leave outside in the high-walled courtyard—
whether he had some notion or whether a god so urged him.

340   Then the enormous rock he lifted and placed as a doorstone;
taking a seat, he milked his sheep and his goats, loud-bleating,
all of them, each in turn, and he set a lamb under each mother.
But when finally, working with speed, he had finished his labors,
two more men he snatched up together and readied his supper.

345   I then started to speak to the Cyklops, standing beside him,
holding in hand dark wine in a cup ornamented with ivy:

      "'Cyklops, here, drink wine, since men's flesh you have just fed on,
so that you know what sort of a drink our galley was bearing;
this I brought you to make libation if you in your pity

350   sent me home; but you rage—no longer is it to be suffered.

Madman, how in the future would anyone else of the many
men in the world come here? For you act not fitly or justly.'
    "So did I say; he took it and drank it down and was hugely
pleased as he drank the sweet drink; and he spoke and demanded a second:
355 'Give me some more, in generous spirit, and tell me your name now
quickly, that I may present you a guest-gift you will rejoice in;
for the Cyklópes as well do the grain-giving lands bear a full rich
wine from the grapes, and the rainfall of Zeus grows them to perfection.
But this wine is distilled of ambrosia, extract of nectar.'
360   "So he spoke; I again poured glistening wine in the goblet;
thrice I brought it and gave it, and thrice he recklessly drank it.
But when the wine had at last got into the mind of the Cyklops,
then I spoke and addressed him in these words, subtle and soothing:
'Cyklops, you have inquired my glorious name: I will tell you
365 now what it is, and you give me a guest-gift, just as you promised.
Nobody is my name, yes, Nobody what I am called by
both my mother and father and all of the other companions.'
    "So did I say; straightway he answered in pitiless spirit:
'Nobody last of the men I will eat, just after his comrades—
370 all those others before him; and this I will give as a guest-gift.'
Thus, then slumping away he fell on his back, and he lay there
twisting his great thick neck to one side; he was taken at once by
sleep, that queller of all; and the wine burst up from his gullet,
gobbets of man flesh too, as he vomited, heavy with drinking.
375 Then I drove the sharp club down underneath many red embers
till it became very hot; and to all the companions I spoke in
words of encouragement, lest anyone back out in his terror.
But when the olive-wood cudgel was almost going to catch on
fire, in spite of its being so green, and was dreadfully glowing,
380 then from the fire I carried it closer; around me the comrades
stood at the ready, and into us all a god breathed great courage.
They then, seizing the cudgel of olive wood, pointed and sharpened,
thrust it into his eye, while leaning my body against it
I kept whirling it, much as a man with a boring drill bores some
385 beam for a ship, while those underneath, by gripping a leather
thong each side, help twist it, and it drills ever more deeply—
holding it thus in his eye, that club with the fiery point we
twisted around, and about it the blood poured heated to seething;
all of his eyebrows above and his eyelids were singed by the savage
390 blast of the eyeball aflame, and the eye roots cracked in the blazing.

As when into cold water a man who works as a blacksmith
dips the huge blade of an ax or an adze, and it sputters and hisses,
treating the tool—since this is the cause of the strength in the iron—
so was his eye now sizzling about that olive-wood cudgel.
395 Dreadfully, loudly he cried, and around him the rocks were resounding;
we all fearfully scurried away from him. Out of his eye he
drew the great club, which much of his blood now drenched and polluted.
When with his hands he had thrown it away from himself in a frenzy,
then he clamored aloud to the other Cyklópes, who lived in
400 caverns around his own in the windswept peaks of the mountains.
Hearing the cry, they gathered together from every direction;
standing around his cavern, they asked him what was his trouble:
    "'Why are you so distressed, Polyphémos, that you are exclaiming
through the ambrosial night, so robbing us all of our slumber?
405 No one, surely, against your will has been driving your sheep off!
Nor is there any by guile or by violence aiming to kill you!'
    "Out of his cave then strong Polyphémos returned them an answer:
'Nobody, friends, is by guile and not violence aiming to kill me!'
    "Answering him, they addressed him in winged words, offering counsel:
410 'If then no one is doing you violence, living alone there,
there is no way to avoid a disease great Zeus has assigned you;
nevertheless, you pray to your father, the lordly Poseidon.'
    "So they spoke and departed; the heart inside me was laughing
over the way my name and my excellent scheme had deceived them.
415 Moaning aloud in the agonized pain of his anguish, the Cyklops,
groping about with his hands, first lifted the stone from the doorway;
then he himself sat down in the doorway, spreading his arms out,
so that if anyone went outside with the sheep, he would catch him—
thus no doubt he hoped I would be in my mind so foolish.
420 I however was planning the best way matters could happen,
hoping that I might find some means of avoiding my comrades'
death and my own; all sorts of deceptions and craft I was weaving
as it concerned our lives, since such great evil was near us.
This is the plan which seemed to me then in my spirit the best one:
425 several rams were among his sheep, well-nourished and thick-fleeced,
handsome and bulky, with wool of a dark blue-violet color.
These I quietly fastened together with flexible willows
which that monster had slept on—the Cyklops lawless in spirit—
bound them in threes; and the one in the middle would carry a man out
430 while at its sides both others would walk, so saving the comrades.

Thus each man three sheep would be carrying; as for myself then,
there was a ram that of all of the sheep by far was the finest;
holding to him by the back, in the thick wool under his belly
huddled, I lay; so twisting myself in the wonderful fleece, I
435   held on tight with my hands, persevering with resolute spirit.
So then, making lament, we awaited the glorious morning.

    "Soon as the Dawn shone forth rose-fingered at earliest daybreak,
straightway the males of the flock then started to rush to the pasture,
while all over the sheepfolds the unmilked females were bleating,
440   since their udders were full to the bursting. The master, although he
suffered in terrible pain, kept feeling the backs of the sheep, all
standing erect close by; and the childish fool never noticed
under the breasts of the wool-fleeced sheep how men had been fastened.
Finally, last of the flock, the big ram went out of the doorway,
445   burdened with thick-grown wool and with me, who had schemed so adroitly.
Feeling him under his hands, thus spoke to him strong Polyphémos:

    "'Dear old ram, why thus are you leaving the cave, I wonder,
last of the flock? For before, no sheep ever left you behind them;
rather, the first you grazed on the tenderest blooms of the grasses,
450   striding along in the lead, and the first you arrived at the flowing
rivers, and first you were eager to come back here to the fold when
evening came; yet now you are last of all. Are you in sorrow
over the eye of your master? The cowardly man, with his baneful
comrades, gouged it out, with his wine first quelling my spirit,
455   Nobody, who, I am sure, not yet has escaped from destruction!
How I wish that you thought like us, had also a voice with
which you could say to me where he has hidden himself from my anger!
Then in the cave would his brains fly spattering hither and thither,
as on the ground his body was smashed; my heart would at once grow
460   lighter from all of the evils that no-account Nobody gave me!'

    "So he spoke, and the ram he sent from him, out of the doorway.
When we had gone some distance away from the cave and the courtyard,
first I released myself from the ram, then freed the companions.
Hastily then, of the sheep, long-striding and rich in fat, we
465   rounded up many and drove them forward until at the galley
we had arrived; most welcome we came to our loving companions,
we who had fled from destruction; the rest they mourned and lamented.
I however would not allow weeping—I nodded at each man,
raising my brows—but I bade them quickly to load all the many
470   fine-fleeced sheep on the galley and then sail forth on the sea-brine.

Hastily then they boarded and took their seats at the oarlocks;
sitting in rows, they beat their oars on the silvery sea-brine.
But when I was as far from the land as a man's shout carries,
I then started to call to the Cyklops in words of derision:

475   "'Cyklops, he was no coward, the man whose comrades you were
going to eat by violent force in the hollow cavern!
All too much you would be exposed by your own evil actions,
wretch, since you did not scruple to eat up strangers and guests in
your own house: so Zeus and the rest of the gods have repaid you.'

480   "So did I say; then he in his heart grew even more wrathful;
breaking the topmost peak of a huge high mountain, he threw it,
hurled it so that it fell in front of the dark-prowed galley
only a little and just missed hitting the tip of the rudder;
then, as the rock went down in the water, the sea was dashed upward;

485   suddenly billowing back to the mainland, the wave in a flood tide
carried the ship from the sea and was driving her onto the seashore.
But then, taking a long pole up in my hands as a hook, I
thrust her away, then roused up the comrades, ordering them to
throw their weight on the oars so that we could escape from the evils,

490   nodding at them with my head; and they all leaned into the rowing.
But when twice the original distance of sea we had covered,
then once more I called to the Cyklops; the comrades around me
held me back, one after another, with words of persuasion:

        "'Wretch, now why are you set on enraging a man so savage,

495   who just now, by throwing a missile, has driven the galley
back from the sea to the shore, and we thought right there we would perish?
If he had heard us raising our voices or anyone speaking,
he would have shattered our heads and the beams of the galley to pieces,
hurling a huge rough stone, for with such great strength he could throw it.'

500   "Thus, but they did not sway me in my magnanimous spirit,
but once more I shouted to him in the wrath of my spirit:
'Cyklops, should anyone among men who are mortal inquire of
you concerning your eye and the way it was shamefully blinded,
tell him that it was put out by Odysseus the sacker of cities,

505   son of Laërtes, the man who in Ithaka keeps his dwelling.'

        "So I spoke, and he answered in these words, loudly lamenting:
'Well now, a prophecy spoken of old has indeed come upon me!
Formerly there was a man here, a soothsayer strong and accomplished,
Télemos, Eúrymos' son, who greatly excelled as a prophet;

510   he grew old while furnishing prophecies for the Cyklópes;

all these things, he informed me, would someday come to fulfillment—
thus I would suffer the loss of my sight at the hands of Odysseus.
But I always expected that some man handsome and tall would
come to me here in the cave, endued with the mightiest prowess.
515　Now as it is, one little and powerless no-account man has
gouged my eye from the socket when he with his wine had subdued me.
But come hither, Odysseus, that guest-gifts I may present you,
also exhort the renowned earth-shaker to grant you conveyance,
seeing that I am his son and that he claims he is my father.
520　He of himself, if he wishes, will heal me, and not any other
one of the fortunate gods nor any of men who are mortal.'
　　"So did he say; then I spoke out to him, giving an answer:
'Would that I might so surely bereave you of breath and of life in
sending you down to the palace of Hades, as I am assured that
525　no one will heal your eye, not even the great earth-shaker!'
　　"So did I say; then he called out to the lordly Poseidon,
praying and stretching his hands on high to the star-filled heaven:
'Listen to me now, dark-haired earth-upholding Poseidon:
if in truth I am yours and as my own father you claim me,
530　grant that Odysseus the sacker of cities, the son of Laërtes,
having his home in Ithaka, never return to his homeland.
But if it is his portion to see his friends and to go back
there to his well-built house, back there to the land of his fathers,
badly and late may he come, having quite lost all of his comrades,
535　on some other man's ship, and at home find woe and affliction.'
　　"So did he say in prayer, and the dark-haired deity heard him.
Then once again he lifted a stone, one even more massive;
whirling about, he threw it, and measureless strength he exerted,
hurled it so that it fell in back of the dark-prowed galley
540　only a little and just missed hitting the tip of the rudder.
Then as the rock went down in the water, the sea was dashed upward;
forward the wave bore the ship, so driving her into the seashore.
But when we had arrived at the island, the place where the other
well-benched galleys were waiting together, the comrades were seated
545　round them, grieving for us whom they had been always expecting.
When we arrived at the shore, on the sand we ran out the galley,
then ourselves disembarked on the tide-heaped sand of the seashore.
Driving the Cyklops' sheep from the hollow galley, at once we
shared them, so as we left, no man was deprived of his portion.
550　But as the sheep were divided, the well-greaved comrades accorded

me by myself that ram most excellent; him on the shore I
offered to Kronos' son Zeus of the dark cloud, ruler of all things,
burning the flesh of the thighs; but he took no heed of the victim;
rather he kept on pondering means by which he would ruin
555 all of the well-benched galleys and all of my trustworthy comrades.
So it was that for that whole day till the hour of the sunset,
we sat banqueting there on meat unstinted and sweet wine.
Soon as the sun went down and the shadows of night came upon us,
then we lay down to sleep on the tide-heaped sand of the seashore.
560 Soon as the Dawn shone forth rose-fingered at earliest daybreak,
straightway then I roused up the comrades, bidding them quickly
get themselves on board and at once cast off the stern cables.
Hastily then they boarded and took their seats at the oarlocks;
sitting in rows, they beat their oars on the silvery sea-brine.
565   "Farther along we sailed from the place; in our hearts we lamented—
glad to flee death as we were—the destruction of our dear comrades.

BOOK 10

"Next we arrived at the isle of Aiolia, wherein resided
Aíolos, Híppotas' son, most dear to the gods undying.
His was an island that floated; it all was enclosed by a wall of
bronze unbreakably strong, with a smooth cliff rising beneath it.
5   There also were his children, the twelve all born in the palace,
six of them daughters and six of them sons in the vigor of manhood;
and to his sons he had given his daughters to be their bedmates.
These at the side of their much loved father and virtuous mother
always are feasting, and ready at hand lie numberless dishes.
10   Fragrant with roasting, the palace resounds all around in the courtyard
during the day; and at night, by the side of their virtuous bedmates,
they lie sleeping in blankets on bedsteads corded for bedding.
Theirs was the city to which we came, and the beautiful houses.
He a whole month entertained me and asked about every matter—
15   Ilion city, the Argive ships, the Achaians' returning;
everything I related to him then fitly and truly.
But when at last I inquired of the journey and asked him to send me
forth on the way, he did not say no but prepared us a convoy.
Flaying the skin of a nine-year ox, he gave me the bag this
20   made, with the currents of blustering winds bound tightly inside it—
he had been made the controller of winds by the scion of Kronos,
either to make them stop or to stir them up, as he wanted;
this he bound on the hollow ship with a shimmering silver
cable, that none of the winds might blow from it even a little;
25   then for my sake he sent out a breeze of the west wind, Zephyr,
so that it might bear forward the ships and the men; but it was not
destined to finish the task: by our recklessness we were ruined.

"Nine days then we were sailing, alike in the night and the daytime;
then on the tenth we discerned already the fields of our fathers;
30   we could observe men tending the fires, so near we approached it.

Finally then sweet sleep overcame me, for I was exhausted,
for the ship's sheet I always had handled, nor gave it to other
comrades, that we more quickly would come to the land of our fathers.
Then the companions began to address each other with speeches;
35 they maintained I was carrying silver and gold to my palace,
given to me by great-souled Aíolos, Híppotas' scion.
Thus would one of them say as he looked at another beside him:

"'Well now, this is a man much loved and respected among all
people, of whomsoever the city or country he reaches!
40 Many indeed are the beautiful treasures from Troy he is bringing
back as his booty, and meanwhile we who accomplished the self-same
voyage are journeying homeward with hands that are still quite empty.
Now too, favoring him with his friendship, Aíolos gave him
all these things; come then, let us quickly investigate what these
45 things are, how much silver and gold there is in the skin bag.'
So they said, and the evil advice won over the comrades;
so they loosened the bag, and the winds all rushed out together.
Swiftly the stormwinds seized them and carried them, wailing in anguish,
over the sea and away from the land of their fathers; but I then,
50 being awakened from sleep, in my excellent spirit considered
whether to drop from the galley and die right there in the seaway
or to endure in silence and still be one of the living.
But I endured it and waited and lay down there in the galley,
hiding my face; and the ships were all borne by the baleful stormwinds
55 to the Aiolian island again, as the comrades lamented.

"There we went out onto the land and drew up fresh water;
quickly the comrades took their supper beside the swift galleys.
Finally, when of the food and the drink we all had partaken,
I then, taking a herald and comrade along as attendants,
60 went to the glorious palace of Aíolos; him we discovered
sitting beside his wife and his children and eating his dinner.
We went into the palace, and there by the posts on the threshold
we sat down; in their minds they wondered, and asked us a question:

"'Why have you come here, Odysseus? Has some bad spirit attacked you?
65 We kindheartedly sent you away, in order that you might
come to your country and house and whatever to you is belovèd.'

"So they spoke, and in turn I addressed them, grieving in spirit:
'Evil companions have been my ruin, along with a wretched
slumber; but dear friends, set it all right, for in you is the power.'
70 "So I spoke and addressed them in these soft words of appeasement;

they fell silent, and only the father addressed me an answer:
'Out of the island at once, most loathed among all of the living!
For it is not permitted to me to assist or to convoy
that man who by the fortunate gods is despised and rejected.
75 Out! Since you so despised of the gods undying have come here!'
　　"So he spoke; from the house he sent me heavily groaning.
Farther along we sailed from the place; in our hearts we lamented.
Soon the men's spirits were quite worn out with the pain of the rowing
caused by our folly—the wind no longer appeared as an escort.
80　　"Six full days we were sailing, alike in the night and the daytime;
then on the seventh we came to the high-built city of Lamos,
Laistrygonian Télepylós, where herdsman to herdsman
calls as he drives sheep in; and the one who is outbound answers.
There could a man who did not need sleep gain double the wages—
85 one as a cowherd, the other for pasturing silvery sheep flocks—
since the two roads of the night and the day are so close to each other.
There when we had arrived at a glorious harbor, around which,
all of the way, both sides, does a cliff rise towering upward—
two promontories projecting and opposite, each to the other,
90 reach out into the mouth, so the entrance passage is narrow—
thither within did the rest all bring their tractable galleys;
well inside of the hollow harbor, the vessels were fastened
close to each other, for never in it did a wave swell upward—
neither a great nor a small—but a white calm covered the water.
95 I was alone in keeping my black ship outside the harbor,
there at the outermost mouth; on a rock I fastened her cables.
Climbing a hill, I stood on a rugged and rock-strewn lookout;
therefrom nothing appeared of the labors of men or of oxen;
only a column of smoke we saw rising up from the country.
100 Some of the comrades I sent forth to explore and discover
what sort of men, what eaters of food, might live in the country;
two of the men I chose, and a third I sent as a herald.
　　"Leaving the ship, they followed a smooth road, one where the wagons
carrying wood went down to the town from the heights of the mountains.
105 Soon they met with a girl drawing water, in front of the city;
she was the Laistrygonian King Antíphates' comely
daughter, who down to the fount Artákia's beautiful stream had
come, since it was from there they furnished the city with water.
Standing beside her then they addressed her, making inquiry
110 who was the king of the people and who it was that he governed.

She then pointed at once to the high-roofed house of her father.
When they entered the glorious house, they met an enormous
woman as huge as the peak of a mountain and horribly loathed her.
Quickly she summoned renowned Antíphates home from assembly—
115   he was her husband. For them he plotted a wretched destruction.
Straightway he snatched up one of the comrades and made him his dinner;
meanwhile the other two rushed in flight back down to the galleys.
But he raised the alarm through the city, and hearing it, mighty
Laistrygonians gathered together from every direction,
120   thousands of them, not at all like men, but instead like Giants.
Down from the cliffs they threw great boulders the size that a man can
carry; and quickly a terrible clamor arose from the galleys,
screams of the men they killed, ships crashing together and shattered;
spearing the men like fish, to a gruesome dinner they bore them.
125   While they slaughtered the men inside of the deepwater harbor,
I at the same time, drawing my keen sword out of its thigh sheath,
started to cut at the cable that fastened the dark-prowed galley.
Hastily then I roused up the comrades, ordering them to
throw their weight on the oars so that we could escape from the evils;
130   then with their oars all threw up the seawater, fearing destruction.
So to our joy, my galley escaped from the cliffs overhanging
out to the sea, but the rest were destroyed there, crowded together.

     "Farther along we sailed from the place; in our hearts we lamented—
glad to flee death as we were—the destruction of our dear comrades.
135   Soon we came to the isle of Aiaía; upon it resided
Circè of beautiful hair, dread goddess with speech of a mortal;
she was the own blood sister of murderous-minded Aiétes;
both were of Helios sprung, of the Sun who shines upon mortals,
while their mother was Persè, the child engendered of Ocean.
140   There we silently headed the galley along to the seashore
into a harbor for ships: some god it was who was guiding.
There two days and as well two nights, after disembarking,
we lay eating our hearts in weariness mingled with sorrow.
     "But when the fair-haired Morning had brought full light on the third day,
145   finally, taking along my spear and my keen-edged sword, I
speedily climbed from the ship to a lookout place, to discover
whether I might see labors of men, might hear any voices.
Climbing aloft, I stood on a rugged and rock-strewn lookout;
there to my vision appeared smoke rising from earth of the broad ways,
150   out of the palace of Circè and through dense thickets and woodland.

Then I began to revolve my thoughts in my mind and my spirit,
whether to go and explore, since fiery smoke I had noticed.
So as I pondered the matter, the best course seemed to be this one:
first to the swift ship I would return, to the shore of the deep sea,
155 give the companions a meal, then send some out to explore things.
But on the way, as I came up close to the tractable galley,
then, all alone as I was, some god took pity upon me.
Onto the road, he sent me a great stag, towering-antlered,
which from his woodland pasture was ranging below to the river,
160 going to drink, for the strength of the sun so long had oppressed him.
As he was leaving the wood, I struck at him under the backbone
halfway along his back, and the bronze spear passed straight through him;
screaming, he dropped in the dust, and the life breath flew from his body.
I stepped onto the corpse, then, seizing the bronze spear, drew it
165 out of the wound it had made; on the ground I laid it and left it
there; then quickly I pulled up brushwood and pliable willows;
braiding a rope of a fathom in length, well plaited from either
end, I fastened together the feet of the marvelous creature.
Then I bore it across my back as I went to the black ship,
170 leaning my weight on the spear, since there was no way I could hold it
on one shoulder with one of my hands, for the beast was enormous.
Then I threw it in front of the ship and aroused the companions,
standing beside each man, in words of persuasion and comfort:
    "'Friends, not yet will we be going down, in spite of our sorrow,
175 into the palace of Hades, before our destiny day comes.
But come, while there is plenty to eat and to drink in the swift ship,
let us be mindful of eating and not be wasted with hunger.'
    "So I spoke, and at once they heeded the words I had uttered;
then unveiling their heads on the beach of the desolate sea-brine,
180 they all gazed at the stag, for indeed that beast was enormous.
When by looking at it with their eyes they had taken their pleasure,
carefully washing their hands, they readied a sumptuous dinner.
So it was that for that whole day till the hour of the sunset,
we sat banqueting there on meat unstinted and sweet wine.
185 Soon as the sun went down and the shadows of night came upon us,
then we lay down to sleep on the tide-heaped sand of the seashore.
Soon as the Dawn shone forth rose-fingered at earliest daybreak,
then I called an assembly and spoke among all the companions:
    "'Listen to my words, comrades, despite these evils you suffer.
190 Friends, we never can know where the darkness is or the sunrise,

neither where under the earth the Sun goes who shines upon mortals,
nor where again he rises; but now let us quickly consider
whether there might yet be some plan for us—I do not think so.
Climbing aloft, I saw from a rugged and rock-strewn lookout
195　this is an island; around it the boundless sea is encircled.
Most of the island is quite low-lying, and just in the center,
I with my eyes saw smoke through the dense-grown thickets and woodland.'

　　"So I spoke, and the hearts inside them were utterly shattered,
thinking of Laistrygonian King Antíphates' actions
200　and of the strength of the great-souled Cyklops, eater of man flesh.
Piercingly then they wailed, pouring out great tears in abundance;
nevertheless, no profit to them came out of their weeping.

　　"Next I divided in two the whole troop of the well-greaved comrades,
counting them off, and appointed a leader for each of the sections:
205　one I led, and the other Eurýlochos, godlike in stature.
Putting the lots in a helmet of bronze, we rapidly shook them;
it was the lot of Eurýlochos, mighty in spirit, that sprang out.
He set forth; in his company went twenty-two of the comrades,
making lament; and behind they left us weeping and wailing.
210　Soon, in a forested glen, they came on the palace of Circè,
built of a smooth-dressed stone in a place with a view all around it.
Nearby roaming about it were wolves of the mountains and lions,
which she herself had enchanted by giving them baleful elixirs;
these beasts made no rush of attack at the men, but instead they
215　stood on their hind legs, fawning about them and wagging their long tails.
As when about some lord who is coming from dinner, his dogs run
fawning—for always he brings them morsels to soften their tempers—
so about these men now did the strong-clawed wolves and the lions
fawn; but the men felt terror to see such frightening creatures.
220　Standing within the forecourt of the goddess with beautiful tresses,
they heard Circè inside; in her beautiful voice she was singing,
as she wove to and fro on a great cloth, work that immortal
goddesses do, most delicate, pleasing to see, and resplendent.
Speaking among them opened Polítes, a lord of the people,
225　who was the dearest to me of the comrades, best in devotion:

　　"'Friends, there is someone weaving inside to and fro on a great cloth,
singing a beautiful song, and the whole yard echoes about her,
either a goddess or woman; but let us call to her quickly.'

　　"So he spoke to them all, and they called to her, raising their voices.
230　Throwing the bright doors open, she came out quickly and started

calling the men; in their ignorance they all followed together.
Only Eurýlochos stayed, suspecting that it was deception.
Leading them into the house, she sat them on benches and armchairs;
then for the men she mixed up barley and cheese and green honey,
235　all in Prámneian wine; to the food she added a baneful
drug, so that they would entirely forget the dear land of their fathers.
After she gave it to them and they drank it down, then at once she
struck at the men with her wand and enclosed them all in a pigpen,
since they now had the heads and the hair and the voices and even
240　bodies of swine, but the minds inside were as steady as ever.
So it was they were penned up, weeping; in front of them Circè
threw down acorns to eat, and the fruit of the ilex and cornel—
such is the provender swine who sleep on the ground eat always.

　　"Quickly Eurýlochos came back down to the swift black galley,
245　bringing report of the comrades, the unkind doom they had suffered.
Not one word was he able to utter, as much as he wished to,
stricken at heart as he was with a grief so enormous; his eyes were
filled as the tears welled up, and his soul thought only of wailing.
But when at last we all in astonishment questioned him closely,
250　then he spoke and related the loss of the other companions:

　　"'We went, just as you bade, through the underbrush, brilliant Odysseus;
soon, in a forested glen, we came to a beautiful palace
built of a smooth-dressed stone in a place with a view all around it.
Inside, somebody weaving a great cloth sang in a clear voice,
255　either a goddess or woman; we called to her, raising our voices.
Throwing the bright doors open, she came out quickly and started
calling the men; and in ignorance they all followed together.
Nevertheless I stayed, suspecting that it was deception.
They all vanished together, the whole throng; nor did a single
260　one of them ever appear, for I sat there watching a long time.'

　　"So did he say; and at once I threw my sword, silver-studded,
onto my shoulders, a great bronze blade; and a bow was about them.
Then I bade him to guide me the way back there by the same road,
but with both of his hands he held to my knees and entreated;
265　sorrowing then he spoke, and in these winged words he addressed me:
'Zeus-loved lord, do not take me thither unwilling, but leave me;
for I am sure you will neither return yourself nor will lead back
any companion of yours; but with these men now let us quickly
take our flight, for we yet may escape from the day of affliction.'

270　　"So he spoke; and in turn I addressed him, giving an answer:

'Well then, Eurýlochos, you may remain right here in the same place,
eating and drinking your wine by the hollow and dark-hued galley;
nevertheless, I go, for necessity strongly compels me.'

"So having spoken, I started away from the sea and the galley.
275 But when I was about to pursue my way through the sacred
coppice and reach the great palace of Circè of many elixirs,
then did Hermes, the god of the gold wand, come to encounter
me as I went to the palace, resembling a man in his youthful
years with his first mustache, of the age most graceful and pleasing;
280 taking my hand in his own, he said these words, calling upon me:

"'Where, unfortunate man, are you going alone through the hilltops,
ignorant so of the place? Those comrades of yours in the house of
Circè are kept like hogs, all crowded together in pigpens.
Do you arrive here hoping to free them? You will yourself not
285 go back home, I believe—you will stay where all of the rest are.
But come, I will deliver you out of these evils and save you;
there now, taking this excellent drug, go onward to Circè's
house, so that it from your head might ward off the day of affliction.
I will describe to you all the malevolent cunning of Circè:
290 she will prepare you a potion and throw drugs into your victuals;
but she will not be able to charm you so, for the noble
drug I give you will not let her: each thing I will tell you.
Just at the moment that Circè is thrusting at you with her long staff,
hastily then you, drawing your keen sword out of its thigh sheath,
295 rush toward Circè as if in a rage intending to kill her.
She in terror of you will invite you to bed in her chamber;
do not hesitate then or say no to the bed of a goddess,
so that your comrades she may release, and provide for your own wants.
But first bid her to swear the great oath of the blessèd immortals
300 she is not plotting against you another infliction of evil,
lest when you are stripped naked she make you weak and unmanly.'

"So having spoken, the drug he gave me, the slayer of Argos,
plucking it up from the ground, and he also showed me its nature:
down at the root it was black, but the color of milk was the flower;
305 moly is what it is called by the gods, and for men who are mortal,
hard is the labor to dig it, but all things gods can accomplish.

"Straightway Hermes departed, to go toward lofty Olympos
over the forested island; and so to the palace of Circè
I set forth; and in me as I went was the heart much troubled.
310 Soon I stood at the doors of the goddess with beautiful tresses;

there as I stood I called, and the goddess heard what I uttered.
Throwing the bright doors open, she came out quickly and started
calling; and I went following her, in my spirit lamenting.
Leading me in, she gave me an armchair studded with silver,
315 beautiful, skillfully made; and beneath for my feet was a footstool.
Then she made me a potion to drink in a gold-wrought goblet,
into it throwing a drug: in her heart she was pondering evils.
After she gave it to me and I drank—though it did not charm me—
she struck me with her wand and said these words, calling upon me:
320   "'Go now, get in the pigpen and lie with the rest of your comrades.'
So she spoke, and I, drawing my keen sword out of its thigh sheath,
rushed toward Circè as if in a rage intending to kill her.
Loudly she screamed, ran under the sword to my knees and embraced them;
sorrowing then she spoke, and in these winged words she addressed me:
325   "'Who are you? Whence do you come? What city is yours, and what parents?
I am amazed that you drank these drugs and were not enchanted,
seeing that never were such drugs borne by any man else when
once he had drunk them and over the fence of his teeth they had entered.
There is indeed some unbewitchable mind in your bosom.
330 You are Odysseus, adept and resourceful, whom always the god who
carries the gold wand, slayer of Argos, predicted would come here,
as you returned back homeward from Troy on your swift black galley.
But come, put the sword back in the sheath, then let us together
go in the palace and get into bed, so that when we have mingled
335 there in bed and in love, we may give our trust to each other.'
     "So she spoke, and in turn I addressed her, giving an answer:
'How then, Circè, can you now bid me to deal with you gently,
you who here in your palace have made pigs out of my comrades?
Having me here myself, with a treacherous mind you are bidding
340 me to go into your chamber and get in bed, so that you while
I have been stripped quite naked can make me weak and unmanly.
I will be quite unwilling to get in bed there beside you
if you will not deign, goddess, to swear me an oath of the strongest
you are not planning against me another infliction of evil.'
345   "So I spoke, and at once she swore it, as I had demanded.
But then, when she had sworn and had brought her oath to completion,
I got into the bed, most lovely and splendid, of Circè.
     "Meanwhile the handmaids busied themselves with work in the chambers,
four of them, who are the servants she keeps for herself in the palace.
350 All these women of hers are the issue of springs and of wooded

213

groves and of sacred rivers that flow down into the sea-brine.
One of the four threw over the armchairs beautiful purple
blankets above for the seats, having spread fine cloth underneath them;
meanwhile another one drew into place in front of the armchairs

355 tables of silver, and baskets of gold she put there upon them;
as for the third, she mixed sweet wine, honey-hearted, in silver
mixing bowls, and distributed too gold goblets for drinking;
lastly, the fourth maid brought in water and kindled a blazing
fire there under the great bronze cauldron and heated the water.

360 When in the shimmering cauldron the water was boiling, she sat me
down in the bathtub to wash me, and mixing the water to pleasing
warmth from the cauldron, she poured it over my head and my shoulders,
till from my limbs it had taken the spirit-destroying exhaustion.
When she had bathed me and rubbed me richly with oil of the olive,

365 she threw garments about me, a beautiful cloak and a tunic.
Leading me in, she gave me an armchair studded with silver,
beautiful, skillfully made; and beneath for my feet was a footstool.
Hand-washing water a maid then carried to us in a lovely
gold-wrought pitcher, and over a basin of silver she poured it,

370 so we could wash; nearby she set out a well-polished table.
Carrying food, the revered housekeeper approached us and set it
close to us, many a dish she gladly supplied from her storage;
then she bade us to eat. But to my heart nothing was pleasing;
I sat thinking of different things; my heart boded evil.

375   "Circè, as soon as she noticed that I just sat there and did not
stretch my hands to the food and that powerful sorrow possessed me,
stood there close to my side, and in these winged words she addressed me:
'Why in this way are you sitting, Odysseus, resembling a voiceless
man so, eating your heart, not touching the drink or the victuals?

380 Some other treachery you are expecting, perhaps, but you need not
fear, since I already have sworn you an oath of the strongest.'

    "So she spoke; and in turn I addressed her, giving an answer:
'Circè, indeed what man would he be who, thinking aright, could
ever endure to begin partaking of drink or of victuals

385 till his companions were freed and with his own eyes he had seen them?
But if to drink and to eat you bid me and mean it sincerely,
free them, so that I see with my eyes my trustworthy comrades.'

    "So did I say; then Circè at once went out through the palace
holding her staff in her hand; she opened the doors of the pigpen,

390 then she drove out the men, who were nine-year-old hogs in appearance.

They stood there in a group just opposite; going among them,
some other drug she used to anoint each one of the comrades.
Off of their limbs fell all of the hair that before had been made to
grow by the baleful drug given them by Circé the goddess.
395 Quickly they all turned back into men, now younger than ever,
much more handsome as well, and of mightier size, to behold them.
Then they knew me, and each one took my hand in his handclasp;
over us all came longing to weep, and around us the palace
dreadfully, loudly resounded; the goddess herself felt pity.
400 Straightway, standing beside me, the glorious goddess addressed me:
    "'Zeus-sprung son of Laërtes, Odysseus of many devices,
you go down to the swift ship now and the shore of the deep sea;
first of all drag your ship out onto the land from the water;
next, into caves put all your possessions and all of the tackling;
405 then you yourself come back; lead hither your trustworthy comrades."
    "So she spoke, and the valorous spirit in me was persuaded;
I set out for the swift ship then and the shore of the deep sea.
There on the swift ship, I discovered the trustworthy comrades
raising a piteous moan, pouring out great tears in abundance.
410 As at a time calves bred in the country, around the returning
cows of the herd, which enter the dung yard sated with grazing,
all go skipping together in front of them, nor do the cowpens
hold them in any more, but incessantly lowing, about their
mothers they run, so did they, as with their own eyes they beheld me,
415 pour forth weeping around me, as if to the spirit in them it
seemed they had come back home to the land of their fathers, to rugged
Ithaka's city itself, where they had been gotten and nurtured.
Sorrowing then they spoke, and in these winged words they addressed me:
    "'We are as happy that you have returned to us, Zeus-sprung lord, as
420 if we had reached our houses in Ithaka, land of our fathers;
But come, tell us the tale of the loss of the other companions.'
    "So they spoke; and in turn these comforting words I addressed them:
'First let us drag our ship out onto the land from the water;
next, into caves put all our possessions and all of the tackling;
425 then press onward yourselves, and with me all follow together,
so you may see the companions as they in the sacred abode of
Circè are drinking and eating, for they have food in abundance.'
    "So I spoke, and at once they heeded the words I had uttered;
only Eurýlochos wanted to hold back all the companions;
430 raising his voice he spoke, and in these winged words he addressed them:

215

'Poor friends, where are we going? And why do we want these evils,
following on to the palace of Circè, who surely will turn us
all into hogs, or perhaps into wolves, or again into lions,
so that we keep watch over her great house under compulsion,
435   just as the Cyklops acted the time when into his inner
yard our comrades came and with them went valiant Odysseus;
for by his recklessness they too then came to destruction.'
      "So he spoke, and at once in my mind I began to consider
drawing the keen-edged sword from its sheath on my powerful thigh and
440   cutting his head from his body to throw it down on the ground there,
though we were closely related by marriage. But the companions
held me back, one after another, with words of persuasion:
'Zeus-sprung lord, let us leave him behind now, if you command it,
here by the galley to stay and to keep watch over the galley,
445   while you show us the way to the sacred palace of Circè.'
      "So they spoke, and they went up then from the ship and the seashore;
nor was Eurýlochos left back there by the hollow galley,
but he followed, for he was afraid of my savage reproaches.
      "Meanwhile, there in her house, to the other companions had Circè
450   thoughtfully given a bath and with oil of the olive had rubbed them;
then about them she had thrown fine clothes, wool mantles and tunics;
all of them we found eating a good meal there in the palace.
When they had each looked straight in the face and had known one another,
sorrowing they all wailed, and around them the palace resounded.
455   Straightway standing beside me, the glorious goddess addressed me:
      "'Zeus-sprung son of Laërtes, Odysseus of many devices,
raise no longer the swelling lament—I know without telling
both what pains you have suffered in crossing the fish-thronged seaway,
then what damages hostile men on the land have inflicted.
460   But come, eat the provisions and drink your fill of the wine now,
till such time as again in your breast you have taken the spirit
back as it was when first you were leaving the land of your fathers,
Ithaka, rugged and rocky; for now you are spiritless, wasted,
always remembering such hard wandering; nor is there any
465   spirit at all in your mirth, since so many ills you have suffered.'
      "So she spoke and in us persuaded the valorous spirits.
Then for the whole day through for a year's full circle of seasons,
we sat banqueting there on meat unstinted and sweet wine;
but at the end of the year, when the seasons again were returning,
470   with the decline of the months, as the long days came to completion,

finally, calling me forth, my trustworthy comrades addressed me:
'Charm-struck man, take mind now at last of the land of your fathers,
if it is willed by the heavens that you be saved, that you go back
there to your well-built house, back there to the land of your fathers.'

475 "So they spoke, and the valorous spirit in me was persuaded.
So it was that for that whole day till the hour of the sunset,
we sat banqueting there on meat unstinted and sweet wine;
then when the sun went down and the shadows of night came upon us,
they lay down to their sleep all over the shadowy chambers.

480 "I in the meantime mounted the beautiful bedstead of Circè;
grasping her knees I implored her; the goddess heard what I uttered;
raising my voice I spoke, and in these winged words I addressed her:
'Circè, accomplish for me the agreement you earlier promised,
sending me home; for in me already the spirit is eager,

485 as in the other companions; and my dear heart they are wasting,
woefully groaning around me, the times when you have gone elsewhere.'
    "So I spoke, and at once that glorious goddess responded:
'Zeus-sprung son of Laërtes, Odysseus of many devices,
do not stay any longer against your will in my palace.

490 Yet you first must accomplish a different journey and go down
into the palace of Hades and Perséphonè, honored and dreaded,
seeking prophetic advice of the Theban Teirésias' spirit,
that blind prophet in whom is a mind still fresh in its vigor;
only to him even after his death has Perséphonè granted

495 living intelligent thought; like shadows the rest are aflitter.'
    "So she spoke, and the heart inside me was utterly shattered;
there on her bed I sat down sorrowing, nor did my spirit
wish any longer to live and to look upon Helios' sunlight.
When I had sated myself with groveling, weeping, and groaning,

500 finally then I addressed her in these words, giving an answer:
'What man, Circè, is he who will guide our way on that journey?
No one has ever arrived in Hades' domain on a black ship.'
    "So I spoke, and at once that glorious goddess responded:
'Zeus-sprung son of Laërtes, Odysseus of many devices,

505 do not trouble your heart with desire for a guide on your galley.
Setting the mast upright, then hoisting and spreading the white sails,
sit down; then will the breath of the north wind carry her onward.
But when at last in the ship you have crossed clear over the Ocean,
there is a brush-grown shore and the groves Perséphonè hallows,

510 tall black poplars and willows that cast their fruit unripened.

217

Run out the ship just there on the beach of deep-eddying Ocean;
you yourself go on to the moldering palace of Hades.
There into sorrowful Ácheron flows Pyriphlégethon's fire and
mournful Kokýtos, a branch of the Styx's detestable waters;
515 there is a rock and the junction of those two thundering rivers.
There then, hero, as soon as you draw close in, as I bid you,
dig out a pit of a cubit's extent one way and the other.
Into it then pour out libations to all who have perished,
first a commingling of honey and milk, sweet wine for the second,
520 water the third; and at last white barley you sprinkle upon them.
Then pray hard to the fleeting and strengthless souls of the perished;
say that in Ithaka, when you arrive, you will offer a barren
cow, the best one in your palace, and heap up the pyre with your treasures,
then for Teirésias separately, you will offer an all-black
525 ram, whichever is most outstanding among your sheep flocks.
When to the glorious tribes of the dead you have made your entreaties,
offer a male of the flock and a female also, a black one,
turning their heads toward Érebos; you in the other direction
turn yourself, and set out to the streams of the river; and many
530 shades will arrive there soon, of the bodies of those who have perished.
Straightway then you rouse your companions and tell them to take those
sheep that are lying about, just killed by the pitiless sword blade,
flay their bodies and burn them, and offer the gods their entreaties—
Hades the powerful one, Perséphonè honored and dreaded.
535 Then do you sit there, drawing your keen sword out of its thigh sheath,
nor may you let those fleeting and strengthless souls of the perished
come any nearer the blood, before hearing Teirésias' teachings.
Straightway then will approach you the prophet, the lord of the people;
he will inform you about your road and the length of your journey—
540 and of your homecoming, how on the fish-thronged sea you will travel.'
     "So she spoke, and at once upon us came Dawn of the gold throne.
Circè at once put garments around me, a mantle and tunic;
so too the nymph put on a capacious and shimmering mantle,
graceful and delicate; fastened around her waist was a lovely
girdle of gold, and above on her head she was wearing a head scarf.
545 Going along through the house, I started to rouse the companions,
standing beside each man, with words of persuasion and comfort:
'Now no longer continue to lie here sleeping a sweet sleep;
no, let us go, since Circè the goddess has given directions.'
550   "So I spoke, and the valorous spirits in them were persuaded.

Yet not even from there without loss did I lead the companions.
There was a man, Elpénor, the youngest of them, who was neither
very courageous in battle nor ready and steadfast in judgment;
longing for cool fresh air, in the sacred palace of Circè
555 he lay heavy with wine, well away from my other companions;
hearing the tumult and noise that the comrades made by their movements,
suddenly he jumped up; in his mind he did not remember,
when he started departing, to climb back down the long ladder,
but as he fell headlong from the edge of the roof and the neckbones
560 broke from the joints, his soul went down to the dwelling of Hades.
      "Then as the men were departing I spoke these words there among them:
'Probably you are expecting to go back home to the much loved
land of your fathers; but Circè decrees us a different journey
into the dwelling of Hades and Perséphonè honored and dreaded,
565 seeking prophetic advice of the Theban Teirésias' spirit.'
      "So I spoke, and the hearts inside them were utterly shattered;
there on the spot they sat down wailing and tearing their hair out;
nevertheless, no profit to them came out of their weeping.
But when down to the swift ship then and the shore of the deep sea
570 we went sorrowfully, pouring out great tears in abundance,
meanwhile Circè, who also had gone down close to the black ship,
tethered a male sheep there and a female also, a black one,
easily passing us by: what mortal could look with his eyes on
any god who did not wish to be seen either coming or going?

BOOK 11

"Then when we had arrived down there at the sea and the galley,
first we dragged our ship out into the luminous sea-brine,
set up the mast pole, and hoisted the sails in the dark-hued galley;
bringing the sheep, we loaded them into the hold and ourselves then
5   boarded, lamenting our woes, pouring out great tears in abundance.
Then as a noble companion to follow the dark-prowed galley,
Circè of beautiful hair, dread goddess with speech of a mortal,
sent us a favoring wind which filled up the bellying canvas.
Finally, when on the ship we had seen to each piece of the tackling,
10 we sat down, and the wind and the steersman guided her forward.
All day long were the sails spread out as she ran through the seaway;
then did the sun go down and the ways were all shadowed in darkness.
    "She came then to the ultimate bounds of the deep-flowing Ocean,
where the Kimmerian people are found, their country and city
15 shrouded about by the mist and the clouds, so that never does shining
Helios look down over the land with his radiant sunbeams—
neither whenever he climbs on high to the star-filled heaven,
nor indeed when again out of heaven to earth he is turning—
but a maleficent night spreads over the miserable mortals.
20 There we arrived; then beaching the galley, we carried the sheep out
onto the shore and proceeded along by the current of Ocean,
walking until we came to the place of which Circè had spoken.
There, as the victims were held by Eurýlochos and Perimédes,
straightway then I, drawing my keen sword out of its thigh sheath,
25 dug out a pit of a cubit's extent one way and the other.
Into it then I poured libations to all who had perished,
first a commingling of honey and milk; sweet wine was the second,
water the third; and at last white barley I sprinkled upon them.
I prayed hard to the fleeting and strengthless souls of the perished,
30 said that in Ithaka, when I arrived, I would offer a barren

cow, the best one in the palace, and heap up the pyre with my treasures,
then for Teirésias separately, I would offer an all-black
ram, whichever was most outstanding among our sheep flocks.
When I had thus with entreaties and promises prayed to them, all those
35 tribes of the dead, then seizing the sheep I severed the throat flesh
over the pit; and the blood poured out, black-clouded, and up from
Érebos gathered the shades of the bodies of those who had perished:
young brides, youths unwedded, and men grown old in affliction,
maidens of tenderest years, with the grief yet fresh in their spirits;
40 many as well there were who with bronze-tipped spears had been wounded,
men killed fighting in wars, in accouterments bloody and gore-stained.
These in numbers surrounded the pit, all jostling together,
raising a dreadful and deafening clamor, and green fear seized me.
Straightway then I roused the companions and told them to take those
45 sheep that were lying about, just killed by the pitiless sword blade,
flay their bodies and burn them, and offer the gods their entreaties—
Hades the powerful one, Perséphonè honored and dreaded.
Then did I sit there, drawing my keen sword out of its thigh sheath,
nor would I let those fleeting and strengthless souls of the perished
50 come any nearer the blood before hearing Teirésias' teachings.
       "First however the soul of Elpénor, my comrade, approached me;
not yet under the earth of the broad ways he had been buried,
since we had left his body behind in the palace of Circè
both unwept and unburied: another endeavor constrained us.
55 Seeing him there I wept, in my heart felt sorrow and pity.
Raising my voice I spoke, and in these winged words I addressed him:
'How have you come, Elpénor, down under the murk and the shadows?
You on foot arrived sooner than I with a dark-hued galley.'
       "So I spoke, and he answered in these words, loudly lamenting:
60 'Zeus-sprung son of Laërtes, Odysseus of many devices,
heaven's ill will and unlimited wine subdued me to folly.
I lay asleep in the palace of Circè and did not remember,
when I started departing, to climb back down the long ladder,
but as I fell headlong from the edge of the roof and the neckbones
65 broke from the joints, my soul came down to the dwelling of Hades.
Now I beseech by the ones you left who are far at a distance—
first by your wife and the father who tended you when you were little,
then by Telémachos, whom you left the one son in your palace—
since I know, when you leave this place and the palace of Hades,
70 you will be mooring your well-made ship in the isle of Aiaía,

when you arrive there, lord, be mindful of me, I entreat you;
do not leave me to be henceforth unwept and unburied,
turning your back, lest I bring down upon you the gods' anger;
but having burned me up with the arms that are mine and the armor,
75 heap me a grave mound there on the shore of the silvery sea-brine,
for an unfortunate man to be known by those coming after.
Do these things for my sake, then plant my oar on the grave mound,
that with which I rowed when alive and among the companions.'
   "So he spoke; and in turn I addressed him, giving an answer:
80 'Luckless friend, these things I will do for your sake and accomplish.'
So as we sat, each making reply to the other in somber
words, I held my sword up over the blood on the one side,
while on the other the shade of my comrade talked for a long time.
   "Then came up and approached me the spirit of my dead mother,
85 old Antikleía, who was greathearted Autólykos' daughter,
whom when I parted for sacred Ilion, I had left living.
Seeing her there I wept, in my heart felt sorrow and pity;
yet although I was aching with grief, not then would I let her
come any nearer the blood before hearing Teirésias' teachings.
90   "Then came up and approached me the Theban Teirésias' spirit,
holding a scepter of gold; he knew me, and thus he addressed me:
'Zeus-sprung son of Laërtes, Odysseus of many devices,
why, unfortunate man, do you come here, leaving the shining
light of the sun, to behold these dead, this place without pleasure?
95 But draw back from the pit, and the keen sword hold at a distance,
so I can drink of the blood, then speak to you truth without error.'
   "So he said; I drew back and the keen sword, studded with silver,
thrust back into its sheath; and as soon as he drank of the dark blood,
uttering these words then did the excellent prophet address me:
100 'Sweet homecoming is what you are looking for, brilliant Odysseus;
this will the god make painful for you, since I do not think that
you will elude the earth-shaker, who laid up wrath in his spirit,
goaded to anger because you robbed his dear son of his eyesight.
Nevertheless, you might reach home, though suffering evils,
105 if you are willing to curb your hunger and that of your comrades
from that time when first you are bringing your well-made galley
near the Thrinakian island, escaping the violet seaway;
there you will soon find grazing the cattle and great fat sheep of
Helios, who looks down over all things, listens to all things:
110 these if you leave uninjured and keep your minds on returning,

you may arrive in Ithaka yet, though suffering evils.
But if you injure the cattle, then I foretell the destruction
both of the ship and the comrades; if you yourself should avoid it,
late and unhappily you will return, losing all of your comrades,
115 on some other man's ship; and at home you will come upon troubles,
men overbearing and haughty who now are devouring your substance,
courting your godlike bedmate and giving her presents for marriage;
once you have come back home, their violence you will requite them.
But when there in your palace at last you have slaughtered the suitors
120 either by treacherous guile or by open attack with a sharp sword,
start off, bearing an oar in your hands, well-fitted for rowing;
travel until you arrive at a place where people have never
heard of the sea and they eat no food that is mingled with sea salt;
nor in fact do they know anything about purple-cheeked galleys
125 nor of the well-fitted oars which serve as the wings of a galley.
This unmistakable sign I will tell you, and never forget it:
when on the road you are met by another wayfarer who says that
it is a winnowing fan you hold on your glistening shoulder,
straightway, when in the earth your well-fitted oar you have planted,
130 making oblation of excellent victims to lordly Poseidon,
burning a ram and a bull and a sow-mounting boar in his honor,
then you should go back homeward and sacred hecatombs offer
there to the deathless gods, the immortals who hold the broad heaven,
all of them, one by one; then out of the sea will a death come
135 over you, ever so gently and easily; this it will be which
kills you, tired in a sleek old age; and around you the people
all will be happy and blessèd; the truth unerring I tell you.'
   "So did he say, and in turn I addressed him, giving an answer:
'Doubtless the gods themselves, Teirésias, spun these matters.
140 But come now, tell me this and recount it exactly and fully:
that is the spirit of my dead mother at which I am looking;
she sits close to the blood in silence, without even deigning
either to look her own son in the face or to speak and address me;
tell me, lord, what way she may recognize me as her offspring.'
145   "So did I say, and at once he addressed me, giving an answer:
'Easily I will inform you of this, in your mind I will place it:
whomsoever of all these spirits of those who have perished
you let nearer the blood, he will tell you the truth without error;
but any spirit to whom you refuse it will go back once more.'
150   "So having spoken, the soul of the lord Teirésias entered

into the palace of Hades, for what was ordained he had uttered.
I however continued to stand right there until Mother
came up and drank of the blood, black-clouded, and quickly she knew me;
sorrowing then she spoke, and in these winged words she addressed me:

155 "'How have you come, my child, down under the murk and the shadows
while yet alive? It is hard for the living to look upon these things,
for in the way lie huge wide rivers and terrible currents,
Ocean the first of them all, which someone going on foot can
never traverse, if he does not have any well-built galley.

160 Do you arrive after wandering hither from Troy for a long time
now, in a ship and along with your comrades? Have you indeed not
gone back to Ithaka yet and not seen your wife in the palace?'

"So did she say, and in turn I addressed her, giving an answer:
'Mother, necessity led me to land in Hades' dominion,

165 seeking prophetic advice of the Theban Teirésias' spirit:
for not yet have I neared the Achaian domains nor have set foot
yet in my country; but I have been wandering ever in sorrow
since that time when first I accompanied great Agamemnon
over to Ilion, land of fine horses, to battle the Trojans.

170 But come now, tell me this and recount it exactly and fully:
What doom was it of death long-mourned that defeated and killed you?
Was it a lengthy disease, or did Artemis shooter of arrows
kill you, visiting you with her mild and benevolent missiles?
Tell me then of my father and son also, whom I left there,

175 whether with them my estate yet abides, or whether another
man now has it and they no longer believe I will come back.
Tell me as well of the wife I courted, her mind and intention,
whether she stays with the child, guards everything steadfastly,
or already has married the noblest among the Achaians.'

180 "So I spoke, and at once made answer the lady my mother:
'Even for too long still she remains with a resolute spirit
there in the halls of your palace; the miserable nights and the days are
always wasting away while she keeps letting her tears fall.
Nobody has your noble estate, but Telémachos keeps your

185 property still, at his ease and secure, and presides at the banquets,
equally shared, fit fare for the worthiest judge to partake of;
all of the nobles invite him. Your father remains on his own place
out in the country, nor visits the city, nor has any bedding,
no bedstead, no mantles or covers of shimmering fabric;

190 but in the winter he sleeps right there in the hut where the servants

sleep, in the dirt by the fire, and the clothes on his body are squalid.
Then when summer arrives and the flourishing season of harvest,
everywhere on the slope of his orchard, planted with grapevines,
beds of the dry leaves fallen to earth are arranged for his respite;
195   there in his anguish he lies, in his heart the great sorrow increasing,
longing for you to return, and a harsh old age overtakes him.
For it was thus I perished and thus encountered my doomsday;
no, not there in the halls did the keen-eyed shooter of arrows
kill me, visiting me with her mild and benevolent missiles;
200   nor was it any disease that attacked me, such as above all
takes life force from the limbs with its loathsome pining and wasting;
but it was longing for you and concern for you, brilliant Odysseus,
tender affection for you that bereft me of my sweet spirit.'
    "So did she say; then pondering these things deep in my heart, I
205   wanted to take in my arms that spirit of my dead mother.
Thrice I started for her, as my heart bade me to embrace her;
thrice from my arms she fluttered away like a dream or a shadow.
So in the depths of my heart my sorrow became even sharper;
raising my voice I spoke, and in these winged words I addressed her:
210   "'Why not stay for me, Mother, as I seek now to embrace you,
so even here in Hades' domain, with affectionate arms we
hold each other and both take comfort in cold lamentation?
Or is it some mere phantom that queenly Perséphonè summons
up for me, so that I groan yet longer in sorrow and anguish?'
215   "So I spoke, and at once made answer the lady my mother:
'Oh my child, who beyond all mortals are destiny-ridden!
Not in the least Perséphonè, daughter of Zeus, has deceived you,
but this way is allotted to mortals whenever they perish,
since no longer the thews hold body and bone frame together,
220   but those fleshly remains are consumed by the powerful burning
might of the fire when once from the white bones life has departed,
and like a dream is the fluttering soul flitting out of the body.
But now swiftly return to the light again, keeping in mind all
these things you are observing, to tell your wife of them later.'
225   "So as we stood, each making reply to the other, the women
came and approached—because queenly Perséphonè roused them to do so—
such as were either the wives or the daughters of excellent nobles;
there by the dark blood these came thronging and huddled together.
I took thought of the way to interrogate each of the women.
230   This is the plan which seemed to me then in my spirit the best one:

drawing the long-edged sword from the sheath on my powerful leg, I
would not allow them to drink of the black blood all at the same time,
but they approached in turn, one after another, and each one
told me about her descent, for of all I made the inquiry.

235   "First then I saw Tyro, the child of an excellent father,
who informed me that she was the noble Salmóneus' offspring,
said she was wife, moreover, to Kretheus, Aíolos' scion,
but she had fallen in love with the godly Enípeus River,
which, of the rivers that flow on the earth, by far is the fairest;
240   she by the beautiful streams of Enípeus often would wander.
Likened to him, Poseidon, the holder and shaker of earth, lay
down at the side of the maid in the mouth of the eddying river;
purple and foaming, a wave surged over the two like a mountain,
arching aloft, and concealing from view both the god and the woman.
245   Loosing her maidenly girdle, the god poured slumber upon her.
Straightway after the god had accomplished his amorous deed, he
took her hand in his own and said these words, calling upon her:

          "'Woman, rejoice in our love: as the year moves on in its turning,
you will bear glorious children, for not without fruit the immortals
250   share their embraces; and you watch over the offspring and rear them.
Now go back to the house; stay silent and never disclose this:
know however that I am Poseidon the great earth-shaker.'

          "So did he say, and he plunged down under the billowing sea-brine.
Neleus and Pelias she had conceived of the god, and she bore them.
255   Both of her scions were soon to become strong henchmen of mighty
Zeus: in Iólkos of spacious domains lived Pelias, wealthy
owner of sheep flocks; Neleus dwelt in sandy-soiled Pylos.
Then this queen among women to Kretheus bore other children,
Aison and Pheres and last Amytháon, delighting in horses.

260   "Next after her I saw Antíopè, child of Asópos;
even of Zeus she could boast to have lain in his bed and embraces;
two were the children she bore—one Amphion, Zethos the other—
who were the first to establish abodes in Thebes of the seven
gates and to fortify it, since not without fortification
265   could they have dwelt in Thebes on the broad plain, though they were mighty.

          "Next after her I saw Alkménè, Amphítryon's bedmate,
who bore Herakles, stalwart and bold, with the soul of a lion,
after she bedded with powerful Zeus and enjoyed his embraces.
Mégara also was present, the daughter of high-souled Kreion,
270   whom Amphítryon's scion of vigor unwearying married.

"There too I saw Oídipous' mother, the fair Epikástè,
she who had wrought with an ignorant mind an enormous misdoing,
marrying her own son; he, after he murdered his father,
took her to wife; but the gods soon brought it to light among mortals.
275 But in agreeable Thebes, though suffering woe, by the baneful
will and design of the gods he ruled the descendents of Kadmos.
She went into the dwelling of Hades the strong gatekeeper,
fixing a noose for herself high up at the top of the roof beams,
held by her grief; but she left to the son who survived her the sorrows
280 many and great that a mother's Erínyes, the Furies, accomplish.
    "Chloris as well I saw, most beautiful: Neleus married
her for her beauty, when once he had won her with numberless bride gifts;
she was the lastborn daughter of Amphion son of Iásos,
who once ruled by his might in Orchómenos, Minyan city.
285 She in Pylos was queen and to Neleus bore noble children—
Nestor and Chromios, then Periklýmenos, noble and honored.
After them, virtuous Pero she bore, that marvel to mortals,
courted by all who dwelt thereabout. Yet Neleus would not
give her to any who could not drive out of Phýlakè mighty
290 Íphikles' broad-browed crooked-horned cattle, the fractious and wayward
beasts; and the excellent prophet Melámpous alone undertook it,
driving them out; but an onerous god-sent destiny bound him—
painful and burdensome fetters and cowherds savage and loutish.
But when finally all of the months and the days were completed,
295 after the year had revolved and the seasons again were returning,
finally then did powerful Íphikles give him his freedom;
he spoke all his predictions, and Zeus's design was accomplished.
    "Leda as well I saw, who was once Tyndáreos' bedmate;
she to Tyndáreos bore two offspring, powerful-hearted—
300 Kastor the tamer of steeds, Polydeúkes the noblest of boxers.
Both these heroes the life-giving earth holds, though they are living.
There even under the earth maintaining the honor of Zeus, they
waken to life on alternate days and the rest of the time lie
dead; and the equal of gods' is the honor that they are allotted.
305   "Next thereafter, the wife of Alóeus, Íphimedeía,
I saw, her who is said to have mingled in love with Poseidon;
two offspring she bore to a life of but little duration—
godlike Otos the one, far-famed Ephiáltes the other—
who were the tallest of men brought forth by the grain-giving plowlands,
310 far the most beautiful too, next only to famous Oríon,

since already, when they were but nine years old, nine cubits
broad they were, and in height they had grown up to be nine fathoms.
These two menaced the very immortals who dwell on Olympos,
threatened to stir up strife of impetuous battle against them.
315 Ossa they wanted to pile on Olympos, and then upon Ossa
Pelion, mountain of quivering leaves, as a ladder to heaven.
This they would have achieved had they reached full vigorous manhood;
but by the scion of Zeus whom fair-haired Leto had born they
both were slaughtered before underneath their temples the curly
320 whiskers had bloomed or their cheeks with a blossoming down been covered.

"Phaidra and Prokris as well I saw, and the fair Ariádnè,
murderous-spirited Minos' daughter, whom Theseus once was
taking from Crete to the holy Athenian hill; but he did not
have any joy of the girl, for before that Artemis killed her,
325 acting upon Dionýsos' indictment in sea-washed Dia.

"I saw Klýmenè, Maira, and cruelly harsh Eriphýlè—
gold as the price of her husband the last had esteemed and accepted.
But of them all I will not now speak to you, nor will I name them,
such was the number I saw of the daughters and wives of the heroes;
330 sooner would pass the ambrosial night. But indeed it is time for
sleep now, whether I go on the swift ship, joining the comrades,
or remain here; and the gods and yourselves will provide me a convoy."

So did he say; then all of the people were hushed in silence,
held by the charm of the tale all over the shadowy chamber.
335 Speaking in these words, white-armed Arétè began to address them:
"Men of Phaiákia, how does this man now seem to your liking,
both in appearance and size, in the mind well-balanced within him?
He is indeed my guest, yet each of you shares in the honor;
so do not send him away too hastily, nor to a man thus
340 needy of gifts be scanty in giving them, since in your houses
lie by the will of the gods much wealth and abundant possessions."

Then spoke also to them Echenéos, the elderly hero
who among all the Phaiákian men was of earliest birth date:
"Friends, neither wide of the mark nor away from our expectations
345 speaks our provident lady the queen; now let us obey her.
But Alkínoös now will decide both doing and saying."

Then Alkínoös spoke these answering words and addressed him:
"This is a word indeed to remain so always, as long as
I am alive and I rule the Phaiákians, lovers of rowing.
350 Let our guest now endure, though much he desires to return home,

228

nevertheless, to remain till tomorrow, until I can finish
gathering all of his gifts; and the men will attend to the convoy,
all of them, I above all, since mine is the rule in the country."
    Speaking to him then answered Odysseus of many devices:
355 "Lord Alkínoös, most distinguished among all the people,
even if you should command me to stay for a year in your country,
then should dispatch me a convoy and give me glorious presents,
I would desire it myself; it would be much greater advantage
so with a hand yet fuller to reach the dear land of my fathers;
360 I would indeed be honored the more, more highly belovèd,
by all men who saw me in Ithaka on my arrival."
    Then Alkínoös spoke these answering words and addressed him:
"As we observe you, Odysseus, in no way do we suppose you
one of the cheats or insidious charlatans such as the many
365 men that the black earth feeds and supports, far scattered abroad, who
fashion their lies and inventions from sources that no one could witness.
Grace is upon your words, and an excellent wisdom within them—
like some singer of tales, you have skillfully told us the story
showing the piteous woes of yourself and of all of the Argives.
370 But come now, tell me this and recount it exactly and fully,
whether you saw any godlike comrades of those who with you to
Ilion journeyed together and there encountered their doomsday.
This is a night most wondrously long; not yet is it time we
turn to our sleep in the hall; so tell me your marvelous doings.
375 I would indeed hold out to the glorious morning if you could
still endure to relate your miseries here in the palace."
    Speaking to him then answered Odysseus of many devices:
"Lord Alkínoös, most distinguished among all the people,
there is a time for abundance of words, time also for sleeping.
380 But if you wish still longer to listen, I do not begrudge it,
telling you now about other events yet more to be pitied—
sorrows my comrades suffered, the ones who afterward perished,
who had escaped from the grievous and warlike cry of the Trojans,
then on returning were killed by the will of a treacherous woman.
385   "At that time, after holy Perséphonè scattered the female
souls of the women away, some going in every direction,
then did the soul of the scion of Atreus come, Agamemnon,
bitterly grieving, and others collected around, of the men who
perished with him, encountered their doom in the house of Aigísthos.
390 Quickly he recognized me, as soon as he drank of the black blood.

Piercingly then he wailed, and he shed great tears in abundance,
stretching his hands toward me, as he eagerly reached to embrace me.
But no longer in him were the vigor and potency steadfast
such as before he had had in the flexible limbs of his body.
395 Seeing him there I wept, in my heart felt sorrow and pity:
raising my voice I spoke, and in these winged words I addressed him:
      "'Atreus' glorious scion, the leader of men Agamemnon,
what doom was it of death long-mourned that defeated and killed you?
Was it Poseidon who brought you down as you sailed in your galleys,
400 raising against you a terrible blast of the violent stormwinds?
Or on the dry land were you destroyed by enemy fighters
when from the fields you were driving their cattle and beautiful sheep flocks
or when over their city you fought them and over their women?'
      "So I spoke, and at once he addressed me, giving an answer:
405 'Zeus-sprung son of Laërtes, Odysseus of many devices,
no, Poseidon did not quell me as I sailed in my galleys,
raising against me a terrible blast of the violent stormwinds;
nor on the dry land was I destroyed by enemy fighters;
but Aigísthos it was who wrought my death and destruction;
410 he and my murderous wife called me to his palace and killed me
while I was dining, the way one slaughters an ox at the manger.
So I died a most pitiful death, and around me the other
comrades were killed one after another, as white-tusked pigs are
killed in the house of a wealthy and powerful man for a dinner,
415 either a wedding, a feast, or a sumptuous communal banquet.
You have already encountered the slaughter of many heroic
men killed fighting alone or at war in the violent combat;
but far more in your heart, seeing these things, you would have mourned them,
how we lay there scattered about the full tables and mixing
420 bowls all over the hall, and the whole floor ran with our lifeblood.
Saddest of all was the voice of Kassandra, the daughter of Priam,
which I heard: she was killed by treacherous Klýtaimnéstra
close to my side; then raising my hands, I beat on the earth in
anguish and died with a sword in my body; the bitch-eyed woman
425 turned her back nor would deign, though to Hades' domain I was going,
even to shut my eyes or to close my mouth with her own hands.
So there is nothing at all more dreadful or vile than a woman
who in the thought of her heart meditates this kind of misdoing
like that woman who craftily plotted a deed so indecent—
430 causing the death of the husband she wedded. Indeed I expected

when I arrived back home that at least to the children and servants
I would be welcome, but she with her thoughts of exorbitant evil
poured great shame on herself and as well on women who follow,
all of the female sex, even one whose acts are of virtue.'

435   "So he spoke, and in turn I addressed him, giving an answer:
'Dreadful how violently wide-thundering Zeus has exerted
hatred on Atreus' race from of old by the scheming of women!
Many of us were destroyed on Helen's account, and against you
Klýtaimnéstra was plotting her treason while yet you were far off.'

440   "So I spoke, and at once he addressed me, giving an answer:
'So you, even to your own wife now, never be gentle,
nor disclose to her every matter of which you are certain,
but tell something of it and the rest keep carefully hidden.
But there will be no murder for you from a woman, Odysseus,

445   for a most sound understanding and sensible thoughts in her mind has
noble Ikários' daughter Penelope, thoughtful and prudent.
She was a newlywed bride at the time we left her behind us,
when we went to the war, and upon her breast was a child still
speechless, who I suppose now sits and is numbered among men—

450   fortunate youth, for his own dear father, returning, will see him;
he will embrace his father as well, as is fitting and proper.
Mine was a wife who never allowed me to fill up my eyes with
even a glance at my son; for before I saw him, she killed me.
Something else I will tell you, and you keep this in your mind now:

455   secretly, not in the open, to that dear land of your fathers
bring your galley, because there is faith no longer in women.
But come now, tell me this and recount it exactly and fully,
if perchance you have heard that my son somewhere is alive yet,
whether perhaps in Orchómenos town or in sandy-soiled Pylos,

460   whether perhaps with the lord Meneláos he is, in broad Sparta,
since nowhere on the earth can the noble Orestes have perished.'
    "So he spoke, and in turn I addressed him, giving an answer:
'Atreus' son, why ask me of these things? Nothing I know of
whether he lives or has died; it is bad to say words that are windy.'

465   "So as we stood, each making reply to the other in somber
words and lamenting our woes, pouring out great tears in abundance,
then came near me the spirit of Peleus' scion Achilles,
that of Patróklos and that of the noble Antílochos also,
then that of Ajax, the man who surpassed in beauty and stature

470   all of the Dánaäns other than Peleus' excellent scion.

When that soul of the swift-footed scion of Aíakos knew me,
sorrowing then he spoke, and in these winged words he addressed me:
    "'Zeus-sprung son of Laërtes, Odysseus of many devices,
what still mightier deed, rash man, will you plan in your spirit?
475 How did you dare come down into Hades' dominion, wherein live
dead men lacking their senses, the shadows of wornout mortals?'
    "So he spoke, and in turn I addressed him, giving an answer:
'Peleus' scion Achilles, far greatest among the Achaians,
I have come here in need of Teirésias, if any counsel
480 he might speak, that I might reach Ithaka, rugged and rocky,
since I have not yet neared the Achaian domain, nor have set foot
yet in my country, but ever have woe. But Achilles, there is no
man of the past more blessèd than you, nor yet of the future,
seeing that when you were living, we Argives granted you honors
485 equal the gods'; now here with the shades you are mighty in power.
So even though you are dead, be not too troubled, Achilles.'
    "So I spoke, and at once he addressed me, giving an answer:
'Speak to me not about death so soothingly, brilliant Odysseus;
I would prefer to be working the earth, hired out to another,
490 even a landless man, whose living is far from abundant,
than to be lord over all of the phantoms of those who have perished.
But come now, of that excellent son of mine tell me the story,
whether or not he followed as champion into the battle.
If you have heard anything about excellent Peleus, tell me,
495 whether among those numerous Mýrmidons yet he is honored
or if instead they do him dishonor in Hellas and Phthia
since he is held by his hands and his feet in the trammels of old age;
nor am I there as protector beneath bright Helios' sunbeams,
being the man I was when once in the broad Troäd I
500 slaughtered the best of the fighters, defending the Argive peoples.
If being such I could enter my father's abode but an instant,
then I would make most hateful my might and my terrible hands for
any of those who use him with force and deprive him of honor.'
    "So he spoke, and in turn I addressed him, giving an answer:
505 'First, about excellent Peleus I have heard nothing to tell you;
but of the other, your child Neoptólemos, dearly belovèd,
all of the truth I now will relate to you, just as you bid me,
since it was I myself who upon my hollow and balanced
ship took him out of Skyros to follow the well-greaved Achaians.
510 Then, when in front of the city of Troy we pondered our counsels,

always the first he spoke, and he did not err in advising;
godlike Nestor and I were alone his masters in council.
But then, when we Achaians would fight on the plain of the Trojans,
never did he stay back in the host of the men, in the melee,
515 but far forward he rushed, in his bravery yielding to no one;
many indeed were the men he killed in the terrible combat.
Though of them all I will not now speak to you, nor will I name them,
such was the number of troops he slaughtered defending the Argives,
yet what a man was the hero Eurýpylos, Télephos' scion,
520 whom he killed with a sword; and around him many Keteían
comrades were killed on account of the gifts once given a woman.
He was the handsomest man I have seen after glorious Memnon.
But at the time we went in the horse that Epeíos had built, we
chiefs of the Argives, and I was assigned the command over all things—
525 whether to open the doors of the tight-built ambush or close them—
there then all of the others, the Dánaän leaders and princes,
wiped off tears from their faces; the legs underneath them were trembling;
but as I looked with my eyes, I never at all saw him turn
pallid and lose his beautiful coloring, nor did he ever
530 wipe off tears from his cheeks, but he often implored me to let him
go forth out of the horse; and the hilt of his sword and his spear shaft,
heavy with bronze, he handled, envisioning woe for the Trojans.
But then, after we ransacked the steep-built city of Priam,
taking a share of the loot and a fine prize, onto his ship he
535 went unscathed: he had not been hit by a sharp-pointed brazen
spear nor wounded in hand-to-hand combat, such as in warfare
often occurs while Ares is raging in random destruction.'
    "So I spoke, and the spirit of Aíakos' swift-footed scion
stalked off, moving in long strides over the asphodel meadow,
540 joyful at what I had said, that his son was a glorious hero.
    "Then yet others, the souls of the bodies of men who had perished,
stood there grieving beside me, and each one told me his troubles.
Only the spirit of Ajax the scion of Télamon stood far
distant from me, still angry because of the victory which I
545 won over him when there by the ships I disputed with him those
arms of Achilles, the prize set up by the lady his mother.
Children of Trojans determined the verdict, and Pallas Athena.
How I wish that I never had won in such a contention!
It was because of the arms that the earth closed over a mighty
550 head, that of Ajax, who in his looks and his deeds outrivaled

all of the Dánaäns other than Peleus' excellent scion.
Thus I addressed him, speaking in words of persuasion and comfort:
      "'Ajax, child of the faultless Télamon, even in death you
would not forget your anger at me on account of the baneful
555   armor? The gods made it a great woe for the Argives,
since so mighty a bulwark in you was destroyed: we Achaians,
after you died, incessantly mourned you, as much as we ever
grieved for Achilles the scion of Peleus: nor is there any
other to blame, except Zeus; for the army of Dánaän spearmen
560   he so terribly hated, to bring this doom down upon you.
But come close to me, Lord, so that you may be able to hear my
word and my story; subdue your wrath and your obstinate spirit.'
      "So I spoke, and he gave no reply, but along with the other
souls of the bodies of men who had perished, to Érebos parted.
565   Yet in spite of his wrath, he might have addressed me or I him,
but in the breast inside me the heart still felt a desire for
seeing the spirits of others among those folk who had perished.
      "Minos there I observed, who was Zeus's illustrious scion,
holding a scepter of gold, as he sat there issuing judgments
570   over the dead; they questioned the lord concerning their cases,
sitting and standing about in the broad-gated palace of Hades.
      "Next then, right after him, I noticed enormous Oríon
rounding the wild beasts up all over the asphodel meadow,
those which he had himself once killed in the loneliest mountains,
575   holding in hand his club, bronze-studded, forever unbroken.
      "Títyos also I saw, who was Earth's son, honored and famous;
he lay there on the ground; over nine full roods he was sprawling.
Seated at each of his sides, two vultures were tearing his liver,
plunging inside of the caul; with his hands he could never repel them,
580   for he had dragged off Leto, the glorious consort of Zeus, as
she through lovely Panópeus passed on a journey to Pytho.
      "Then too I saw Tantalos there, with his wretched afflictions,
where he stood in a lake; up against his chin it was splashing.
Thirstily he kept seeking a drink, but he never could get one,
585   since when the old man, wishing to drink, bent over to swallow,
always the water would vanish and be swallowed up, and around his
feet black earth would appear, as a god kept drying the moisture.
Fruit poured down on his head from the trees there, lofty and leafy—
pear trees, fine pomegranate trees, apple trees, glorious-fruited;
590   fig trees laden with sweetness, and olives of flourishing fullness—

234

but when the old man wanted to take them, stretching his hand out,
quickly a wind tossed them to the clouds all dappled with shadows.

    "Then too I saw Sisyphos there, with his wretched afflictions;
he with both of his hands kept pushing uphill a prodigious
595 rock—with his hands and his feet he shoved as he scrambled,
heaving the rock on high to the summit—but always, when he was
almost pushing it over the crest, with force it rebounded;
swiftly again to the flatland the shameful and pitiless stone rolled.
Then once more he would heave it, exerting his strength as the sweat poured
600 off of his limbs; dust rose from his head bent downward in labor.

    "Next after him I recognized Herakles, strong and courageous—
only his phantom, for he himself is among the immortal
gods enjoying abundance, with Hébè of beautiful ankles,
daughter of powerful Zeus and of Hera, whose sandals are golden.
605 Souls of the dead like birds kept clamoring loudly about him,
scattering every way in fright; black night he resembled,
holding his bare bow ready, upon its bowstring an arrow,
dreadfully glaring around like one who will shoot any moment.
Terrible round and about his chest was the baldric, a sword belt
610 wrought out of gold, and upon it marvelous things had been fashioned:
bears, wild boars of the forest, and savagely glowering lions;
conflicts and hard-fought battles and murders and slaughters of heroes.
Would that the man who conceived with his craft that terrible baldric
never had crafted the work, nor ever will craft any other!
615 Quickly he recognized me when he with his eyes had observed me;
sorrowing then he spoke, and in these winged words he addressed me:

    "'Zeus-sprung son of Laërtes, Odysseus of many devices,
ah, poor wretch, you also endure some evil misfortune,
such as the one I suffered beneath bright Helios' sunbeams.
620 I was a scion of Zeus, son of Kronos, and nevertheless had
boundless affliction, for I was subjected to one who was mortal,
much my inferior; difficult tasks he inflicted upon me.
Once he dispatched me hither to lead out the dog, for no other
task, he considered, would ever be harder for me to accomplish;
625 yet I led up the dog, took him from the dwelling of Hades—
Hermes himself escorted me hither, and bright-eyed Athena.'

    "So having spoken he went back into the palace of Hades.
I however continued to stand right there, in the hope some
other would come, of the heroes who perished in earlier ages.
630 Now I would have beheld those earlier men, as I wanted—

Theseus first and Peiríthoös too, the gods' glorious offspring—
but before that, those numberless tribes of the perished about me
thronged with a dreadful and deafening clamor, and green fear seized me,
lest some head of a Gorgon, an ugly and terrible monster,
635 queenly Perséphonè send upon me from the dwelling of Hades.
Straightway then I went on the galley and bade the companions
get themselves on board and at once cast off the stern cables.
Hastily then they boarded and took their seats at the oarlocks;
then on the river of Ocean a swell of the current conveyed us,
640 rowing at first with the oars, but a fair wind blew on us later.

BOOK 12

"But then, after the galley had left that stream of the river
Ocean and come once more to the billowing sea of the broad ways
and to the isle of Aiaía, on which are the home and the dancing
floors of the early-born Dawn and the place of the sun at its rising,
5   when we arrived at the shore, on the sand we ran out the galley,
then ourselves disembarked on the tide-heaped sand of the seashore;
there on the beach we slept and awaited the glorious morning.

"Soon as the Dawn shone forth rose-fingered at earliest daybreak,
then I bade the companions to go to the palace of Circè
10   so they could bring to the galley the body of dead Elpénor.
Quickly we cut down logs where the shoreline jutted the sharpest,
then we buried him, grieving, and shed great tears in abundance.
But then, when we had burned up the dead man's body and weapons,
heaping a grave mound there and upon it dragging a pillar,
15   we then planted his well-shaped oar on the top of the grave mound.

"So we attended to each of the matters; nor as we returned from
Hades' domain did Circè ignore us, but quickly she came down,
carefully dressed and prepared, and with her came household servants
carrying bread and abundance of meat and of glistening red wine.
20   Thus then, standing among us, the glorious goddess addressed us:

"'Foolhardy men, who have gone down alive to the dwelling of Hades,
thus twice dying, when others among men die but the one time.
But come, eat the provisions and drink your fill of the wine now,
right here, all day long; and tomorrow as Dawn is appearing,
25   you will set sail: I will tell you about your voyage and show you
everything, so that by no wretched and wicked devices
either at sea or on land you will suffer affliction and sorrow.'

"So she spoke and in us persuaded the valorous spirits.
So it was that for that whole day till the hour of the sunset,
30   we sat banqueting there on meat unstinted and sweet wine.

Soon as the sun went down and the shadows of night came upon us,
they lay down to their sleep on the shore by the ship's stern cables.
Me, however, she took by the hand, and apart from my much loved
comrades sat me, and lay down beside me, and asked me of each thing;
35   everything I related to her then fitly and truly.
Finally Circè the queen spoke words like these and addressed me:
   "'Thus these things are all brought to completion; but you now listen,
hear what I say, and a god will himself cause you to recall it.
First as you go on your way you will come to the Sirens, who always
40   seek to enchant all men, whoever arrives at their island.
That man who without knowing approaches the Sirens and hears their
voices, for him his wife and his infant children will never
stand at his side when he goes back home nor rejoice at his coming;
but with a high clear thrilling refrain those Sirens enchant him
45   as they sit in the meadow; around them is heaped an enormous
number of men who are rotting, the skin falling off of their bodies.
But drive past them and onward; and softening honey-sweet wax by
kneading it, stop up your comrades' ears, so that none of the others
listen to them; but if you should yourself keep wanting to listen,
50   then let them bind you tight hand and foot, upright on the mast box
in the swift ship, with the ends of the rope tied fast to the mast pole,
so you can listen in blissful delight to the songs of the Sirens.
Should you beseech your companions and give them orders to free you,
let them instead then fasten you down with additional bindings.
55   "'Then when past them and onward the comrades have driven the galley,
from that point I will now no longer continue advising
which of the two ways you will be following: you must yourself take
counsel in your own mind; but about both ways I will tell you.
For in one place there are rocks overhanging the sea, and against them
60   roar huge billows of Ámphitrítè, the dark-faced goddess;
these are called Planktai, Wandering Rocks, by the blessed immortals.
There no creatures with wings pass by, not even the timid
doves which carry to Zeus our father ambrosial victuals,
never, but always the sheer smooth rock takes one from among them;
65   but then another is sent by the father to make up the number.
That place never a ship full of men has arrived and escaped from;
rather, the timbers of ships and the bodies of men are alike tossed
hither and yon by the waves of the sea and the ruinous firestorms.
Past it indeed one seafaring ship did manage the voyage—
70   she was the Argo, renowned among all, as she sailed from Aiëtes.

She also would have been thrown swiftly upon the enormous
rocks but was sent on past by Hera, for she loved Jason.
    "'Then on the other way, there are two crags; and of these, one reaches
up to the great wide sky with a sharp peak; around it a dark blue
75 cloud stands; never does this draw back, nor ever does clear sky
hold to the peak of the crag, not even in summer or autumn;
nor could a man, a mere mortal, ascend it or stand on its summit,
never, although he had twenty hands, twenty feet for the climbing.
For it is smooth sheer rock, as if polished on every surface.
80 There in the midst of the crag is a cave all misty and murky,
turned to the quarter of dusk, toward Érebos; this is the place which
you would be steering your hollow ship past, brilliant Odysseus.
Never could even a vigorous man who shot with his bow from
out of a hollow ship reach up to the wide-mouthed cavern.
85 There inside dwells Skylla, appallingly howling and snarling;
hers is a voice that resembles the yelp of an unweaned puppy,
but she herself is a horrible monster; and no one would ever
take any pleasure to see her—not even a god—if he met her.
Twelve legs hang from her body, and all unjointed and dangling;
90 six necks also she has, very long, with a fearful and ugly
head on each of the necks; and in each head, teeth are in three rows,
thick-set, crowded together, and full of the darkness of slaughter.
Down in the hollow cave she plunges as far as her middle,
while her heads she holds outside of the dreadful abysm.
95 There she fishes and searches around her crag for the dolphins,
dogfish, and any more sizable creature, if ever she catches
one of the multitudes blustering Ámphitrítè is feeding.
There no sailors can boast that they ever escaped with a vessel
quite unharmed; for in each of her heads, that monster is bearing
100 one of the men she has snatched right out of a dark-prowed galley.
    "'You will observe that the second crag lies much lower, Odysseus,
close to the other, and you might shoot across it with an arrow.
Growing upon it and blooming with leaves is a great wild fig tree;
under it sacred Charýbdis is sucking the black seawater.
105 Thrice each day she expels it, and thrice she dreadfully sucks it
back down: never must you be found there when she is sucking,
since then even the shaker of earth could not save you from evil.
But sail swiftly along very close to the headland of Skylla,
driving your ship on past, since it is at least far better
110 six of the comrades to mourn in your galley than all at the same time.'

"So did she say; then I spoke out to her, giving an answer:
'Come now, goddess, if you can indeed say this to me truly,
whether in some way I may escape from destructive Charýbdis
while I ward off the other when she makes prey of my comrades.'

115   "So I spoke, and at once made answer the glorious goddess:
'Obstinate man! Is your heart once more so concerned with the deeds of
war and its toil? Will you not yield even to gods undying?
She is in fact not mortal but rather immortal in evil,
fearful and cruel and savage, and not someone to be fought with;
120   nor is there any defense—by far the best course is to flee her.
For if you stay very long by the cliff in helmet and armor,
I am afraid that again she will rush out upon you and seize you;
then for her numerous heads, of the men she will take the same number.
But drive forcefully onward and call on Krátaïs loudly,
125   Skylla's mother, who bore her to be an affliction to mortals;
she will prevent her from making the second attack she would rush to.

"'Then you will come to the isle of Thrinakia, there where the many
cattle of Helios graze and the great fat sheep, in the pastures—
seven the herds of his cattle, as many the beautiful sheep flocks,
130   each one fifty in number; and none of them bear any offspring,
nor do they ever diminish; and goddesses serve as the herders—
nymphs with beautiful hair, Lampétië and Phaëthoúsa,
born to the High Lord Helios by resplendent Neaíra.
When that lady their mother had born these daughters and raised them,
135   she sent them to inhabit the distant Thrinakian island,
there to keep watch of the sheep and the crooked-horned cows of their father.
These if you leave uninjured and keep your minds on returning,
you may arrive in Ithaka yet, though suffering evils.
But if you injure the cattle, then I foretell the destruction
140   both of the ship and the comrades; if you yourself should avoid it,
late and unhappily you will return, losing all of your comrades.'

"So she spoke, and at once upon us came Dawn of the gold throne.
Then that glorious goddess returned up into the island.
Straightway then I went on the galley and bade the companions
145   get themselves on board and at once cast off the stern cables.
Hastily then they boarded and took their seats at the oarlocks;
sitting in rows, they beat their oars on the silvery sea-brine.
Then as a noble companion to follow the dark-prowed galley
Circè of beautiful hair, dread goddess with speech of a mortal,
150   sent us a favoring wind which filled up the bellying canvas.

240

Finally, when on the ship we had seen to each piece of the tackling,
we sat down, and the wind and the steersman guided her forward.
Then I spoke and addressed the companions, grieving in spirit:
"'Friends, not only for one or for two is it needful to know these
155 prophecies uttered to me by Circè the glorious goddess;
now therefore I will tell you, that knowing of them we may either
die or avoid our death and escape from the fate that is threatened.
This is the first of her orders: the song of the marvelous Sirens
we must carefully shun, and as well their flowery meadows;
160 only myself she ordered to hear their voices; but bind me
tightly in tough harsh bonds so that there, upright on the mast box,
I stand firm, with the ends of the rope tied fast to the mast pole.
Should I beseech you ever and give you orders to free me,
you should instead then fasten me down with additional bindings.'
165   "So it was that I spoke and revealed all this to the comrades;
meanwhile the well-built galley arrived at the isle of the Sirens,
speedily sailing ahead, for the favoring breezes impelled her.
Suddenly then did the wind stop blowing, and there was a windless
calm all over the sea as a god lay the waves in a slumber.
170 Quickly the comrades stood, then furling the sails of the galley,
stowed them away in the hollow ship; straightway at the oars they
sat and with blades smooth-polished of fir wood whitened the water.
Meanwhile I with my keen bronze sword cut wax from a large round
cake into small-sized pieces and kneaded them well in my stout hands.
175 Quickly the wax grew softer as that great pressure compelled it
and as the rays of Hypérion's son, Lord Helios, warmed it;
going to all in turn I stopped up the ears of the comrades.
They at once bound me tight hand and foot, upright on the mast box
there in the ship, with the ends of the rope tied fast to the mast pole;
180 they themselves sat beating their oars on the silvery sea-brine.
But when we were as far from the isle as a man's shout carries,
speedily driving, the swift-sailing galley did not escape notice
as she approached them; a sweet clear song they started to sing me:
"'Come to us here, the Achaians' renown, much honored Odysseus,
185 drawing the ship right in, so that you to our voices may listen.
This is a place past which in his dark ship no one has ever
driven, before from our lips he has heard the melodious voices;
but having taken delight, he goes on greater in knowledge.
We know all of the things that the Argive troops and the Trojans
190 there in the broad Troäd by the gods' wills labored and suffered;

we know all that is on the much nourishing earth generated.'

    "They spoke, wafting their beautiful voices across, and my spirit
wanted to listen to them, and I bade the companions to free me,
nodding at them with my brows; they fell yet more to their rowing.

195   Then straightway standing up, Eurýlochos and Perimédes
bound me tighter and fastened me down with additional bindings.
When we had finally sailed on past them and then from the galley
we no longer were hearing the voice or the song of the Sirens,
then straightway my trustworthy comrades removed from their ears that

200   wax with which I had stopped them and set me free from my bindings.

    "When we had left that island behind us, then of a sudden
I saw smoke and a great high wave, and I heard a loud roaring.
Out of the hands of the terrified comrades all of the oars flew,
noisily splashing the currents of water; the galley remained right

205   there, since they with their hands no longer were moving the sharp oars.
Going along through the ship I started to rouse the companions,
standing beside each man, with words of persuasion and comfort:

    "'Friends, hitherto we have not been ignorant yet of afflictions;
no more evil is this, in fact, than the time that the Cyklops

210   penned us up in his hollow cave by his violent power;
but yet even from there by my valor and counsel and wit we
made our escape, and I think these things too we will remember.
Come now, just as I say, let all of us heed and obey it.
You with your oars keep beating the turbulent depth of the sea-brine,

215   while at the oarlocks holding your seats, so that Zeus may in some way
grant that we take our flight and escape this ruin before us.
Steersman, thus do I bid you: because you manage the steering
oar on the hollow ship, put this in your heart and remembrance:
keep on heading the ship outside of the spume and the swelling

220   breakers, and steer your course for the crag, lest she begin rushing
yonder before you know it and into disaster you plunge us.'

    "So I spoke, and at once they heeded the words I had uttered.
Nothing I said about Skylla, the insurmountable danger,
lest the companions, despite my orders, in terror should leave off

225   rowing and shelter themselves inside all huddled together.
Then indeed I forgot about Circè's difficult order,
when she commanded that I not arm myself for a struggle;
dressing myself instead in my glorious armor and taking
two long spears in my hands, I went on the deck of the galley

230   nearest the prow, since it was from there I supposed rock-dwelling

Skylla would first be seen, who would bring such bane to my comrades.
Nowhere at all was I able to glimpse her; my eyes became weary
gazing at every place in the sea cliff misty and murky.

    "Thus we were sailing along in the narrows, lamenting and wailing;
235 Skylla was on one side; on the other was sacred Charýbdis—
dreadfully she kept sucking and swallowing down the saltwater;
then whenever she vomited forth, like a pot on a great fire,
all would be roaring and seething with turbulence—high on the topmost
peaks of the crags both sides of the strait was the seafoam falling.
240 But then, when yet again she would swallow the salt seawater,
she would appear all seething inside, and around her the rock was
dreadfully bellowing; down underneath her, the earth with its dark blue
sand would appear to the eyes of the comrades; and green fear seized them.
So toward her we kept on looking, and fearing destruction;
245 meanwhile out of the hollow galley were six of my comrades
snatched by Skylla, the ones who in might of their hands were the strongest.
So as I looked back into the swift ship, toward the companions,
I already discerned their feet and their hands up above us
as on high they were lifted; and they called out to me, shouting,
250 speaking my name for the last time then, much grieving in spirit.
As when upon some headland a fisherman using a long rod
throws out morsels of meat as the bait for the littler fishes,
casting the horn of a field ox out to the sea as a line shield,
then as he takes one, throws it on shore all gasping and writhing,
255 so to the rocks now, gasping and writhing, the comrades were lifted.
There in the doorway then she devoured them as they kept screaming,
stretching their hands toward me in their last most terrible struggle.
That was the one most piteous thing I saw with my eyes while
searching the paths of the sea, out of all the afflictions I suffered.
260   "But when we had escaped from the rocks and from fearful Charýbdis,
Skylla as well, then quickly we came to the excellent island
held by the god; therein were the beautiful broad-browed cattle,
many and fine fat flocks of the High Lord Helios' keeping.
Then indeed, while out on the sea in the dark-hued ship, I
265 heard the loud lowing of cattle as they were returned to the farmyard,
also the bleating of sheep; and the words came into my spirit,
those that the blind soothsayer, the Theban Teirésias, uttered,
those of Aiaían Circè, for both had insistently ordered
me to avoid this island of Helios who delights mortals.
270 Then I spoke and addressed the companions, grieving in spirit:

"'Listen to my words, comrades, despite these evils you suffer,
so that about Teirésias' prophecies I may inform you,
and of Aiaían Circè's, for they insistently ordered
me to avoid this island of Helios who delights mortals;
275   for, they declared, therein a most terrible evil awaits us.
No, keep driving the black ship out and away from the island.'
   "So I spoke, and the hearts inside them were utterly shattered.
Straightway then in malevolent words Eurýlochos answered:
'You are relentless, Odysseus, surpassing in strength, and your limbs are
280   never fatigued—no doubt you are made entirely of iron—
you who will not even let your companions, exhausted with labor
and with a longing for sleep, go out on the land where again we
might in the tide-washed isle make ready a savory dinner,
but as we are, in the swift-falling night you bid us to wander,
285   driven away from the isle on the seaway misty and murky.
After the nightfall, dangerous winds, the destroyers of vessels,
start up. Where could a man get away from a sheer destruction
if some tempest of wind came down upon him of a sudden—
Notos the south wind or Zephyr the blusterer, those that above all
290   break ships up into bits, though the sovereign gods do not wish it?
But instead let us now take heed of the darkness of nighttime;
let us prepare our dinner, remaining beside the swift galley;
then, embarking at dawn, we will sail out onto the broad sea.'
   "So Eurýlochos spoke, and the other companions assented.
295   Straightway I was aware that a god was devising us evils;
raising my voice I spoke, and in these winged words I addressed him:
'Being alone as I am, Eurýlochos, how you compel me!
But come, all of you now must swear me an oath of the strongest:
if somehow we should find some herd of his cattle or mighty
300   flock of his sheep, no man in the evil of recklessness will
slaughter a cow or a sheep, not one of them: rather, in quiet
ease eat only the victuals that deathless Circè provided.'
   "So I spoke, and at once they swore it, as I had demanded.
But then, when they had sworn and had brought their oath to completion,
305   there in a hollow harbor we anchored the well-made galley,
close to some sweet fresh water; at once from the galley the comrades
disembarked, then skillfully they made ready a dinner.
When they had quite satisfied their appetites, drinking and eating,
then they remembered and started lamenting our much loved comrades,
310   those whom Skylla had snatched from the hollow galley and eaten;

244

over the men as they wailed there came a delectable slumber.
But in the night's third watch, when the stars turned down toward setting,
then as we slept, cloud-gathering Zeus set turbulent stormwinds
raging in furious tempest; the land and the seaway alike he
315 hid in a thick cloud cover, and night rushed down from the heavens.
Soon as the Dawn shone forth rose-fingered at earliest daybreak,
bringing the ship on shore, to a hollow cavern we dragged her;
there were the beautiful seats of the nymphs and the floors for their dancing.
Then I called an assembly and spoke among all the companions:
320   "'Friends, now since there is plenty to eat and to drink in the swift ship,
let us hold off from the cattle, lest something of evil we suffer;
these are the cattle and great fat sheep of a god to be dreaded,
Helios, who looks down over all things, listens to all things.'
    "So I spoke, and the valorous spirits in them were persuaded.
325 All month Notos the south wind steadily blew, nor did any
other wind ever arise except for the east and the south winds.
So for as long as they still had plenty of food and of red wine,
they held off from the cattle, desiring to go on living.
But when all of the stores from the galley at last were depleted,
330 then they went on the hunt, of necessity ranging the country,
taking whatever came into their hands, both fishes and game fowl,
using their bent fishhooks, because hunger afflicted their stomachs.
Then I went away into the island, in order that I might
ask of the gods whether one might show me a way for returning.
335 But having gone through the island and left the companions behind me,
carefully washing my hands where there was a shelter from winds, I
raised my prayer to the gods, all those who live on Olympos;
onto me then they poured sweet sleep, down over my eyelids.
Meanwhile Eurýlochos broached this evil advice to the comrades:
340   "'Listen to my words, comrades, despite these evils you suffer:
every manner of dying is hateful to miserable mortals,
but most wretched by hunger to die and encounter our doomsday.
But come now, let us drive off the best among Helios' cattle,
offering them to the gods, the immortals who hold the broad heaven.
345 If we should ever arrive in Ithaka, land of our fathers,
we will at once to the High Lord Helios build a resplendent
temple and put inside it our offerings many and noble;
if he instead in feelings of rage for his lofty-horned cattle
wants to destroy our ship, and the other gods follow his wishes,
350 I would prefer all at once by gulping a wave to lose life breath

than to be drained of my strength a long time on a desolate island.'
　　"So Eurýlochos spoke, and the other companions assented.
Then straightway they drove off the best among Helios' cattle,
bringing them nearer; for not very far from the dark-prowed galley,
355　grazing the grass, were the beautiful crooked-horned broad-browed cattle.
There around them they stood; to the gods they raised their entreaties,
plucking the tenderest leaves from an oak tree, lofty and leafy,
for on the well-benched galley they had no more white barley.
Straightway, after they prayed, they slaughtered the victims and flayed them,
360　then they cut off the thighs and in thick fat covered them over,
making two layers, and morsels of flesh they fastened upon them;
nor did they have any wine to pour on as the victims were burning,
but made water libations; and all of the innards they roasted.
After the thighbones burned and the men partook of the entrails,
365　then they cut up the rest, and on stakes they spitted the pieces.
　　"Finally, after delectable sleep flew away from my eyelids,
I set forth to the swift ship then and the shore of the deep sea.
But on the way, as I came up close to the tractable galley,
then did the pleasant aroma of flesh new-roasted surround me;
370　raising a moan, I called out loud to the gods undying:
'Oh Father Zeus and the rest of the fortunate gods, ever-living,
how to my ruin have you thus lulled me in pitiless slumber!
Such an enormous deed my comrades devised as they waited.'
　　"Swiftly to High Lord Helios then went, bearing report how
375　we had slaughtered his cows, Lampétiè, nymph of the long robe.
Then straightway in the wrath of his heart he addressed the immortals:
'Oh Father Zeus and the rest of the fortunate gods, ever-living,
work my revenge on the men of Odysseus the son of Laërtes,
who in their arrogance killed those cattle of mine over which I
380　always rejoiced as I climbed on high to the star-filled heaven,
then also when again out of heaven to earth I was turning.
If for my cattle to me they pay no fitting requital,
sinking to Hades' domain, I will shine on those who have perished.'
　　"Answering him in return spoke forth the cloud-gathering god Zeus:
385　'Helios, do you instead keep shining among the immortals
and among mortals, the men who dwell on the grain-giving plowland.
Their swift ship I will strike with a scintillant bolt of my lightning
soon, in the midst of the wine-dark seaway, and break it to pieces.'
This I heard from Kalýpso, the goddess with beautiful tresses,
390　she herself having heard it, she said, from the messenger Hermes.

246

"Then when I had arrived down there at the sea and the galley,
standing by each in turn, I rebuked them; nevertheless, no
remedy we could discover: the cattle already were slaughtered.
Straightway then to the comrades the gods showed manifest omens:
395   hides of the cattle were creeping; the flesh on the spits began mooing,
that both roasted and raw; and the lowing was like that of cattle.

"Then for the next six days my trustworthy comrades were feasting
there on the best of the cattle of Helios which they had stolen.
But when Zeus son of Kronos to those days added the seventh,
400   finally then did the wind stop raging and blowing a tempest;
going on board straightway, we sailed out onto the broad sea,
raising the mast upright and the white sails hoisting upon it.
When we had left that island behind us and there was no other
land in sight anywhere, but the sky and the sea all around us,
405   then was a dark cloud raised by the scion of Kronos and stationed
over the hollow ship; and the sea turned murky beneath it.
Not much time did she keep running on, for the west wind Zephyr
suddenly came down shrieking and blowing a powerful tempest;
then from the mast a tumultuous storm gust tore off the forestays,
410   both of the ropes, and the mast fell backward, and all of the gear was
thrown down into the hold; at the stern of the galley the mast pole
crashed on the head of the steersman and instantly battered together
all of the bones of his head, and at once he dropped like a tumbler
down from the deck, and his valorous spirit abandoned the bone frame.
415   Zeus then thundered and hurled at the galley a bolt of his lightning;
struck by the lightning of Zeus, the entire ship spun in a circle,
brimstone filling her up; and the comrades fell from the galley.
Then like cormorants, crows of the sea, they were carried about on
waves all around the black galley: the god took away their returning.

420   "I kept walking about in the ship, till the surge of the waves had
loosened the sides from the keel; thus stripped quite bare the waves bore it.
Out of the keel was the mast pole shattered, and down upon that then
tumbled the backstay, which was a rope strong-braided of oxhide—
therefore with it I fastened together the keel and the mast pole;
425   sitting on them, I was carried ahead by the ruinous stormwinds.

"Finally then did the west wind leave off blowing a tempest;
quickly the south wind came; for my heart it carried affliction,
lest I should once more measure the way to destructive Charýbdis.
All that night I was carried along; then just at the sunrise,
430   back to the headland of Skylla I came and to dreadful Charýbdis,

who that moment was sucking and swallowing down the saltwater;
but then, raising myself high up on the tall wild fig tree,
there I held, like a bat I clung to it—neither was any
place I could set my feet in security, nor could I climb it,

435 since its roots held far from my feet and the branches were lifted
high and were massive and long, so that they overshadowed Charýbdis.
There I steadily held till the time that the mast and the keel she
vomited upward again; and to me so longing they came back
late—when a man gets up from assembly to go to his dinner

440 after deciding the numerous quarrels of youthful contenders,
that indeed was the time those timbers appeared from Charýbdis.
Then from above letting go of my hands and my feet, I was borne down
into the midst of the water and plunged out beyond the long timbers;
sitting upon them then, with my hands I paddled the narrows.

445 Not again now did the father of men and of gods let Skylla
see me, for else I would never have fled from a sheer destruction.

  "Nine days then I was carried from there; on the tenth in the nighttime
to the Ogygian island the gods brought me, where Kalýpso
dwells, of the beautiful hair, dread goddess with speech of a mortal.

450 There she loved me and saw to my wants. Why tell you this story?
I have already recounted it yesterday, here in your palace,
both to yourself and your virtuous wife; and to me it is hateful
telling again some tale that has once been told to perfection."

BOOK 13

So did he say; then all of the people were hushed in silence,
held by the charm of the tale all over the shadowy chamber.
Then Alkínoös spoke these answering words and addressed him:
"Seeing, Odysseus, that you have at last come here to my bronze-floored
5 high-roofed house, I believe that without any other reverses
you will return to your home, though much indeed you have suffered.
These things now I will say to each man of you, urging to action
all you chiefs who are drinking the glistening wine of the elders
always, here in the palace, and hearing the tales of the singer:
10 clothes for our guest lie here in a coffer of exquisite polish,
also gold of most intricate crafting and all of the other
gifts that the counselors of the Phaiákians put inside it.
Come now, let us each give him a great tripod and a cauldron
man by man, and collect from the people the price of the presents,
15 for to one man unpaid such generous giving is painful."
So Alkínoös spoke, and his words found favor among them;
then they departed to rest for the night, each one to his own house.
Soon as the Dawn shone forth rose-fingered at earliest daybreak,
carrying bronzeware useful to men they sped to the galley.
20 Going himself through the ship, Alkínoös sacred in power
stowed it away well under the benches, that none of the comrades
while they wielded their oars in driving ahead would be hampered.
Then they went to Alkínoös' house to prepare for a dinner.
Now for the people, a bull Alkínoös sacred in power
25 offered to Kronos' son Zeus of the dark cloud, ruler of all things.
Burning the flesh of the thighs, they dined on a sumptuous dinner,
taking delight, and among them was singing the godlike singer
held in esteem by the people, Demódokos. Meanwhile Odysseus
turned his head to the radiant sun very often, for he was
30 eager for it to go down: he wanted to start on the journey.

So when a man feels longing for supper—his wine-dark oxen
all day over the field have been dragging the well-jointed plowshare—
welcome to him does the light of the sun go down, so that he may
go to his home for his supper, and while he is going his knees ache,

35   so for Odysseus the light of the sun went down very welcome.
Straightway then he addressed the Phaiákians, lovers of rowing;
but to Alkínoös mainly he spoke to declare what he wanted:
     "Lord Alkínoös, most distinguished among all the people,
make libation and send me away untroubled, and may you

40   fare well: now have the things that my heart most wished been accomplished,
means of conveyance and gifts most dear; may the gods in the heavens
make them blessings for me. When I go back home, may I find my
wife quite blameless, with those who are dear to me healthy and happy.
Then may you who remain bring comfort and cheer to your wedded

45   wives and your children, and may the gods make prosperity follow
all your endeavors, and may no evil be found in your people."
     So did he say; they all then assented and bade that it be so,
granting the stranger conveyance, for properly he had addressed them.
Finally then did mighty Alkínoös speak to the herald:

50   "Mix up wine in the bowl, Pontónoös, then pour it out for
all these men in the hall, so that, praying to Zeus our father,
we may convey this guest back home to the land of his fathers."
     So did he say; Pontónoös, mixing the wine, honey-hearted,
served it to all as he stood beside them; they poured a libation

55   out to the fortunate gods, the immortals who hold the broad heaven,
right from the chairs where they sat. Then stood up noble Odysseus;
into the hand of Arétè he placed his two-handled goblet;
raising his voice he spoke, and in these winged words he addressed her:
"Now may you fare well, Queen, unceasingly, up to the time old

60   age shall arrive, then death: those things all people must suffer.
I now take my departure, but you have joy in the household,
in your children and people and King Alkínoös also."
     So spoke noble Odysseus and went out over the threshold.
Mighty Alkínoös sent forth one of his heralds with him to

65   lead him the way to the swift ship then and the shore of the deep sea.
Women attendants Arétè dispatched to accompany him there:
one of them carried a well-washed mantle as well as a tunic;
then to a second she handed the well-made coffer to carry;
third came another one taking the red wine out and the victuals.

70   Then when they had arrived down there at the sea and the galley,

straightway the glorious escorts received those presents and put them
into the hollow galley, with all of the drink and the victuals.
Then for Odysseus they spread out above on the deck of the hollow
galley a rug and a cover, that he might sleep unawakened,
75 just at the stern; and he went himself on the galley and lay down
silently. They sat down, each one in his place at the oarlocks,
all in order, and then from the hole in the stone unfastened the cable.
When to the rowing they bent, with the oar blades tossing up sea-brine,
onto the eyes of Odysseus a sleep fell, gentle and grateful,
80 sweetest of sleeps, unawaking, and death most closely resembling.
Meanwhile the galley—as when on a plain four stallions, together
harnessed, have all been roused to a run by the blows of a whiplash,
leap up high in a gallop and swiftly accomplish the journey—
so was the stern of the ship raised up, and behind her was seething
85 darkly a great high wave of the deep sea rumbling and booming.
Safely and steadily she ran ahead: not even a hawk or
falcon, the nimblest of creatures with wings, would have stayed her companion,
so very swiftly she ran as she cut through waves of the deep sea,
bearing a man with a mind most like to the gods' in devices;
90 many the pains in his heart in the time gone by he had suffered,
cleaving a way through battles of men and the troublesome billows;
now quite still he was sleeping, of all he had suffered forgetful.

   Just at the time when rises the brightest of stars, that above all
comes and announces the light of the dawn in the earliest daybreak,
95 finally then did the seafaring ship touch shore on the island.

   There is a harbor in which an old man of the sea-brine, Phorkys,
lives, in the Ithakan country; the two promontories around it
rise from the sea in abrupt steep headlands but slope to the harbor.
These are protection against the enormous waves that the squally
100 winds raise outside; and inside, without any cable the well-benched
galleys can stay whenever they come near enough to be anchored.
Up at the head of the harbor, its long leaves spread, is an olive
tree; nearby is a cavern, delightfully misty and shadowed,
sacred retreat of the nymphs called Naíades, nymphs of the fountains.
105 There inside of the cavern are two-handled vases and mixing
vessels of stone; and to them come bees to deposit their honey.
Inside also are stone-wrought looms, very long, and upon them
nymphs weave fabric of deep-sea purple, a wonder to look at.
Inside are waters that always flow. Two doors it possesses:
110 one to the north wind pointed, providing an entrance for people;

one also, more divine, to the south wind—never do men go
into the cave this way, but the passage is for the immortals.
  There, as they knew of the harbor before, they drove in the galley;
she then ran clear up to the half of her length on the seashore,
115 speeding—of rowers so strong were the arms that were driving her forward.
They stepped out of the well-benched galley and onto the dry land;
first from the hollow ship they lifted and carried Odysseus,
taking along with the hero the rug and the shimmering cover,
set him there on the sand, still quite overcome in his slumber.
120 Then they took out the goods that the noble Phaiákians gave him,
when he had left to go home, by the working of great-souled Athena.
These they placed in a heap right next to the trunk of the olive
tree, well out of the road, lest some wayfarer perchance should
come upon them and despoil them before Odysseus awakened.
125 Then they started to go back home. But the shaker of earth had
never forgotten the threatening words he had earlier spoken,
menacing godlike Odysseus; and he asked Zeus for his counsel:
  "Oh Father Zeus, no longer will I here among the immortal
gods be honored when mortals there are who show me no honor,
130 those Phaiákians, though from my own blood they are descended.
I had decided that now, when Odysseus had suffered so many
ills, he would go back home—his return I never had wholly
taken from him, for before you promised and nodded agreement—
they brought him as he slept in a swift ship over the seaway,
135 then in Ithaka set him and gave him numberless presents,
treasures of bronze and of gold in abundance and well-woven garments,
much, so much that Odysseus from Troy could never have brought it
if he had come unharmed with his own fair share of the booty."
  Answering him in return spoke forth the cloud-gathering god Zeus:
140 "Well, earth-shaker of widespread strength, what word do you utter!
Not in the least do the gods dishonor you. It would be harsh for
us to assail with dishonors the oldest of gods and the noblest.
If giving in to his might and his violence, one of those men is
failing to honor you, yours is the vengeance forever hereafter.
145 Do whatever you wish and whatever your heart finds pleasing."
  Speaking to him then answered the great earth-shaker Poseidon:
"Lord of the dark cloud, I would at once act just as you tell me
but that I always respect your spirit, avoiding its anger.
What I wish is to smash the Phaiákians' beautiful ship as
150 home from the convoy now on the seaway misty and murky

she is returning—so they might cease and desist from providing
convoy to men—and to hide their city behind a huge mountain."
    Answering him in return spoke forth the cloud-gathering god Zeus:
"Brother, to me in my spirit the best way seems to be this one:
155   just when all of the people observing the ship from the city
see her driving ashore, then turn her into a stone that
looks like a swift ship close to the land, so that all of the people
marvel; but do not hide their city behind a huge mountain."
    But then, soon as the great earth-shaker Poseidon had heard this,
160   straightway to Scheria, where the Phaiákians live, he set forth.
There he waited; the seafaring ship came close to the island,
speedily running ahead; and beside her came the earth-shaker;
turning her into a stone, he rooted her there to the bottom,
pressing her down with the flat of his hand, and away he departed.
165   Then began speaking in these winged words, each one to the others,
those men famed for their ships, the Phaiákians, long-oar wielders—
thus would one of them say as he looked at another beside him:
"Well! Who was it that fastened the swift ship down in the seaway
while she was driving for home? Just now she had made her appearance."
170   So would one of them say, as they did not know what had happened.
Then Alkínoös spoke and addressed them, giving them counsel:
"Well now, a prophecy spoken of old has indeed come upon me,
that of my father, who used to predict that Poseidon would one day
grudge it of us that for every man we provide safe convoy—
175   said that a beautiful ship of Phaiákian men on the way back
home from a convoy once on the seaway misty and murky
he would smash and would hide our city behind a huge mountain.
So did the old man say; now this is all being accomplished.
Come now, just as I say, let all of us heed and obey it:
180   cease the conveyance of every man when anyone ever
comes to our city; and then, let us make sacrifice to Poseidon,
choosing the best twelve bulls from the herd, so that he in his mercy
might not hide our city behind an immense tall mountain."
    So did he say; they feared the prediction and made the bulls ready.
185   So for the people and land, the Phaiákian leaders and princes
stood there raising their supplicant prayers to the lordly Poseidon,
gathered around his altar.—And meanwhile noble Odysseus
woke from his sleep in the land of his fathers and did not know it,
he had been gone so long; for the goddess Pallas Athena,
190   daughter of Zeus, poured round him a mist, so that she might make him

unrecognizable, then might tell him of all the conditions,
so that his wife, his friends, and his townsmen would not recognize him,
not till the suitors had given requital for every trespass.
Therefore everything looked different now to their master,
195   pathways uninterrupted and harbors to anchor all vessels,
towering rocks and luxuriant trees profusely ablossom.
Quickly he sprang to his feet, stood viewing the land of his fathers;
then straightway he uttered a groan; with the palms of his hands he
struck at his thighs, both sides, and in these words made lamentation:
200   "Ah me, what are the people whose land this time I have come to?
Are they bold and offensive and violent, lacking in justice,
or are they kindly to strangers, endowed with a god-fearing conscience?
Where shall I take these many possessions? And as for myself, where
now shall I wander? I wish they had stayed in their own place,
205   with the Phaiákians: I would have met with another exalted
king who would have received me as friend, sent me on my journey.
Now I neither can see where to put them, nor can I simply
leave them here on the beach, lest they become booty for others.
Well now, I can be sure the Phaiákian leaders and princes
210   were not quite altogether so prudent in counsel or honest,
leading me off to a different land; they said they would take me
over to Ithaka, bright in the sun, but they did not achieve it.
Now may Zeus the protector of supplicants punish them, he who
oversees other men too, chastising whoever transgresses.
215   But come now, let me count up my treasures and see if they did not
carry off some for themselves when they left in the hollow galley."
        So he spoke, and the beautiful tripods then and the cauldrons
he counted up, and the gold and the garments of elegant weaving.
Nothing of them did he miss; but he mourned for the land of his fathers,
220   creeping along on the shore of the deep sea rumbling and booming,
heavy with lamentation. But close to him then came Athena,
seeming in shape like a man in his youth, some herder of sheep flocks,
tender and delicate—just such looks as the children of lords have—
wearing a well-made mantle in two folds over her shoulders;
225   sandals she wore on her glistening feet; in her hand was a spear shaft.
As he observed her Odysseus rejoiced, and he came up to meet her;
raising his voice he spoke, and in these winged words he addressed her:
        "Friend, since you are the first I have met with here in this country,
greetings to you, and without any evil intent may you meet me—
230   rather, preserve these things, and preserve me too, for I make my

prayer to you as to a god, and I come to your knees in friendship.
Truthfully speak to me now about these things, so that I know well
what is this land, what country, and what men here are the natives.
Is it perhaps some sun-bright island, or is it a foreland
235   sloping away from the fertile mainland and down to the sea-brine?"
        Speaking to him made answer the goddess bright-eyed Athena:
"You are a simpleton, stranger, or else from afar you have come here,
if indeed you are asking about this land: it is not so
nameless as you imply, for the people who know it are many,
240   whether of those who have their abodes toward dawn and the sunrise
or among those in the west toward dusk, all misty and murky.
It is a rough land, true, not fit for the driving of horses;
yet it is not very poor, even though not broad in extension.
For on the island is food in wondrous abundance, and on it
245   wine grows too; there is always rain and a nourishing dewfall.
It is an excellent pasture for cattle and goats; there is timber,
every sort, and upon it are yearlong watering places.
Therefore, stranger, as far off as Troy has Ithaka's name gone,
which they say is a long way away from the land of Achaia."
250   So she spoke; he rejoiced, much-suffering noble Odysseus,
taking delight in the land of his fathers as it was described by
Pallas Athena the daughter of Zeus who carries the aegis.
Raising his voice he spoke, and in these winged words he addressed her,
though he did not speak truth but instead held back on his story,
255   always wielding the thought in his breast with the greatest of cunning:
"I have indeed heard talk about Ithaka even in broad Crete,
far off over the sea; now I myself have arrived here
with these goods that you see; and as many I left with my children,
fleeing to exile after I murdered Idómeneus' much loved
260   son Orsílochos swift on his feet, who had always in broad Crete
triumphed over all grain-eating men in swiftness of running—
killed him because he wanted to take away all of my booty
won from the Trojans, for which such pains in my heart I had suffered
cleaving a way through battles of men and the troublesome billows,
265   since I would not do his father the favor to serve as his henchman,
there in the Trojans' domain, but instead led other companions.
Him as he came back in from the fields I struck with a bronze-tipped
spear, having waited in ambush close to the road with a comrade;
it was a very dark night which covered the sky, so that no man
270   noticed us there, and his life I took without anyone knowing.

But then, when I had killed that man with my sharp bronze weapon,
straightway boarding a ship, to the lordly Phoenician crew I
made supplication and gave them loot to their hearts' satisfaction;
I implored them to take me to Pylos and set me ashore there
275 or to illustrious Elis, in which the Epeíans are rulers.
Then however the force of the wind drove them from those places—
wholly against their will, for they did not wish to deceive me.
So after wandering thence, we at last came here in the nighttime.
Hastily we rowed into the harbor; in none of us was there
280 even a thought about dinner, as much as we wanted to take it;
but as we were, we all disembarked from the galley and lay down.
Finally then sweet sleep overcame me, as I was exhausted;
out of the hollow galley they took my possessions and put them
down in the place I was lying asleep on the sand of the seashore.
285 Then they embarked and departed to well-inhabited Sidon;
meanwhile I was left here in this land, in my spirit lamenting."

So did he say; then, smiling, the goddess bright-eyed Athena
stretched out a hand to caress him; she likened her form to a woman
beautiful, noble in stature, and skilled in glorious handwork;
290 raising her voice she spoke, and in these winged words she addressed him:
"Crafty indeed would he be, a real trickster, whoever outstripped you
in all manner of wiles, even if some god were against you—
obstinate, various-minded, insatiably clever, not even
here in your land would you ever desist from your lying and cheating,
295 telling the fraudulent tales that are dear to your soul from the ground up.
But come now, let us talk no longer of this, for we both are
skilled in our cunning: as you among all mortal men are the best by
far in counsel and speeches, so I among all of the gods am
famous for wit and for wily devices; but you did not know me,
300 Pallas Athena the daughter of Zeus, who always, in all your
labors and woes, stand right at your side, watch over your safety,
I who made you belovèd of all the Phaiákian people.
Now I have come here so that with you I may weave some scheme, then
hide those treasures away that the noble Phaiákians gave you
305 when you departed for home—it was by my thought and intention—
speak to you too of the numerous woes you are destined to suffer
here in your well-built house: of necessity you are to bear them.
Neither to any among all the women and men in the palace
say you have finally come from your wandering; rather in silence,
310 suffering many afflictions, endure men's violent doings."

　　　　Speaking to her then answered Odysseus of many devices:
"It is most difficult, goddess, for even the cleverest mortal,
when he meets you, to know you; for anything you may resemble.
This I know very well, that before, you treated me kindly,
315　while in Troy we were fighting a war, we sons of Achaians.
But when at last we ransacked the steep-built city of Priam,
we went away in the ships, and a god dispersed the Achaians;
then I never beheld you, daughter of Zeus, or discerned you
coming aboard my galley to ward off any affliction,
320　but with the heart much wounded inside of my breast I would always
keep on roaming about till the gods freed me from my troubles—
till that time in the fertile land of Phaiákian men you
gave me heart with your words and yourself led me to the city.
Now at your knees, by your father I supplicate you—for I do not
325　think I have landed in sun-bright Ithaka, but to another
land have again been diverted; I think you are teasing and mocking,
when you tell me I am, so that you may delude my spirit—
tell me whether in truth I have reached the dear land of my fathers."
　　　　Speaking to him made answer the goddess bright-eyed Athena:
330　"Always indeed you have in your breast some thought such as this one;
therefore now, when you are unhappy I cannot forsake you,
seeing that you are polite, keen-witted, and firm of intention.
For very gladly would some other man, come back from his travels,
hurry to go to his dwelling to see his wife and his children.
335　You however desire not even to learn or ask questions
yet, until you make proof of your bedmate, who is as ever
sitting inside your house and for whom both the days and the nights are
always dolefully wasted away in the tears she is shedding.
Never at all I doubted your case, but I knew in my heart that
340　you would return to your home, having quite lost all your companions;
nevertheless I did not want to contend with Poseidon,
who is my father's brother, who laid up wrath in his spirit,
goaded to anger because you robbed his dear son of his eyesight.
Come, I will show you the layout of Ithaka, so that you trust me.
345　This is the bay where abides an old man of the sea-brine, Phorkys;
here at the head of the harbor, its long leaves spread, is an olive
tree; nearby is a cavern delightfully misty and shadowed,
sacred retreat of the nymphs called Naíades, nymphs of the fountains.
This to be sure is the spacious and high-arched cavern in which you
350　used to perform for the nymphs many hecatombs full and effective;

that peak there is in fact Mount Nériton, clad in its forests."
      So having spoken, the goddess scattered the mist, and the land showed.
Then indeed he rejoiced, much-suffering noble Odysseus,
happily greeting the country and kissing the clod-rich plowland.
355   Straightway he uttered a prayer to the nymphs while lifting his hands up:
"Naíades, nymphs of the springs, you daughters of Zeus, I could never
think I would look upon you; for the present, rejoice in my loving
prayers; yet we will as well give gifts, as so often aforetime,
if the spoil-plundering daughter of Zeus most graciously lets me
360   go on living myself and my dear son raises to manhood."
      Speaking to him then answered the goddess bright-eyed Athena:
"Take heart—do not allow these matters to trouble your spirit,
but in the deepest recess of the marvelous cave let us straightway
place these treasures in safety, where they may await your returning.
365   Then ourselves let us think of the best way matters could happen."
      So having spoken, the goddess went into the shadowy cavern,
searching around in the cave for recesses; and meanwhile Odysseus
brought it all nearer, the gold and the indestructible bronze ware,
also the well-made clothes the Phaiákians gave him at parting;
370   then he put them away, and a stone was placed in the door by
Pallas Athena the daughter of Zeus who carries the aegis.
      Both of them then sat down by the trunk of the sacred olive
tree and began to consider the arrogant suitors' destruction.
Speaking to him then opened the goddess bright-eyed Athena:
375   "Zeus-sprung son of Laërtes, Odysseus of many devices,
take thought how you may lay your hands on the shameless suitors
who for the last three years have been lording it over your palace,
courting your godlike bedmate and giving her presents for marriage;
she over your homecoming is always mourning in spirit;
380   holding out hope to them all, to each man she offers her promise,
sending them messages, while her own mind holds other intentions."
      Speaking to her then answered Odysseus of many devices:
"Ah me! I would indeed most surely have died by an evil
doom right here in my halls, like Atreus' son Agamemnon,
385   if about all this, goddess, you had not fitly informed me.
But come, weave some scheme so that I may repay them their evils;
you stand beside me and put audacity into my spirit,
just as when we undid Troy's glistening circlet of towers.
Bright-eyed goddess, if you were as eagerly standing beside me,
390   willingly I would in fact fight even against three hundred

men with you, lady and goddess, if you would be ready to aid me."
　　Speaking to him then answered the goddess bright-eyed Athena:
"I will indeed stay close to your side, I will never forget you,
all of the time we are bent on this business: yes, and I think this
395　vast earth soon will be spattered about with the blood and the brains of
some of the men, those suitors who now are devouring your substance.
Come, I will make you unrecognizable now to all mortals:
first on your flexible limbs your beautiful skin I will shrivel;
then on your head I will ruin the light brown hair, and in tatters
400　dress you, such that a man who saw you wear them would shrink from;
next I will cloud those eyes, until now so noble in beauty,
so that to all of the suitors you seem ill favored and wretched—
and to your bedmate as well as the child you left in your palace.
As for yourself, before anything else, go visit the swineherd
405　who is the guard of the pigs and to you feels loyal as ever;
he is a friend to your child and to constant Penelope also.
You will discover him sitting beside your pigs, which are seeking
provender close to the Ravens' Rock by the spring Arethoúsa,
feeding to please their hearts on the acorns and drinking the shadowed
410　water, the things which nourish the fat on hogs to abundance.
You stay there and inquire about each thing, sitting beside him.
Meanwhile to Sparta, the country of beautiful women, will I go
summon Telémachos home, your son so belovèd, Odysseus;
to Lakedaímon of spacious domains, Meneláos' abode, he
415　went to find out what news there is of you, whether you live still."
　　Speaking to her then answered Odysseus of many devices:
"Why did you not tell him—for you know all things in your spirit?
Was it perhaps so that he too wanders and suffers afflictions
out on the desolate seaway and other men eat up his substance?"
420　　Speaking to him then answered the goddess bright-eyed Athena:
"Now as concerns that boy, in your heart be not overanxious.
I myself was his guide, so that he might garner a noble
fame going there; and he has no trouble but sits in the house of
Atreus' son at his ease; by his side lie gifts in abundance.
425　Meanwhile the young men sit on a dark ship waiting in ambush,
wanting to kill him before he arrives in the land of his fathers.
No such thing, I am certain, will happen, before earth covers
some of the men, those suitors who now are devouring your substance."
　　Thus when Athena had spoken to him, with her wand she touched him:
430　first on his flexible limbs his beautiful skin she shriveled;

then on his head she ruined the light brown hair, and she covered
all of his limbs with the skin of a man grown old and decrepit;
next she clouded his eyes, until then so noble in beauty;
then she put other clothes around him, a foul rag and a tunic
435 tattered to pieces and filthy, with foul smoke noisomely sullied;
then in a swift-footed deer's great hide stripped clean of its hair she
wrapped him about, and she gave him a staff and a pitiful knapsack
riddled with slashes and holes, with a rope well-twisted to hold it.

Thus, their planning completed, the two of them parted; and she then
440 went to divine Lakedaímon, in search of the son of Odysseus.

BOOK 14

Meanwhile up from the harbor Odysseus was taking the rough path
over the forested land through hills to the place where Athena
showed him the excellent swineherd lived, he who, of the servants
noble Odysseus possessed, most carefully guarded his substance.
5   There he found him sitting in front on the porch where the courtyard
lay with a high wall built around it in a place with a wide view,
handsome and large, and a clearing surrounded it; this had the swineherd
built himself for the pigs while his master was out of the country,
at some distance away from his mistress and agèd Laërtes,
10 quarrying stones for the wall, and he used thornbushes for coping.
Just outside he had driven in stakes one way and the other,
close-set, crowded in files, of the black core cut from an oak tree;
then inside of the yard twelve pigsties he had constructed,
set quite close to each other, as beds for the swine; and in each one
15 fifty of these ground-slumbering hogs were enclosed and protected,
females tending their young; but the males all passed the night outside,
they being fewer by far, for the godlike suitors were ever
eating them, cutting them down in number, as always the swineherd
sent them the best among all those hogs well-nourished and fattened.
20 So of the males there were now three hundred and sixty remaining;
near them the dogs, very like wild animals, always were sleeping,
four of them, who had been reared by the swineherd, leader of people.
As for himself, on the soles of his feet he was fastening sandals,
cutting the hide of an ox of a suitable color; the other
25 swineherds had gone out herding the pigs one way or another,
three of them; as for the fourth, he had sent him away to the city
under constraint: he was taking a boar to the arrogant suitors,
so, having made sacrifice, they could sate their hearts on the swine flesh.
All of a sudden the clamorous dogs caught sight of Odysseus;
30 loudly they barked as they rushed upon him, but Odysseus with ready

wit sat down on the ground; from his hands he let fall the cudgel.
There by his own pen he would have suffered a pain most shameful
but that the swineherd, hastily following them on his swift feet,
rushed to the courtyard gate; from his hands he let fall the oxhide.

35   Shouting at them, he scattered the dogs one way or another,
rapidly volleying stones, and at once he spoke to his master:
     "Old man, surely the dogs would have almost torn you to pieces
all of a sudden, and you would have showered reproaches upon me.
So have the gods now given me other afflictions and sorrows,

40   since for a godlike master I sit here grieving and making
lamentation, and these sleek hogs I am rearing for other
men to consume, while that one is no doubt longing for victuals,
roaming a city and land of a people of alien language,
if he perhaps still lives, still looks upon Helios' sunlight.

45   But come follow me into the hut, old sir, so that once you
quite satisfy your heart with the food and the wine, you may tell me
where you have come from now, how many the woes you have suffered."
     So said the excellent swineherd and led him into his cabin;
taking him in, he gave him a seat, first strewing some shaggy

50   branches and over them spreading the unshorn skin of a wild goat,
shaggy and broad, from his own bedstead, and Odysseus rejoiced that
he had received him so, and said these words, calling upon him:
"May Zeus grant to you, friend, and the rest of the gods who live always,
what you especially want, so heartily you have received me."

55   Then in answer to him you spoke, Eumaíos the swineherd:
"Stranger, for me it would not be right to dishonor a stranger
though one baser than you came, for every stranger and beggar
has the protection of Zeus; and a gift, though little, but welcome,
lies in our power to give, since this is the custom of servants

60   always, fearful whenever they have young men as their masters
governing them; for the gods have detained that man from returning,
him who would have befriended me kindly and given me treasures
such as a master in gentle benevolence gives to a servant—
his own house and a family lot and a much wooed woman—

65   who toils hard for his lord, and a god too prospers the labor,
as he has prospered for me this labor that I persevere in.
Therefore much would the master have given me had he grown old here;
but he is lost! Oh, would that the kindred of Helen had perished,
brought to their knees, since many a man's knees she has unsinewed!

70   For to exalt Agamemenon's honor he also had gone to

262

Ilion, land of fine horses, that he might battle the Trojans."
 So he spoke, and at once with a belt he bound in his tunic;
then he went to the sties where the herds of his swine were all penned up;
choosing from there two hogs, he brought both inside and killed them.
75 Then he singed them and carved them; on stakes he spitted the pieces.
When he had roasted it all, to Odysseus he took it and set it
close to him, hot on the spits, then strewed white barley upon it.
When he had mixed up honey-sweet wine in an ivy-wood wine bowl,
facing him he himself sat, and he spoke these words to arouse him:
80 "Eat now, stranger, the food that a servant is able to give you,
young pork; meanwhile the sleek fat hogs are devoured by the suitors,
nor in their hearts do they think of divine supervision or pity—
deeds so cruel and reckless the fortunate gods do not favor;
no, they honor the justice of men and the virtuous actions.
85 Even if hostile men, strong enemies, go and invade some
foreign dominion and Zeus grants them much booty and plunder,
loading it onto their ships they leave and return to their own homes—
even on their hearts falls strong fear of divine supervision.
These men surely have learned—they have heard some rumor from heaven—
90 that man's wretched destruction, for they do not want in the proper
manner to court his wife nor to go back home, but at ease they
eat up his goods in arrogant wantonness, stopping at nothing,
seeing that however many the nights and the days Zeus sends down,
never they sacrifice one sole victim or even two only;
95 as for the wine, they draw it off freely and wantonly waste it.
For beyond words is the size of his livelihood: none of the heroes
had so big a one, neither of those on the shadowy mainland,
nor here in Ithaka; nor among mortals do twenty together
have such measureless wealth. In fact, I will tell you the numbers:
100 there on the mainland, twelve herds of cattle; as many the sheep flocks;
so too the droves of his swine, and as many the widespread goat flocks,
which both strangers and his own herdsmen take out to pasture.
Here on the island the widespread goat flocks, eleven in all, are
pasturing far from the city, and good men see to their keeping—
105 every day each brings some animal in to the suitors
always, choosing the well-nourished goat which seems to him finest.
As for myself, I watch over these swine here and protect them;
carefully choosing from all of the hogs, I send them the finest."
 He spoke; gratefully eating and drinking the meat and the wine in
110 haste and in silence, Odysseus was nourishing bane for the suitors.

When he had finished the meal and had pleased his heart with the victuals,
filling the cup out of which he had drunk, to the swineherd he gave it
brimful of wine—and the other received it, rejoicing in spirit.
Raising his voice he spoke, and in these winged words he addressed him:
115   "Friend, what man was it then who used his resources to buy you,
one so exceedingly wealthy and mighty as you have recounted?
You say he to exalt Agamemnon's honor has perished—
tell me, in case it chance that I know one such as you speak of.
For Zeus only can know, and the rest of the gods who live always,
120   if I have seen him and might bring news; I have roamed many places."
         Speaking to him then answered the swineherd, leader of people:
"Old man, never was there any wanderer who has arrived here
carrying news about him who persuaded his wife and his dear son.
In any case, such wandering men in need of relief will
125   tell false stories and are not willing to say what the truth is.
Yes, whoever arrives in the country of Ithaka, roaming,
makes his way to my mistress; and there he babbles his falsehoods.
She in her kindness receives him well and inquires of the details;
then as she makes lamentation, the tears fall down from her eyelids,
130   as is right for a wife when her husband is lost in a strange land.
Quickly would you also, old man, make up such a story
if somebody would give you a mantle and tunic as clothing.
But as for him, already the dogs and the swift-flying birds must
surely have torn the skin off of the bones, and the spirit has left them,
135   or in the seaway fish have devoured him; all of his bones lie
out on the mainland now, in the deep sand covered and hidden.
So out there he has perished, and many the pains he has made for
all of his friends thereafter, especially me, for I will not
find so gentle a master again, wherever I travel—
140   no, not even if back at the house of my father and mother
I should arrive, where first I was born, where they themselves raised me.
Nor do I mourn for them now so deeply, as much as I yearn to
see them with my own eyes back there in the land of my fathers;
no, I am held by a longing for him who is absent, Odysseus.
145   Though he is not here, stranger, I feel much awe as I say his
name, for he loved me greatly and cared about me in his spirit;
yet I call him my brother and lord even when he is distant."
         Then spoke answering him much-suffering noble Odysseus:
"Friend, since you altogether deny it and still do not think that
150   he is about to return, and your spirit is ever mistrustful—

yet not so will I say it in mere words but with an oath, that
thus is returning Odysseus: and let the reward for the good news
be mine straightway after he comes and has entered his palace;
clothe me then in a mantle and tunic, the finest apparel.
155 Though I am much in need, before that day I will take nothing.
Equally hateful to me as are Hades' gates is the man who
yields to his poverty so that he babbles agreeable falsehoods.
Zeus be witness the first of the gods, and this table of friendship,
also the hearthstone of faultless Odysseus to which I have come now:
160 all these things will be brought to fulfillment as I am declaring.
Sometime within this same moontide will Odysseus arrive here—
one moon just having waned and the next moon just at its onset.
He will return to his house and exact his revenge on whoever
there are depriving his wife and his glorious son of their honor."

165   Then in answer to him you spoke, Eumaíos the swineherd:
"Old man, never will I pay you a reward for the good news,
nor will Odysseus again come back to his house; but at ease now
drink your wine; let us think about other things. Do not remind me
further about those, for in my breast my heart is afflicted
170 painfully anytime someone mentions my kindhearted master.
As for your oath, we will let it alone, though I hope that Odysseus
finally will come back, as both I and Penelope want him,
so too agèd Laërtes and godlike Telémachos wish it.
Unforgettingly now I mourn for the son that Odysseus
175 fathered, Telémachos: after the gods raised him like a sapling—
so that I thought among men he would be to his own dear father
nothing inferior, marvelous both in body and beauty—
then some immortal afflicted the mind well-balanced within him,
or else it was a man; and he left to seek news of his father,
180 going to sacred Pylos; the glorious suitors await in
ambush for him as he comes back homeward, so that the race of
godlike Arkeisios dies, is in Ithaka utterly nameless.
Nevertheless let us leave him alone, whether he be taken
or he escape and the hand of the scion of Kronos protect him.
185 But come now, old man, you tell me about your own sorrows—
truthfully speak to me now about these things, so that I know well:
Who are you? Whence do you come? What city is yours, and what parents?
Then upon what sort of ship did you come here? How did the sailors
bring you to Ithaka? What did they claim as their names and their nation?
190 For it was certainly not on foot, I suppose, that you came here."

Speaking to him then answered Odysseus of many devices:
"These things I will indeed now tell you exactly and fully.
If now there were sufficient provisions to last us a long time—
victuals and sweet wine both—so that we might stay in the cabin
195 quietly eating our meals while others were doing the labor,
in that case, till a whole year passed I could easily keep on
telling the tale of the cares of my heart yet never complete it,
all those miseries which by the will of the gods I have suffered.
     "Mine is a race, I tell you, for whom broad Crete is the homeland.
200 I was the child of a prosperous man; there were numerous other
sons also in the house, of legitimate birth; by a wedded
wife they were nourished and born—I was born of a mother acquired as
concubine; yet did the scion of Hylax, Kastor, of whom I
claim my descent, prize me as he did his legitimate offspring.
205 At that time, as a god by the people of Crete he was honored
for his success and his wealth and his sons so famous in glory.
Then however the powers of death came upon him and bore him
off to the palace of Hades; his proud high-spirited children,
having divided his goods, cast lots to determine the portions;
210 little indeed was the part they gave and the house they assigned me.
Yet I married a wife from among men rich in possessions,
thanks to my valorous strength, since I was not idle or worthless,
nor would I flee from a battle; but now at the end it is all gone.
Nevertheless I think if you look you can see from the stubble
215 what was the grain, for an ample abundance of misery holds me.
Ares himself endowed me with courage, and so did Athena,
power to break through ranks whenever I chose for an ambush
excellent men, thus sowing the seeds of the enemy's anguish.
Never in me did the valorous heart anticipate dying,
220 but I would leap out far in the foremost and take with my spear that
man of the enemy who in his running was slower than I was.
Such I was in the fighting, but never did I love working
nor any household tending that brings up glorious children.
But instead it was well-oared ships that were dear to me always,
225 also battles and arrows and javelins, skillfully crafted—
baleful things that indeed cause others to shudder in terror.
Yet they were dear to me—maybe a god put them in my spirit,
since each different man takes pleasure in different actions.
Even before those sons of Achaians departed for Troy, I
230 served nine times as the leader of men and of swift-faring galleys

going against outlanders, and much was the loot that I met with.
Some of it, pleasing the spirit, I chose, then afterward got much
more by lot; and my house grew quickly; and soon thereafter
I had become respected and feared among all of the Cretans.
235 But at the time wide-thundering Zeus concocted the hateful
journey that would unsinew the knees under many a fighter,
then they urged upon me and renowned Idómeneus both to
lead them forth in the galleys to Ilion; nor was there any
means by which to refuse—the harsh talk of the people compelled us.
240 There nine years we were fighting the war, we sons of Achaians;
but in the tenth we ransacked the city of Priam and started
homeward then with the ships, and a god dispersed the Achaians.
But for myself, poor wretch, Zeus Counselor plotted afflictions;
for I remained there, taking delight in my children and wedded
245 wife and the treasures I carried, for one month only, and then my
spirit demanded that I take ship and depart toward Egypt,
fully equipping the galleys, along with my godlike comrades.
Nine ships then I equipped, and the people were quickly collected.
Then for the next six days my trustworthy comrades continued
250 feasting, and numerous victims I gave them, in order that they might
sacrifice them to the gods and as well make ready their dinners.
Then on the seventh day we boarded the galleys and started
sailing from broad Crete under a steady and favoring north wind,
effortlessly, as if going downstream, so that never a single
255 one of my galleys was injured, but quite unscathed and unailing
we sat there, and the wind and the steersmen guided us forward.
On the fifth day we arrived in the fair-flowing river of Egypt;
inside the river of Egypt I anchored the tractable galleys.
Then straightway, to begin, I ordered the trustworthy comrades
260 there by the galleys to stay and to keep watch over the galleys,
also commanded the scouts to go up to the lookout places.
They soon yielded to wanton excess, and pursuing their impulse,
suddenly started to ransack the beautiful fields of the men of
Egypt and carried away their women and innocent children,
265 killing the men. Then quickly the outcry came to the city;
there they heard the commotion and just at the earliest daybreak
came against us—with the footmen and chariots all of the plain filled,
and with the flashing of bronze; then Zeus the great thunderbolt-hurler
threw foul panic among my companions, and none could endure to
270 stand there facing the foe; for on all sides evils beset us.

There they killed a large number of us with their sharp bronze weapons;
others they led off living, to work for them under compulsion.
Zeus however himself brought about in my spirit a notion,
thus—I wish I rather had died and encountered my doomsday
275 there in Egypt, for still more trouble was waiting to take me—
straightway then from my head I put off the well-made helmet,
dropped my shield from my shoulders, the spear from my hand I threw down.
Then I went in the way of the king, in front of his horses;
clasping his knees I kissed them, and he took pity and spared me,
280 onto his chariot put me, and homeward carried me weeping.
Many a man came rushing at me with a spear made of ash wood,
eager to kill me at once, for indeed they were dreadfully angered.
Yet he kept them away, so showing respect for the wrath of
Zeus the protector of strangers, who hates foul deeds above all things.
285   "In that place I stayed seven years, and I gathered together
many possessions among the Egyptians, for all of them gave some.
But when the eighth year came in the course of the seasons' revolving,
then there came a Phoenician man, well-skilled in deceptions,
one of those cheats who had wrought much ill already among men.
290 He by his cunning persuaded and led me until in Phoenicia
we had arrived, at the place where lay his own house and possessions.
There at his home I remained for a year's full circle of seasons.
But when finally all of the months and the days were completed,
after the year had revolved and the seasons again were returning,
295 he put me on his seafaring ship and to Libya took me,
falsely advising that I might carry with him a good payload,
so once there he could sell me and get an enormous profit.
Under constraint I went on the ship, though I was suspicious.
She ran ahead then, under a steady and favoring north wind,
300 in midsea, above Crete; but for them Zeus plotted destruction.
When we had left Crete far in the distance and there was no other
land in sight anywhere, but the sky and the sea all around us,
then was a dark cloud raised by the scion of Kronos and stationed
over the hollow ship; and the sea turned murky beneath it.
305 Zeus then thundered and hurled at the galley a bolt of his lightning;
struck by the lightning of Zeus, the entire ship spun in a circle,
brimstone filling her up; and the crew all fell from the galley.
Then like cormorants, crows of the sea, they were carried about on
waves all around the black galley: the god took away their returning.
310 Zeus however himself, though I had great pain in my spirit,

then put into my hands that dark-prowed galley's enormous
mast unbroken and strong, that I might yet flee from affliction.
This I embraced in my arms and was borne by the winds of destruction,
carried ahead nine days; on the tenth, in the darkness of nighttime,
315   to the Thesprotians' country a great wave billowing brought me.
There the Thesprotians' ruler, the hero Pheidon, provided
all of my needs unpaid, for his own dear son came upon me
quite overcome by cold and exhaustion and guided me homeward,
holding me up with his hand till we came to the house of his father;
320   then he at once put garments around me, a mantle and tunic.
There I heard of Odysseus; for that king said he had shown him
welcome and made him his friend on his way to the land of his fathers.
Also he showed me the many possessions Odysseus had gathered,
treasures of bronze and of gold and of iron, laborious metal.
325   Even to ten generations would these feed, each in succession—
such great treasures of his lay there in the halls of the ruler.
He said Odysseus had gone to Dodóna in order to listen
there to the counsel of Zeus from the oak tree, lofty and leafy,
how he could go back homeward to Ithaka's fertile dominion
330   now he had long been away—in the open or else in secret.
In my presence he swore—in his house poured out a libation—
there was a ship drawn down to the sea, and the comrades were ready
who would convey him back to the much loved land of his fathers.
But before that he sent me away, for a ship of Thesprotian
335   men chanced then to set sail for Doulíchion, wealthy in wheat fields.
There to Akastos the king he bade them give me conveyance
carefully; but in their minds an iniquitous plot about me found
favor, that I yet come to the utmost pain of affliction.
So when the seafaring galley had sailed far out from the mainland,
340   straightway for me they started devising the day of enslavement.
First they took off my mantle and tunic, the clothes I was wearing;
then they put other clothes around me, a foul rag and a tunic
tattered to pieces, at which with your own eyes you are now looking.
They in the evening landed at sun-bright Ithaka's farmsteads;
345   there they bound me and tied me down in the well-benched galley
tightly, with cord well-twisted and strong; then they, disembarking,
hastily took their evening meal on the shore of the deep sea.
Then however the gods themselves unfastened my bindings
easily; wrapping my head all around in a rag to conceal it,
350   I slid down on the plank, well-polished, and lowered my chest just

into the sea, and with both of my hands I started a breaststroke,
swimming, and so got out very quickly, away from the others.
When I had climbed to a place with a copse of thick-flowering bushes,
cowering, I lay down; they meanwhile, mightily groaning,
355 wandered in search; but as nothing of profit, or so it appeared, would
come from additional looking, they finally went once again back
onto the hollow galley: the gods themselves had concealed me
easily; then they led me and brought me along to the homestead
of an intelligent man, for my lot now still is to live on."

360   Then in answer to him you spoke, Eumaíos the swineherd:
"Ah, unfortunate stranger, the spirit in me you have troubled,
telling me all these things, how much you have suffered and wandered.
Yet I believe it without due order—nor will you persuade me—
when you speak of Odysseus. Why need such a person as you are
365 fruitlessly tell these lies? I know myself very fully
of the return of my lord, how he by all of the gods was
hated so much that they did not bring him down among Trojans
or in the arms of his friends after he had wound up the warfare.
Then would a funeral mound have been heaped by all the Achaians;
370 so for his son also had he won great fame for the future.
Now ingloriously has he been snatched up by the stormwinds.
I meanwhile live apart with the pigs here, nor do I ever
go to the city except when prudent Penelope sometimes
asks me to come in town when a message has come in from somewhere.
375 But then they sit there at my side and inquire of the details,
both those who are lamenting about their lord so long absent
and those who take joy in devouring his goods without payment.
But no pleasure for me it is to inquire or to question,
since one time an Aitolian man tricked me with a story:
380 he after killing a man, then wandering far on the earth, had
finally come to my house; I embraced him, treated him kindly.
He told me that in Crete, at Idómeneus' house, he had seen him
making repairs on the galleys of his which stormwinds had shattered;
he said he would return in the summer or else in the autumn,
385 carrying many possessions, along with his godlike comrades.
You too, old man, heavy with grief, as a spirit has led you
here to me, make no effort to please me with lies or to charm me:
not for that reason will I show honor to you or befriend you—
Zeus the protector of guests I fear, and for you I feel pity."
390   Speaking to him then answered Odysseus of many devices:

"Certainly you have a mind in your breast that is very suspicious,
such that the oath I swear cannot bring you around or persuade you.
But come now, let us make an agreement—for both of us let our
witnesses be hereafter the gods who inhabit Olympos—
395 if your master at last comes back home, here to his palace,
you will provide me a mantle and tunic as clothing and send me
off to Doulíchion, where my heart most wishes to travel.
If instead your master should not come back as I tell you,
set your servants upon me to throw me over a great cliff,
400 so that another who comes here begging will shrink from deceiving."
     Then in answer to him you spoke, Eumaíos the swineherd:
"Stranger, for me this surely would be great honor and virtue
here among men, both now in the present and then in the future,
when I had led you here to my cabin and given you guest-gifts,
405 nevertheless I killed you and took away your dear life breath!
Then with a good heart I would be praying to Zeus, son of Kronos!
Now it is time for our supper, and may the companions at once come
into the hut, so that we can make ready a savory dinner."
     These things then they spoke and addressed each one to the other;
410 then did the sows come near, and with them came men who were swineherds.
There in their regular sties they penned up the sows for the night's rest;
deafening clamor arose from the swine all crowded in pigpens.
To his companions the excellent swineherd called out an order:
"Bring in the best of the pigs, so that I for our guest from a distant
415 country may kill it, and we will enjoy it as well who a long time
now for the white-tusked pigs have been suffering hardship and labor;
meanwhile others are eating our work up quite without payment."
     So having spoken, with pitiless bronze he split up the firewood;
into the hut they guided a pig, well-fattened, of five years.
420 Then they made it stand by the fireplace, nor did the swineherd
slight or forget the immortals, for he used excellent judgment:
rather, to open the rite, hairs cut from the head of the white-tusked
pig he threw on the fire while praying to all of the gods for
various-minded Odysseus to come back home to his palace.
425 Raising himself, with an oak chunk left from the splitting he struck it;
breath went out of the pig, and at once they butchered and singed it,
cutting it up into joints; and the swineherd started by fixing
morsels from all of the limbs on the thick fat wrapped on the thighbones.
These they threw on the fire with barley meal sprinkled upon them;
430 then they cut up the rest, and on stakes they spitted the pieces;

when they had carefully roasted the meat and had taken the spits out,
then on platters in generous heaps they placed them; the swineherd
stood to apportion the meat—for his mind was skillful in justice—
seven in all were the shares into which he divided the morsels.
435   One share then for the nymphs of the place and for Maia's son Hermes
he set aside with a prayer, and the rest to each man he apportioned.
But with the whole long cut from the chine of the white-tusked pig he
honored Odysseus, and so he delighted the heart of his master.
Thus then spoke and addressed him Odysseus of many devices:
440   "May you be equally dear, Eumaíos, to Zeus our father
as to myself, that you honor a man like me with the best things."
Then in answer to him you spoke, Eumaíos the swineherd:
"Eat up, ill-starred stranger, and take your pleasure in all these
things that we have here: this will a god give, that will he let go,
445   as in his heart he wishes; for all things he may accomplish."
Thus, and he burned the first offering meats for the gods who live always,
poured a libation of glistening wine; to the hands of Odysseus,
sacker of cities, he transferred the cup, then sat with his own share.
Bread was provided to them by Mesaúlios, one whom the swineherd,
450   all by himself, had acquired while his master was out of the country,
making the purchase apart from his mistress and agèd Laërtes;
he with his own resources from Taphian sailors had bought him.
They put forth eager hands to partake of the food lying ready.
When they had quite satisfied their appetites, drinking and eating,
455   then was the bread cleared away by Mesaúlios; eagerly they went
off to their beds, having eaten their fill of the bread and the roast meat.
Night came on very bad, in the dark of the moon; for the whole night,
Zeus rained; always wet, the strong west wind, Zephyr, was blowing.
Then among them said Odysseus, to make some proof of the swineherd—
460   whether he might take off his mantle and give it to him or
urge it of one of his comrades, since he cared greatly about him:
"Listen to me, Eumaíos and all you other companions.
Bragging a bit I will tell you a tale, for the madness of wine is
urging me, which sets even a man who is thoughtful to singing
465   much and to laughing with small provocation and drives him to dancing.
Often as well it throws out a word that were better unspoken;
but since I have now started to speak out, I will hide nothing.
How I wish I were young and my strength yet steady within me,
as at the time under Troy we mustered and led up an ambush.
470   Those who led were Odysseus and Atreus' son Meneláos;

I was with them as the third in command, since they themselves asked me.
But then, when we arrived at the city and under the steep walls,
all of us, there in the thick brushwood that surrounded the fortress,
huddling beneath our armor among dense reeds in the marshland,

475 lay down; then as the north wind dropped, harsh night came upon us,
freezing the blood; and the snow which fell from above was as dense as
hoarfrost, while on the shields all around, ice thickened to clusters.
There did all of the others, who had both mantles and tunics,
sleep all night at their ease—with their shields they covered their shoulders.

480 But I, when I had gone with the comrades, had foolishly left my
mantle, for I did not think I would be cold even without it;
I went along taking only a shield and a shimmering waist guard.
But in the night's third watch, when the stars turned down toward setting,
finally then I spoke to Odysseus, who lay there beside me,

485 nudging his side with my elbow—at once he heeded and listened:
'Zeus-sprung son of Laërtes, Odysseus of many devices,
soon I will be no more with the living; the wintery cold is
wearing me down, for I have no mantle; a spirit beguiled me
only a tunic to wear; there is no way out any longer.'

490 So did I say; then this was the plan he conceived in his spirit—
such was the man he was in advising as well as in fighting—
speaking to me in a soft low voice, these words he addressed me:
'Hush now, lest some other among the Achaians should hear you.'
Propping his head on his elbow then, these words he addressed them:

495 'Hear me, friends: a divine dream came to me now in my slumber.
Since we have come very far from the ships, is there anyone who would
go ask Atreus' son Agamemnon, the shepherd of people,
whether he might urge more of the men from the galleys to come here?'
So did he say; then up sprang Thoas the son of Andraímon

500 swiftly, and put from his body his mantle of Tyrian purple;
leaving, he ran to the ships, while I lay there in his clothing,
happily resting, until shone down on us Dawn of the gold throne.
So now, would I were young and the strength yet steady within me!
Somebody here in the swineherd's house might give me a mantle,

505 both on account of our friendship and out of respect for a good man;
now men scorn me because I wear foul clothes on my body."

    Then in answer to him you spoke, Eumaíos the swineherd:
"Old man, that is indeed a most excellent tale you have told us;
not one word you have spoken unfitly or lacking in profit.

510 Therefore neither of clothes nor of other things you shall be lacking

such as befit a long-suffering supplicant when he approaches—
now: but again in the morning your own rags you will be flaunting.
For our clothes are not many, the mantles and changes of tunics
here in the cabin, to wear, but for each man only the one set.
515 But when at last he comes back home, the dear son of Odysseus
then of himself will provide you a mantle and tunic as clothing,
also send you wherever your heart and your spirit command you."

    So he spoke and arose, and he laid out a bed for the stranger
close to the fire, and upon it he threw sheep's fleeces and goatskins.
520 There did Odysseus recline; then over him he threw a mantle,
thick, close-woven, and large, that was lying at hand as an extra,
so he could wear it whenever a terrible tempest was raging.

    So in the hut lay sleeping Odysseus; and close to his side lay
down to their slumber the young men also; but not to the swineherd
525 was it a pleasure to lie there apart from the pigs for the night's rest,
but he prepared instead to go out, and Odysseus was happy
that he would take such care of his livelihood while he was absent.
First his sharp-pointed sword he threw on his powerful shoulders,
then as a shelter from wind he put on a thick heavy mantle,
530 picked up the unshorn skin of a goat that was big and well nourished,
took a sharp javelin also, from dogs and from men a protection.
He set forth to lie down in the place where the white-tusked pigs slept
under a hollow rock in a shelter against the cold north wind.

BOOK 15

To Lakedaímon of spacious domains now Pallas Athena
went, to recall to the mind of greathearted Odysseus' brilliant
son his return to his home and to urge him to leave on the journey.
She found Telémachos there and the excellent scion of Nestor,
5   taking their rest in the porch of the glorious lord Meneláos.
Still was the scion of Nestor subdued in a soft mild slumber,
though sweet sleep was not holding Telémachos; but in his spirit
through the divine night, cares for his father were keeping him wakeful.
Standing beside him there thus spoke to him bright-eyed Athena:
10   "No more, Telémachos, can it be good to stray far from your palace,
leaving behind your possessions and such men there in the household
so overbearing as those, lest they be dividing and eating
everything you possess—then you will have fruitlessly journeyed.
But now rouse the great crier of war Meneláos to send you
15   quickly away, so you find your virtuous mother at home still.
For already in fact her father and brothers are urging
her to be married at last to Eurýmachos: all of the suitors
he outdoes with his gifts and increases his presents for marriage.
Do not let her against your will take wealth from the palace—
20   for as you know, so inclined is the heart in the breast of a woman:
she will desire to enrich the household of whomever she marries,
while of her earlier children and that dear husband she wedded,
once he is dead, no more does she take any thought or ask questions.
But now, going yourself, each piece of your property you should
25   trust to whoever appears best suited among the maidservants,
till such time as the gods make known your illustrious bedmate.
Here is another such word I will say; put this in your spirit.
Strongly the best of the suitors in ambush wait in the channel
which from the Ithakan isle divides Samè, rugged and rocky,
30   wanting to kill you before you return to the land of your fathers.

275

But it will not be so, I believe; earth sooner will cover
many a one of the suitors who now are devouring your substance.
But keep holding the well-made galley away from the islands,
sailing as well by night; whatever immortal it is who
35 guards and defends you will send wind blowing behind on the galley.
Straightway upon your arrival at Ithaka's first promontory,
hasten the galley and all the companions along to the city;
you yourself, meanwhile, go immediately to the swineherd
who is the guard of the pigs and to you feels loyal as ever.
40 There take rest for the night; then urge him to go to the city
so that to prudent Penelope he may deliver a message,
saying that you are alive and have come in safety from Pylos."
    When she had said these things, she departed to lofty Olympos.
Out of his sweet sleep then he awakened the scion of Nestor,
45 rousing him up with a kick of his foot; these words he addressed him:
"Wake up, scion of Nestor, Peisístratos; bringing the whole-hoofed
steeds, to the chariot yoke them, so we may accomplish the journey."
    Thus did the scion of Nestor, Peisístratos, speak in his answer:
"Though we long for the journey, Telémachos, surely we cannot
50 drive off now through the shadowy night; soon it will be morning.
But wait here till the gifts be carried and placed on the car by
Atreus' son Meneláos, the hero renowned as a spearman,
then with benevolent words he speaks to us, sending us homeward.
For during all of his days is a guest most apt to remember
55 such a hospitable man who furnishes tokens of friendship."
    So he spoke, and at once upon them came Dawn of the gold throne.
Close to them there then came the great crier of war Meneláos,
having arisen from bed beside Helen of beautiful tresses.
Then, as he noticed him there, straightway the dear son of Odysseus,
60 moving in haste, put onto his body his shimmering tunic;
over his stalwart shoulders the hero threw a capacious
mantle, and went out the door; then standing beside Meneláos,
so did Telémachos speak, the dear son of the godlike Odysseus:
"Atreus' son Meneláos, the Zeus-loved lord of the people,
65 send me away right now to the much loved land of my fathers,
since right now is my spirit desirous of journeying homeward."
    Answering him then spoke the great crier of war Meneláos:
"Surely, Telémachos, I will not keep you here for a long time
if you desire to go home; indeed I would censure another
70 man entertaining a guest who showed excess in his friendship

as one excessive in hatred: in all things, measure is better.
Equal, indeed, are the evils of urging a guest to depart who
does not want to, and holding him back when he wishes to travel—
offer your love to a guest who is present and speed him at parting.
75 But wait here till I bring out the gifts, place them on the car box—
good ones, as you will observe with your eyes. My wife I will order
quickly to ready a meal of the plentiful food in the storage.
It is not only distinction and honor but also advantage,
eating a meal before traveling far on earth's measureless surface.
80 If you desire in Hellas to tour and the middle of Argos,
so that I too may accompany you, I will harness the horses,
then guide you to the cities of mankind; no one will ever
send us away as we came—he will give us a present to carry,
either a tripod of beautiful bronze, perhaps, or a cauldron,
85 maybe a couple of mules or a gold-wrought goblet for drinking."
    Thoughtful Telémachos then spoke out to him, giving an answer:
"Atreus' son Meneláos, the Zeus-loved lord of the people,
I want now to return to my country, for when I departed,
I left no one behind me to watch and protect my belongings;
90 neither in seeking my godlike father should I be ruined,
nor should any of those fine treasures be lost from my palace."
    But then, when the great crier of war Meneláos had heard this,
speaking at once he ordered his wife and the maids of the household
quickly to ready a meal of the plentiful food in the storage.
95 Then Eteóneus, son of Boëthoös, came and approached him,
when he had risen from bed, for he dwelt not far from his master.
Him the great crier of war Meneláos commanded to kindle
fire and prepare roast meat; he heard and did not disobey him.
As for the lord, he went downstairs to a sweet-smelling chamber,
100 not by himself, for with him went Helen and young Megapénthes.
But when they had arrived down there where the treasures were lying,
then did Atreus' son lay hold of a two-handled goblet,
also ordered his son Megapénthes to take up a mixing
vessel of silver; and Helen herself stood next to the boxes
105 inside which were the robes she had made, all brightly embroidered.
One of them, lifted and carried by Helen the splendor of women,
which was the loveliest in its adornment as well as the largest,
shone forth bright as a star; it had lain there under the others.
Then they set out to go back up through the palace until they
110 came to Telémachos; thus light-haired Meneláos addressed him:

"As in your heart you are longing, Telémachos, now to go homeward,
may Zeus bring it to pass, the loud-thundering husband of Hera.
I will present you, of all of the gifts which lie in my palace,
treasures of mine, that one which is finest and far the most honored:
115 I will present you a well-made wine bowl which is entirely
fashioned of silver; with gold are the rims on it skillfully finished;
it is a work of Hephaistos that valorous Phaídimos gave me—
he the Sidonians' king, whose palace provided me shelter
when I visited there; I wish to bestow it on you now."
120   So as he spoke, in his hand was the hero, Atreus' scion,
placing the cup, two-handled; and meanwhile strong Megapénthes
carried and placed in front of him there that shimmering wine bowl
fashioned of silver; and Helen of beautiful cheeks stood near him
holding the robe in her hands and said these words, calling upon him:
125 "I also have a gift, dear child, this one, to present you,
token of Helen's own hands, for the hour of your lovely espousals,
then to be worn by your bride; meanwhile let it lie in the palace,
kept by your own dear mother. From me, farewell as you go back
there to your well-built house, back there to the land of your fathers."
130   So as she spoke, in his hands she placed it; he gladly received it.
These things then did the hero Peisístratos place in the car box
as he received them, and wondered in spirit at all he was seeing.
Into the house light-haired Meneláos escorted the young men.
Then at once they seated themselves on benches and armchairs.
135 Hand-washing water a maid then carried to them in a lovely
gold-wrought pitcher, and over a basin of silver she poured it,
so they could wash. Near them she laid out a well-polished table.
Carrying food, the revered housekeeper approached them and set it
close to them, many a dish she gladly supplied from her storage.
140 Nearby, Boëthoös' son cooked meat and divided the portions,
while Meneláos' illustrious son poured wine for the diners.
They put forth eager hands to partake of the food lying ready.
When they had quite satisfied their appetites, drinking and eating,
then did Telémachos and the illustrious scion of Nestor,
145 yoking the team, climb onto the chariot bright with adornment,
out of the courtyard gate and the echoing portico drove it.
Atreus' scion accompanied them, light-haired Meneláos;
he in his right hand carried along for them wine, honey-hearted,
in a gold goblet, that they might make libation at parting;
150 standing in front of the horses he spoke, with a gesture to pledge them:

"Now, young men, farewell, and to Nestor the shepherd of people
give my greeting; to me like a father he was in his kindness
while in Troy we were fighting the war, we sons of Achaians."
    Thoughtful Telémachos then spoke out to him, giving an answer:
155 "Certainly, Zeus-loved lord, when I go back there I will tell him
all these things you have spoken; and would that I also, returning
homeward to Ithaka, finding Odysseus at last in the palace,
might say how having met at your hand all manner of friendship
I come, bringing as well so many and excellent treasures."
160   As these words he was speaking, a bird flew by on his right hand;
it was an eagle that carried a huge white goose in its talons
out of a farmyard, a tame one; and shrieking, the men and the women
followed along; then, when it was close to the watchers, it rushed up
just to the right in front of the chariot. As they observed it,
165 they were delighted; in every breast did the heart grow warmer.
Speaking to them thus opened Peisístratos, scion of Nestor:
"Tell us now, Meneláos, the Zeus-loved lord of the people,
whether for us or for you yourself a god showed this omen."
    So he spoke; Meneláos belovèd of Ares considered
170 how he could say what he thought in the right way, giving an answer.
But in advance of him, long-robed Helen addressed them in these words:
"Hear me: I will deliver a prophecy, as the immortals
send it into my mind, and I think this will be accomplished.
As this bird, from the peak where it had its race and begetting,
175 came down, snatching and bearing away a goose reared in the household,
so will Odysseus, when much he has suffered and far he has wandered,
go back home and exact his vengeance, or else he already
has arrived home and is nurturing evil for all of the suitors."
    Thoughtful Telémachos then spoke out to her, giving an answer:
180 "Thus Zeus bring it to pass, the loud-thundering husband of Hera—
so even when I am there I will pray to you as to a goddess!"
    Thus, and he laid his whip on the horses, and they very quickly
hastened away to the plain in their eagerness, out through the city.
All that day they were shaking the yoke they carried about them.
185 Then did the sun go down and the ways were all shadowed in darkness;
soon thereafter they came into Phérai, to Díokles' palace;
he was the son of Ortílochos, whom great Álpheios fathered.
There they rested the night, and he gave them guests' entertainment.
    Soon as the Dawn shone forth rose-fingered at earliest daybreak,
190 yoking the team, they climbed on the chariot bright with adornment,

out of the courtyard gate and the echoing portico drove it,
wielding the whip, nor against their wishes the horses were speeding.
Soon thereafter they came to the steep-built city of Pylos;
then did Telémachos speak these words to the scion of Nestor:

195 "Nestor's son, if you can, will you promise me now to achieve this
word of mine? We can avow ourselves to be friends from a long time
through the friendship of our fathers; and then too, we are the same age;
then this journey will add yet more to our oneness in spirit.
Do not take me beyond my ship, Zeus-nourished, but leave me

200 there, lest the old man hold me against my will in the palace,
wanting to show his affection; I must go home very quickly."

So he spoke; in his spirit the scion of Nestor considered
how in the way most proper to promise him this and achieve it.
So as he pondered the matter, the best course seemed to be this one:

205 turning the horses toward the swift ship and the shore of the deep sea,
he unloaded upon the ship's stern the magnificent presents,
all of the garments and gold Meneláos had given the young man.
Then to arouse him to action, in these winged words he addressed him:
"Go aboard now, and give orders to all the companions to set forth

210 quickly, before I arrive at the house and report to the old man.
For in fact I know very well in my mind and my spirit
how overbearing his temper will be: he will never release you
but will himself come here to invite you; nor do I think that
he will go back without you; as it is, he will be very angry."

215 So having spoken, he went on, driving the fair-maned horses
up to the Pylians' city, and quickly arrived at the palace.
Rousing the comrades to action, Telémachos gave out the orders:
"Comrades, set in order the tackle inside the black galley,
then let us board it ourselves, so that we may accomplish the journey."

220 So did he say; they carefully listened to him and obeyed him;
hastily then they boarded and took their seats at the oarlocks.
Then as he busied himself in praying and offering victims,
there by the stern of the ship, to Athena, a man from a distant
land came close, who for killing a man was in exile from Argos.

225 He was a prophet, and as for descent, he was sprung from Melámpous,
who had at one time dwelt in Pylos, the mother of sheep flocks.
Wealthy, he lived among Pylian folk in an opulent palace;
then he had come to a country of strangers, in flight from his own land,
also from great-souled Neleus, the noblest of all men living,

230 who had kept back by force, till a whole long year was completed,

much of his substance; and meanwhile Melámpous in Phýlakos' halls was
bound in wearisome bondage and suffering mighty afflictions
first for the daughter of Neleus and then for the terrible madness
put in his mind by the goddess Erinys, the smiter of houses.
235 Yet he fled from his doom, and he drove loud-bellowing cattle
over to Pylos from Phýlakè, paying with shameful exertion
godlike Neleus' price; and the woman he took to his brother,
there in the halls, for a wife, then went to a country of strangers,
to horse-nourishing Argos, for there it now was appointed
240 that he should keep his dwelling and rule over numerous Argives.
There he wedded a wife and erected a high-roofed palace,
then Antíphates fathered and Mantios, powerful scions.
Next in turn Antíphates sired greathearted Oïkles;
son to Oïkles was Ámphiaráos, the rouser of people,
245 whom in his heart Zeus, lord of the aegis, as well as Apollo
loved with all love; but he did not arrive at the threshold of old age
but was destroyed in Thebes on account of the bribes that his wife got.
He in his turn had sons, Amphílochos and Alkmaíon.
Mantios too was a father—he sired Polypheídes and Kleitos.
250 Kleitos, however, because of his beauty, was carried away by
Dawn of the gold throne, so that he might be among the immortals,
while great-souled Polypheídes Apollo created a prophet,
best by far among mortals, when Ámphiaráos had perished.
To Hyperésia he migrated, in wrath at his father;
255 there he lived, and he uttered his prophecies there to all mortals.
      That was the man whose son, by name Theoklýmenos, then came
close to Telémachos, taking his stand there; him he discovered
pouring libations and uttering prayers by the swift black galley.
Raising his voice he spoke, and in these winged words he addressed him:
260 "Friend, since here in this place I have found you offering victims,
I entreat by the victims you burn and the god and as well by
your own head and by those of the friends who accompany you now,
tell me the truth as I ask my questions, conceal from me nothing:
Who are you? Whence do you come? What city is yours, and what parents?"
265   Thoughtful Telémachos then spoke out to him, giving an answer:
"These things, stranger and friend, I will tell you exactly and fully.
I am of Ithakan stock, my father Odysseus, if ever
he was alive; by now he has perished in wretched destruction.
Therefore now having taken companions along, and a black ship,
270 I set forth to inquire of my father, who long has been absent."

Then in return godlike Theoklýmenos spoke and addressed him:
"So I too am away from my country—a man of my tribe I
slaughtered, of whom there are numerous brothers and kinsmen
in horse-nourishing Argos who mightily rule the Achaians.
275   So to escape my death and the blackness of doom at their hands, I
take flight, since my destiny now is to wander among men.
But take me on your ship, since I as a fugitive beg you,
so that they may not kill me; for I know well they pursue me."
    Thoughtful Telémachos then spoke out to him, giving an answer:
280   "Now from the balanced ship I will not thrust you who desire it;
come then; there you will find entertainment such as we have still."
    So having spoken to him, he took the bronze spear from the other;
there longways on the deck of the tractable galley he laid it;
then he himself straightway went onto the seafaring galley.
285   There in the stern he took his seat, and beside himself he
made Theoklýmenos sit; they loosened the ship's stern cables.
Then to arouse them to action, Telémachos bade the companions
lay their hands on the gear; they eagerly heeded his orders.
Lifting the pine-hewn mast, they fitted it into the hollow
290   mast box, stood it upright, and then bound it fast with the forestays,
hoisted the glistening sail with the ropes well plaited from oxhide.
Then was a favoring wind sent down by bright-eyed Athena,
rushing along through the air in a blustery gale, so that swiftly
running, the ship would accomplish her course on the salt seawater.
295   Close by Krounoi they went and the beautiful stream of the Chalkis.
    Then did the sun go down and the ways were all shadowed in darkness;
hurried along by breezes from Zeus, she headed for Phéai,
then by illustrious Elis, in which the Epeíans are rulers.
Thence he drove her ahead to the Thoai, Sharp-pointed Islands,
300   pondering whether he would flee death or be taken a captive.
    Meanwhile those in the cabin—Odysseus, the excellent swineherd—
ate their meal, and the other men also were eating beside them.
When they had quite satisfied their appetites, drinking and eating,
thus did Odysseus among them speak to make proof of the swineherd—
305   whether he yet would befriend him kindly and bid him to stay on
there at the pig farm still or would urge him to go to the city:
"Listen to me, Eumaíos and all you other companions:
early at dawn I am eager to leave here and go to the city;
there I will beg, so that I will not wear down you and your comrades.
310   Only advise me well and provide me a guide who is skillful,

one who can lead me there; in my need I will wander about all
over the city, for someone to offer me bread and a cupful.
Then too, should I arrive at the dwelling of godlike Odysseus,
I would be speaking to prudent Penelope, bringing a message,
315　also mingling with those overbearing and arrogant suitors,
seeing if they, with their plentiful food, might give me a dinner.
I would do quickly and well among them whatever they wanted.
For I say to you plainly, and you take notice and heed me:
through the good graces of Hermes the messenger, him who apportions
320　to the endeavors of all mankind their grace and their glory,
no other mortal could even compete with me doing the housework,
neither in skillfully lighting a fire nor in splitting the kindling,
nor in the carving and roasting of meat, nor in pouring the wine out,
all such service as men of the lower sort do for their betters."

325　　Deeply disturbed, you spoke to him then, Eumaíos the swineherd:
"Ah me, stranger, what is this notion that into your mind has
entered? Apparently there on the spot you long to be slaughtered,
if indeed you are wishing to enter the throng of the suitors,
whose outrages and violence reach to the iron-bright heaven!
330　No such beggars as you are the men who work as their servants;
no, they are men in their youth, well-dressed in mantles and tunics;
always their heads have been oiled to a shine; their faces are handsome,
those who work under them; moreover, their well-polished tables
ever with bread, with meat, and with wine are heavily loaded.
335　Stay here instead, since nobody here is annoyed by your presence,
neither myself nor anyone else I have as a comrade.
But when at last he comes back home, the dear son of Odysseus
then of himself will provide you a mantle and tunic to dress in,
also send you wherever your heart and your spirit command you."

340　　Answering him then spoke much-suffering noble Odysseus:
"May you be equally dear, Eumaíos, to Zeus our father,
as to myself, that you stop my roaming and terrible hardships!
No other evil is greater for mortals than wandering rootless,
but on account of the damnable belly, malignant afflictions
345　men have, any to whom come roaming and trouble and anguish.
Now as you hold me here and you bid me to stay for the young man,
come then, tell me concerning the mother of godlike Odysseus,
also his father, whom, parting, he left on the threshold of old age,
whether perhaps they still are alive under Helios' sunbeams
350　or they have died already and dwell in the palace of Hades."

Thus in his answer addressed him the swineherd, leader of people:
"These things, friend, I will certainly tell you exactly and fully.
Still is Laërtes alive, and to Zeus he always is praying
that at the last his spirit may waste from his limbs in his dwelling,

355 since unbearable grief he feels for his child who is absent
and for the virtuous wife he wedded, who perishing caused him
terrible woe, plunged him in an old age raw and untimely.
It was in grief for the loss of her glorious son that she perished
by the unhappiest death—may nobody die in the same way

360 who as a friend dwells here in the house and behaves as a friend does!
Now so long as she yet was alive, although she was grieving,
I liked often to ask about her and to make my inquiries,
since herself she had reared me along with her virtuous daughter,
long-robed Ktímenè, whom she had brought forth last of her children.

365 It was with her I was nurtured, and not much less was I favored.
But when the two of us came to our youthful and lovely adulthood,
her they gave in marriage in Samè and got many bride gifts;
as for myself, she gave me a mantle and tunic as clothing,
dressed me in very fine ones, for my feet too furnishing sandals,

370 then sent me to the fields; in her heart most dearly she loved me.
Now I am lacking in all these things; but the blessèd immortals,
favoring me, make prosper the labor that I persevere in,
whence I have eaten and drunk and have given to people I honor.
Nothing agreeable ever is now to be heard from the mistress,

375 neither of word nor of deed, for on that house evil has fallen,
men overbearing and reckless; the servants are sorely in want of
talking in front of the mistress and learning of various matters,
also eating and drinking, and afterward carrying something
out to the fields, which always rejoices the hearts of the servants."

380   Speaking to him then answered Odysseus of many devices:
"Well, what a little one you must have been, Eumaíos the swineherd,
when you wandered away so far from your country and parents!
But come now, tell me this and recount it exactly and fully,
whether the wide-wayed city of people was captured and ransacked,

385 that in which your father and reverend mother were dwelling,
or instead you were captured when out with the sheep or the cattle
all by yourself, by enemy men who brought you in ships to
sell you in this man's house, and he gave them a price that was worth it."
     Thus in his answer addressed him the swineherd, leader of people:

390 "Friend, since about these things you are asking and making inquiry,

listen in silence for now, take pleasure and sit there drinking
wine: these nights are unending at present, and some can be sleeping,
even as those who enjoy it can listen; and you do not need to
take to your bed before time—even too much sleep can be boring.
395   But of the others, whoever his heart and his spirit command him,
go sleep outside the cabin; tomorrow as Dawn is appearing,
after he breakfasts, let him go follow the swine of our master.
Meanwhile, here in the cabin as we keep eating and drinking,
we two now will enjoy each other's afflictions and sorrows
400   as we recall them; for even in pains can a man take pleasure
later in life, when much he has suffered and far he has wandered.
This I will say about what you are asking and making inquiry:
There is an island that men call Syria—you may perhaps have
heard of it—lying above Ortýgia, out where the sun turns,
405   not very great in the number of people, but still quite a fine place,
teeming in cattle and sheep, full of wine and prolific in grain crops.
Never does poverty visit the people, and never is any
other disease found there that is hateful to miserable mortals;
rather, when each generation of men grows old in the city,
410   then does Apollo, whose bow is of silver, with Artemis come and
kill them, visiting them with their mild and benevolent missiles.
In that place are two cities, between which all is divided;
over them both one man held sway as the king, my own father,
Ktésios, Órmenos' scion, a man most like the immortals.
415   "There did Phoenicians arrive, those men far famed for their galleys,
swindlers who carried with them in their black ship plenty of trinkets.
There was a woman, Phoenician-born, in the house of my father,
beautiful, noble in stature, and skilled in glorious handwork,
yet the Phoenicians, sly with experience, tricked and beguiled her.
420   First, as she laundered her clothes by the hollow galley, a seaman
mingled with her in bed and affection, which cozen the minds of
all of the female sex, even one whose acts are of virtue.
Then he inquired of her who she was, where she had now come from;
she then pointed at once to the high-roofed house of my father;
425   'Sidon the bronze-rich city is where I boast to have come from;
daughter I am to Arýbas, a man overflowing with riches.
But men snatched me and carried me off with them, pirates from Taphos,
as from the pasture I came back home; they carried me here to
sell me in this man's house; he gave them a price that was worth it.'
430   "Speaking to her made answer the man she had secretly lain with:

285

'Well, would you now be ready to go with us back to your own home,
so you may look on the high-roofed house of your father and mother
and on themselves? For they still are alive and are still called wealthy.'
    "Thus did the woman address him, in these words giving an answer:
435 'These things, sailors, in fact might happen, if you would be willing
only to pledge with an oath to return me safe to my own home.'
    "So she spoke; and they all then swore her an oath, as she bade them.
But then, when they had sworn and had brought their oath to completion,
thus said the woman among them, in these words giving an answer:
440 'Now keep silent, and let no one of your comrades address me
even a word if he happens to come upon me on a pathway
or at a fountain, perhaps, lest somebody go to the old man's
house and report it to him and then he, suspecting, would bind me
fast in wearisome bondage; for you he would meditate ruin.
445 Keep in your heart my words; make haste to buy goods for the journey;
but when the galley is finally loaded and full of provisions,
quickly to me in the house let somebody come with a message;
for I will bring gold also, whatever I then can lay hands on.
One thing more I would willingly give you as fare for the journey,
450 for in the palace am I now rearing the nobleman's offspring,
so quick-witted, who always is running along with me outdoors;
him I would take on the galley, and he would then bring you enormous
profit wherever you gave him for sale among alien people.'
    "When she had said these things, she went to the beautiful palace;
455 nevertheless, for the whole long year, they stayed in our country,
trading for many provisions to put in the hollow galley.
But when the hollow galley was loaded for them to go homeward,
then they sent out a messenger taking the woman a message.
This man, crafty and shrewd, came up to the house of my father
460 bringing a necklace of gold that was strung with pieces of amber.
There in the chambers, the servant girls and the lady my mother
fondled the chain in their hands; with their eyes they looked at it closely,
then they offered his price. To the woman he silently nodded.
When he had nodded to her, he went to the hollow galley;
465 then by the hand she took me and led me out of the palace;
there in the forecourt she found cups still sitting, and tables,
left by the men who had dined in the house and attended my father;
they to the session had gone, to attend the debate of the people.
Three of the cups she quickly concealed in the folds of her bosom,
470 bearing them off, while I unthinkingly, heedlessly followed.

286

Then did the sun go down and the ways were all shadowed in darkness;
rapidly walking, we soon had arrived at the glorious harbor,
inside which was the swift-running ship of the men of Phoenicia.
Then they, boarding the ship, sailed out on the watery pathway,
475　after they put us on board; Zeus sent down favoring breezes.
Six days then we were sailing, alike in the night and the daytime,
but when Zeus son of Kronos to those days added the seventh,
then that woman was smitten by Artemis shooter of arrows;
into the bilge in the hold she fell with a splash, like a sea tern.
480　Out of the ship, to become fresh prey for the seals and the fishes,
they threw her, while I remained there, in my spirit lamenting.
Ithaka then they reached, borne ahead by the wind and the water;
there Laërtes acquired me by paying the price with his treasure.
So it was that I came to behold this land with my own eyes."
485　　This word then in reply spoke Zeus-descended Odysseus:
"Now most deeply, Eumaíos, the heart in my breast you have troubled,
telling me all these things, what pains in your heart you have suffered.
Even along with the evil has Zeus set good things before you,
since after suffering much, you came to the house of a kindly
490　man who in fact has provided you plenty for eating and drinking,
caring for you, and the life you are living is noble; but only
after I wandered among many cities of men have I come here."
　　Such things then they spoke and addressed each one to the other,
nor did the two of them sleep very much time, only a little;
495　quickly the Dawn of the fair throne came.—But Telémachos' comrades,
coming to land, first slackened the canvas and took down the mast pole
speedily; wielding their oars, they rowed the ship in to the mooring.
They threw over the anchoring stones, made fast the stern cables,
then themselves disembarked on the tide-heaped sand of the seashore,
500　readied their dinner, and mingled the glistening wine with water.
When they had quite satisfied their appetites, drinking and eating,
speaking among them thoughtful Telémachos started the discourse:
"You men now keep driving the black ship on to the city;
meanwhile I will at once go visit the fields and the herdsmen.
505　When I have looked at my farms, I will come to the city, at sunset,
then in the morning will set before you a reward for the voyage,
excellent feasting on meat and on wine most sweet in the drinking."
　　Then in return godlike Theoklýmenos spoke and addressed him:
"Where shall I go, dear child? Whose house shall I visit among those
510　owned by the men who in rock-strewn Ithaka govern the people?

Shall I instead go straight to the house of yourself and your mother?"
　　Thoughtful Telémachos then spoke out to him, giving an answer:
"I would advise you in other conditions to go to our palace—
not in the least does it lack hospitality. But for yourself now
515　it would be worse, since I will not be there, nor will my mother
see you, for not very often she shows herself to the suitors
there in the house, but apart in her high room works at her weaving.
But I will tell you of somebody else whom you may go visit:
he is Eurýmachos, provident Pólybos' glorious scion—
520　these days much like a god do the Ithakan people regard him,
for by far is he best of the men; most eagerly he is
seeking to marry my mother and have the estate of Odysseus.
But of all this knows Zeus the Olympian, dwelling in heaven,
whether before that marriage he bring him a day of affliction."
525　　As these words he was speaking, a bird flew by on his right hand;
it was a falcon, Apollo's swift messenger, plucking a pigeon
which he held in his claws; on the ground midway from the galley
up to Telémachos he kept strewing the feathers he pulled out.
Then Theoklýmenos summoned him forth from the other companions,
530　took his hand in his own, and said these words, calling upon him:
"Surely, Telémachos, not without god the bird flew on your right hand;
soon as I saw it approach, I realized it was an omen.
There is no lineage nobler than yours, more fitted for kingship,
here in the Ithakan land: no, you are most powerful always."
535　　Thoughtful Telémachos then spoke out to him, giving an answer:
"May this word now, stranger and friend, be brought to fulfillment!
Thereon you would at once be aware of my love and of many
presents from me, so someone who met you would call you blessèd."
　　So having said, he called to Peiraíos, a trusty companion:
540　"Klytios' scion Peiraíos, in all things else you obey me
best among all the companions who went with me over to Pylos;
so now also for me take home this stranger as guest-friend;
treat him with kindly affection and honor, until I arrive there."
　　Thus Peiraíos renowned as a spearman spoke as an answer:
545　"Surely, Telémachos, even if you were to stay here a long time,
I would attend to him: no hospitality he will be lacking."
　　So he spoke, and he boarded the galley and bade the companions
get themselves on board and at once cast off the stern cables.
Hastily then they boarded and took their seats at the oarlocks.
550　　Under his feet now Telémachos fastened his beautiful sandals;

then he took his powerful spear, well-pointed with sharp bronze,
up from the deck of the galley; and they cast off the stern cables.
Pushing to sea, they sailed to the city, exactly as they were
told by Telémachos, much loved scion of godlike Odysseus.
555 Swiftly his feet bore him as he walked, till he came to the farmyard;
there were his swine, great numbers; among them also the noble
swineherd rested the night, with benevolent thoughts for his masters.

BOOK 16

Meanwhile those in the cabin—Odysseus, the excellent swineherd—
early at dawn rekindled the fire, made ready the breakfast;
then they sent out the drovers along with the swine they were herding.
Seeing Telémachos, straightway the clamorous dogs began fawning,
5   nor did they bark as he came up closer; and noble Odysseus
took note how the dogs fawned as the noise of the two feet reached him.
Straightway he spoke to Eumaíos; in these winged words he addressed him:
"Surely, Eumaíos, a comrade of yours is approaching the cabin—
or some other acquaintance—because your dogs are not barking,
10   but they fawn about him; I am hearing the thud of his footsteps."
    All of his words he had not yet said when his own dear son stood
there in the porch of the cabin; the swineherd jumped up, astonished.
Out of his hands fell both of the jars with which he was busy
mixing the glistening wine; and he went straight up to his master,
15   gave him a kiss on his head and on both of his beautiful bright eyes,
then on both of his hands; and a great tear fell from his eyelid.
Just as a father in loving benevolence welcomes a dear son
who in the tenth year comes back home from a faraway country,
his sole child and his darling, for whom much grief he has suffered,
20   so now Telémachos, godlike in beauty, the excellent swineherd
kissed and embraced all over, as one who had fled from destruction.
Then as he wept he spoke, and in these winged words he addressed him:
    "You have arrived, sweet light, dear Telémachos; never again I
thought I would see you once you had gone in the galley to Pylos.
25   But come now, enter in, dear child, so that I may rejoice my
heart once more to behold you, returned from abroad, in my cabin.
For not often do you come out to the fields and the herdsmen,
but among townsmen you stay, since so in your heart you delight in
keeping your eyes on the cursèd and ruinous throng of the suitors."
30   Thoughtful Telémachos then spoke out to him, giving an answer:

[handwritten margin note: odysseus has to stand there and watch him hug his son]

"Papa, it shall be so—and for your sake now I have come here,
so I can see you with my own eyes and can hear what you tell me,
whether my mother remains in the palace or whether another
man already has made her his wife, and the bed of Odysseus
35   lies without sleepers perhaps, holds nothing but hideous cobwebs."
      Thus in his answer addressed him the swineherd, leader of people:
"Even for too long still she remains with a resolute spirit
there in the halls of your palace; the miserable nights and the days are
always wasting away while she keeps letting her tears fall."
40   Thus then when he had spoken, he took the bronze spear from the young man,
who straightway went into the cabin and crossed the stone threshold.
Just as he entered, his father Odysseus was yielding his own seat;
quickly Telémachos spoke from the other side, checking the action:
"Friend, sit down where you were; we will look for a seat in another
45   place in our cabin, and this man here at my side will provide it."
      So he spoke, and Odysseus returned and sat down, and the swineherd
spread for him light green brushwood beneath, on top of it fleeces.
There then also was seated the much loved son of Odysseus.
Straightway the swineherd set by the two men platters of roasted
50   meat that they had left over from earlier when they had eaten,
bread also that he hastily heaped up high in the baskets.
When he had mixed up honey-sweet wine in an ivy-wood wine bowl,
he himself sat down facing and opposite godlike Odysseus.
They put forth eager hands to partake of the food lying ready.
55   When they had quite satisfied their appetites, drinking and eating,
finally then did Telémachos speak to the excellent swineherd:
      "Papa, now where has this stranger arrived from? How did the sailors
bring him to Ithaka? What did they say were their names and their nation?
For it was certainly not on foot, I suppose, that he came here."
60   Then in answer to him you spoke, Eumaíos the swineherd:
"Certainly, child, the whole tale I will tell you fully and truly.
He makes claim of himself that of broad Crete he is an offspring,
but, as he says, he has wandered among many cities of mortals,
roaming about, for a god spun such things out as his portion.
65   Just now, having escaped from a ship of Thesprotian sailors,
he has arrived at my cabin, and I give him to your keeping.
Do as you wish: he declares as a supplicant he has approached you."
      Thoughtful Telémachos then spoke out to him, giving an answer:
"These, Eumaíos, are most heart-anguishing words you have spoken!
70   How can I possibly welcome the stranger as guest in the palace?

I am myself quite young and cannot yet trust to my hands for
keeping away any man when he first starts doing me outrage.
As for my mother, her heart is divided and weighs two courses:
whether she will stay here at my side, take care of the household,
75   thus respecting her husband's bed and the voice of the people;
whether she finally goes with the noblest among the Achaians
who pays court to her here in the palace and gives the most presents.
But as regards this stranger, as he has arrived at your dwelling,
I will attire him in mantle and tunic, the finest apparel,
80   also give him a two-edged sword, for his feet provide sandals,
then I will send him wherever his heart and his spirit command him.
But if you will, take care of him now, keep him in your cabin;
I will myself send out here clothing and all the provisions
he will consume, so that he will not wear down you and your comrades.
85   I would indeed not allow him to go to the palace among those
suitors, for they are possessed too much of infatuate outrage;
I fear they would insult him: to me it will be cruel anguish.
It is in fact very hard to achieve anything for a single
man among many, though he be mighty, for they are much stronger."
90   Then spoke answering him much-suffering noble Odysseus:
"Dear friend, since it is certainly proper for me to make answer,
as I was listening, my own heart was indeed lacerated,
such are the things you say of the suitors contriving their reckless
deeds in the palace against your will, though you are so worthy.
95   Tell me, are you subdued quite willingly, or do the people
hate you here in the land in response to a god's injunction?
Or do you lay some blame on your brothers, on whom any man should
put his trust in a fight, even if a great quarrel arises?
How I wish, with the heart that I have, I were youthful as you are
100   or were the offspring of noble Odysseus—or even himself might
come back home from his roaming, for there is a measure of hope yet.
Straightway then might a foreigner cut off the head from my body
if I did not show all of those men what evil to them I
was when I came to the halls of Odysseus the son of Laërtes.
105   Yes, and if I all alone were subdued by them in their numbers,
then much rather would I be slaughtered in my own palace,
dying instead of forever observing these scandalous actions,
guests outrageously treated and battered, and women attendants
men keep shamelessly dragging about in the beautiful palace,
110   wine being drawn off, wasted, and men who are eating the food up

wholly in vain, to no purpose, on business never accomplished."
　　Thoughtful Telémachos then spoke out to him, giving an answer:
"These things, stranger and friend, I will tell you exactly and fully.
All of the people are not my enemies, nor are they angry,
115　nor do I lay any blame on my brothers, on whom any man should
put his trust in a fight, even if a great quarrel arises.
So has the scion of Kronos arranged our line to be single—
one son only, Laërtes, did old Arkeisios father;
one son he in turn fathered, Odysseus; and then in the halls one
120　son did Odysseus beget, and he left never having enjoyed me.
Therefore now beyond counting the enemies are in the palace.
All of the highborn chieftains who lord it over the islands,
over Doulíchion, Samè, and also wooded Zakýnthos,
those men too who in rock-strewn Ithaka govern the people,
125　all these seek my mother in marriage and wear out the household.
She will neither reject this odious marriage, nor can she
make herself carry it through; meanwhile they eat and destroy this
household of mine. And indeed they will soon put me to the slaughter.
Nevertheless on the knees of the gods these matters are resting.
130　Papa, in haste go now to Penelope, thoughtful and constant;
tell her that I am quite safe and that I have arrived here from Pylos.
I will remain in the cabin myself; then you return hither,
when you have told her only; and let no other Achaian
learn of the message, for many of them are devising me evils."
135　　Then in answer to him you spoke, Eumaíos the swineherd:
"I know, I understand; to a sensible man you are talking.
But come now, tell me this and recount it exactly and fully:
shall I go the same path as a messenger now for Laërtes,
miserable man, who while he was grieving so much for Odysseus
140　yet looked after the farm and along with the slaves in the house kept
eating and drinking whenever the heart in his breast would demand it;
but these days, from the time you went in the galley to Pylos,
he, so they say, no longer is eating or drinking in that way,
nor does he look to the farm, but in lamentation and sorrow
145　sits there grieving; the flesh keeps wasting away from his bone frame."
　　Thoughtful Telémachos then spoke out to him, giving an answer:
"Yet more painful; but let him alone, in spite of our sorrow;
for if all things somehow had been given to mortals to choose from,
first we would set our choice on a day of return for my father.
150　But after telling the news, you return, and do not in the fields go

wandering, searching for him; instead, you speak to my mother,
tell her to send the housekeeper, her servant, as soon as she ever
can in secret, for she may deliver the news to the old man."
      So he said, rousing the swineherd, who laying his hands on his sandals
155 fastened them under his feet to depart for the city. Athena
did not ignore Eumaíos the swineherd leaving the farmstead;
but she approached quite near; she had likened her form to a woman
beautiful, noble in stature, and skilled in glorious handwork.
Outside the door of the hut she stood and appeared to Odysseus;
160 nor did Telémachos look at her head on, nor did he know her—
for in no way do the gods make manifest showing to all men—
it was Odysseus who saw, and the dogs too; they were not barking;
whining in fear, they slunk to the farthest side of the farmstead.
She with her brows made a signal, and noble Odysseus perceived it;
165 he came out of the house, outside the great wall of the farmyard,
then stood close to her side; and in these words Athena addressed him:
      "Zeus-sprung son of Laërtes, Odysseus of many devices,
now it is time—say a word to your son; no longer conceal it,
so that when you have contrived destruction and doom for the suitors,
170 both of you go to the glorious city; and I will myself not
long be away from your side—I am ready and eager for battle."
      So having spoken, Athena at once touched him with her gold wand.
Then to begin, she put on his shoulders a cloak and a tunic,
both well cleaned, and augmented his stature and youthful appearance.
175 Dark once more was his skin, and the flesh of his cheeks became solid;
also the beard he wore on his chin turned blacker in color.
When she had wrought these things, she departed again; and Odysseus
went back into the cabin. His dear son marveled to see him;
fearing that he was a god, his eyes he quickly averted.
180 Raising his voice he spoke, and in these winged words he addressed him:
      "Stranger, to me you appear quite different now than before this.
Different clothing you have, and your skin is no more the same color.
Surely indeed you are one of the gods who hold the broad heaven;
now be gracious, that we may provide you pleasing oblations,
185 presents as well, wrought finely of gold; show mercy and spare us!"
      Answering him then spoke much-suffering noble Odysseus:
"I am indeed no god—why liken me to the immortals?
But your father I am, for whose sake you, weeping and moaning,
suffering many afflictions, endure men's violent doings."
190   So having spoken, he kissed his son; he was letting a tear fall

down from his cheek to the ground, though before he had been unyielding.
Then did Telémachos—for he could not yet believe him his father—
quickly return him an answer; in words like these he addressed him:
"You are most certainly not my father Odysseus, but some god
195   charms me, so that I groan yet longer in sorrow and anguish.
For in no way could a man who was merely a mortal contrive it,
using his own mind only, unless some god should in person
come to him, ready and willing to make him a young or an old man.
For just recently you were an old man, vilely appareled;
200   now you resemble the gods, the immortals who hold the broad heaven."
    Speaking to him then answered Odysseus of many devices:
"It is not seemly, Telémachos, when in the cabin is your own
father, to marvel beyond all measure or be too astonished.
For be sure there will come to you here no other Odysseus—
205   such as he is, I am; far wandering, suffering evils,
I have returned in the twentieth year to the land of my fathers.
What you have seen is the work of Athena, the driver of plunder,
who has made me whatever she wishes—for she has the power—
one time quite like a beggar in semblance and then at another
210   time like a man in his youth and with beautiful clothes on his body.
It is indeed quite easy for gods who hold the broad heaven
either to glorify or to disfigure a man who is mortal."
    So having spoken, he sat back down; and Telémachos started
clasping his excellent father and weeping and letting the tears flow.
215   Thus in the two men longing arose for lamenting and mourning;
shrilly they wailed, more constantly, throbbingly even than cries of
birds, sea eagles or hook-clawed vultures, from whom have the offspring
been snatched off by farmers before they grew into fledglings.
So they were sorrowing, letting the tears flow under their eyebrows.
220   Now would the light of the sun have gone down on the lamentation
had not Telémachos suddenly spoken, addressing his father:
"In what sort of a ship, dear father, was it that the sailors
brought you to Ithaka? What did they say were their names and their nation?
For it was certainly not on foot, I suppose, that you came here."
225   Answering him then spoke much-suffering noble Odysseus:
"Certainly, child, this tale I will tell you fully and truly.
They were Phaiákians, famed for their ships, who brought me, and they give
other men also conveyance, whoever arrives in their country.
They brought me as I slept in a swift ship over the seaway,
230   then in Ithaka set me, and gave me glorious presents,

treasures of bronze and of gold in abundance and well-woven garments;
now, by the grace of the gods, these things lie stored in the caverns.
I have arrived here now by the will and advice of Athena,
so that we might take counsel about our enemies' slaughter.

235 But come, number for me those suitors, and tell me about them,
so that I know how many they are, which men are among them;
soon then, when in my flawless mind I have pondered the matter,
I can decide if the two of us might be able to face them
acting alone, without others, or if we should also seek others."

240   Thoughtful Telémachos then spoke out to him, giving an answer:
"Father, for years I have always heard of your great reputation,
both as a spearman of powerful hands and in prudence of counsel;
but it is too much, what you have said; awe holds me—it could not
be that two men should alone fight men so strong in such numbers.

245 For in truth there are not just ten of the suitors, nor twice ten,
but far more than that. Soon you will know how many are here now.
First, from the isle of Doulíchion come fifty-two of the suitors,
youths wellborn and select; six bondsmen follow to serve them.
Next, from the island of Samè have come here twenty-four young men.

250 Then, from the isle of Zakýnthos are twenty young sons of Achaians.
Lastly, from this very Ithaka twelve come, all of the noblest;
Medon the herald accompanies them, and the godlike singer,
two of their servants as well, both skillful at carving the roast meat.
If we attack all those in the house, I fear your revenge for

255 violence, now you have come, will for us be bitter and dreadful.
No, take thought whether you can discover another defender,
somebody who in resolute spirit would aid and protect us."
     Answering him then spoke much-suffering noble Odysseus:
"Well then, I will now tell you, so give your attention and listen:

260 take thought whether for us now Athena, with Zeus the great father,
will be sufficient or whether I must discover some other defender."
     Thoughtful Telémachos then spoke out to him, giving an answer:
"Those indeed are the noblest defenders of whom you have spoken,
both of them seated above in the clouds, both holding dominion

265 over all other men also and over the gods undying."
     Answering him then spoke much-suffering noble Odysseus:
"Those are indeed two gods who will not be aloof from the mighty
clash of the battle a very long time when the power of Ares,
there in my halls, is brought to the test between us and the suitors.

270 But as for you now, go when the dawn first makes its appearance

back to the palace and join those haughty and arrogant suitors;
later the swineherd will bring me also along to the city,
closely resembling a beggar, an ancient and miserable vagrant.
If in the house they treat me dishonorably, let the dear heart
275 deep in your breast endure it as long as I suffer afflictions,
even if they through the house drag me by the feet out the doorway
or if they pelt me with missiles: you still keep watching and hold back.
Though to be sure you should urge them to cease their mindless behavior,
speaking in words mollifying and gentle; but never will they give
280 credence to you, for the day of their destiny stands very near them.
Something else I will tell you, and you keep this in your mind now:
soon as Athena, the lady of many contrivances, puts it
into my mind, I will nod with my head to you; when you observe it,
pick up such of the weapons of battle as lie in the great halls;
285 carry them off to a nook of a high-built chamber and stow them
all there; then you will put off the suitors with soft and beguiling
speeches as soon as they miss them and ask you questions about them:
'Out of the smoke I have put them, for they no longer resemble
what they were when Odysseus departed for Troy and forsook them
290 but have become quite foul, so much has the fire's breath reached them.
Then too, Kronos' son put in my mind this fear even greater:
deep in your wine cups, you might stir up a quarrel among you,
then you would wound each other and bring disgrace on the banquet
and on your courting, for iron itself draws a man to employ it.'
295 But for the two of us only, a couple of swords and of spears you
leave there to take in our hands, and a couple of shields made of oxhide,
so we can rush at the suitors and seize them; and Pallas Athena
then will be casting a charm over them, Zeus Counselor also.
Something else I will tell you, and you keep this in your mind now:
300 if in fact you are really my son and are born of our own blood,
then let nobody hear that Odysseus is there in the palace;
let not Laërtes know about this, no, neither the swineherd,
let no one of the house servants know, nor Penelope even.
But you only and I will discover the minds of the women;
305 we will as well make trial of many among the menservants,
find where anyone honors us both in his heart and reveres us,
also those who neglect and dishonor you who are so youthful."
     Thus did his glorious son speak out to him, giving an answer:
"Father, indeed you will learn what spirit I have when the right time
310 comes, I am sure, for no slackness of will holds me in the slightest.

But I am also certain that what you suggested will not be
useful to either of us, and I urge you to think of it further.
For in vain a long time you would go about testing each person,
visiting all of our farms; meanwhile, at their ease in the palace,
315 they are devouring our goods in their arrogance, stopping at nothing.
Nevertheless, I urge you to learn for yourself of the women,
which ones bring you dishonor and which ones yet remain guiltless;
as for the men, I would not myself want us to go visit
them at their cabins to test them, but tend to that business later,
320 if in truth you have learned some omen from Zeus of the aegis."
          Such things then they spoke and addressed each one to the other.
Then to the Ithakan harbor proceeded the well-built ship which
carried Telémachos homeward from Pylos with all of his comrades.
Finally, when they arrived inside of the deepwater harbor,
325 straightway then they dragged the black ship up onto the dry land,
while proudhearted attendants began unloading the armor;
quickly they carried the beautiful presents to Klytios' dwelling.
Then they sent off a herald to go to the house of Odysseus,
so that a message to prudent Penelope he could deliver,
330 saying Telémachos was in the fields and had bidden the galley
sail on up to the city, that so the magnificent queen would
not be frightened in spirit and shed soft tears from her eyelids.
          So the two met each other, the herald and excellent swineherd,
as a result of the very same message they bore to the lady.
335 But when they had arrived at the house of the godlike ruler,
there in the midst of the women attendants the herald addressed her:
"Now already has your dear son, Queen, come to the country."
But to Penelope, standing beside her, the swineherd reported
everything that her own dear son had enjoined him to tell her.
340 But then, when he had said all he had been told to deliver,
he went away to the pigs, and he left that courtyard and palace.
          Then in their hearts were the suitors afflicted and utterly downcast;
they went out of the palace along the great wall of the courtyard,
then they took their seats right there in front of the gateway.
345 It was Eurýmachos, Pólybos' son, who was first to address them:
"Oh friends, what a great exploit Telémachos now has accomplished
insolently, this journey! We thought he would never achieve it.
But come now, let us drag to the sea a black galley, our best one,
then collect sailors to serve as the oarsmen, so they may at once go
350 carry a message to those in our ship to return home swiftly."

He had not yet said all when Amphínomos noticed the galley,
as from his place he turned, inside of the deepwater harbor;
crewmen were holding the oars in their hands and were taking the sails down.
Merrily he began laughing and spoke these words to his comrades:

355　"We will not need to dispatch any message, for they are inside now.
Either it was some god who told them, or they of themselves caught
sight of the other ship passing, but they were not able to catch her."

So did he say; then, rising, they went to the shore of the deep sea.
Quickly they started to drag the black ship up onto the dry land,

360　while proudhearted attendants began unloading the armor.
To the assembly they went in a throng, and they did not allow that
anyone else sit down with them there, of the young or the old men.
Then among them thus spoke Antínoös, son of Eupeíthes:
"Oh what a shame how the gods have delivered this man from affliction!

365　Day by day did the lookouts sit on the wind-swept headlands,
one man always succeeding another; and then at the sunset,
never we passed any night on the dry land, but on the seaway
sailing in our swift ship we awaited the glorious morning,
setting our watches to ambush Telémachos, so we could kill him

370　when we had seized him; but meanwhile a god has guided him homeward.
But let us who are here lay plans for a wretched destruction
now for Telémachos; let him not flee from us, for I believe that
while that man is alive these labors will not be accomplished.
For of himself he is skilled in deliberate counsel and cunning,

375　nor do the people at all bear favor to us any longer.
But come quickly, before he can bring the Achaians together
in the assembly—for not in the least, I am sure, will he slacken,
but he will be outraged; he will stand among all of them telling
how we devised for him utter destruction and did not catch him.

380　Hearing about our evil contrivances, they will not praise us;
I am afraid they will do us evil and drive us away from
our own land, so that we must go to a country of strangers.
Let us forestall him and take him in fields quite far from the city
or on the road, and ourselves lay hold of his living and substance,

385　fairly dividing them up among all of us; as for the palace,
that we would give to his mother to hold and to him who should wed her.
If this speech is not pleasing to you, but instead you prefer that
he continue to live and to keep all the wealth of his fathers,
then we should not be eating away his goods in their pleasing

390　plenty and gathering here; rather each man must from his own house

court her and seek her with marriage presents; and she would in that case
marry the man who gives her the most and comes destined to wed her."
    So did he say; then all of the suitors were hushed into silence.
Straightway raising his voice, Amphínomos spoke and addressed them,
395 glorious son of the great lord Nisos, Arétias' offspring;
he was the leader among those suitors who came from the grain-rich
grassy Doulíchion isle; to Penelope he was the one who
pleased above all in his speeches, for he used excellent judgment.
He with benevolent wisdom addressed them, giving them counsel:
400 "Friends, I would not myself in any way ever desire to
murder Telémachos; it is most terrible, killing a kingly
progeny. Yet let us ask the advice of the gods to begin with.
If indeed the decrees of the great god Zeus do approve it,
I will myself kill him and command all others to do so;
405 but if the gods turn away from the deed, I demand that we stop it."
    So Amphínomos spoke, and his words found favor among them.
Straightway arising, they went back into the house of Odysseus;
having arrived, they took their seats on smooth-polished benches.
    Then other things were devised by Penelope, thoughtful and prudent—
410 showing herself to the suitors of such overbearing presumption,
for she knew of the ruin that threatened her child in the palace—
Medon the herald reported to her what he heard of their counsels.
Down to the hall she descended along with her women attendants.
When she had come down there to the suitors, the splendor of women
415 stood by the pillar supporting the roof beams, stoutly constructed,
holding in front of her cheeks as a veil her shimmering head scarf.
Then to Antínoös she said these words, calling upon him:
"Wanton Antínoös, schemer of bane, they say even so that
you are the best of the men of your age in the Ithakan land at
420 giving advice and at speaking; but you have in fact not been so.
Madman, why do you plot for Telémachos death and destruction
nor pay any attention to supplicants, those for whom Zeus stands
witness? It is not righteous to plot such ills for each other.
Do you not know, one time your father as fugitive came here,
425 fearing the men of the land? For indeed they were dreadfully angered,
seeing that he joined up with the Taphian pirates and harried
those Thesprotians who were allied with our people in friendship.
So they wanted to ruin him utterly, hammer his heart out,
then moreover to eat up his great and agreeable living.
430 It was Odysseus who stayed and restrained them, much as they wished it.

His house now without payment you eat; his wife you are courting;
his is the son you would kill—so huge is the sorrow you cause me.
But I tell you to stop it and order the others to do so."
    Speaking to her then answered Eurýmachos, Pólybos' scion:
435 "Noble Ikários' daughter Penelope, thoughtful and prudent,
take heart, do not allow these matters to trouble your spirit.
That man does not exist, nor will ever exist, nor will be born
who on Telémachos your dear son will lay hands to destroy him,
never while I am alive on the earth and am seeing the daylight.
440 For I say to you plainly, and this thing will be accomplished:
straightway that man's dark-hued blood will be flowing around my
spear shaft, since very often the sacker of cities Odysseus
sat me too on his knees while putting some pieces of roasted
meat in my hands, then holding the red wine up to refresh me.
445 Therefore to me among all mankind is Telémachos dearest
far and away, and I urge that he not be frightened of death, at
least from the suitors; but if from the gods, it cannot be evaded."
    He spoke, cheering her up, but himself was devising the murder.
She then started to climb to her glistening upstairs chamber;
450 there she lamented Odysseus, the husband she loved, till a pleasant
slumber was cast down over her eyes by bright-eyed Athena.
    Then in the evening, the excellent swineherd returned to Odysseus
and to his son, who were readying dinner with careful attention,
killing a year-old pig as an offering. Meanwhile Athena
455 stood there close to the side of Odysseus the son of Laërtes;
touching his head with her wand, she once more made him an old man,
clothed his body in miserable garments, in fear that the swineherd
might, as he looked at him, know who he was, then go with the news to
constant Penelope, nor would he keep it in mind as a secret.
460   It was Telémachos then who first said a word to address him:
"Noble Eumaíos, you come. What news is abroad in the city?
Are the presumptuous suitors within already, returned from
ambush, or do they watch for me yet as I come back homeward?"
    Then in answer to him you spoke, Eumaíos the swineherd:
465 "I was not greatly concerned such things to inquire and to question,
going about in the city; my heart kept urging me swiftly,
once I had told her the message, to get on the way and return here.
There moreover a comrade of yours, a swift messenger, joined me;
he was the herald who first recounted the news to your mother.
470 But there is something else that I know—with my eyes I observed it.

Just now over the city, above on the summit of Hermes,
as I was going along, I saw a swift galley advancing
straight on into our harbor; and numerous men were inside it;
heavily loaded it was with shields and with double-curved spear blades.
475 Those I thought were the men you mention, but I do not know it."
      So he spoke; and the sacred strength of Telémachos, smiling,
glanced with his eyes at his father, but still he avoided the swineherd.
Then when they had completed the work and had readied the dinner,
they dined, nor of the well-shared meal were their hearts at all wanting.
480 When they had quite satisfied their appetites, drinking and eating,
they took thought of their rest and accepted the present of slumber.

BOOK 17

Soon as the Dawn shone forth rose-fingered at earliest daybreak,
straightway under his feet then fastened his beautiful sandals
noble Telémachos, much loved scion of godlike Odysseus;
then he took up a powerful spear which fitted his handgrip.
5 He set out for the city and spoke these words to the swineherd:
"Papa, at once I will go to the city, in order that Mother
see me; for I do not think she ever will bring to a stop her
bitter and loathsome wailing and tearful lamentation,
not till she can behold me in person. But thus do I bid you:
10 lead this miserable stranger along to the city, that he may
beg for his dinner, and there whoever may want to will give him
bread and a cupful of wine; there is no way I can put up with
every man that I meet, such pains in my heart I am feeling.
And if the stranger becomes quite furious, that will be even
15 worse for himself. As for me, plain truth is what I prefer saying."
Speaking to him then answered Odysseus of many devices:
"Friend, I do not myself have any desire to be kept here.
Yes, for a beggar a city is better by far than the country
when he begs for his meal; and whoever may want to will give me.
20 For no longer am I of the age to remain in the farmyard,
so as to follow a master's behest in all that he orders.
You go on; this man you are bidding will give me his guidance
straightway, when I am warm from the fire and the heat of the sunshine.
For these clothes I am wearing are dreadfully vile, and I fear lest
25 frost of the dawn overcome me—you say it is far to the city."
So he spoke, and Telémachos went straight out through the farmyard,
striding on swift feet forward and nourishing bane for the suitors.
Then when he had arrived in the house well-built as a dwelling,
putting his spear down there, he leaned it against a tall pillar;
30 then he himself went into the palace and crossed the stone threshold.

First by far to observe him there was the nurse Eurykleía,
while she was spreading the fleeces upon the elaborate armchairs;
starting to weep, she ran straight up to him then, and around her
gathered the other maidservants of steadfast-hearted Odysseus,
35 giving affectionate welcome by kissing his head and his shoulders.
Prudent Penelope then came down from her upstairs chamber—
Artemis now she resembled, or Aphrodítè the golden—
then in her arms embracing her dear son, she began weeping,
gave him a kiss on his head and on both of his beautiful bright eyes.
40 Sorrowing then she spoke, and in these winged words she addressed him:
"You have arrived, sweet light, dear Telémachos; never again I
thought I would see you once you had gone in the galley to Pylos,
leaving in secret, against my will, to seek news of your father.
But come, tell it to me, however it came to your notice."
45 Thoughtful Telémachos then spoke out to her, giving an answer:
"Mother of mine, do not stir lamentation in me nor arouse my
heart in my breast, since I have escaped from a sheer destruction;
but now, when you have bathed and have put clean clothes on your body,
going upstairs to your chamber along with your women attendants,
50 all of the gods then promise that hecatombs full and effective
you will devote them, if somehow Zeus should accomplish requital.
Now I will go to the place of assembly, so I may invite that
stranger, the man who came in my company hither from Pylos.
I sent him in advance and along with my godlike comrades,
55 told Peiraíos to take him ahead on up to the palace,
treat him with kindly affection and honor till I could arrive here."
So he spoke, and in her was the word unwinged for an answer.
But then, when she had bathed and had put clean clothes on her body,
all of the gods she promised that hecatombs full and effective
60 she would devote them, if somehow Zeus would accomplish requital.
Then did Telémachos start on his way, on out through the palace,
holding a spear, and together with him went two of his swift hounds.
Marvelous then was the grace poured down over him by Athena;
all of the people were gazing in wonder at him as he came on.
65 Then the presumptuous suitors at once came thronging about him,
speaking in fine smooth words, but at heart they plotted him evils.
He however avoided the whole large throng of the suitors,
but where Mentor was sitting and Ántiphos and Halithérses,
who from the very beginning had been his father's companions,
70 there he went and sat down; they asked him for all of the details.

Close to their side now approached Peiraíos, renowned as a spearman,
bringing the stranger along through the town to the place of assembly;
nor did Telémachos turn from the stranger for long, but stood near him.
It was Peiraíos then who first said a word to address him:

75   "Urge your women, Telémachos, quickly to come to my dwelling,
so I can send to you here those gifts Meneláos presented."
　　Thoughtful Telémachos then spoke out to him, giving an answer:
"We do not know, Peiraíos, the way these matters will happen.
If the presumptuous suitors who stay in the palace should ever

80   kill me in secret and then share out all the goods of my fathers,
I want you, much rather than those, to possess and enjoy them.
If it is I, however, who breed for them death and destruction,
happily bring them to me in the palace, and I will be happy."
　　He spoke; into the house he led the long-suffering stranger.

85   Soon as the two had arrived in the house well-built as a dwelling,
first having laid their mantles aside on benches and armchairs,
they stepped into the well-polished tubs and were given a washing.
When maidservants had bathed them and rubbed them with oil of the olive,
they threw garments about the two men, wool mantles and tunics;

90   they stepped out of the basins and took their seats on the benches.
Hand-washing water a maid then carried to them in a lovely
gold-wrought pitcher, and over a basin of silver she poured it,
so they could wash; near them she set out a well-polished table.
Carrying food, the revered housekeeper approached them and set it

95   close to them, many a dish she gladly supplied from her storage.
Opposite him, by the hall's roof pillar, his mother was sitting;
back in her seat she reclined as she turned fine yarn from a distaff.
They stretched forth eager hands to partake of the food lying ready.
When they had quite satisfied their appetites, drinking and eating,

100 speaking among them opened Penelope, thoughtful and prudent:
　　"Now to my upstairs chamber, Telémachos, I will be going,
there I will lie on the bed that has been an occasion for weeping,
always stained with the tears I shed, from the time that Odysseus
parted with Atreus' scions to Ilion; you were not even

105 willing, before the presumptuous suitors had entered the palace,
clearly to tell me the news of your father's return, if you heard some."
　　Thoughtful Telémachos then spoke out to her, giving an answer:
"Certainly, Mother, the tale I will tell you fully and truly.
We first journeyed to Pylos, to Nestor, the shepherd of people;

110 he in his high-raised palace received me kindly and treated

me with a gentle regard, as a father would welcome his own son
newly arrived from a long hard journey abroad—so did he then
treat me with gentle affection, along with his glorious children.
But as to steadfast-hearted Odysseus, he said he had never
115 heard of him either as living or dying from any earth-dweller.
Onward to Atreus' son Meneláos, renowned as a spearman,
he then sent me with horses and chariots, skillfully jointed.
Once there, I saw Helen of Argos, the woman for whose sake
Argives and Trojans endured, by the gods' will, many afflictions.
120 Straightway then the great crier of war Meneláos inquired of
me what need I had had to have come to divine Lakedaímon.
I then related to him the whole business fully and truly.
Finally then he addressed me in these words, giving an answer:
'Shameful to think what strong-hearted man is the one whose bed they
125 want to be bedded in, they themselves being spiritless cowards!
So when a doe having fawns newborn, still sucking her sweet milk,
lulls them to sleep in a thicket, the lair of a powerful lion,
then goes off to the grassy ravines and the spurs of the mountain,
seeking her forage, and then, when he comes back into his covert,
130 both on the brood and the mother he visits a hideous doomsday,
so upon those men Odysseus will visit a hideous doomsday.
Oh Zeus, father of all, and Athena as well and Apollo,
would that he might be such as he was when in well-built Lesbos
he stood up in a contest and wrestled with Phílomeleídes—
135 strongly he gave him a fall, so that all the Achaians exulted.
Would that Odysseus in such a condition could mix with the suitors!
Then they all would become quick-dying and bitterly married!
As for the things you inquire and entreat of me, never would I say
anything swerving away from the truth nor ever deceive you,
140 but whatever the facts the unerring old man of the sea said,
not one word of it all will I hide from you now or conceal it.
He saw him on an island, he said, with his dreadful afflictions,
there in the house of Kalýpso, a nymph who keeps him beside her
forcibly. He is unable to leave for the land of his fathers,
145 since neither well-oared ships does he have near at hand nor companions
who might serve to convey him across the broad back of the deep sea.'
So spoke Atreus' son Meneláos, renowned as a spearman.
When I had done these things, I departed for home; the immortals
gave me a wind and to my dear fatherland swiftly conveyed me."
150   So he spoke, and in her he roused up the heart in her bosom.

Then also godlike Theoklýmenos spoke and addressed them:
"Honored and virtuous wife of the son of Laërtes, Odysseus,
no clear knowledge he has; but attend to this word that I tell you,
for in good truth I will utter a prophecy; I will hide nothing.
155   Zeus be witness the first of the gods, and this table of friendship,
also the hearthstone of faultless Odysseus, to which I have come now,
that already Odysseus is here in the land of his fathers;
yes, he is sitting or moving and learning of these foul actions
somewhere, and he is engendering evils for all of the suitors.
160   Such was the sign of the bird I observed at the time I was sitting
there on the well-benched ship; to Telémachos then I declared it."
    Prudent Penelope then spoke answering words and addressed him:
"May this word now, stranger and friend, be brought to fulfillment!
Thereupon you would at once be aware of my love and of many
165   presents from me, so someone who met you would call you blessèd."
    Such things then they spoke and addressed each one to the others.
Meanwhile all of the suitors in front of the house of Odysseus
were entertaining themselves in hurling the disk and the goat spear,
just as before, on the well-smoothed grounds, in shameless presumption.
170   When it was mealtime then and from everywhere in the fields were
coming the sheep and they drove them into the farmyard as always,
finally Medon spoke to the suitors, for he was the herald
who was most pleasing to them, who waited on them at their dinner:
"Young men, since you have all entertained yourselves with the contests,
175   now come into the house, so that we may prepare us a dinner.
For it is no bad thing for a meal to be taken in season."
    So did he say; then, rising, they went and obeyed what he told them.
Soon as the men had arrived in the house well-built as a dwelling,
first having laid their mantles aside on benches and armchairs
180   they made sacrifice then of the full-grown sheep and the fat goats,
sacrificed sleek hogs also, as well as a cow from the ox herd—
thus they readied the meal.—But Odysseus as well as the noble
swineherd aroused themselves to go in from the fields to the city.
Speaking between them opened the swineherd, leader of people:
185   "Friend, since you are so eagerly wanting to go to the city
this very day, as my lord gave order—and even if I would
like to be able to leave you here as the guard of the farmyard,
but that I hold him in honor and fear him, that afterward he might
blame me for it; the reproaches of masters are risky and painful—
190   but come now, let us go, for the day is indeed for the most part

307

past, and as you will soon find, toward evening it will be colder."
    Speaking to him then answered Odysseus of many devices:
"I know, I understand; to a sensible man you are talking.
But now let us be off; you guide me yourself the whole journey.
195 Give me a staff, if perchance you have had one cut for your own use,
which will support my weight; for the road, they say, is a rough one."
    Thus, and about his shoulders he threw his pitiful knapsack,
riddled with slashes and holes, with a rope well-twisted to hold it.
Then Eumaíos gave him a staff that was pleasing and handy.
200 Both now went on their way, and behind them the dogs and the herdsmen
stayed there guarding the farm; he led to the city his master
closely resembling a beggar, an ancient and miserable vagrant
propped on a staff, who was wearing the vilest of clothes on his body.
    But when, going ahead on the rugged and rock-strewn pathway,
205 they were approaching the city and came to the beautiful flowing
fountain, skillfully made, whence water was drawn by the townsmen,
which Ithakos once fashioned and Néritos too and Polýktor—
there about it was a coppice of poplars that grow by the water,
all of the trees in a circle; the pure cold water was flowing
210 down from the rock up above it; and also above was an altar
built to the nymphs, where every traveler offered oblations—
there did Melánthios, Dolios' son, then come upon them while
driving the goats that were best by far among all of the goat flocks
as a main meal for the suitors; with him came two of the herdsmen.
215 Seeing the two, he began to abuse them and spoke and addressed them
shameless and violent words, and he stirred up the heart of Odysseus:
    "Now does an utterly worthless man lead one who is worthless,
so always is it thus that a god brings a like to a like man.
Where are you leading this wild pig now, despicable swineherd,
220 this obnoxious beggar who scavenges meals and defiles them,
who is for standing at many a doorpost, rubbing his shoulders,
begging for scraps from the table and never for swords or for cauldrons?
If you gave him to me to be made my guard of the farmyard,
he would be sweeping the pens out and taking the kids green fodder,
225 then by drinking the whey, he would build up powerful thigh flesh.
But since mischievous actions are what he has learned, he will not be
willing to come near work; instead he will want to go begging
over the district and seeking to feed his insatiable belly.
But I say to you plainly, and this thing will be accomplished:
230 should he ever arrive at the palace of godlike Odysseus,

there will indeed be many a stool worn out on his ribs when
thrown at his head from the hands of the men all over the palace."
     So he spoke, and as he passed by, in his folly he kicked him
right on the hip; but he did not buffet him out of the pathway;
235 rather he stayed unmoved; and Odysseus was pondering over
whether to leap upon him, with his staff then bashing his life out,
or to lift him by the middle and dash his head on the hard earth.
But he endured it and kept it back in his mind; and the swineherd,
glaring, rebuked him and prayed in a loud voice, lifting his hands up:
240 "Nymphs of the spring, you daughters of Zeus, if ever Odysseus
burned to your honor and pleasure the thighbones of lambs or of young goats,
wrapping them in rich fat, then accomplish the thing I am praying:
let that man come back, let a god lead him to his homeland.
Then he would soon send scattering all of the glorious trappings
245 which in your insolent pride you bear as you always are roaming
here in the town, and the flocks are destroyed by iniquitous herdsmen."
     Speaking to him made answer Melánthios, herder of goat flocks:
"Well now, see how he talks, this hound so skilled in malignance!
Someday I on a dark-hued well-benched galley will carry
250 him far from Ithaka, where he would get me a plentiful fortune.
Would that Apollo whose bow is of silver today in the halls would
shoot down Telémachos or that he might be killed by the suitors,
just as Odysseus has lost faraway his day of returning."
     So did he speak, and he left them there going quietly onward.
255 But as he went, he quickly arrived at the house of his master.
Straightway then he entered and took his seat with the suitors,
facing Eurýmachos, for it was he who especially liked him.
Those who were serving the meal placed near him a portion of roast meat;
carrying bread, the revered housekeeper approached him and set it
260 so he could eat.—When Odysseus approached with the excellent swineherd,
they came close and stood still; and around them sounded the music
out of the hollow lyre, for among them Phemios now had
struck up a song. Then taking his hand, he spoke to the swineherd:
"This is indeed, Eumaíos, the beautiful house of Odysseus,
265 easy to see and to recognize even among many others.
One part leads right into another; the walls and the coping
finish the courtyard well, and the double gates closing the doorways
give it security too; no man with his arms could subdue it.
I can be sure there are numerous men now taking their dinner
270 inside, since smoke rises from it, since also a lyre is

sounding, the instrument made by the gods to accompany feasting."
          Then in answer to him you spoke, Eumaíos the swineherd:
"You know easily, since you are otherwise not without shrewdness.
But come, let us discuss this business, how it should happen.
275   Either do you go first in the house well-built as a dwelling,
going among those suitors, and I will remain here outside;
or if you want, you stay here, and I will go inside before you.
But do not take very long, lest someone observing you outside
hit you or drive you away; such things I would urge you to think of."
280   Answering him then spoke much-suffering noble Odysseus:
"I know, I understand; to a sensible man you are talking.
But you go in before me, and I will remain here outside,
since I am not in the least unacquainted with blows or with missiles.
Mine is a heart of endurance, for many an ill have I suffered
285   both on the waves and in war: let this be added upon them.
But there is still no way of concealing the ravenous belly,
cursèd and baneful, that gives mankind so many afflictions;
on its account are the well-benched ships made ready for sailing
over the desolate sea, to bring evil to men who are hostile."
290   Such things then they spoke and addressed each one to the other.
There was a dog lying near who lifted his head and his ears up—
Argos, steadfast-hearted Odysseus' dog that he once had
reared but he did not enjoy, for he sooner had parted for sacred
Ilion. Sometime past had the young men taken him hunting
295   after the wild goats out in the fields and the deer and the rabbits;
now he was lying neglected—his master so long had been absent—
there on the plentiful dung of the mules and the oxen that had been
heaped in abundance in front of the gates till it could be carried
off by Odysseus' servants to fertilize some of his broad fields.
300   There lay Argos the dog, infested with ravaging dog ticks.
Finally, when he perceived that Odysseus had come up beside him,
wagging his tail he fawned over him, and he laid both ears back;
nevertheless, no longer had he enough strength to approach his
master. But looking away from the dog, he was wiping a tear off,
305   easily keeping Eumaíos from seeing, and asked him a question:
          "This is a marvel, Eumaíos, the dog who lies on the dunghill.
He is quite handsome in body, and yet I cannot be certain
whether he used to be swift in running to match his appearance
or was a dog like those which men are accustomed to have at
310   table, the sort which masters will keep on account of their beauty."

Then in answer to him you spoke, Eumaíos the swineherd:
"This indeed is the dog of a man who faraway perished.
If he were still such now in his body as well as his actions
as he was when Odysseus departed for Troy and so left him,
315 then you would marvel at once as you saw his speed and his prowess.
No wild animal ever escaped from him deep in the deepest
forest when he was pursuing, for he was most skillful at tracking.
Now he is held by affliction: his master has died in another
country; the household women are careless, and they do not tend him.
320 So indeed servants, whenever their lords no longer command them,
then no longer are willing to go on properly working.
For it is true wide-thundering Zeus takes half of the virtue
out of a man at the time he is seized by the day of enslavement."
    So having said, he entered the house well-built as a dwelling.
325 He walked straight through the palace to find the illustrious suitors.
But as for Argos, the doom of his black death finally took him
straightway when in the twentieth year he had looked on Odysseus.
    Godlike Telémachos then was the first by far who had noticed,
coming along through the palace, the swineherd; quickly he nodded,
330 calling him over to him; and in turn he, looking around him,
picked up a stool that was set where the carver would sit when carving
much roast meat for the suitors who took their meals in the palace.
Taking it over, he set it close to Telémachos' table,
opposite him, then sat down himself; and the dinner attendant
335 brought him a portion and set it there and served bread from a basket.
    Right after him then entered Odysseus into the palace,
closely resembling a beggar, an ancient and miserable vagrant,
propped on a staff, who was wearing the vilest of clothes on his body.
He sat down on the ash-wood threshold inside the doorway,
340 leaning his back on a pillar of cypress wood that a workman
once had skillfully planed, made straight by stretching a chalk line.
Calling him over, Telémachos spoke these words to the swineherd,
seizing and lifting a whole big loaf from the beautiful basket,
roast meat also, as much as his arms held round it could carry:
345 "Take these things to the stranger and give them to him, and exhort him
also to go among all of the suitors and beg even more food.
Modest demeanor is no good thing in a man who is needy."
    So he spoke, and the swineherd went when he heard what he told him;
straightway, standing beside him, in these winged words he addressed him:
350 "Stranger, Telémachos gives these things to you; then he exhorts you

311

also to go among all of the suitors and beg even more food.
Modest demeanor is no good thing, so he says, in a beggar."
    Speaking to him then answered Odysseus of many devices:
"Lord Zeus, now among men may Telémachos ever be blessèd;
355   may all things be his fortune that he in his spirit may wish for."
    So he spoke, and in both of his hands he received it and placed it
there in front of his feet, on top of the pitiful knapsack.
Then he ate, as the singer was singing to them in the palace.
When he had eaten his meal and the godlike singer had finished,
360   there in the hall were the suitors arousing a din; but Athena
stood there close to the side of Odysseus the son of Laërtes,
urging him on to collect his pieces of bread from the suitors,
so he would know which ones were the righteous and which were the lawless;
yet even so she would not keep any of them from disaster.
365   He went begging of each man then, from the left to the right side,
stretching his hand all directions, as if he had long been a beggar.
They took pity and gave him bread, and they marveled to see him;
each inquired of the others of him—who he was, where he came from.
Speaking to them made answer Melánthios, herder of goat flocks:
370   "Listen to me, you who of the glorious queen are the suitors,
hearing about this man; for indeed I have seen him before now.
It was the swineherd, you may be sure, who guided him hither;
but I do not know clearly the land he claims he was born in."
    So did he say; Antínoös spoke and berated the swineherd:
375   "Oh most notable swineherd, and why have you brought this fellow
here to the city? Are there not vagrants enough for us, other
wretched importunate beggars who scavenge at meals and defile them?
Or do you take it so lightly that men are devouring your master's
livelihood, gathering here, and invite this man in addition?"
380   Then in answer to him you spoke, Eumaíos the swineherd:
"Though you are noble, Antínoös, what you have spoken is not good.
Who then, going himself, invites from abroad any stranger
ever, unless he is one of the masters who work for the public—
either a prophet, a healer of ills, or a skilled woodworker,
385   even a singer, inspired by the gods, who delights by his singing?
For among men on the measureless earth all these are invited;
no one would ever invite some beggar to eat up his own goods.
But it is always you who are harshest of all of the suitors
here to Odysseus' servants, especially me. But I do not
390   care about that in the least while constant Penelope still is

living, and godlike Telémachos too, right here in the palace."
    Thoughtful Telémachos then spoke out to him, giving an answer:
"Silence! And do not answer the man by speaking at such length.
This Antínoös has a bad habit of always provoking
395   men with injurious words, and he also rouses the others."
    Then to Antínoös these winged words he spoke, and addressed him:
"Kindly you treat me, Antínoös, just as a father his own son,
you who bid me dismiss this stranger and guest from the palace,
speaking in words of constraint—may a god not cause it to happen!
400   Take food, give to him; I do not grudge it; indeed I command it.
Be not at all in awe of my mother in this, nor of any
servant besides among those in the palace of godlike Odysseus.
But in your breast there is certainly no such gracious intention—
you want rather to eat much more than to give to another."
405   Then in return Antínoös spoke to him, giving an answer:
"Tongue-proud Telémachos, reckless in temper—for so have you spoken!
If now all of the suitors should hand him as much as you tell us,
then for at least three months would the house keep him at a distance."
    He said; from under the table he lifted a stool that was lying
410   there, where he placed his glistening feet as he feasted, and showed it.
All of the other men gave him then—so filling his knapsack—
pieces of bread and roast meat, and Odysseus was ready to go back
soon to the threshold, again quite freely to prove the Achaians.
Standing beside Antínoös then, these words he addressed him:
415   "Give, friend; you do not seem to be meanest among the Achaians
in my sight, but the best, since you have a kingly appearance.
Therefore you should be giving more generous portions of bread than
others; and I all over the measureless earth will exalt you.
For in the past I also was fortunate, lived in a wealthy
420   house among men, and on many occasions I gave to a vagrant
freely, whoever he was and whatever he came to me needing.
I had numberless servants and numerous other possessions—
it is with such things men live well and for them are called wealthy.
But Zeus, scion of Kronos, destroyed this—somehow he wished to.
425   He dispatched me to travel, along with far-wandering pirates,
over to Egypt, a long hard voyage, so I would be ruined.
Inside the river of Egypt I anchored the tractable galleys.
Then straightway, to begin, I ordered the trustworthy comrades
there by the galleys to stay and to keep watch over the galleys,
430   also commanded the scouts to go up to the lookout places.

They soon yielded to wanton excess, and pursuing their impulse,
suddenly started to ransack the beautiful fields of the men of
Egypt and carried away their women and innocent children,
killing the men. Then quickly the outcry came to the city;
435   there they heard the commotion and just at the earliest daybreak
came against us—with the footmen and chariots all of the plain filled,
and with the flashing of bronze; then Zeus the great thunderbolt-hurler
threw foul panic among my companions, and none could endure to
stand there facing the foe; for on all sides evils beset us.
440   There they killed a large number of us with their sharp bronze weapons;
others they led off living, to work for them under compulsion.
Me however in Cyprus they gave to a stranger they met with,
Dmetor, the son of Iásos, who ruled by force over Cyprus.
Thence have I come here now in this way after suffering hardships."
445   Then in return Antínoös spoke to him, giving an answer:
"What is the god who has brought this pain, this spoiler of dinner?
Stand as you are in the middle, and stay there away from my table,
lest you soon should arrive in a sorrier Egypt or Cyprus,
such is the bold-faced beggar you are, so utterly shameless.
450   One man after another, you stand beside all, and they give you
recklessly, idly, for no restraint do they feel nor compunction,
favoring you with another man's goods, since each has plenty."
        Drawing away, thus answered Odysseus of many devices:
"Oh what a shame—your mind is no match for your outward appearance!
455   From your own household you would not even give salt to your servant,
you who now sit at another man's table and yet cannot bear to
break off a morsel of bread to give me, when there is such plenty."
        So he spoke; in his heart was Antínoös even more wrathful,
looking from lowering brows, and in these winged words he addressed him:
460   "Now I am sure you will never again go back through the palace
honorably or unscathed, when you speak such scurrilous insults."
        So did he say, then, throwing the stool, he struck his right shoulder
low down, close to the back; and he stood there just as a stone would,
steadfast, nor did Antínoös' missile cause him to stumble.
465   Silently shaking his head, he secretly plotted him evil.
Going again to the threshold, he sat there, putting the well-filled
knapsack down at his side; and he spoke these words to the suitors:
"Listen to me, you who of the glorious queen are the suitors,
so I can say such things as the heart in my breast is demanding.
470   There is indeed no pain in the heart, nor is there any sorrow,

at such times as a man joins battle about his possessions,
making defense of his cattle or white-fleeced sheep, and is wounded.
But Antínoös struck me because of my odious belly,
cursed and baneful, that gives mankind so many afflictions.

475   But if perchance there be any gods and avengers for beggars,
may his ordained death come to Antínoös sooner than marriage."
      Then spoke answering him Antínoös son of Eupeíthes:
"Stranger, be silent and sit there and eat your food or go elsewhere,
lest these youths drag you through the halls for the things you are saying,

480   seizing your foot or your hand, lacerating your skin all over."
      So he spoke; and they all were exceedingly vexed and reproachful;
such are the words which one of the arrogant youths would have spoken:
"It was not well, Antínoös, hitting the miserable vagrant—
cursèd you are if perchance he is some god dwelling in heaven.

485   Yes, it is true that the gods, in the likeness of strangers from distant
lands, take forms of all sorts, then go around visiting cities,
keeping a watch on the malice of men and as well on their fairness."
      Thus did the suitors address him; he took no heed of their speeches.
But in Telémachos' heart was the great grief ever increasing

490   over the blow, but he cast no tears on the ground from his eyelids.
Silently shaking his head, he secretly plotted them evil.
      Meanwhile, soon as the prudent Penelope heard that the man had
just been struck in the hall, she spoke to her women attendants:
"Would that Apollo the glorious archer would strike at the other!"

495   Thus did the housekeeper, old Eurýnomè, speak as an answer:
"Yes, if indeed fulfillment would come to the prayers that we utter,
not one man of them all would arrive at the fair-throned Morning."
      Prudent Penelope then spoke answering words and addressed her:
"Hateful they all are, Mamma, for they are devising us evils.

500   As for Antínoös, he is especially like a dark spirit of ruin:
there is a miserable stranger who wanders about in the palace
begging for food from the men, for necessity bids him to do so;
therefore all of the others have filled his knapsack and given;
this one hit him beneath the right shoulder by throwing a footstool."

505   Such words then she was speaking among her women attendants,
sitting above in her chamber; but noble Odysseus was dining.
Then she summoned the excellent swineherd, and thus she addressed him:
"Come now, noble Eumaíos, and go to the stranger and bid him
come up here, so that I may befriend him warmly and ask him

510   whether of steadfast-hearted Odysseus he somewhere has heard or

seen anything with his eyes, for he seems a far-wandering person."

    Then in answer to her you spoke, Eumaíos the swineherd:
"If the Achaians for your sake, Queen, would at least be silent!
Such good stories he tells, he would charm the dear heart in your bosom.
515 For in my hut three nights I had him and kept him for three days,
for he had come to me first when running away from a galley.
Yet he has not yet finished recounting the tale of his hardships.
As when a man keeps watching a singer who learned from the gods his
knowledge and skill and who sings such tales as are pleasing to mortals—
520 they are insatiably eager to listen to him as he sings them—
so did this man charm me as he sat close by in my chambers.
He informs me that he is a family friend of Odysseus
and that he dwells in Crete, where live the descendants of Minos.
It is from there he has now come this way, suffering hardships,
525 rolling incessantly forward; he claims to have heard of Odysseus—
he is nearby in the fertile land of Thesprotian people;
he is alive and is carrying homeward plenty of treasures."

    Prudent Penelope then spoke answering words and addressed him:
"Go now, summon him here, that himself he can tell me directly.
530 Let those men keep playing their games as they sit in the doorways
or right here in the house, since they are so mirthful of spirit.
For their ample possessions are lying untouched in their houses,
plenty of bread and sweet wine; these their house servants are eating;
day after day in our house they keep on coming and going,
535 killing for victims the sheep and the sleek fat goats and the oxen;
drinking the glistening wine, they revel in festival fashion,
heedlessly, idly, and much has been wasted, for now there is no man
such as Odysseus was to defend this household from ruin.
But were Odysseus to come and arrive in the land of his fathers,
540 he with his son would avenge the men's violence quickly and surely."

    So she spoke; and Telémachos sneezed out loud, and the palace
terribly echoed around with the sound; and Penelope, laughing,
straightway spoke to Eumaíos; in these winged words she addressed him:
"Go as I said now, summon the stranger to come up and see me.
545 Do you not see that my son just sneezed about all I was saying?
Therefore not unaccomplished may death soon be for the suitors,
all of them, nor may a one ward off his death and his doomsday.
Something else I will tell you, and you keep this in your mind now:
if I discover that all he says is the truth and unerring,
550 I will attire him in mantle and tunic, the finest apparel."

So she spoke, and as soon as he heard it, the swineherd departed;
going to stand by Odysseus, in these winged words he addressed him:
"Stranger and father, the prudent Penelope calls you to go there—
she is Telémachos' mother; her heart enjoins her to question
555   you about news of her husband, although she suffers distresses.
If she discovers that all you say is the truth and unerring,
she will attire you in mantle and tunic, the clothes that indeed you
need above all. Then also begging for bread through the country,
you will provision your belly: whoever may want to will give you."
560   Then spoke answering him much-suffering noble Odysseus:
"I would at once, Eumaíos, be willing to tell the whole truth to
noble Ikários' daughter Penelope, thoughtful and prudent—
I know well about him, for the same sad fate we have suffered.
But I am fearful before this muster of dangerous suitors,
565   whose outrages and violence reach to the iron-bright heaven.
For even now, as I went through the house, not planning or doing
anyone evil, when this man struck me and gave me affliction,
neither Telémachos nor any other could offer protection.
Therefore counsel Penelope now to remain in the palace
570   waiting, in spite of her eager desire, till the hour of the sunset;
then let her ask me about her husband's day of returning,
making me sit down nearer the fire, for the garments I wear are
wretched, as you yourself know—it was you I first supplicated."
So he spoke; and as soon as he heard it, the swineherd departed.
575   Straightway as he stepped over the threshold, Penelope asked him:
"Do you not bring him, Eumaíos? And what is the vagrant's intention?
Does he perhaps fear someone excessively, or is he feeling
shamed otherwise in the house? But a bashful tramp is a bad one."
Then in answer to her you spoke, Eumaíos the swineherd:
580   "He speaks measure and reason, as anyone else would be thinking
who would escape from the violent actions of men so audacious.
But he asks you to stay here and wait till the hour of the sunset.
This way also would be for yourself, Queen, greatly the better,
speaking alone to the stranger and hearing the story he tells you."
585   Prudent Penelope then spoke answering words and addressed him:
"Not without sense is the stranger's thinking, however it turns out.
For among mortal mankind there certainly never were any
men so presumptuous, plotting and practicing deeds of such rashness."
Thus it was she addressed him; the excellent swineherd departed
590   back to the throng of the suitors when she had said all she intended.

317

Straightway in these winged words to Telémachos he began speaking,
keeping his head near his, so as not to be heard by the others:
"Dear child, I am now leaving to watch my pigs and those other
things, your living and mine; all these things here are in your care.
595   First of all, see to your own preservation, and keep it in mind lest
you be injured, for many Achaians are plotting us evils—
may Zeus cause their destruction before such harm can befall us!"
      Thoughtful Telémachos then spoke out to him, giving an answer:
"Papa, let it be so; you go when you finish your supper;
600   but come back in the morning and bring us beautiful victims.
Meanwhile all these things shall be my care, and the immortals'."
      So he spoke; on a well-polished stool again sat down the other.
When he had quite replenished his spirit with eating and drinking,
he set off for the pigs and departed from courtyard and palace
605   crowded about with the feasters; and they were enjoying themselves with
dancing and song, for the dusk of the day already was coming.

BOOK 18

There was a communal beggar who came in now—through the town of
Ithaka he was accustomed to beg; he was known for his ravenous belly,
for his continuous eating and drinking; in him there was neither
prowess nor potency, but his physique was enormous to look at.

5   Arnaios was his name, for the lady his mother had given
him that name at his birth; but the young men all called him Iros,
since like Iris he used to run errands when anyone bade him.
He came intent on chasing Odysseus away from his own house,
and he began to revile him; in these winged words he addressed him:

10 "Move from the door, old man, lest soon by the foot you be dragged off.
Do you not notice the men all winking at me as a signal,
calling upon me to drag you away? Yet I am ashamed to.
Up now, lest this quarrel of ours soon turn to a fistfight!"

    Looking from lowering brows said Odysseus of many devices:

15 "Strange man, I am not doing or telling you anything evil,
nor do I grudge anyone who gives, so much has been taken.
This threshold is enough to hold both of us, nor have you any
call to begrudge other men, for it seems to me you are a vagrant,
just as I am; it is only the gods who proffer us blessings.

20 Now with your fists do not challenge me too much, lest you enrage me,
lest, old man that I am, I sully your breast and your lips with
bloodstains—then I would have an abundance of peace, and tomorrow
more yet, since I am sure you would never return for a second
time back here to the house of Odysseus the son of Laërtes."

25   Raising his voice in wrath, thus spoke to him Iros the vagrant:
"Oh what shame how the swine goes rattling along in his speeches,
like some old oven woman! But I should devise for him evils—
beat him with both of my hands, knock all of the teeth from his jaws out
onto the ground, like those of a sow which ruins the grain crop.

30 Gird up your clothes right now, so that all these men may observe us

while we battle. But how could you fight with a man who is younger?"
So were the two men then, in front of the high-built doorway,
there at the smooth threshold, wholeheartedly, fiercely contending.
Then as the sacred might of Antínoös noticed the two men,
35 merrily he began laughing and spoke these words to the suitors:
"Friends, there has never before been anything like this happen,
such is the entertainment a god has now brought to the palace!
That old stranger and Iros are starting a quarrel between them,
going to war with their fists. But at once let us set them together!"
40 So he spoke, and the suitors all sprang to their feet in laughter,
crowding together around those two foul-garmented beggars.
Then among them thus spoke Antínoös son of Eupeíthes:
"Listen to me now, valorous suitors, so I can say something.
Here on the hearth fire lie these bellies of goats that we stuffed with
45 savory suet and blood, then set them there for our dinner.
Now whichever of these men wins and is proven the better,
let him come up and stand here and take whichever he wishes.
Then he will always dine with us too; we will let no other
beggar man join us here in the halls, imploring our favors."
50 So Antínoös spoke, and his words found favor among them.
Then with a trick in his mind said Odysseus of many devices:
"Friends, there is no way, surely, a man who is older and worn with
sorrow can fight with a younger; and yet my villainous belly
urges me on, so that under his blows I fall down vanquished.
55 But come, all of you now must swear me an oath of the strongest,
that nobody, to show his favor to Iros, will strike me,
reckless and heavy of hand, and for him use force to subdue me."
So he spoke, and they all then swore it, as he had demanded.
But then, when they had sworn and had brought their oath to completion,
60 thus did the sacred strength of Telémachos speak and address them:
"Stranger, if now your heart and your valorous spirit are urging
you to ward off this man, you should not be fearful of any
other Achaian; for he who strikes you will fight against many.
I myself am the host, and the two kings give their approval,
65 both Antínoös and Eurýmachos, men who are thoughtful."
So he spoke; they were all in agreement. Straightway Odysseus
girded about his privates the rags he was wearing and showed his
thighs to be handsome and large; and the breadth of his shoulders appeared, as
well as his chest and the well-knit strength of his arms; and Athena
70 stood close by and augmented the limbs of the shepherd of people.

Thereat all of the suitors were hugely impressed and astonished;
thus would one of them say, as he looked at another beside him:
"Quickly will Iros, un-Irosed, have evil that he himself brought on,
such was the great thigh muscle the old man showed from his tatters."

75   So they spoke, and the heart in Iros was dreadfully shaken.
Nevertheless, he was girded and forcibly led by the servants,
terrified so that the flesh all over his body was trembling.
Then Antínoös jeered and said these words, calling upon him:
"You would as well not be, ox-braggart, nor ever have been born,

80   if indeed you are trembling at him and so dreadfully frightened,
this old man, worn down by the trouble and grief he has met with.
But I say to you plainly, and this thing will be accomplished:
if this man wins out over you and is proven the better,
in a black ship I will throw you and send you across to the mainland,

85   to King Échetos, worker of ruin to all who are mortal;
there he will cut off your nostrils and ears with a harsh bronze sword blade,
tear off your privates and give them raw to the dogs to be eaten."
So he spoke, and the trembling that gripped his limbs was yet stronger.
Into the middle they led him, and both men lifted their hands up.

90   Thus then pondered the matter much-suffering noble Odysseus,
whether to strike so the soul would abandon him there as he fell down,
whether to stretch him out on the ground by striking him gently.
So as he pondered the matter, the best course seemed to be this one,
gently to strike him, so the Achaians would not be suspicious.

95   They both put up their hands, and on his right shoulder then Iros
hit him; he under the ear, on the neck, hit Iros and crushed his
bones inside, and at once from his mouth red blood came gushing;
bellowing he fell down in the dust, and his teeth crashed together,
as he was kicking the ground with his feet; the illustrious suitors

100   lifted their hands and were dying with laughter; and meanwhile Odysseus,
gripping his foot, dragged him through the doorway till in the courtyard
he had arrived, and the portico doors; by the wall of the court he
seated him leaning against it and into his hand put a long staff;
raising his voice he spoke, and in these winged words he addressed him:

105   "Sit right there from now on, so keeping the pigs and the dogs off;
do not be any longer the chieftain of strangers and beggars,
wretch that you are, or you may well win yet greater affliction."
Thus, and about his shoulders he threw his pitiful knapsack,
riddled with slashes and holes, with a rope well-twisted to hold it.

110   Going again to the threshold, he sat there; the suitors were laughing

sweetly as they went in, and they made him welcome with speeches;
111a such are the words which one of the arrogant youths would have spoken:
"May Zeus grant to you, stranger, as well as the other immortal
gods, what most you desire and whatever is dear to your spirit,
now you have stopped that ravenous fellow from roaming about all
115 over the district; for soon we will take him across to the mainland,
to King Échetos, worker of ruin to all who are mortal."
    Thus he spoke, so that noble Odysseus rejoiced at the omen.
Then Antínoös set down before him a large belly pudding
filled with the suet and blood stuffed in; Amphínomos also
120 picked two bread loaves out of the basket and set them beside him;
drinking his health from a cup made of gold, these words he addressed him:
"Welcome, father and stranger; and may good fortune attend you
ever hereafter; but now you are gripped by many afflictions."
    Speaking to him then answered Odysseus of many devices:
125 "You are indeed, so it seems, Amphínomos, sound in your judgment;
such was your father, because I have heard of his fine reputation—
Nisos, Doulíchion's lord—to be both well meaning and wealthy;
his they say you were born; you seem like a man of discretion.
So I will speak to you now: you give your attention and hear me.
130 Nothing of slighter account than a man does the earth ever nurture,
even among all creatures on earth both breathing and creeping;
for he believes he will never be suffering ills in the future
while gods grant him his prowess and still he can set his limbs moving;
but whenever the fortunate gods bring sorrows upon him,
135 these he bears, though against his will, with a heart of endurance.
For of the men who dwell on the earth, such a mood does the mind have
as is the day that the father of gods and of mankind brings them.
There was a time even I should have been among men who are blessèd;
yielding to might and coercion, I did many things that were reckless,
140 since I had put my trust in my father as well as my brothers.
Therefore, never at all should a man be heedless of justice
but in quiet preserve the gods' gifts, whatever they give him.
Such are the reckless acts I see these suitors contriving—
they lay waste the possessions, dishonor the wife, of a man who
145 not much longer will be, I tell you, away from his loved ones
nor from his fatherland now—he is quite close by. May a god soon
lead you away to your home, and may you not have to encounter
that man when he returns to the much loved land of his fathers.
For I am certain that not without blood will the suitors and he be

150　parted and leave off fighting when he comes into his palace."
　　　　So he spoke, then making libation, the honey-sweet wine he
　　drank, and he put the cup back in the hands of the marshal of people.
　　Sorrowing deep in his heart, Amphínomos went through the palace,
　　shaking his head, for his spirit indeed foreboded disaster.
155　Yet even so he did not flee fate, for Athena had bound him
　　too to be quelled by the hands and the spear of Telémachos' prowess.
　　Then he again sat down on the armchair whence he had risen.
　　　　Straightway the goddess bright-eyed Athena put into the mind of
　　noble Ikários' daughter Penelope, thoughtful and prudent,
160　now to appear to the suitors, that she might yet even further
　　open the hearts of the suitors to love and that she would be honored
　　more than before she had been in the eyes of her son and her husband.
　　Idly she laughed, to her maid spoke these words, calling upon her:
　　"Now my heart is desiring, Eurýnomè, as it has never
165　done before this, to appear to the suitors, although they are hateful.
　　I would as well say a word to my child, that it might be better
　　not to be always mingling among the presumptuous suitors,
　　who speak nicely to him but devise foul deeds for the future."
　　　　Thus did the housekeeper, old Eurýnomè, speak as an answer:
170　"Certainly all this, child, you speak as is fitting and proper.
　　Go now, speak to your child this word, no longer conceal it,
　　once you have washed your skin and your cheeks also have anointed;
　　do not go down thus, with your face all ravaged and foul with
　　tearstains, since it is bad to be mourning so endlessly, always.
175　For it is true your child is already the age that you most have
　　prayed the immortals that you might see him become, full-bearded."
　　　　Prudent Penelope then spoke answering words and addressed her:
　　"No, Eurýnomè, much as you care for me, do not persuade me
　　this way, to wash my skin and anoint myself with an unguent.
180　For it is true that the gods who possess Olympos destroyed my
　　beauty and charm, from the time he left in the hollow galleys.
　　But go bid my maids Autónoë and Híppodameía
　　come to me, so they can stand at my side down there in the great hall.
　　Not by myself will I go among men, since I am ashamed to."
185　So she spoke; the old woman at once set off through the palace,
　　taking the women her message and bidding them come in a hurry.
　　　　Then other things were devised by the goddess bright-eyed Athena;
　　sweet was the slumber that she poured down on Ikários' daughter;
　　she leaned backward and slept, and the joints of her limbs were all loosened,

190   there on the couch as she lay; and the splendor of goddesses meanwhile
gave her ambrosial gifts, so the Achaians would marvel to see her.
First she cleansed and embellished her beautiful face with a fragrant
balm of ambrosial beauty, the sort fair-wreathed Kythereía
rubs on herself when she goes to the ravishing dance of the Graces;

195   also she made her taller and ampler of body to look at,
caused her as well to be whiter than ivory sawn for a statue.
These things having accomplished, the splendor of goddesses parted.
Out of the hall then approached her the white-armed women attendants,
talking as they came on, and the sweet sleep lifted and left her.

200   Then with her hands she wiped off her cheeks and began to address them:
"Now in my terrible anguish a soft sleep covered me over.
How I wish that a death so soft chaste Artemis now would
give me at once, so that I no more with the grief in my heart would
keep on wasting my life as I long for a much loved husband's

205   manifold virtue, for he was outstanding among the Achaians."
    So she spoke, and went down from her glistening upstairs chamber,
not by herself, for together with her went two of her handmaids.
When she had come down there to the suitors, the splendor of women
stood by the pillar supporting the roof beams, stoutly constructed,

210   holding in front of her cheeks as a veil her shimmering head scarf;
standing with her there, one at each side, were the virtuous handmaids.
Then were the men's limbs loosened, their hearts enchanted with passion;
they all loudly were praying to lie in the bedding beside her.
It was Telémachos whom she addressed, her son so belovèd:

215   "Now are your mind and intentions, Telémachos, steady no longer;
while you were still quite a child, in your mind you were better at thinking;
now when you are grown up and have come to the measure of manhood,
so that the child of a fortunate man somebody would think you—
one who came from abroad—on observing your stature and beauty,

220   yet your mind no longer is righteous, nor are your intentions,
such is the shameful deed that has just been done in the palace—
you have allowed this stranger and guest to be treated so badly.
How is it now if the stranger and guest who here in our palace
sitting should suffer so much brutality, bitter and painful?

225   Then among men you would bring on yourself disgrace and derision."
    Thoughtful Telémachos then spoke out to her, giving an answer:
"Mother of mine, I cannot reproach you for feeling this anger;
I am at heart quite conscious of everything; I have noticed
better and worse deeds both, though before this I was still childish.

230 Nevertheless, I cannot be sure about all that is prudent;
for as they sit one side and the other devising their evils,
these men make me distracted, and I have no one to help me.
But the contention between that stranger and Iros did not turn
out as the suitors desired—the old man was the stronger in prowess.

235 Oh Zeus, father of all, and Athena as well and Apollo,
so too now may it be for the suitors who stay in our palace—
may they nod their heads, overcome, some out in the courtyard,
some inside of the house, with the limbs in each of them loosened—
just as for Iros the vagrant, who out at the gate of the courtyard

240 now sits nodding and lolling his head, like a man who is drunken,
nor is he able to stand up straight on his feet nor to go back
home, wherever his home might be, for his limbs are all loosened."

Such were the things they spoke and addressed each one to the other.
Then Eurýmachos spoke to Penelope, uttering these words:

245 "Noble Ikários' daughter Penelope, thoughtful and prudent,
if now all the Achaians throughout Iásian Argos
saw you, there would be yet more suitors to take their dinner
here in your house in the morning, since you stand out among women
both in appearance and size, in the mind well-balanced within you."

250 Prudent Penelope then spoke out to him, giving an answer:
"No, Eurýmachos, all my distinction in beauty and body
was destroyed by the deathless gods when the Argives boarded
galleys for Ilion—then with them went my husband Odysseus.
If that man were to come back home, my life he would care for;

255 greater would be the renown I have, more splendid, in that case.
Now I mourn, so much is the evil a god sent against me.
But at the time he parted, forsaking the land of his fathers,
picking my right hand up by the wrist, he spoke to me these words:
'Dear wife, because I cannot believe that the well-greaved Achaians

260 all will be coming from Troy back home quite well and uninjured—
for as they say, indeed, those Trojans are men who do battle,
whether as throwers of spears or as shooters of arrows or else as
drivers of swift-footed chariot horses, the ones who determine
fastest of all the great issue of war's impartial contention—

265 therefore I do not know if the god will restore me or whether
I will be killed there in Troy; here everything is in your charge.
Hold in your memory, here in the halls, my father and mother,
even as now or yet more, since I will be absent and far off.
But then, when you behold our child an adult, full-bearded,

270   marry whomever you wish to and leave your household behind you.'
       So he spoke at the time; now this is all being accomplished.
       There will indeed be a night when a hateful marriage will come to
       me, unhappy, accursed, whom Zeus has bereaved of her blessings.
       But this terrible grief comes over my heart and my spirit:
275   what you suitors are doing is not what justice devised in
       earlier times for the men who wished to pay court to a noble
       woman, a rich man's daughter, and vie for her, each with the others.
       Such are the men who themselves bring up with them cattle and fat sheep,
       meals for the friends of the lady, and give her glorious presents;
280   but they never consume without payment the goods of another."
              So she spoke; he rejoiced, much-suffering noble Odysseus,
       that she extracted from them their gifts and enchanted their hearts with
        words mollifying and bland, but her mind held other intentions.
              Answering her then spoke Antínoös son of Eupeíthes:
285   "Noble Ikários' daughter Penelope, thoughtful and prudent,
       as to the gifts which any Achaian is wishing to bring here,
       take them, since it cannot be good to refuse any present.
       Never will we go back to our earlier farm work nor elsewhere,
       not until you be wed to the noblest among the Achaians."
290   So Antínoös spoke, and his words found favor among them.
       Then each one of them sent out a herald to bring back presents.
       One to Antínoös carried a robe, very large and embroidered
       beautifully; twelve brooches in all were fastened upon it,
       made out of gold, all fitted with clasps well bent for securing.
295   One to Eurýmachos straightway brought an elaborate necklace,
       golden and strung with pieces of amber—the sun it resembled.
       Two of Eurýdamas' servants returned to him carrying earrings—
       each of three clustering droplets—from which great glamour was shining.
       Then also from the lord Peisander, the son of Polýktor,
300   one of his servitors carried a necklace, a lovely adornment.
       Other magnificent presents were brought by the other Achaians.
       Then did the splendor of women ascend to her upstairs chamber;
       following her were the handmaids who carried the beautiful presents.
              They then turned their minds to the dance and delectable singing,
305   playing to please themselves, and awaited the evening's onset.
       While they were taking their pleasure, the evening gloom came upon them.
       Straightway then they set three braziers up in the great hall,
       so that they might give light, and around them laid dry firewood
       seasoned a long time, utterly parched, new-split with a bronze axe.

310 Mingled with them were the torches that steadfast-hearted Odysseus'
    maids took turns holding up for the light they gave; and among them
    he himself spoke, Zeus-nourished Odysseus of many devices:
    "Maids of Odysseus, the master who now so long has been absent,
    go along now, back into the house where the august queen is;
315 there at her side, twist wool from the distaff, do her some pleasure,
    sitting with her in the chamber, or else with your hands card raw wool.
    Meanwhile, I will be furnishing light here for all of these people,
    even if they should desire to remain till the fair-throned Morning,
    never will they overcome me; for I am devoutly enduring."
320   So did he say; they broke out laughing and looked at each other.
    Shamefully then by Melántho of beautiful cheeks he was scolded,
    her whom Dolios fathered; Penelope saw to her welfare,
    bringing her up like a daughter, and giving her toys to her liking;
    yet even so in her mind was no thought of Penelope's sorrow,
325 but with Eurýmachos now she would mingle affection and make love.
    She it was who with words of reproach now scolded Odysseus:
    "Impudent stranger, you must be a man whose wits have been knocked out—
    you do not wish to depart, go sleep at the house of the bronzesmith
    or at a public resort, but in this house here you are saying
330 so many things among so many men so boldly and are not
    frightened at heart. Wine seizes your brains, or perhaps it is always
    this sort of mind you have, that you speak so idly and vainly.
    Are you beside yourself that you beat down Iros the vagrant?
    Take heed, lest some other man better than Iros should stand up
335 soon who would beat you about your head with his heavy and huge hands,
    then send you from the palace, defiled by many a bloodstain."
        Looking from lowering brows said Odysseus of many devices:
    "Soon I will go to Telémachos, bitch, and report to him there what
    words you have said, so that he might straightway cut you to pieces."
340   So as he spoke, with his words he terrified all of the women.
    They went off through the house, and the limbs of each one became looser
    from the alarm; for they thought it the truth, these things he had spoken.
    He meanwhile stood there by the fiery braziers, keeping
    light while looking at all of the men; but the heart in his breast was
345 pondering other proceedings that would not be unaccomplished.
        By no means did Athena permit that the arrogant suitors
    keep their deeds from heart-anguishing outrage, so even greater
    pain might enter the heart of Odysseus the son of Laërtes.
    It was Eurýmachos, Pólybos' son, who was first to address them;

350 speaking abuse of Odysseus, he roused his comrades to laughter:
"Listen to me, you who of the glorious queen are the suitors,
so I can say such things as the heart in my breast is demanding.
Not ungodly has this man come to the house of Odysseus;
no, for it seems to me now that the light of the torches is coming
355 from his own head, for on it is no hair, not even the slightest."
　　Thus, and he also spoke to Odysseus the sacker of cities:
"Stranger, would you be willing, if I should hire you, to labor
out at the edge of the fields—and the pay I give will suffice you—
gathering stones for the fences and nurturing trees to grow taller?
360 As for your bread there, I would provide you a regular portion,
also dress you in clothes; for your feet I would furnish the sandals.
But since mischievous actions are what you have learned, you will not be
willing to come near work; instead you will want to go begging
over the district in order to feed your insatiable belly."
365 　　Speaking to him then answered Odysseus of many devices:
"Would that a contest of labor, Eurýmachos, might be between us,
when in the springtime season the days grow longer and longer,
out in the meadow; and I would be holding a well-bent sickle;
you would be holding the same, so that we could be tested at labor,
370 keeping a fast till the evening shadows, with plenty of grass there.
Or if instead there were oxen to drive, they being the finest,
tawny and huge in body, and both well filled with their fodder,
equal in age and in plowing, the power in them not decrepit,
thus over four full measures the clods gave way to the plowshare—
375 then you would see whether I cut forth a continuous furrow.
Or if the scion of Kronos should somewhere raise up a battle
this very day, and a shield and two spears I had for the fighting,
also a helmet entirely of bronze well fitting my temples,
then you would see me mingling in battle along with the foremost—
380 nor would you then make speeches to me so abusing my belly.
But you are most outrageous, the mind in you is unbending—
doubtless you think yourself to be someone weighty and potent
only because you consort with these few men, none of them noble.
But if Odysseus should come and arrive in the land of his fathers,
385 quickly indeed would the doors, although in fact very broad ones,
be too narrow for you as you took flight out through the forecourt."
　　So he spoke; in his heart was Eurýmachos even more wrathful,
looking from lowering brows, and in these winged words he addressed him:
"Wretch, I will soon cause evil to you for the way you are speaking

390   such things now among so many men so boldly and are not
frightened at heart; wine seizes your brain, or perhaps it is always
this sort of mind you have, that you speak so vainly and idly.
Are you beside yourself that you beat down Iros the vagrant?"
So having spoken, he picked up a footstool. Quickly Odysseus
395   sat at the knees of Amphínomos, lord of Doulíchion, feeling
fear of Eurýmachos; it was the wine server then that he struck on
his right hand, so that onto the ground fell clanging the pitcher;
as for the man, he fell on his back in the dust and was groaning.
There in the shadowy hall were the suitors arousing an uproar;
400   thus would one of them say as he looked at another beside him:
"How I wish that the stranger had strayed elsewhere and before he
came been killed—that way he would never have raised such tumult!
Now that we quarrel about these beggars, no more in the noble
banquet will there be pleasure, for ever the worst is the winner."
405   Thus did the sacred strength of Telémachos speak and address them:
"You fools! You are demented and hide in your hearts no longer
what you have eaten and drunk; it is one of the gods who has roused you.
But having thus dined well, go away to your houses and lie down,
when your own hearts bid you to do so—I drive away no man."
410   So he spoke, and they all kept biting their lips with their teeth in
wonder at hearing Telémachos now, he was talking so boldly.
Then Amphínomos spoke and addressed them, giving them counsel—
he was the glorious son of lord Nisos, Arétias' scion:
"Friends, no man should become enraged at a thing that is spoken
415   justly and so use quarrelsome words when giving an answer.
Do not at all maltreat this stranger nor yet any other
servant among those here in the palace of godlike Odysseus.
But come now, let the wine server pour the first drops in the goblets,
so we can pour libation and go to our homes and our slumber;
420   as for the stranger, let him go into the halls of Odysseus,
now, to Telémachos' care; it is his dear house he has come to."
So did he say, and the word he spoke pleased all of the suitors.
Doing their bidding, the hero Moulios mixed up a wine bowl—
he the Doulíchian herald who was Amphínomos' servant—
425   then he passed it around to them all in order; and pouring
offerings out to the fortunate gods, they drank of the sweet wine.
When they had made libations and drunk whatever their hearts wished,
then they departed to rest for the night, each one to his own house.

BOOK 19

Meanwhile noble Odysseus remained right there in the palace;
he, and Athena with him, were devising the death of the suitors.
Straightway in these winged words to Telémachos he began speaking:
"All of the weapons of battle, Telémachos, we should at once stow
5   inside; then you will put off the suitors with soft and beguiling
speeches as soon as they miss them and ask you questions about them:
'Out of the smoke I have put them, for they no longer resemble
what they were when Odysseus departed for Troy and forsook them
but have become quite foul, so much has the fire's breath reached them.
10   Then too, a god put into my mind this thought even greater:
deep in your wine cups, you might stir up a quarrel among you,
then you would wound each other and bring disgrace on the banquet
and on your courting, for iron itself draws a man to employ it.'"
So he spoke, and Telémachos heeded his much loved father.
15   Calling her out of the house, he spoke to the nurse Eurykleía:
"Come, Mamma, give me your help; keep out of the halls the maidservants,
so I may stow in an inside chamber the arms of my father,
beautiful ones, untended, that smoke in the palace has tarnished
since my father departed, for I myself was too childish.
20   These I now would bestow where the breath of the fire will not reach them."
Then spoke giving an answer the much loved nurse Eurykleía:
"Certainly, child, I hope that you sometime lay hold of prudence
so that you care for the household and keep safe all your possessions.
But come, who will go after a light and then carry it for you?
25   You will not let come forth any maids who might have borne torches."
Thoughtful Telémachos then spoke out to her, giving an answer:
"This same stranger; for I will not let someone who has taken
bread of mine do no work, even though from afar he has come here."
So he spoke; and in her was the word unwinged for an answer;
30   she put bars on the door of the house well-built as a dwelling.

Jumping up, quickly Odysseus along with his glorious son then
started to carry the helmets, the strong-bossed shields, and the pointed
spears inside of the house; and before them Pallas Athena
made them a beautiful light; she was holding a gold-wrought lantern.
35 Quickly Telémachos spoke and addressed these words to his father:
"Father, immense is the marvel that I with my eyes am beholding:
strangely but surely the walls of the hall and the beautiful bases,
also the fir-wood beams and the towering pillars that hold them,
shine to my eyes as resplendent as if it were fire that was flashing.
40 Surely within there is one of the gods who hold the broad heaven."
     Speaking to him then answered Odysseus of many devices:
"Silence, and keep this back in your mind, and do not ask questions.
This in truth is the way of the gods who inhabit Olympos.
But as for you, go now to your bed, while I stay behind here,
45 so as to stir up the maids, and your mother as well, even further;
mourning and weeping for me, about everything she will ask me."
     So he spoke, and Telémachos started away through the palace,
under the blaze of the torches, to go lie down in his chamber,
where he had rested before, any time sweet sleep came upon him.
50 There now also he lay and awaited the glorious morning.
Meanwhile noble Odysseus remained right there in the palace;
he, and Athena with him, were devising the death of the suitors.
     Prudent Penelope then came down from her upstairs chamber,
Artemis now she resembled, or Aphrodítè the golden.
55 Close to the fire, in the place she sat, they put her an armchair,
inlaid with spirals of silver and ivory; this had the craftsman
called Ikmálios fashioned; beneath for the feet was a footstool
which he had joined to the chair; over all was a great fleece spread out.
It was upon this armchair that prudent Penelope sat now.
60 Out of the hall did the white-armed maidservants then start coming,
taking away much leftover bread and removing the tables,
also the goblets from which those arrogant men had been drinking.
Throwing the fire to the ground from the braziers, they began heaping
much more firewood upon them to use for both heating and lighting.
65 Straightway Melántho again for the second time scolded Odysseus:
"Stranger, will you even now all night be giving us trouble,
prowling about through the palace, and keep on ogling the women?
Go out of doors instead, you wretch, and be grateful for dinner!
Otherwise you may be going outdoors when struck by a firebrand!"
70 Looking from lowering brows said Odysseus of many devices:

331

"Madwoman, why do you set upon me in rancorous spirit?
Is it because I am dirty and wear foul clothes on my body,
begging about the whole district? Necessity drives me to do it.
Such in fact is the portion of beggars and wandering people.

75   For in the past I also was fortunate, lived in a wealthy
house among men, and on many occasions I gave to a vagrant
freely, whoever he was and whatever he came to me needing.
I had numberless servants and numerous other possessions—
it is with such things men live well and for them are called wealthy.

80   But Zeus, scion of Kronos, destroyed this—somehow he wished to.
Therefore you take heed now, woman, lest all of the charming
beauty you lose in which you excel now among the maidservants,
lest your mistress perhaps get angry and treat you unkindly,
or lest Odysseus return, since there is a measure of hope yet.

85   If in fact he has perished and never will have a homecoming,
yet is his child already, Telémachos, thanks to Apollo,
equal to him; in his house, no woman of reckless misdoings
ever escapes his notice, since he is no longer so childish."

       Such were the words he uttered; and prudent Penelope heard him,
90   then she scolded the maid and said these words, calling upon her:
"Not in the least, you brazen and shameless bitch, you escape me,
doing your monstrous deed: you shall wipe it off on your own head.
All this you knew well, for you listened to me as I said it,
how, right here in my house, I was going to ask of the stranger
95   what of my husband he knew, since I incessantly mourn him."

       Thus, and she spoke this word to Eurýnomè, her housekeeper:
"Bring me a chair here now, Eurýnomè, spread with a sheep fleece,
so that the stranger can sit here and tell me his tale and can listen
also to what I say; I am eager to ask him some questions."

100   So she spoke; very quickly a well-polished armchair the woman
brought there and set in place and upon it spread out a sheep fleece.
Then on the seat sat down much-suffering noble Odysseus.
Speaking among them opened Penelope, thoughtful and prudent:
"Stranger, to start with, I will myself now ask you a question:
105   Who are you? Whence do you come? What city is yours, and what parents?"
       Speaking to her then answered Odysseus of many devices:
"Lady, among men here on the measureless earth there is no one
who would abuse you, for truly your glory has reached the broad heaven,
much like that of a blameless king who, fearing the gods, holds
110   sway as the lord over men both many and mighty in valor,

332

one who justly upholds good laws; and the rich black earth brings
forth both barley and wheat, and with fruit are the trees heavy-laden,
so do his flocks bear young without fail, and the sea provides fish, all
coming from his good rule, and the people beneath him prosper.
115   So about anything else, inquire of me now in your palace,
but of my race or the land of my fathers do not ask questions,
so that you may not fill my heart yet fuller with sorrows
when I remember; for I am a man of much woe, and I do not
need to sit here in the house of another lamenting and making
120   moan, since it is far worse to be mourning incessantly, always.
One of your handmaids or you yourself might want to reproach me,
say it is out of a mind made heavy with wine that my tears flow."
      Prudent Penelope then spoke out to him, giving an answer:
"Stranger, whatever I had of distinction in beauty and body
125   was destroyed by the deathless gods when the Argives boarded
galleys for Ilion—then with them went my husband Odysseus.
If that man were to come back home, my life he would care for;
greater would be the renown I have, more splendid, in that case.
Now I mourn, so much is the evil a god sent against me.
130   All of the highborn chieftains who lord it over the islands,
over Doulíchion, Samè, and also wooded Zakýnthos,
also those who dwell around Ithaka, bright in the sunshine,
seek me in marriage against my wishes and wear out the household.
Therefore neither to strangers nor supplicants am I attentive
135   nor in the least to the heralds, who work for the good of the people;
but in the depths of my heart I pine away, wanting Odysseus.
They keep hastening marriage, and I keep spinning deceptions.
First some god inspired in my mind the idea of a mantle;
putting the great loom up in my chamber, I set about weaving
140   delicate fabric of amplest measure, and thereupon told them:
'Young men, suitors for me, since noble Odysseus has perished,
wait, hold off from the marriage you urge upon me, until I can
finish the mantle, lest all of the yarn be uselessly wasted.
It is a burial robe for the hero Laërtes, for when he
145   falls in the ruinous doom of his death so long in the mourning,
lest in the town some woman among the Achaians reproach me
that this man who acquired so much should be lying unshrouded.'
So I spoke, and the valorous spirits in them were persuaded.
Then each day I would weave at the loom, enlarging the fabric,
150   while each night I undid it, when torches I had set beside me.

So three years by my craft I fooled and convinced the Achaians,
but when the fourth year came with the passing of hours and of seasons,
with the decline of the months, when many a day was completed,
finally they, by the help of the maids, those shameless bitches,
155 coming upon me, caught me and shouted reproaches together.
Thus I completed the cloth unwillingly, under compulsion.
Now I can neither escape this marriage, nor can I discover
any contrivance besides; my parents are eagerly urging
me to be married; my son is incensed at them eating our living,
160 as he observes it, for he is already a man who can quite well
take good care of a house of the sort to which Zeus grants honor.
Nevertheless, tell me your descent and the place that you come from,
since you are not sprung out of the oak or the rock of the proverb."
    Speaking to her then answered Odysseus of many devices:
165 "Honored and virtuous wife of the son of Laërtes, Odysseus,
will you not leave off, ever, inquiring about my ancestry?
Yet I will tell you plainly, and so you will give me to greater
sorrows than those I have, for such is the rule when a man has
been outside of his country as long as I now have been absent,
170 roaming among many cities of mortals and suffering sorrows.
Nevertheless I will tell you the things you ask and inquire of.
There is a land called Crete, in the midst of the wine-dark seaway,
lovely and fertile, and girt by the sea flood; within it are many
people, in fact past counting; the cities are ninety in number;
175 every language is mixed with the others; therein are Achaians,
there greathearted Original Cretans, Kydonians also,
Dorians triply divided, and noble Pelasgian people,
one of their towns the great city of Knossos; and therein Minos
reigned as the king nine years—great Zeus was his intimate fellow—
180 father of that greathearted Deukálion who was my father.
Me and the lordly Idómeneus both Deukálion fathered.
But it was he who along with the scions of Atreus went to
Ilion, sailing the well-curved ships; my glorious name is
Aithon—I was the later in birth; he was older and braver.
185 There it was that I looked on Odysseus and gave him a guest-gift.
For in fact he was carried to Crete by the force of a stormwind,
when he was set toward Troy, past Máleia driving him off course;
he made land at Amnísos, wherein is Eileíthyia's cavern,
in a most difficult harbor, and barely escaped from the tempest.
190 Seeking Idómeneus, he straightway went up to the city,

334

for, he informed them, he was his guest-friend, dear and respected.
But already the tenth or eleventh dawn was upon him
since in his curved ships sailing to Ilion he had departed.
So I brought him along to my house, and I well entertained him,
195   kindly befriending him there—in the house were abundant provisions.
Then to himself and the other companions who followed him thither
I gave barley and glistening wine that I got from the people,
cattle to sacrifice too, so their appetites might be contented.
There for a twelve-day stay those noble Achaians were waiting,
200   for the great north wind Boreas held them and would not allow them
even to stand on the earth; some cruel divinity roused it.
When on the thirteenth day the wind dropped, they started their voyage."
    So did the numerous falsehoods he told seem like a true story.
Tears flowed down from her then as she listened; her body was melted.
205   Just as the snow melts down on the topmost peaks of the mountains—
Euros the east wind melts it when Zephyr the west wind has heaped it—
then as the snow keeps melting the rivers are flowing replenished,
so now her beautiful cheeks as the tears flowed down them were melting,
while she wept for her husband, who sat at her side. But Odysseus,
210   though in his heart he pitied his wife who for him was lamenting,
yet did his eyes stay steady, as if made of horn or of iron,
under his lids, untrembling; his tears he concealed by his cunning.
But then, when she had taken her comfort in tearful lamenting,
once more giving an answer she spoke these words and addressed him:
215   "Now then, as to your story, I think I will test you, stranger,
whether it really is true that along with his godlike comrades
you in your halls entertained my husband, as you have been saying.
Tell me, what were the sorts of apparel he wore on his body;
what was he like himself, those also with him as his comrades?"
220   Speaking to her then answered Odysseus of many devices:
"Lady, indeed it is hard to relate to you, such is the length of
time since parting; for it is already the twentieth year from
when he started from there and departed the land of my fathers.
Nevertheless I will tell you the picture my spirit imagines.
225   Noble Odysseus was wearing a mantle of wool, deep purple,
folded in two; and the breast pin of gold on it had been fashioned
with twin sockets. The face of the brooch was an elegant figure:
it was a hound that was holding a dappled fawn in his forepaws,
looking at it as it panted; and all men wondered at seeing
230   how, though they were of gold, the dog gazed at the fawn he was throttling

335

while with its feet it struggled and frantically tried to escape him.
As for the tunic he wore on his body, I saw that it glistened
much like the shimmering over the dried-out skin of an onion,
such was the silky refinement; the light was as bright as the sunshine.
235 Many indeed were the women admiringly gazing upon it.
Something else I will tell you, and you keep this in your mind now:
I do not know if Odysseus had worn these clothes from his own home
or some comrade had given him them as he boarded the swift ship—
or it perhaps was a friend from abroad, for to many Odysseus
240 used to be friends, for among the Achaians few men were his equal.
There I gave him a sword made of bronze and a beautiful double
mantle of purple, as well as a tunic with fringes around it,
then with due honor I sent him away on his well-benched galley.
He had a herald as well, who was somewhat older than he was,
245 following him; what manner of man he was I will tell you.
He had shoulders that sloped, was a dark-skinned man, wooly-headed,
named Eurybátes, and more than the other companions Odysseus
held him in honor, for he was a match to himself in his thinking."
He spoke, stirring in her yet greater desire for lamenting
250 as she perceived to be certain the tokens Odysseus had shown her.
But then, when she had taken her comfort in tearful lamenting,
finally answering him she spoke these words and addressed him:
"Now for me, stranger, although you before were an object of pity,
here in this palace of mine you will be both dear and respected,
255 for it was I myself who gave him the garments you tell of,
folding them up in my room; I fastened the glistening breast pin
on as adornment for him. But I never again will receive him
when he returns to his house and the much loved land of his fathers.
So by a mischievous fate on a hollow galley Odysseus
260 parted to see Evililion, that place not to be mentioned."
Speaking to her then answered Odysseus of many devices:
"Honored and virtuous wife of the son of Laërtes Odysseus,
no more now devastate your beautiful skin, neither waste your
heart in lamenting your husband—though not in the least would I blame you.
265 For indeed any woman will mourn when she loses her wedded
husband, to whom, having coupled in love, she has brought forth children—
even one not like Odysseus: the gods they say he resembles.
But leave off your lamenting, and mark this word of mine closely:
this is the truth unerring I tell you, and I will hide nothing,
270 how I have heard already about the return of Odysseus—

he is nearby in the fertile land of Thesprotian people;
he is alive and is bringing the many and excellent treasures
he went begging throughout that land. But his trustworthy comrades
he has lost, and his hollow ship, on the wine-dark seaway,
275   leaving Thrinakia Island; for odious he had become to
Zeus and to Helios too, whose cattle the comrades had slaughtered;
thus they all were destroyed on the seaway surging and dashing.
Riding the keel of the ship, he was thrown by a wave on the mainland,
in the Phaiákians' land—to the gods those people are kindred.
280   They in their hearts as if he were a god then honored him greatly;
many a gift they gave him and wanted themselves to escort him
homeward safe and unharmed; and a long time since would Odysseus
have been here, but it seemed to his mind this course would be better,
getting together possessions by going about many countries.
285   For of advantage and profit, Odysseus, of men who are mortal,
knows a great deal—no other man even would give him a contest.
So to me then the Thesprotians' king, great Pheidon, narrated.
In my presence he swore—in his house poured out a libation—
there was a ship drawn down to the sea, and the comrades were ready
290   who would convey him back to the much loved land of his fathers.
But before that he sent me away, for a ship of Thesprotian
men chanced then to set sail for Doulíchion, wealthy in wheat fields.
Also he showed me the many possessions Odysseus had gathered.
Even to ten generations would these feed, each in succession—
295   such great treasures of his lay there in the halls of the ruler.
He said Odysseus had gone to Dodóna in order to listen
there to the counsel of Zeus from the oak tree, lofty and leafy,
how he could go back home to the much loved land of his fathers
now he had long been away—in the open or else in secret.
300   So as you see from my tale, he is safe, already is coming;
he is quite close, nor away from his friends and the land of his fathers
will he be gone very long; in fact this oath I will give you.
Zeus be witness the first—of the gods, he is highest and greatest—
also the hearthstone of faultless Odysseus, to which I have come now:
305   all these things will be brought to fulfillment as I am declaring.
Sometime within this same moontide will Odysseus arrive here,
one moon just having waned and the next one just at its onset."
    Prudent Penelope then spoke answering words and addressed him:
"May this word now, stranger and friend, be brought to fulfillment!
310   Thereupon you would at once be aware of my love and of many

presents from me, so that someone who met you would call you blessèd.
But in my heart it seems to me this will be how it will happen:
neither again to his home will Odysseus return, nor will you find
any escort, since here in the household are no such masters

315 such as Odysseus was among men, if he ever existed,
who could dispatch respectable strangers as well as receive them.
But come, maidservants, give him a wash, lay down for him bedding—
bedstead first, then mantles and covers of shimmering fabric—
so that sufficiently warm he arrives at the Dawn of the gold throne;

320 then very early at dawn you will give him a bath and anoint him,
so that within at Telémachos' side, he may think of his dinner,
as he sits in the palace; and it will be painful to any
spirit destroyer among them who troubles him—he will accomplish
nothing at all any more, even if he is dreadfully angry.

325 Otherwise how would you learn of me, stranger, if I among other
women am most outstanding in mind and in circumspect counsel,
if you, squalid and dirty and dressed in the vilest of garments,
sit in the palace to dine? Men flourish the briefest of seasons.
When some person is heartless himself and his thinking is heartless,

330 then all people invoke on him curses for pain in his future
while he is living, and when he is dead all mock and deride him;
but when a person is faultless himself and his thinking is faultless,
then do his guest-friends carry his fame far abroad to remotest
regions among all peoples, and many men say he is noble."

335   Speaking to her then answered Odysseus of many devices:
"Honored and virtuous wife of the son of Laërtes Odysseus,
hateful to me such mantles and covers of shimmering fabric
ever have been since first from the snow-clad mountains of Crete I
took my leave when I went on board of the long-oared galley;

340 I will lie down as before, those nights I passed without sleeping.
For in fact there was many a night in a comfortless bed I
passed, and I lay there awaiting the Dawn, resplendent and fair-throned.
Neither to me in my heart such water for washing the feet is
pleasing at all, nor upon these feet of mine shall any woman

345 lay her hands among those who are working for you in the household,
not unless there is an elderly woman, astute and devoted,
one who has suffered in spirit as many afflictions as I have;
then if she laid her hands on my feet, I would make no objection."
     Prudent Penelope then spoke answering words and addressed him:

350 "Stranger and friend—for a man so thoughtful has never arrived more

welcome to me of the strangers who came from abroad to my household,
so very wisely do you speak thoughtfully all that you utter—
there is indeed an old woman of mine with a mind full of counsel,
she who tended and nursed that man so unhappy, and reared him,
355 after receiving him into her hands when his mother first bore him—
she will be washing your feet, although her strength is but feeble.
But come now, stand up, Eurykleía, sagacious and prudent,
wash this man the same age as your master—and doubtless Odysseus
now already is such in his feet, in his hands such also,
360 for in affliction do mortals become more rapidly agèd."
    So did she say; then holding her face in her hands, the old woman
shed hot tears from her eyes, and the word she spoke was of mourning:
"Ah me, child, I am helpless to succor you. Surely above all
men Zeus hated you most, though you had a god-fearing spirit,
365 since no one among mortals to Zeus the great thunderbolt-hurler
ever has burnt fat thighbones or hecatombs chosen, in such great
numbers as those you presented to him as you prayed that you might reach
old age sleek and contented and raise your son to be noble.
Only from you has he now quite taken your day of returning.
370 Thus him too, I suppose, have the women of faraway strangers
mocked and derided, whenever he came to their glorious houses,
just as at you these bitches are all of them mocking and jeering,
so that you now, to avoid their insults and many reproaches,
do not allow them to wash you; but willing I am, and am asked by
375 noble Ikários' daughter Penelope, thoughtful and prudent.
So I will wash your feet for Penelope's sake and as well for
your own sake, for the heart inside of my breast is aroused by
sorrowing. But come now, pay heed to the word I address you:
many the strangers have been, long-suffering, who have arrived here,
380 yet I am sure I have never before seen one who resembles
him as in body, in voice, and in feet you resemble Odysseus."
    Speaking to her then answered Odysseus of many devices:
"So do they say, old woman, whoever have seen with their own eyes
both that man and myself, that indeed we closely resemble
385 each to the other, as you have yourself just noticed and told me."
    So he spoke; the old woman then took up a glittering basin
which she used in foot washing and poured in plenty of water,
cold to begin, then added the hot to it. Meanwhile Odysseus
stayed in his seat by the hearth; then quickly he turned to the darkness,
390 for in his heart he suddenly thought that as soon as she touched him,

she would discover his scar and the facts of the case would be open.
Coming up close, she was washing her master and quickly discovered
that very scar which a boar inflicted on him with its white tusk
when to Autólykos once and his sons he had gone, to Parnassos.
395 He was his mother's illustrious father, excelling all men in
thieving and sly oath taking; to him the god Hermes himself had
given the talent, for he had been pleased by the thighbones the man had
burnt him, of lambs and of kids, and was eager to show him his favor.
Once Autólykos journeyed to Ithaka's fertile dominions;
400 there he found that a child had been recently born to his daughter;
then as her father had finished the meal, Eurykleía had laid her
offspring down on his knees and said these words, calling upon him:
"Now, Autólykos, find for yourself some name to bestow on
this dear child of your child; he is one who has been much prayed for."
405   Then in answer to her Autólykos spoke and addressed them:
"Son-in-law and my daughter, bestow this name that I tell you.
Seeing that I who have come here now am detested by many,
odious on the much nourishing earth both to men and to women,
so let his name be Odysseus the odious: but as to my part,
410 when he reaches adulthood and comes to the house of his mother's
family there on Parnassos, in which I keep my possessions,
many of these I will give him and send him back to you happy."
         Thus came Odysseus, that he might give him the glorious presents.
Him Autólykos welcomed, the sons of Autólykos also,
415 taking his hand in their own and addressing him words of affection.
Old Amphithéa, his mother's mother, embracing Odysseus,
gave him a kiss on his head and on both of his beautiful bright eyes.
Then Autólykos called to his glorious sons and commanded
them to make ready the meal; they listened to what he was urging.
420 Straightway an ox, a male five years old, they led in the dwelling,
flayed it and got it prepared, dismembering all of the carcass;
skillfully cutting it up, on stakes they spitted the pieces,
then they carefully roasted the meat and divided the portions.
So it was that for that whole day till the hour of the sunset,
425 they dined, nor of the well-shared meal were their hearts at all wanting.
Soon as the sun went down and the shadows of night came upon them,
then they lay down to rest and accepted the present of slumber.
         Soon as the Dawn shone forth rose-fingered at earliest daybreak,
they set forth to go hunting, the dogs and the men themselves, those
430 sons of Autólykos; noble Odysseus as well went along with

them, and together they came to the steep high mount of Parnassos,
mantled in forest, and swiftly the windy ravines they ascended.
Helios then was beginning to strike at the plowlands, arisen
out of the silently flowing abysmal stream of the Ocean,
435   when at a forested canyon the beaters arrived; and before them
tracking the quarry, the dogs were advancing; and after them came those
sons of Autólykos; noble Odysseus as well went along with
them, much nearer the dogs; a long-shadowing spear he was shaking.
There in the thick undergrowth of a copse was a huge boar lying.
440   This no watery might of the blustering winds ever blew through,
nor with its beams did the radiant sun ever strike to the bottom,
nor did the rain penetrate it all of the way, for it was so
thick; inside, an enormous abundance of leaves had collected.
But to the boar came noise from the feet of the dogs and the huntsmen
445   as upon him they were driving; against them out of the thicket,
bristling the hair on his back, and the fire in his eyes bright-glaring,
he stood close to the huntsmen; the first of them all was Odysseus
rushing the boar while lifting his long spear high in his stout hand,
eager to deal him a wound; but the boar got ahead of him, striking
450   over the knee, and he scooped out much of the flesh with a tusk by
thrusting obliquely at him, though he did not reach the man's thighbone.
Hitting him on the right shoulder, Odysseus wounded the creature,
so that the point of the glittering spear passed onward and through him.
Squealing he dropped in the dust, and the life breath flew from his body.
455   First with the boar the dear sons of Autólykos busied themselves, then
skillfully bound up the wound of Odysseus, faultless and godlike,
while they were holding his dark blood back with an incantation
sung on it; quickly they went to the dwelling of their dear father.
Him Autólykos healed, and the sons of Autólykos also,
460   excellently, and providing him then with glorious presents,
speedily sent him rejoicing away to his own dear country,
Ithaka. When he returned, his father and reverend mother
welcomed him back to his home; they asked about all that had happened,
how he had suffered the wound; and to them he related it fully,
465   told how the boar with its white tusk wounded him while he was hunting,
when he had gone with the sons of Autólykos up to Parnassos.
      This scar now the old woman, as she with the palms of her hands was
touching him, knew by its feel and let go of the foot she was holding;
into the basin his shin fell down, and the bronze clattered loudly;
470   back to one side it tipped, on the ground so spilling the water.

Pleasure and sorrow at once laid hold of her mind, so that both eyes
filled with the tears she shed; and her vigorous voice became silent.
Taking his beard in her hand, she spoke these words to Odysseus:
"Certainly, dear child, you are Odysseus; but not even I could
475   recognize you before every part of my lord I had handled."

So she spoke; to Penelope then her eyes she directed,
wanting to let her know that her own dear husband was inside.
She however could not look her in the face nor perceive her,
for her perception Athena was turning aside. But Odysseus,
480   groping for her with his hands, took hold of her throat with the right one,
as with the other he pulled her closer to him and addressed her:
"Mamma, now why do you want to destroy me? For you are the one who
brought me up at your breast; now, suffering many afflictions,
I have returned in the twentieth year to the land of my fathers.
485   But since you have perceived, and a god put it into your spirit,
hush, lest somebody else in the halls discover my presence.
For I say to you plainly, and this thing will be accomplished:
if a god under my hand brings down the illustrious suitors,
nurse though you are, I will not hold off from you when I am set on
490   killing the others, the women and maidservants, here in my palace."

Then spoke answering him Eurykleía, sagacious and prudent:
"Oh my child, what a word has escaped from the fence of your teeth now!
You know well that my spirit is steady in me and unyielding,
how I will hold out just as a fixed stone would or as iron.
495   Something else I will tell you, and you keep this in your mind now:
if a god under your hand brings down the illustrious suitors,
then I will tell you about these women who serve in the palace,
those who bring you dishonor and also those who are guiltless."

Speaking to her then answered Odysseus of many devices:
500   "Mamma, now why are you speaking of them to me? You do not need to;
I will observe for myself quite well, find out about each one.
Keep your story in silence; entrust to the gods what will happen."

So he spoke; the old woman at once set off through the palace,
fetching the foot-washing water; for all of the first had been tipped out.
505   When she had washed him and rubbed him richly with oil of the olive,
once more nearer the fire was his chair drawn up by Odysseus,
so he could warm himself, but the scar he concealed in his tatters.
Speaking among them opened Penelope, thoughtful and prudent:
"Stranger, again I will ask you myself of a matter, a small one,
510   for in fact it will soon be the hour for the pleasures of slumber—

sleep is delightful, whomever it grips, even if he is grieving.
Me however a god has endowed with a grief beyond measure:
during the day, I take my pleasure lamenting and mourning,
seeing to my own tasks and to those of the maids in the household;
515 but when the night comes on, when sleep grips all of the others,
I lay there in my bed, and about my quick-beating heart crowd
sharp anxieties which torment me as I am lamenting.
As Pandáreos' daughter, the nightingale, singer of greenwood,
raises her beautiful song when spring has but recently started,
520 sitting among thick-flowering foliage deep in the forest,
often she varies her strain while pouring her many-trilled song out,
raising lament for her dear son Ítylos, child of Lord Zethos,
whom with a sword one day she killed in maniacal folly—
so my heart is divided and starts one way, then the other,
525 whether I stay with my child, keep vigilant watch over all these
things I possess, these maids, this mighty and high-roofed palace,
thus respecting my husband's bed and the voice of the people;
whether I finally go with the noblest among the Achaians
who pays court to me here in the halls, gives numberless bride gifts.
530 While he still was a child, still weak in his thinking, my son would
never allow me to marry, forsaking the house of my husband;
now when he is grown up and has come to the measure of manhood,
he is imploring me even to go back home from the palace,
fretting about the possessions of his the Achaians are eating.
535   "But come now and interpret a dream of mine, after you hear it:
Here in my house I have twenty geese who are eating the wheat up
out of the water trough; I am rejoicing at them as I see it.
Down from a peak then came an enormous and hook-beaked eagle;
all of their necks he broke, and he killed them; they in a heap lay
540 piled in the hall, and the bird soared up in the bright and divine air.
Then—it was still in the dream—I started to weep and bewail them;
women with beautiful tresses, Achaians, were gathered around me,
as I woefully mourned for my geese that the eagle had slaughtered.
He however returned, and he perched on the jut of a rafter;
545 then in the voice of a mortal, he checked my tears and addressed me:
'Be of good heart now, widely renownèd Ikários' daughter;
this is no dream, but a genuine vision that will be accomplished:
those same geese are the suitors, and formerly I was the eagle
which as an omen you saw; I have come back now as your husband,
550 who will inflict on all of the suitors a hideous doomsday.'

343

So did he say; then quickly the honey-sweet slumber released me;
as I was glancing around, I observed that the geese in the halls were
feeding on wheat from the trough, just where they had earlier eaten."
    Speaking to her then answered Odysseus of many devices:

555 "It is impossible, lady, to twist this dream to another
meaning, interpreting it; since it was Odysseus himself who
told you the way it will happen: their ruin is plain for the suitors,
all of them, nor may a one ward off his death and his doomsday."
    Prudent Penelope then spoke answering words and addressed him:

560 "Stranger, of difficult meaning are dreams, and of endless confusing
stories, and they are not all fulfilled for the people who have them.
For they are double, the portals of dreams so feeble and fleeting:
there is one set made of horn, and of ivory work is the other;
as to the dreams which pass through the fine-sawn ivory portals,

565 they are illusory, bearing a tale that will not be accomplished;
as to the others that pass outside through the well-polished horn gates,
they bring truth to fulfillment, whenever a mortal may see them.
But I am sure it was not through these that a dream so astounding
came to me—that to my son and to me would indeed be welcome!

570 Something else I will tell you, and you keep this in your mind now:
there will a dawn soon come most evil of name that will take me
out of the house of Odysseus; for now I will set up a contest,
having to do with the axes that that man, here in his palace,
used to stand up in a row, all twelve, like a shipwright's trestle;

575 then he would stand at a distance and shoot through them with an arrow.
This is the contest which I will now set up for the suitors.
He who is nimblest at bending the bow with his hands to the bowstring,
then through all twelve axes is able to shoot the one arrow,
him I will follow as spouse, so leaving behind me the house where

580 I was a bride, so lovely, so full of the goods of existence—
I feel sure I will always remember it, even when dreaming."
    Speaking to her then answered Odysseus of many devices:
"Honored and virtuous wife of the son of Laërtes, Odysseus,
now no longer put off this contest here in the palace.

585 For I am sure that Odysseus of many devices will come here
sooner than these men manage the bow so skillfully fashioned,
bending it well to the string, then shooting a shaft through the iron."
    Prudent Penelope then spoke answering words and addressed him:
"If you, stranger, would like to delight me, sitting beside me

590 here in the halls, sleep never would be poured over my eyelids.

But in fact there is no way possible people can always
be without sleep; for to everything the immortals have dealt out
portions befitting to mortals upon the grain-nourishing plowlands.
Now to my upstairs chamber to take rest I will be going;
595 there I will lie on the bed that has been an occasion for weeping,
always stained with the tears I shed, from the time that Odysseus
parted to see Evililion, that place not to be mentioned.
There will I lie down now; meanwhile you lie in this palace,
spreading your bed on the ground or else getting the servants to place it."
600   So having spoken, she climbed to her glistening upstairs chamber,
not by herself, for together with her went the others, her handmaids.
Going upstairs to her chamber along with her women attendants,
there she lamented Odysseus, the husband she loved, till a pleasant
slumber was cast down over her lids by bright-eyed Athena.

BOOK 20

Meanwhile noble Odysseus retired to his rest in the forecourt,
under him spreading an untanned oxhide, placing upon it
many a fleece of the sheep the Achaians had offered as victims;
over him, when he lay down, Eurýnomè threw on a mantle.

5 There in his heart for the suitors Odysseus was pondering evils
while he was lying awake. Then out of the palace the women
came, those who had before been going to bed with the suitors,
each entertaining the others with laughter and happy amusements.
But as for him, in his breast was a heartfelt anger arising;

10 much he was pondering over the thoughts in his mind and his spirit,
whether to spring upon them and accomplish the death of each woman
or to allow them to lie once more with the arrogant suitors
this last, final occasion; the heart inside him was growling.
Just as a bitch who has taken a stand by her powerless puppies

15 growls at a man that she does not know and is eager to fight him,
so was he growling inside, indignant at their wicked actions.
Striking himself on the breast, he spoke to his heart in reproval:
"Steady, my heart, and endure: you suffered another more shameful
thing on the day that the Cyklops, resistless in power, was eating

20 those strong comrades of mine; you endured till Nobody's cunning
led you away from the cavern in which you expected to perish."
So he spoke in his breast as he pressed the appeal on his own heart.
Therefore his heart held, bound by persuasion; and ever unblenching
so it endured; he himself kept twisting one way and the other.

25 As when a man keeps shifting a paunch that has been stuffed full with
suet and blood, in a huge fire's blaze, one way and the other
turning it over, and wishes for it to be rapidly roasted,
so did he twist one way and the other and kept meditating
how he could manage to lay his hands on the shameless suitors,

30 being but one against many. Athena, descending from heaven,

346

came up close to him there; she had likened her form to a woman;
standing above his head, she spoke these words and addressed him:
"Why do you wake, who beyond all mortals are destiny-ridden?
This is in fact your house; in the house this woman is your wife;
35   as for the child, he is surely the son anybody would long for."
        Speaking to her then answered Odysseus of many devices:
"Certainly all this, goddess, you speak as is fitting and proper.
Yet there is this that the heart in my breast still keeps meditating,
how I can manage to lay my hands on the shameless suitors—
40   being but one, while they in the palace are always together.
Then a more difficult thing in my breast I keep meditating—
thus: if indeed, by the succor of you and of Zeus, I should kill them,
where would I go to escape? I ask you to think about these things."
        Speaking to him made answer the goddess bright-eyed Athena:
45   "Obstinate man! Some people will trust an inferior comrade,
though he is mortal, and knows no counsel as crafty as mine is;
I am a god, however, who keep a continual watch on
you in all of your trials; and this I will say to you plainly: .
if in fact there were fifty battalions of men who are mortal
50   standing around us, eagerly striving to kill us in battle,
even from them you would drive their cattle away and their fat sheep.
But allow slumber to take you; a pain this is, to be watching
all night, lying awake; you will soon rise out of your troubles."
Such words when she had spoken, she poured sleep over his eyelids;
55   straightway the glorious goddess herself went back to Olympos.
        While he was held by slumber, releasing the cares from his spirit,
loosing his limbs, his devoted and virtuous wife was awakened;
there in her soft bed she sat up, and she wept and bewailed him.
But then, when in her heart she was quite satisfied with her weeping,
60   first did the splendor of women to Artemis make her entreaty:
"Artemis, august goddess and daughter of Zeus, how I wish that
you by striking my chest with an arrow would take out the life breath
now, this moment, or else that a stormwind seizing upon me
then would be gone from here, bearing me forth on the vaporous pathways,
65   casting me down at the mouth of the back-flowing river of ocean,
just as it was when the stormwinds seized Pandáreos' daughters,
girls whose parents the gods had destroyed, so that they were forsaken
there in the palace, as orphans; and bright Aphrodítè provided
nourishment, giving them cheese, sweet honey, and wine to their pleasure.
70   Hera to them moreover beyond all women presented

347

beauty and sensible minds; chaste Artemis granted them stature;
how to do glorious handcraft work they were taught by Athena.
Then, when bright Aphrodítè ascended to lofty Olympos,
so as to seek for the girls the fulfillment of flourishing marriage,
75 praying to Zeus the great thunderbolt-hurler, who knows about all things
well—what is fated and what not fated for men who are mortal—
that was the time those maidens were all snatched up by the stormwinds,
who gave them to the hateful Erinyes to be taken care of;
so may the gods with Olympian dwellings annihilate me now,
80 or may the fair-haired Artemis strike me down, so that I go
under the hateful earth with my mind's eye still on Odysseus,
lest I gladden the thoughts of another, inferior husband.
But an endurable evil possesses a person whenever
somebody weeps all day, without cease in her heart is lamenting,
85 yet sleep holds her at night; for of all it makes her forgetful,
both of the good and the evil, when it comes over her eyelids.
But now even the dreams that a god sent against me are evil,
since last night there was sleeping beside me a man who resembled
him as he was when he went with the army; and therefore my heart felt
90 joyful, for I did not think it a dream but a genuine vision."
   So she spoke, and at once upon her came Dawn of the gold throne.
There to her voice as she wept kept listening noble Odysseus;
then as he pondered her words, it seemed to his heart that already
now she had recognized him and beside his head she was standing.
95 So he gathered the mantle and fleeces on which he was lying,
laid them down on a chair in the hall, then taking the oxhide
out, laid it on the ground, and to Zeus prayed, lifting his hands up:
"Zeus our father, if willing at last you gods have conveyed me
over the dry and the wet to my land, when much you had harmed me,
100 let someone among those who are waking impart me an omen,
speaking within, and without let a portent of Zeus appear also."
   So he spoke in his prayer; Zeus Counselor heard him and heeded;
straightway then he sounded his thunder from shining Olympos,
high aloft out of the clouds, so that noble Odysseus was joyful.
105 Out of the house nearby where the shepherd of people had set up
mills was an omen of words dispatched by a woman, a miller—
sitting at them, twelve women in all were engaged in the labor,
barley and wheat meal they were producing, the marrow of people.
Now were the others asleep, since they were through grinding their wheat meal;
110 only the one had not finished, for she was the weakest among them;

stopping her mill, she spoke this word as a sign to her master:
"Zeus our father, who rule as the lord of the gods and of mankind,
loudly you sounded your thunder from out of the star-filled heaven,
nor is a cloud anywhere; as a sign you show this to someone.
115 Even for me, though wretched, fulfill this word that I utter:
may those suitors on this very day for the last and the final
time in the house of Odysseus partake of a pleasurable dinner,
they indeed who have loosened my knees in heart-anguishing labor
making the barley meal; for the last time now may they banquet!"
120 So did she say; then noble Odysseus rejoiced at the omen,
as at the thunder of Zeus; for the guilty, he thought, would be punished.
      There in the beautiful house of Odysseus, the rest of the handmaids
gathered together and kindled a weariless fire on the hearthstone.
Out of his bed then rising, Telémachos, godlike in manhood,
125 put on his clothing and hung his keen-edged sword on his shoulder;
under his glistening feet he fastened his beautiful sandals;
then he took up his powerful spear, well-pointed with sharp bronze.
Going to stand on the threshold, he spoke and addressed Eurykleía:
"Mamma dear, how have you honored the stranger and guest in our palace?
130 Given him food and a bed? Or instead does he lie uncared for?
That is the way my mother can be, though a sensible woman—
she is impulsive in showing respect to the one who is worse of
men who are mortal; the better she sends from the house without honor."
      Then spoke answering him Eurykleía, sagacious and prudent:
135 "Child, now I wish you would not lay blame upon her who is blameless.
For as he sat there, wine he was drinking as long as he wanted;
as to the food, no more was he hungry, he said, for she asked him.
Afterward, when he at last began thinking of bed and of sleeping,
she then ordered the women attendants to spread out his bedding;
140 he however, like one who is utterly woeful and hapless,
had no wish to be going to sleep on a bed or in blankets,
but on the untanned hide of an ox and on fleeces of sheep he
slept outside in the forecourt; and we put a mantle upon him."
      So she spoke; and Telémachos set forth out of the palace,
145 holding his spear, and together with him went two of his swift hounds.
He went on to the meeting, to join with the well-greaved Achaians.
Meanwhile the women attendants were called by the glorious woman
old Eurykleía the daughter of Ops, offspring of Peisénor:
"Come now; some of you busy yourselves in sweeping the palace,
150 sprinkle the floor, then throw on the well-made armchairs the purple

349

coverlets; others of you get busy with sponges and wipe off
thoroughly all of the tables and then go clean out the wine bowls,
also the well-wrought cups, double-handled; and others among you
go to the spring after water and come back bringing it quickly.

155 For it will not be long that the suitors are gone from the palace;
they will arrive quite early, for all take part in this feast day."
So did she say; they carefully listened to her and obeyed her.
Twenty of them went out to the spring with its deep dark water,
while right there in the palace the others were skillfully working.

160 Into the house came haughty menservants, and they then started
splitting the firewood well and expertly; and shortly the women
came back up from the spring; just after them entered the swineherd,
driving in three fat swine, those which were the best of the whole herd.
These he allowed to go search out food in the lovely enclosure,

165 while he himself in gentle and kind words spoke to Odysseus:
"Dear friend, do the Achaians regard you with greater respect now,
or do they slight you still in the house, as before they were doing?"
Speaking to him then answered Odysseus of many devices:
"Surely I wish that the gods, Eumaíos, would punish the outrage

170 which in their recklessness these arrogant men have been wreaking
here in another man's house, and they have no share of discretion."
Such were the things they spoke and addressed each one to the other.
Then did Melánthios, herdsman of goats, come up and approach them,
driving the goats that were best by far among all of the goat flocks

175 for the repast of the suitors; with him came two of the herdsmen.
These goats under the echoing portico then they tethered,
while he himself spoke out to Odysseus in words of derision:
"Stranger, will you even now in the house be giving us trouble,
begging your keep of the men, and will you not get along outdoors?

180 As for the two of us, I am quite sure we will never be parted
till we have tested our fists, since you are without due order
when you are begging; and other Achaians as well hold banquets."
He said; Odysseus of many devices returned him no answer;
silently shaking his head, he secretly plotted him evils.

185 Third then coming to them was Philoítios, leader of people,
driving a sterile heifer and fat goats in for the suitors.
These had been carried across by ferrymen, those who provide for
other men also conveyance, whoever arrives at their landing.
These beasts under the echoing portico then he tethered,

190 while he himself stood close to the swineherd, making inquiry:

"What new stranger is this who has come so recently, swineherd,
here to our palace? And who are the people he claims to derive from?
Where does his family live now, and where are the fields of his fathers?
He is ill fated but seems in stature a king and a leader.
195 Yet it is true that the gods bring pain to far-wandering mortals,
anytime—even for kings—they spin out sorrow and hardship."
    Thus, and he greeted him then with his right hand, standing beside him.
Raising his voice he spoke, and in these winged words he addressed him:
"Welcome, father and stranger; and may good fortune attend you
200 ever hereafter; but now you are held by many misfortunes.
Oh father Zeus, there is no other god more baneful than you are!
You do not show any pity for men when once you beget them,
when they plunge in the midst of affliction and miserable hardships.
I began sweating as soon as I thought, my eyes became tearful,
205 when I remembered Odysseus, because he too, I suppose, is
wearing old rags like these as he wanders about among mankind,
if he perhaps still lives, still looks upon Helios' sunlight.
If he has died already and dwells in the palace of Hades,
ah me then for the faultless Odysseus, who set me in charge of
210 cattle, a young boy still, in the Képhallénians' district.
Now that stock has become quite numberless, nor among men has
anyone's breeding of broad-browed cattle produced such an increase;
these are the ones which strangers command me to bring to themselves for
eating, and do not care in the least for the child in the palace,
215 nor do they quake at the gods' supervision; for they are already
eager to share out the wealth of the lord who long has been absent.
But it is this that the heart in my own dear breast is revolving
often, that while his son is alive, it would be a great evil
going away to the country of others and taking the cattle
220 there among alien men; yet this is more dreadful, to stay here
taking in charge those cattle for other men, suffering hardships.
Certainly I would have fled long since and arrived at another
proud-souled king, since this is no longer a place to put up with;
but of the luckless man I think still, if coming from somewhere
225 he might cause those suitors throughout his palace to scatter."
    Speaking to him then answered Odysseus of many devices:
"Oxherd, since you seem like a man neither evil nor senseless—
I am myself well aware what wisdom has entered your spirit—
therefore I will say this, and a great oath swear you upon it:
230 Zeus be witness the first of the gods, and this table of friendship,

also the hearthstone of faultless Odysseus, to which I have come now—
while you are still inside it, Odysseus will come to his dwelling;
then with your own eyes, should you desire it, you will observe those
suitors be slaughtered who here in the palace are playing the masters."

235   Speaking to him then answered the herdsman, tender of cattle:
"Stranger and friend, may the scion of Kronos accomplish your saying!
Then you would learn what strength I have and what hands to employ it!"
So in like fashion Eumaíos was praying to all of the gods for
various-minded Odysseus to come back home to his palace.

240   Such things then they spoke and addressed each one to the others,
while for Telémachos' death and destruction the suitors were making
ready their plots; but a bird came over their heads on the left side—
it was a high-flying eagle; a tremulous dove it was holding.
Then Amphínomos spoke and addressed them, giving them counsel:

245   "Friends, this plan of ours now never will run true to our wishes,
plotting Telémachos' murder; instead, let us think about feasting."
So Amphínomos spoke, and his words found favor among them.
When they had gone back into the palace of godlike Odysseus,
first having laid their mantles aside on benches and armchairs,

250   they made sacrifice then of the full-grown sheep and the fat goats,
sacrificed sleek hogs also, as well as a cow from the ox herd.
Then they roasted the innards and shared them out, and the wine they
blended in mixing bowls; and the swineherd passed out the goblets.
Bread also they were served by Philoítios, leader of people,

255   piled in beautiful baskets; the wine was poured by Melántheus.
They stretched forth eager hands to partake of the food lying ready.
Managing things to their profit, Telémachos seated Odysseus
well inside of the strong-built hall, close by the stone threshold,
setting an ugly old stool for him there and a little low table.

260   Near him placing a share of the innards and pouring the wine out
into a gold-wrought goblet, he spoke these words and addressed him:
"Sit right here in your place with the men while drinking your wine now.
I myself will defend you against the insults and the fists of
all of the suitors at need; since this is in no way a public

265   house but the house of Odysseus, and it was for me that he gained it.
But as for you now, suitors, restrain your hearts from abuses
and from your fists, so as not to arouse any rancor or fighting."
So he spoke; and they all kept biting their lips with their teeth in
wonder at hearing Telémachos now, he was talking so boldly.

270   Then among them thus spoke Antínoös son of Eupeíthes:

"Let us Achaians accept this word of Telémachos, even
though it is harsh—in saying these things, he threatens us gravely.
Zeus son of Kronos would not let us do it, or we would have stopped him,
here in the halls, before now, though he is an eloquent speaker."

275   Thus Antínoös spoke; to his words he paid no attention.
Meanwhile up through the town a divine hecatomb for the gods was
led by the heralds; the long-haired men, the Achaians, were gathered
under the shadowy grove of Apollo who shoots from a distance.
      When they had roasted the outermost flesh and had taken the spits out,
280   then they divided the portions and dined on a sumptuous dinner;
those who were serving the meat set down by Odysseus a portion
equal to what they received themselves, since it had been ordered
so by Telémachos, much loved scion of godlike Odysseus.
      By no means did Athena permit that the arrogant suitors
285   keep their deeds from heart-anguishing outrage, so even greater
pain might enter the heart of Odysseus the son of Laërtes.
There was among those suitors a man most lawless in spirit—
he had been named Ktesíppos; he made his dwelling in Samè.
He was confiding his hopes for success in abundant possessions
290   when he courted the wife of Odysseus, who long had been absent.
He was the one who then spoke out to the arrogant suitors:
"Listen to me now, valorous suitors, so I can say something.
Long since now has the stranger been getting a share, as is proper,
equal to ours, since it is not noble or just to be treating
295   guests of Telémachos lightly, whoever may come to this dwelling.
But come, I will present him a guest-gift too, so that he may
offer a present himself to the bathwater pourer or else to
some other servant of those in the palace of godlike Odysseus."
      So having said, in his large strong hand he picked up an ox hoof
300   out of the basket it lay in, and threw it; Odysseus avoided
it by easily ducking his head, and he smiled in his spirit
grimly, sardonically, as it struck the strong wall of the palace.
Thus did Telémachos speak to Ktesíppos in words of reproval:
"This was indeed, Ktesíppos, a better thing now for your spirit,
305   you did not strike this stranger; for he has avoided the missile.
For with my keen-edged spear, in the midriff I would have struck you;
then would your father, instead of a wedding, have worked on arranging
funeral rites for you here. So nobody show any ugly
deeds in my house; for already I notice them all and I know which
310   ones are the good, which worse, though before I was still quite childish.

353

Nevertheless these deeds we still are enduring as we keep
seeing the sheep flocks slaughtered, the wine being drunk, and the victuals
always devoured; for indeed it is hard for one man to check many.
But come, do me no harm any longer, with hostile intention;
315 if now you are indeed with a bronze sword eager to kill me,
I would desire even that myself; it would be much better
rather to die than forever to see these scandalous actions,
strangers abusively treated and battered, and women attendants
shamefully harried about by the men in the beautiful palace."

320   So did he say; then all of the people were hushed in silence;
finally then Ageláos the son of Damastor addressed them:
"Friends, no man should become enraged at a thing that is spoken
justly and so use quarrelsome words when giving an answer.
Do not at all maltreat this stranger nor yet any other
325 servant among those here in the palace of godlike Odysseus.
But to Telémachos and to his mother a word that is milder
I would address, if to both of their hearts it would give any pleasure.
For so long as the hearts in your breasts could keep on expecting
various-minded Odysseus to come back home to his palace,
330 then it was not blameworthy to wait for him nor to restrain us
suitors who come to the house, since that would have been much better
if to the country Odysseus returned, came back to his palace;
now it is finally clear that he never will have a homecoming.
But come, sit by your mother and put this counsel before her:
335 'Marry the man who is noblest, the one who provides the most presents,'
so that in happiness you will control all the goods of your fathers,
eating and drinking, and she may be tending the house of another."

     Thoughtful Telémachos then spoke out to him, giving an answer:
"Now by Zeus, Ageláos, as well as the pains of my father,
340 who far distant from Ithaka, surely, has died or yet wanders,
not in the least I oppose my mother's marriage but bid her
marry whomever she wishes, and I will give numberless presents.
I would be shamed if I drove her unwilling away from the palace,
speaking in words of constraint—may a god not cause it to happen!"

345   So did Telémachos speak; in the suitors Pallas Athena
roused unquenchable laughter and caused their minds to be addled.
Now they were laughing with jaws which seemed like somebody else's;
spattered with blood was the meat they ate, and the eyes of them all were
filled as the tears welled up; and their souls thought only of wailing.
350 These words then godlike Theoklýmenos uttered among them:

354

"Miserable men! What evil is this you suffer? In night your
heads, your faces, and down to the knees underneath are enshrouded;
lamentation is kindled, and over your cheeks are tears flooding;
sprinkled with blood are the beautiful walls and the bases of pillars;
355 phantoms are crowding the porch, and the courtyard also is crowded,
ghosts who are parting for Érebos under the dusk; and the sun has
perished from out of the sky as a baneful mist overspreads it."
    So he spoke, and at him they all began merrily laughing.
It was Eurýmachos, Pólybos' son, who was first to address them:
360 "Out of his mind is the stranger arrived from abroad just lately.
Come, young men, let us quickly escort him out of the palace,
so he may go to assembly, for here it seems to him nighttime."
    Then in return godlike Theoklýmenos spoke and addressed him:
"No, Eurýmachos, I do not ask you to furnish me escorts.
365 I have eyes, and I have ears too, and both feet to convey me,
also a mind in my breast that is not so shabbily fashioned.
These I will use to go out, since I am aware of the evil
coming upon you, which not one of you suitors will flee from
nor will avoid, you who in the palace of godlike Odysseus,
370 doing to men such violent deeds, plot follies so reckless."
    So he spoke and went out of the house well-built as a dwelling;
then he came to Peiraíos, who welcomed him gladly and kindly.
Straightway all of the suitors, as each one looked at the others,
taunted Telémachos over his guests by laughing about them.
375 Such were the words which one of the arrogant youths would have spoken:
"No one, Telémachos, has less luck with his strangers and guest-friends,
seeing that one of them you have here is a scavenging vagrant,
victuals and wine he is always wanting, and not in the least is
skillful in works or in bodily strength, but a weight on the farmland.
380 As for the other one now, he stood and began prophesying.
But if you trust me a little, it might be much to your profit:
putting the strangers upon some galley of numerous oarlocks,
let us to Sicily send them—a worthwhile price it would fetch you."
    Thus those suitors would say; to their words he paid no attention,
385 but at his father he looked in silence and always was keeping
watch for the time he could lay his hands on the shameless suitors.
    Putting a beautiful stool just opposite where they were sitting,
noble Ikários' daughter Penelope, thoughtful and prudent,
listened to all that was spoken by each man there in the palace.
390 For indeed they were laughing as they made ready a banquet

355

pleasant and sweet to the heart, since they had killed numerous victims.
No other supper could ever be made more joyless than this one
which that powerful man and the goddess were soon to be setting
there for the suitors; for they were the first to devise such scandals.

BOOK 21

Then did the goddess bright-eyed Athena put into the mind of
noble Ikários' daughter Penelope, thoughtful and prudent,
now to set up for the suitors the bow and the silver-gray iron,
there in Odysseus' halls, as a contest, starting the slaughter.
5   So she descended the steep high stairway, down from her quarters,
when in her large strong hand she had taken the beautiful brazen
well-curved key of the door, on which was an ivory handle.
She set forth with her women attendants to go to the inmost
storeroom—it was in there that her lord's possessions were lying:
10   treasures of bronze and of gold and of iron, laborious metal.
Therein also were lying a back-springing bow and a quiver,
holder of shafts, in which there were many maleficent arrows—
gifts given him by a friend who in Lakedaímon had met him,
Íphitos, Eúrytos' scion, a man who was like the immortals.
15   These two men in Messénè already had met one another,
while in the house of sagacious Ortílochos. There had Odysseus
gone in pursuit of a debt which all of the people had owed him:
for out of Ithaka men of Messénè had stolen and borne off
sheep, three hundred, and shepherds, in galleys of numerous oarlocks.
20   It was for them that Odysseus had gone a long way on his mission,
while still a boy, for his father and others, the elders, had sent him.
Íphitos came there searching for horses, the twelve of his females
which he had lost, at their teats young mule-colts, patient in labor.
They were the ones which later would be for him death and disaster
25   when he came to the dwelling of Zeus' son powerful-hearted
Herakles, who was a man well practiced in monstrous actions:
he in his own house murdered the man, though a guest and a stranger.
Cruel, he neither respected the gods' oversight nor the table
which he himself set near him; and afterward, when he had killed him,
30   he kept hold of the mares with the powerful hooves in his palace.

Seeking them, Íphitos met with Odysseus and gave him the bow which
in times past great Eúrytos carried and which he had later
left to his son at the time he died in his high-built palace.
Him had Odysseus given a sharp sword then and a strong spear;
35 it was the start of a firm close friendship; but never at table
they entertained each other; before that, Zeus' son murdered
Íphitos, Eúrytos' scion, a man who was like the immortals,
him who had given the bow; but afterward noble Odysseus
when to the war he went on the dark-hued galleys would never
40 take it along, but he left it to lie in his halls, a reminder
there of a well-loved friend, and he carried it when in his country.
    Finally then, when the splendor of women arrived at the chamber,
she went over the threshold carved out of wood that a workman
once had skillfully planed, made straight by stretching a chalk line,
45 fitting the doorposts and putting upon them shimmering door leaves;
straightway then from the hook she quickly unfastened the bolt strap,
then inserted the key, and the bar of the door struck upward,
pushing it out of the latch; and the doors groaned loud as a bull which
feeds on the grass of a meadow—so loud did the beautiful doors now
50 sound when struck by the key—then quickly were they spread open.
She stepped up on the high-raised platform; there were the coffers
standing, and inside these sweet-scented apparel was lying.
Reaching from where she stood, she lifted the bow from its hanger,
taking the bow case too, a resplendent one that enclosed it.
55 There on the spot she sat, then putting it down on her knees, she
plaintively, stridently wailed while taking the bow of her lord out.
But then, when she had taken her comfort in tearful lamenting,
she set forth to the hall to go join the illustrious suitors,
holding in hand that bow, back-springing, as well as the quiver,
60 holder of shafts, in which there were many maleficent arrows.
Handmaids carried a basket for her, in which there was iron
lying aplenty, and bronze, all prizes acquired by the master.
When she had come down there to the suitors, the splendor of women
stood by the pillar supporting the roof beams, stoutly constructed,
65 holding in front of her cheeks as a veil her shimmering head scarf;
standing with her there, one at each side, were the virtuous handmaids.
Straightway then to the suitors she spoke; these words she addressed them:
    "Listen to me now, valorous suitors, who always are vexing
this house, using it up, incessantly eating and drinking,
70 while my husband is absent a long time; nor is there any

other account you are able to make in the way of a pretext,
only that you are desiring to marry me, take me as bedmate.
But come, suitors, and act, since this is a prize that appears now:
for as a test I will set the great bow of the godlike Odysseus.
75 He who is nimblest at bending the bow with his hands to the bowstring,
then through all twelve axes is able to shoot the one arrow,
him I will follow as spouse, so leaving behind me the house where
I was a bride, so lovely, so full of the goods of existence—
I feel sure I will always remember it, even when dreaming."
80   So she spoke, and she bade Eumaíos, the excellent swineherd,
now to set up for the suitors the bow and the silver-gray iron.
Then as he wept Eumaíos received them, setting them down there;
also the oxherd wailed, as he looked on the bow of his master.
Then Antínoös jeered and said these words, calling upon them:
85 "Childish yokels, who think of no more than the day that is passing!
Miserable men, why now do you pour out tears, and the woman's
heart in her breast why stir to commotion? Enough as it is her
heart lies low in affliction because she has lost her dear husband.
But now sit there in silence devouring your dinner, or else go
90 out of the house and lament, while leaving the bow in its place to
be a decisive test for the suitors, for I do not think this
well-polished bow can at all be easily bent to the bowstring.
For among all these men in the house there is certainly no man
such as Odysseus was—I saw him myself, with my own eyes;
95 well I remember the time, though I was a boy and still childish."
      So he spoke, but the heart in his breast yet hoped for success in
bending the bow to the bowstring and shooting a shaft through the iron.
But in fact, it was he who would first be tasting an arrow
out of the hands of the faultless Odysseus, the man he was slighting
100 now as he sat in the palace and stirred up all of the comrades.
Thus did the sacred strength of Telémachos speak and address them:
      "Oh! Zeus scion of Kronos has made me utterly witless!
It is my own dear mother who says, although she is prudent,
that some other man she will now follow, forsaking this palace.
105 Yet in the witlessness of my heart I laugh and am happy!
But come, suitors, and act, since this is a prize that appears now—
no such woman as she now exists in the land of Achaia,
neither in sacred Pylos nor Argos nor yet in Mykénè,
neither in Ithaka island itself, nor upon the dark mainland.
110 This you yourselves know well; what need have I, praising my mother?

But come, do not evade it with pretexts nor turn away from
stringing the bow any longer, that we may observe what happens.
Yes, even I myself might make an attempt at the bow now;
should I manage to string it and shoot my shaft through the iron,
115 then I would not be pained if the lady my mother should leave me
here in the palace to go with another, as I would be left here
able to win already my father's beautiful prizes."
    He spoke; then from his shoulders he took his mantle of purple
as he jumped up, and his sharp sword also he took from his shoulders.
120 Then to begin he stood up the axes, for all of them digging
one long trench though the hall, and he made it straight with a chalk line,
tamping the earth around them; and amazement seized all, observing
how he stood them in order, for never before had he seen it.
He stepped onto the threshold and stood there trying the bow out:
125 thrice he caused it to quiver as he kept straining to bend it;
thrice he slackened his strength—in his heart he ever was hopeful
that he could fasten the bowstring and shoot his shaft through the iron.
Pulling it now with his strength for the fourth time, he would have strung it
but that Odysseus nodded and stopped him, though he was eager.
130 Then did the sacred strength of Telémachos speak and address them:
"Oh what shame! I will turn out, surely, a coward and weakling;
else I am still too young and cannot yet trust to my hands for
keeping away any man when he first starts doing me outrage.
But come, you who in strength are in fact more able than I am,
135 make an attempt at the bow now, and let us accomplish the contest."
    So did he say, then putting the bow from himself on the ground, he
leaned it against the two wings of the door, well-planed and close-fitted;
there also on the beautiful handle he leaned the swift arrow;
then he again sat down on the armchair whence he had risen.
140 Then among them thus spoke Antínoös son of Eupeíthes:
"All of you comrades rise, from the left to the right in order,
starting at once from the place where wine is poured out by the server."
    So Antínoös spoke, and his words found favor among them.
It was Leiódes who first stood up now, the scion of Oinops;
145 he was their sacrifice augur and sat by the beautiful wine bowl
always, away in a corner; and only to him were their reckless
follies detestable—all of the suitors he used to admonish.
He was the first man then who took up the bow and swift arrow.
He stepped onto the threshold and stood there trying the bow out,
150 nor did he string it, for sooner than that, by pulling he tired his

hands, unhardened and tender; and then he spoke to the suitors:
"Friends, I cannot string this—let somebody else now take it.
This is a bow that is soon to bereave many excellent men of
spirit and life breath, since it is certainly better by far to
155 die than to go on living and miss the one thing for whose sake we
always are gathering here, that we every day are expecting.
Even at this time now, someone still hopes in his spirit,
keeps on wanting to marry Penelope, wife of Odysseus.
When however the bow has been seen as it is and attempted,
160 then let him turn to another among all the fair-robed Achaians,
woo her and seek her with courtship presents; and she would in that case
marry the man who gave her the most and came destined to wed her."
　　Such were the words he spoke; then putting the bow from himself, he
leaned it against the two wings of the door, well-planed and close-fitted;
165 there also on the beautiful handle he leaned the swift arrow;
then he again sat down on the armchair whence he had risen.
Then Antínoös jeered and said these words, calling upon him:
"What is this word, Leiódes, escaping the fence of your teeth now!
It is a wretched and terrible one—I am outraged to hear it—
170 if this bow is indeed to bereave many excellent men of
spirit and life breath, since you yourself are not able to string it.
For it was no such man you were born to the lady your mother
as to be capable ever of drawing the bow and the arrows;
but soon others among the illustrious suitors will string it."
175 So he spoke, and he called to Melánthios, herder of goat flocks:
"Come now, Melánthios, kindle a fire for us inside the palace,
then put near it a good long bench and upon it some fleeces;
bring out a great round cake of the tallow that lies in the storeroom,
so when the young men have heated it up and have rubbed it with suet,
180 we might make an attempt on the bow and accomplish the contest."
　　He spoke; Melánthios kindled a weariless fire very quickly,
then brought in and put near it a bench and upon it some fleeces,
brought out too a great round of the tallow that lay in the storeroom.
Heating it up, the youths made their attempt at the bow, but they were not
185 able to fasten the string—they were far too weak to achieve it.
Still Antínoös held back and godlike Eurýmachos also;
they were the chiefs of the suitors and best by far in their prowess.
　　Meanwhile two of the men had departed together, as comrades,
out of the palace—the oxherd and swineherd of godlike Odysseus.
190 After them noble Odysseus himself came out of the palace.

But then, when they were all outside of the doors and the courtyard,
raising his voice, he addressed them in words mollifying and gentle:
"Oxherd and you too, swineherd—shall I now speak to you something
or keep it to myself? My spirit is bidding me say it.

195 How would you make a defense for Odysseus if he were to come here
all of a sudden from somewhere and some god guided him homeward?
Then would it be for the suitors you fought or instead for Odysseus?
Speak out now in the way that your heart and your spirit command you."
       Speaking to him then answered the herdsman, tender of cattle:

200 "Zeus our father, if only you bring this wish to fulfillment—
let that man come back; let a god lead him to his homeland!—
then you would learn what strength I have and what hands to employ it!"
       So in like fashion Eumaíos was praying to all of the gods for
various-minded Odysseus to come back home to his palace.

205 But when he had determined that these men's minds were unfailing,
then he at once made answer, and in these words he addressed them:
"I am home—yes, it is I, since, having endured many evils,
I have returned in the twentieth year to the land of my fathers.
Now I discover as I come back that of all of the servants,

210 only the two of you wished it; for I have heard none of the others
praying for me to return once more and arrive in the palace.
What it will be for you both, I will now speak fully and truly:
if a god under my hand brings down the illustrious suitors,
then for the two of you I will get wives and provide you possessions,

215 houses as well, built close to my own; and to me in the future
you will be comrades, friends of Telémachos, even his brothers.
Come now, something besides I will show you, a manifest token,
so that you know me for certain and so in your hearts you can trust me:
it is a scar that a boar inflicted on me with its white tusk

220 when with the sons of Autólykos once I went to Parnassos."
       So having spoken, he drew his tatters away from the huge scar.
Those two, when they had seen it and each thing well had considered,
burst out weeping and threw their arms around skillful Odysseus,
giving affectionate welcome by kissing his head and his shoulders.

225 So also were their heads and their hands then kissed by Odysseus.
Now would the light of the sun have gone down on the lamentation
had not Odysseus himself restrained them, addressing them these words:
"Stop this wailing and lamentation, lest somebody see it
as he is leaving the palace and then tell those who are inside.

230 Go in, rather, one after another and not all together;

I will go first, you after. And let this serve as the signal:
all of the others within, those who are illustrious suitors,
will not allow that to me be given the bow and the quiver;
still, you carry the bow through the hall then, noble Eumaíos,
235 putting it into my hands, then bidding the women attendants
onto the close-fitting doors of the hall put bars to secure them;
even if any of them should within hear groaning or noises
made by the men inside of these walls of ours, then not at all should
she go out, but remain right there at her work in silence.
240 Noble Philoítios, you I order to close up the courtyard
doors with a bar, then speedily fasten the binding around it."
　　So having said, he entered the house well-built as a dwelling;
then he went and sat down on the bench whence he had arisen.
Inside too went both of the servants of godlike Odysseus.

245 　　Now was Eurýmachos wielding the bow in his hands already,
heating it this side and that in the blaze of the fire, but he could not
fasten the string even so, and his valorous heart swelled hugely.
Wrathfully thus he spoke and said these words, calling upon them:
"Oh shame! Here is a woe for myself and for all of the suitors;
250 though I am grieved, it is not so much for the marriage I sorrow,
since there are numerous other Achaians, the women in this same
sea-girt Ithaka first, then those in the rest of the cities;
no, it is rather if we are deficient so far in the strength of
godlike Odysseus that we are incapable even of stretching
255 string on his bow—a disgrace for the men of the future to hear of!"
　　Answering him then spoke Antínoös, son of Eupeíthes:
"It will not be that way, Eurýmachos; you yourself know it.
For just now is the festival day of the god in the district,
holy indeed—who would string bows then? No, peaceably rather
260 put it away; but it might be as well to leave all of the axes
standing in place, for I do not think anyone will be coming
into the hall of Odysseus the son of Laërtes to steal them.
But come now, let the wine server pour the first drops in the goblets,
so we can make libation and then put away the great curved bow;
265 early at daybreak summon Melánthios, herder of goats, and
bid him to bring she-goats, far the best among all of the goat flocks,
so having offered the thighs to Apollo the glorious archer,
we might make an attempt on the bow and accomplish the contest."
　　So Antínoös spoke, and his words found favor among them.
270 Heralds at once poured over their hands clean water for washing;

young men filled to the brim great wine bowls, ready for drinking,
then poured wine into all of the cups to begin the observance.
When they had made libation and drunk whatever their hearts wished,
then with a trick in his mind said Odysseus of many devices:

275 "Listen to me, you who of the glorious queen are the suitors,
so I can say such things as the heart in my breast is demanding.
Now of Eurýmachos first and of godlike Antínoös also
do I entreat—since he too has said words fitting and proper—
let the bow be for the present; entrust to the gods what will happen;

280 then in the morning the god will give strength to whomever he wishes.
But come, give me the well-polished bow now, so that among you
I may try out my hands and my strength, to discover if I still
have such force in my flexible limbs as I had in the past or
whether by roaming and lack of good care I already am ruined."

285 So he spoke, and they all were exceedingly vexed and reproachful,
fearing that he might bend that well-polished bow to the bowstring.
Then Antínoös jeered and said these words, calling upon him:
"Miserable stranger, in you is no mind, not even a little;
are you not satisfied how at your ease you are dining among us

290 highborn men, nor are wanting for dinner, but even can hear what
we are discussing and how we are saying it? There is no other
stranger, and surely no beggar, who listens to what we are saying.
It is the honey-sweet wine which brings you to grief, as it injures
others as well who take it in gulps, not drinking in measure.

295 It was the wine which made Eurýtion, glorious Centaur,
maddened against greathearted Peiríthoös once in his palace,
when he had come to the Lapiths; with wine in his mind he was maddened,
then in his frenzy he wrought great harm in Peiríthoös' palace;
grief took hold of the heroes, and leaping upon him they dragged him

300 outside, out through the forecourt, and then with the pitiless bronze they
cut off his ears and his nostrils; and he, become mad in his spirit,
went on bearing about in his volatile heart a great madness.
Out of it came the contention between those men and the Centaurs,
but it was first for himself, when heavy with wine, he found evil.

305 So I declare for you too great trouble if ever you put that
string on the bow; for indeed no courtesy you will encounter
here in this country of ours; in a black ship then we will send you
to King Échetos, worker of ruin to all who are mortal,
quickly—from there you would not be saved. No, quietly stay here

310 drinking; do not seek quarrels with men who are younger than you are."

Prudent Penelope then spoke answering words and addressed him:
"It is not noble or just, Antínoös, so to be treating
guests of Telémachos lightly, whoever may come to this dwelling.
Do you expect, if the stranger should fasten the string on the mighty
315　bow of Odysseus, in confidence both of his hands and his power,
he would then take me away to his home, there make me his bedmate?
Certainly it is not what he himself in his breast is expecting.
Let not any of you on that account grieve in your spirit
while you are banqueting here, since not in the least is it seemly."

320　　Speaking to her then answered Eurýmachos, Pólybos' scion:
"Noble Ikários' daughter Penelope, thoughtful and prudent,
we do not think he will take you away with him; it is not seemly.
But it is shame we feel at the gossip of men and of women,
lest some other Achaian of meaner descent should be saying,
325　'Far inferior men are now courting the wife of the faultless
man and cannot even bend his well-polished bow to the bowstring;
rather another, a beggar and wandering man who arrived here,
easily fastened the string to the bow, then shot through the iron.'
So they will say; and to us such words will be shame and dishonor."

330　　Prudent Penelope then spoke answering words and addressed him:
"No, Eurýmachos, there is no way that the men who dishonor,
eating it up, this house of a man so noble will have good
fame here among our people—so why take this as a censure?
Now this stranger is both very large in stature and well built;
335　as to descent, he claims to be son of a wellborn father.
But come, give him the well-polished bow now, that we may observe him.
For I say to you plainly, and this thing will be accomplished:
if he should fasten the string and Apollo should give him the glory,
I will attire him in mantle and tunic, the finest apparel,
340　and a sharp javelin give him, from men and from dogs a protection,
also a two-edged sword; for his feet I will furnish the sandals;
then I will send him wherever his heart and his spirit command him."

　　Thoughtful Telémachos then spoke out to her, giving an answer:
"Mother mine, as to the bow, no man of Achaia has greater
345　power than I have to give and deny it to any I wish to—
no, not those who in rock-strewn Ithaka govern the people,
nor those ruling the islands towards horse-pasturing Elis;
none of the men will prevent me against my will, if I wish to
give this bow outright to be carried away by the stranger.
350　But go back to your room and devote more care to your own work,

weaving and spinning, the loom and the distaff, bidding your handmaids
busy themselves with their labor; the men will attend to the bow now,
all of them, I above all, since mine is the rule of the household."
    Struck with astonishment then, she went back up to her chamber,
355 for to her heart she had taken the thoughtful remarks of her offspring.
Going upstairs to her chamber along with her women attendants,
there she lamented Odysseus, the husband she loved, till a pleasant
slumber was cast down over her lids by bright-eyed Athena.
    Now the curved bow had the excellent swineherd taken and carried,
360 but in the hall then all of the suitors were shouting together.
Such are the words which one of the arrogant youths would have spoken:
"Where are you taking the curved bow now, you miserable swineherd,
madman? Soon swift dogs that you raised yourself will be eating
you amid swine, quite alone and forsaken of men, if Apollo
365 shows us his favor, as well as the rest of the gods who live always."
    So they spoke; and he took it and put it again in the same place,
fearful because in the hall so many were shouting together.
Quickly Telémachos, threatening him from the other side, shouted:
"Papa, keep bringing the bow; you will not do well to heed all men;
370 take care lest, though younger, I chase you away to the pastures,
showering you with stones; in strength I am greatly your better.
Would that above all these who are here in the palace the suitors,
both in my hands and my vigorous strength I were that much better!
Then I would soon send each of them wretchedly off on a journey
375 out of this palace of ours, since they are devising us evils."
    So he spoke, and at him they all began merrily laughing,
all of the suitors, and so gave over the furious wrath they
felt for Telémachos; taking the bow through the palace, the swineherd
placed it in skillful Odysseus' hands while standing beside him.
380 Calling her out of her room, he spoke to the nurse Eurykleía:
"Thus does Telémachos bid you to do now, wise Eurykleía:
onto the close-fitting doors of the hall put bars to secure them;
even if any of them should within hear groaning or noises
made by the men inside of these walls of ours, then not at all should
385 she go out, but remain right there at her work in silence."
    So he spoke; and in her was the word unwinged for an answer;
she put bars on the doors of the house well-built as a dwelling.
    Then in silence Philoítios hurried outside of the palace,
there straightway he barred up the gates of the strong-walled courtyard.
390 Under the porch there was lying a tractable galley's papyrus

cable, with which he fastened the gates; then he himself entered.
There he went and sat down on the bench whence he had arisen,
keeping his eye on Odysseus, who now kept handling the great bow,
turning it every direction and testing one side and the other,

395 fearing that worms could have eaten the horn while the master was absent.
Thus would one of them say as he looked at another beside him:
"He is for sure an admirer of bows—yes, even an expert.
No doubt either in his own house there are such things lying
or else he is intending to make one, so in his hands he

400 turns it one side and the other, the vagabond practiced in evils."
    Thus would somebody else of the arrogant young men answer:
"Would that he might encounter success to as great a degree as
now he ever is able to bend this bow to the bowstring!"
    So those suitors were saying; Odysseus of many devices,

405 once he had taken the great bow up and had looked it all over—
as when a man who has talent and skill at the lyre and at singing
easily stretches a string to a peg just recently fitted,
tightening both of the ends of the twisted and flexible sheep gut—
so did Odysseus fasten the string on the bow without effort.

410 Taking it up in his right hand then, he tested the bowstring;
pleasantly under his hand it sang like the voice of a swallow.
Great grief then came over the suitors; the skin of them all turned
color; and Zeus began mightily thundering, showing his portents;
then much-suffering noble Odysseus rejoiced at the omen

415 he had been sent by the scion of Kronos of crooked devices.
He picked up a swift arrow that lay nearby on the table,
naked and loose—for the others were lying inside of the hollow
quiver: of these the Achaians were soon to be given a trial.
Putting it up to the bridge, he drew back the string and the notches;

420 right from the bench he was sitting upon he fired off the arrow,
aiming it straight towards them, and of all of the axes he did not
miss any helve hole right from the first; but the bronze-heavy arrow
went straight out through the end; to Telémachos then he said these words:
"Never, Telémachos, does this stranger who sits in your palace

425 cause you shame—not a whit of my aim I missed, nor a long time
labored at stringing the bow; even yet my strength remains steadfast,
not as the suitors have said, dishonoring me with their insults.
Now is the time too that the Achaians command that a meal be
made in the daylight and then take pleasure with other amusements,

430 singing and playing the lyre, since these are adornments of dining."

   Thus; with his brows he nodded; about him then was a sharp sword
girt by Telémachos, much loved scion of godlike Odysseus;
onto his spear then casting his hand, he took his position
close to him there by the armchair, equipped with the glittering bronze arms.

BOOK 22

Stripping the rags from his body, Odysseus of many devices
leapt on the great threshold; he was holding the bow and the quiver
still full-laden with arrows; the swift shafts quickly he poured out
there in front of his feet as he spoke these words to the suitors:
5 "This was indeed a decisive contest that now is completed!
As to another mark which no man has been able to hit yet,
now I will know if I strike it—Apollo bestow what I pray for!"
    Thus he spoke; at Antínoös then he aimed a sharp arrow.
He was in fact just starting to lift up a beautiful goblet,
10 twin-eared, fashioned of gold—in his hands already he held it—
so he could drink of the wine; and he took no thought in his heart of
slaughter; for who could imagine that one sole man among many
men then banqueting there, even if he were mighty in power,
ever would bring upon him so evil a death and such black fate?
15 He was Odysseus' target—his throat he hit with the arrow
so that the point, penetrating the delicate neck, passed through it.
Off to the side he slumped, and the cup fell out of his hand, so
stricken he was; then out of his nostrils a jet of his mortal
blood came heavy and viscous; and quickly the table he pushed from
20 him, kicking it with his foot, on the ground thus spilling the victuals,
messing and fouling the bread and the roast meat. Then did the suitors
rouse an uproar in the house as they looked at the man who had fallen;
out of their chairs they sprang; through the house they rushed in a panic,
glancing around at the well-built walls in every direction;
25 nowhere at all was a shield or a stout spear there to be taken.
Thus they berated Odysseus, addressing him words full of anger:
    "Stranger, at men you shoot to your own hurt; no other contests,
ever, will you take part in—assured is your sheer destruction.
For in fact you have just now slaughtered the man who by far was
30 best of the Ithakan youths, so that right here vultures will eat you."

So each man of them guessed, for in fact they thought that he had not
willfully slaughtered the man; and the poor fools never suspected
how on all of the suitors the grim death bindings were fastened.
Looking from lowering brows said Odysseus of many devices:

35   "Oh you dogs, you believed I would have no return and would not come
home from the land of the Trojans, and so you have pillaged my household;
so you have taken to bed by force those women, the handmaids;
so though I was alive my wife you illicitly courted;
neither the gods you feared, the immortals who hold the broad heaven,

40   nor any vengeance that men might bring upon you in the future.
Now on all of you suitors the grim death bindings are fastened!"

So did he say, and a green fear seized upon all of the suitors;
each looked round for a place to escape from a sheer destruction;
only Eurýmachos spoke and addressed him, giving an answer:

45   "If you in truth are Odysseus the Ithakan who have arrived here,
justly you speak about all these things the Achaians committed—
many a reckless deed in your halls, much too in the country.
But already the man lies low who was guilty of all those
things, Antínoös; for it was he who incited these misdeeds,

50   not so much that he wanted or felt a great need for the marriage;
other things rather he schemed, which Kronos' son never accomplished,
so that he might himself be king in the country of well-built
Ithaka, even could murder your son by setting an ambush.
Now he has died in accord with his destiny: spare your own people

55   therefore, and we in the land hereafter will give satisfaction,
paying for everything we have eaten and drunk in your household,
each for his own part bringing indemnity worth twenty oxen,
giving you bronze to repay you and gold, to the point that your heart is
softened: until then no one will blame you at all for your anger."

60   Looking from lowering brows said Odysseus of many devices:
"Not even if you gave me, Eurýmachos, all the paternal
goods which now you possess, then others you added from elsewhere,
not even so would I yet restrain my hands from the slaughter,
not till the suitors have given requital for every trespass.

65   Now with you lies this choice: to engage in face-to-face combat
or to take flight, whoever would flee from his death and his doomsday.
But I believe no man will escape from a sheer destruction."

So he spoke, and their limbs and the hearts inside them were loosened.
Then for a second time yet Eurýmachos spoke out among them:

70   "Friends, I am sure this man will not hold his invincible hands back,

but now, since he has taken the well-polished bow and the quiver,
there from the smooth threshold he will shoot it until he has killed us,
every man of us present; but let us remember our war craft.
Draw out your swords, put tables in front of your bodies, defending
75 them from the swift-fated arrows; at him let us all in a body
sally, that we might force him away from the doors and the threshold;
then through the town we would go, and a cry might quickly be started,
so this man may perhaps for the last time now have been shooting."
      So having spoken to them, he drew his keen sword from the scabbard,
80 bronze, well whetted on both of its edges, and leapt at the other
yelling a terrible yell; at the same time, noble Odysseus
shot off an arrow and struck him square in the chest by the nipple,
driving the swift shaft into the liver; and out of his hand he
cast his sword to the ground, as he sprawled out over the table,
85 doubled up, falling in death, on the ground thus spilling the victuals,
also the two-handled goblets; the earth he beat with his forehead,
racked by the pain in his breast; then, kicking with both of his feet, he
set the chair shaking, and over his eyes death-mist came pouring.
      Then Amphínomos hurtled himself against famous Odysseus,
90 rushing at him headlong, and he drew out his sword, sharp-pointed,
hoping that he would surrender the doors; but Telémachos now was
swifter than he in striking at him from behind with a bronze-tipped
spear in the midst of his shoulders, and on through the chest he drove it.
Falling, he crashed to the earth, hitting ground with his whole broad forehead.
95 Jumping away then, Telémachos left the long-shadowing spear shaft
there in Amphínomos; greatly he feared that another Achaian,
as he drew out the long-shadowing spear, might thrust with his sword at
him while rushing against him or strike at him while he was stooping.
Quickly he set out running and speedily came to his father.
100 There at his side he stood, and in these winged words he addressed him:
"Father, to you right now I will bring two spears and a shield out,
also a helmet entirely of bronze well fitting your temples;
I will myself go put on armor, and I will give other
arms to the swineherd and oxherd—to be armed surely is better."
105   Speaking to him then answered Odysseus of many devices:
"Run then, bring them to me, while arrows I have to defend me,
lest since I am alone they force me out of the doorway."
      So he spoke, and his own dear father Telémachos heeded;
he set out for the chamber in which lay glorious armor.
110 Four of the shields he carried, and eight spears, out of the storeroom;

four of the helmets as well, bronze-plated and crested with horsehair.
Bearing them, he set out, and he speedily came to his father,
then it was he who was first in putting the bronze on his body.
So did the two menservants as well don beautiful armor,
115   taking their stand by ingenious various-minded Odysseus.
       As for himself, for as long as he still had shafts to defend him,
so long there in his house did he keep on shooting at suitors,
always hitting his mark; and they dropped down one by another.
Then when the arrows had been used up by the lord who was shooting,
120   as for the bow, against one of the pillars supporting the strong-built
palace he leaned it to stand there next to the wall, bright-gleaming;
then he placed on his shoulders a shield four-layered of oxhide;
onto his powerful head he fitted a well-made helmet,
crested with horsehair—the plume on top of it fearfully nodded;
125   two of the valorous spears he picked up, headed with sharp bronze.
       Now in the well-made wall there happened to be a small side door,
right on top of the threshold, that gave access to a passage
out of the strong-built palace; and it had well-fitted door leaves.
This had Odysseus commanded the excellent swineherd to look to,
130   taking his stance nearby; it alone was a way of approaching.
Then Ageláos addressed them, to all of them giving his word out:
"Friends, is there nobody now who will go up out of the side door,
then to the people report, so a cry might quickly be started?
So this man may perhaps for the last time now have been shooting."
135   Speaking to him made answer Melánthios, herder of goat flocks:
"There is no way, Zeus-bred Ageláos; the beautiful courtyard
doors are too fearfully near, and the mouth of the passage is narrow—
one man, if he were valiant, could hold off all the attackers.
But come now, I will carry you armor from out of the storeroom
140   so you can arm; for in there, I imagine, and not any other
place has Odysseus along with his glorious son put the armor."
       So having spoken, Melánthios, herder of goat flocks, started
climbing aloft through vents of the hall to the rooms of Odysseus.
Out of the chamber he took twelve shields, and of spears the same number,
145   so many helmets as well, bronze-plated and crested with horsehair;
he set forth, and he speedily brought them to give to the suitors.
Then in Odysseus the limbs and the heart inside him were loosened
as he observed them putting on armor and taking the long spears,
brandishing them in their hands—it appeared to him now a huge labor.
150   Straightway in these winged words to Telémachos he began speaking:

"There is for sure some woman, Telémachos, here in the palace
rousing against us an evil attack, or Melánthios does so."
   Thoughtful Telémachos then spoke out to him, giving an answer:
"Father, in this it is I who was negligent—nobody else is
155   blamable—I left open the close-fitted doors of the chamber,
leaning apart; then one of these men was a better observer.
Go now, noble Eumaíos, and close up the doors of the chamber,
also observe if indeed it is one of the women who does this
or if Melánthios, scion of Dolios, does it, as I think."
160   Such things then they spoke and addressed each one to the others;
meanwhile Melánthios, herder of goat flocks, returned to the chamber
so he could bring fine armor; the excellent swineherd perceived him;
then he at once spoke out to Odysseus, as he was beside him:
"Zeus-sprung son of Laërtes, Odysseus of many devices,
165   there is indeed that villainous man whom we were suspecting
going again to the chamber: you tell me the truth of the matter,
whether to kill him myself, providing that I am the stronger,
or instead bring him to you, so that he may pay the requital
now for the numerous crimes which he has devised in your palace."
170   Speaking to him then answered Odysseus of many devices:
"Now the illustrious suitors shall I and Telémachos keep on
holding inside of the halls in spite of their desperate struggle.
You two pinion his feet and his hands, all twisted behind him;
throw him into the room; to his back then fasten some lumber;
175   onto the man himself tie a strong rope fast, tight-twisted,
hoisting him up the high pillar and bringing him close to the roof beams,
so that he long stays living and suffers the cruelest torments."
   So did he say; they carefully listened to him and obeyed him;
they set forth to the chamber unseen by the man, who was inside.
180   He now deep in the chamber was searching a corner for weapons;
those two stood there waiting for him, each side by the doorposts.
Then as Melánthios, herder of goat flocks, stepped on the threshold,
carrying out in one of his hands a fine four-horned helmet
and in the other a broad old shield much spattered with mildew,
185   that of the hero Laërtes, who carried it when he was youthful—
there it had lain some time, and the stitches were loose on the hand straps;
rushing upon him, the two men seized him, and then by the hair they
dragged him inside; on the floor they threw him grieving in spirit.
With heart-anguishing bindings his feet and his hands they fastened,
190   twisting them thoroughly, strongly behind him, as they had been told by

373

agèd Laërtes' son, much-suffering noble Odysseus,
then to the man himself tied a strong rope fast, tight-twisted,
hoisting him up the high pillar and bringing him close to the roof beams.
Mocking and jeering at him you spoke, Eumaíos the swineherd:

195 "Now for the whole night surely, Melánthios, you will be keeping
watch as you take your rest in a soft bed such as befits you.
Nor will the early-born Dawn of the gold throne ever escape your
view as she comes from the streams of the Ocean, the time you would drive in
goats to the suitors, for them to make ready a feast in the palace."

200 So he had been left there stretched tight in the murderous bindings.
Both of them put on armor; and closing the shimmering doors, they
went back down to ingenious various-minded Odysseus.
There did they all stand breathing their valor—the ones on the threshold
four men only, but those inside the house many and noble.

205 Then came up and approached them Athena the daughter of great Zeus,
making herself like Mentor in speaking as well as appearance.
As he beheld her Odysseus rejoiced; this word he addressed her:
"Mentor, defend me from ruin, be mindful of your dear comrade,
who was accustomed to do you honor, for you are my own age."

210 He spoke, thinking that it was the rouser of armies Athena.
Opposite him in the palace the suitors were shouting together;
first to rebuke her spoke Ageláos the son of Damastor:
"Mentor, do not let Odysseus with mere words talk you around to
fighting against us suitors, providing himself a defender.

215 For in this way I think our purpose will soon be accomplished:
when we have finally killed these men, both the son and the father,
then you too will be slaughtered along with them, such are the things you
plan to do here in the halls—with your own head you will requite it.
But then, when with the bronze we have stripped you all of your powers,

220 all your possessions, whatever you have both inside and outside,
we will combine with the goods of Odysseus, and never allow your
sons to remain in the palace and live here, and neither your daughters
nor your virtuous wife will see Ithaka, going about here."

So he spoke; in her spirit Athena was dreadfully angered;

225 thus she berated Odysseus, addressing him words full of anger:
"Steady no longer, Odysseus, the strength you had, and the valor,
when over white-armed Helen, the child of an excellent father,
you with the Trojans were fighting for nine years, always relentless.
Many indeed were the men you killed in the terrible combat;

230 by your counsel was taken the wide-wayed city of Priam.

How is it now, when you have arrived at your home and possessions,
going against these suitors you wail for a warrior's valor?
Come over here, old friend, stand by me and witness my actions,
so you can see what kind of a man among enemy men is
235 Mentor Álkimos' son, in paying you back for your kindness."
      She spoke, not yet giving the victory wholly to one side;
rather, she went on making a proof of the strength and the valor
still, of Odysseus himself and as well of his glorious offspring.
Then she herself flitted up to a roof beam high in the smoky
240 palace and sat there aloft to be seen in the form of a swallow.
      Then were the suitors aroused by Damastor's son Ageláos;
also Eurýnomos, Démoptólemos, and Amphimédon,
talented Pólybos too, and Peisander the son of Polýktor;
for it was these who were easily best of the suitors in prowess,
245 best among those who still were alive, still fighting for life breath;
some already the bow and the showering arrows had brought down.
Then Ageláos addressed them, to all of them giving his word out:
"Friends, this man will at last now hold his invincible hands back.
Mentor has gone, indeed, after uttering boasts that were empty;
250 they are the only ones left out there in front of the doorway.
Therefore now, let us not all throw long spears at the same time;
but come, six of you first hurl spears at him, hoping that Zeus might
grant that Odysseus at once be hit and that we achieve glory.
Then from the rest there will be no trouble, when that one has fallen."
255 So he spoke; and they all threw spears in the way he had bidden,
eagerly; all of the throws were made utterly vain by Athena—
one of the men thus struck at the pillar sustaining the well-built
hall of the palace; another one hit on the door, tight-fitted;
onto the wall fell the bronze-heavy ash-wood spear of another.
260 Straightway, after the men had avoided the spears of the suitors,
speaking among them began much-suffering noble Odysseus:
"Friends, for myself I would say right now is the time that we also
hurl our spears at the throng of the suitors, because they are keenly
seeking to kill us and add that deed to their earlier evils."
265 So he spoke; and the sharp-pointed spears they all began throwing,
aiming them straight. It was Démoptólemos then that Odysseus
killed; Euryádes, Telémachos slaughtered; Elátos, the swineherd
slew. Peisánder was killed by the herdsman, tender of cattle.
When these men had together all bitten their teeth on the vast earth,
270 into a corner away in the palace retreated the suitors;

then out rushed the four others and took their spears from the corpses.
Then their sharp-pointed spears did the suitors again start hurling
eagerly; most of the throws were made utterly vain by Athena—
one of the men thus struck at a pillar sustaining the well-built
275 hall of the palace; another one hit on the door, tight-fitted;
onto the wall fell the bronze-heavy ash-wood spear of another.
But Amphimédon wounded Telémachos' hand at the wrist by
grazing it—only the outermost skin did the bronze point injure.
Hurling a long spear over the shield of Eumaíos, Ktesíppos
280 wounded his shoulder; it flew on over and fell to the ground there.
Those who surrounded Odysseus, sagacious and various-minded,
now began throwing their sharp-pointed spears at the throng of the suitors.
Then was Eurýdamas struck by the sacker of cities Odysseus;
Pólybos too, by the swineherd; Telémachos hit Amphimédon;
285 then Ktesíppos was struck by the herdsman, tender of cattle,
square in the chest, and Philoítios spoke out boasting above him:
"Oh Polythérses' son, you lover of mockery, never
yield so completely to folly and speak so grandly, but rather
leave all speech to the gods, since they are much stronger than you are.
290 This is a guest-gift now in exchange for the hoof of an ox you
once gave godlike Odysseus as he went about in his palace."
So said the herdsman of crooked-horned cattle; and meanwhile Odysseus
thrust with a long spear, wounding the son of Damástor at close range.
Likewise Telémachos wounded Leiókritos, son of Euénor,
295 square in the flank with a spear, and the bronze drove on through the body;
he fell flat on his face, hitting ground with his whole broad forehead.
Then did Athena at last raise up the man-slaughtering aegis
high on the roof overhead; and the minds of the men were affrighted.
They took flight all over the hall, like cows of a herd when
300 they are stampeded about by a gadfly rushing and darting
when in the springtime season the days grow longer and longer.
Meanwhile the others, as eagles with strong-curved talons and hooked beaks
come down out of the mountains and swoop on birds that are smaller—
cowering down from the clouds to the plain their quarry are driven;
305 stooping upon them there they slaughter them; nor is there either
rescue for them or escaping; and men feel joy at the hunting—
so they, rushing upon those suitors all over the palace,
struck one after another; and miserable was the groan which
rose from the heads thus stricken; the whole floor ran with their lifeblood.
310 Rushing at him, Leiódes took hold of the knees of Odysseus;

making his supplication, in these winged words he addressed him:
"Now I implore you, Odysseus: respect me and show me your mercy;
never, I say, have I spoken or done any one of the women
here in the house any reckless thing; but I always was checking
315 others—in fact, any one of the suitors who acted in that way.
Yet they never would heed me to keep their hands out of evils,
so in their recklessness they meet with a hideous doomsday.
I among them was an augur and never an actor, but I will
fall now: for deeds well done, there never is gratitude later."

320   Looking from lowering brows said Odysseus of many devices:
"If you are boasting indeed to have been among them as an augur,
then no doubt you would often have uttered a prayer in the palace
that the completion of sweet homecoming be far from me always
and that my dear wife, going with you, give birth to your children;
325 even for that you may not flee a death most hateful and anguished."

So having said, in his large strong hand he picked up a sword which
lay before him on the ground just where Ageláos had thrown it
when he was killed; and with it he cut through his neck in the middle,
so that his head lay mingled with dust even while he was speaking.

330   Still was the singer, the scion of Terpes, attempting to flee from
black death, Phemios, who by compulsion had sung for the suitors.
There he stood, and he held in his hands his lyre with the clear tone,
close to the side door, pondering over two ways in his spirit—
whether to slip from the palace and take his seat at the strong-built
335 altar of great Zeus, god of the court, where many an ox thigh
once Laërtes had burnt in oblation, and so had Odysseus,
or to rush up to Odysseus and clasp his knees in entreaty.
So as he pondered the matter, the best course seemed to be this one:
he would take hold of the knees of Odysseus the son of Laërtes.

340 Straightway, carefully laying the hollow lyre on the ground just
there by the mixing bowl and the armchair studded with silver,
he rushed up to Odysseus and clasped his knees in entreaty.
Making his supplication, in these winged words he addressed him:
"Now I implore you, Odysseus: respect me and show me your mercy;
345 there will be sorrow for you yourself in the future if you should
murder a singer like me, who sing for the gods and for mortals.
I am in fact self-taught; my lays has a god implanted,
every sort, in my mind; I am suited for singing before you
as for a god; so do not be so eager for cutting my head off.
350 So would Telémachos tell you of this, your son so belovèd,

377

how not willing at all nor desiring a thing, I frequented,
here in your palace, the suitors and sang among them at their banquets;
they were too many and strong, and they brought me here by compulsion."
    So did he say, and the sacred strength of Telémachos heard him;
355 hastily then he spoke to his father who stood there beside him:
"Hold off, and do not wound with a bronze sword one who is guiltless.
Let us as well spare Medon the herald—a man who would always
watch over me when I was a child still, here in our palace—
if he has not been killed by Philoítios or by the swineherd,
360 or unless he met you while you in the palace were raging."
    So did he say; he was heard by Medon, sagacious and knowing;
under an armchair he lay hiding himself, and the new-flayed
skin of a cow he had put on about him, avoiding a black fate.
Quickly arising from under the chair, he took off the cowhide;
365 then to Telémachos rushing, he clasped his knees in entreaty;
making his supplication, in these winged words he addressed him:
"Friend, it is I, the same man; hold back, and say so to your father,
lest with his sharp bronze sword and his powerful might he destroy me,
feeling such furious rage at the suitors, the men who have ravaged,
370 here in the halls, his possessions, the fools who showed you no honor."
    Smiling at him, thus uttered Odysseus of many devices:
"Be of good heart now, since this man has protected and saved you,
so that you know in your heart and report it as well to another
how it is better by far to do good deeds than to do bad ones.
375 But now go from the palace and sit there away from the slaughter
out in the court, both you and the versatile singer of stories,
while in the house I busy myself with whatever I need to."
    So he spoke; and the two set forth to go out of the palace.
Both of them then sat down outside by the altar of great Zeus,
380 looking about them, always expecting that they would be slaughtered.
    So was Odysseus looking about in the palace, to see if
any man still was alive and concealed and avoiding a black fate.
But he observed how all of the men, great numbers of them, had
fallen in blood and in dust, like fish when the fishermen take them
385 up in their many-holed nets, then drag them out on the curving
beach from the silvery sea-brine; and all of the fishes are longing
still for the waves of the sea when they on the sand have been heaped up—
out of their bodies is radiant Helios taking the life breath.
So it was that the suitors were heaped up one on another.
390 Then to Telémachos thus said Odysseus of many devices:

"Go now, Telémachos, summon to me the old nurse Eurykleía,
so I can utter the word I have in my spirit to tell her."
     So he spoke, and his own dear father Telémachos heeded;
shaking the door to arouse her, he called to the nurse Eurykleía:
395 "Rise, come hither, old woman of ancient birth—it is you who
here in this palace of ours keep watch of the women attendants.
Come now—it is my father who calls you to tell you of something."
     So did he say; and in her was the word unwinged for an answer;
but she opened the doors of the house well-built as a dwelling,
400 then set forth, with Telémachos going before as the leader.
Then she discovered Odysseus among dead bodies of slain men,
spattered and fouled with the blood and the battle gore, much like a lion
who stalks off after feeding himself on an ox of the pasture;
all of his breast and as well his cheeks both sides of the muzzle
405 are quite covered with blood, and to look at his face is most fearful—
so on his feet and his hands up above was Odysseus bespattered.
When she beheld those corpses and all the unspeakable blood, she
started her victory shout, since great was the work that she witnessed,
but was restrained by Odysseus and held back, much as she wished it;
410 raising his voice he spoke, and in these winged words he addressed her:
"Keep this joy in your heart, old woman, do not shout triumph;
it is not piety so to exult over men who are slaughtered.
These has the doom of the gods brought low, and detestable actions,
for to no person who lives on the earth they showed any honor,
415 neither the base nor the noble, whatever man might have approached them;
so in their recklessness they meet with a hideous doomsday.
Come now, tell me about these women who serve in the palace,
those who bring me dishonor and also those who are guiltless."
     Then spoke giving an answer the much loved nurse Eurykleía:
420 "Certainly, child, this tale I will tell you fully and truly.
Fifty in all are the women of yours who are here in the palace,
servants to whom we have taught how to work at the tasks of the household,
chores like carding the wool, and of servitude, how to endure it.
Twelve among these in all have embarked on shameless behavior;
425 neither myself nor even Penelope they have shown honor.
Only of late has Telémachos grown to adulthood; his mother
never allowed him to be in command of the women attendants.
But come now, I will go upstairs to the shimmering chamber,
so I may tell your wife, upon whom some god has sent slumber."
430   Speaking to her then answered Odysseus of many devices:

379

"Do not awaken her yet; but inside, tell those of the women
who in the past have devised such shameless behavior to come here."
    So he spoke; the old woman at once set forth through the palace,
taking the women his message and bidding them come in a hurry.
435   Calling Telémachos meanwhile, as well as the oxherd and swineherd,
over to him, he spoke, and in these winged words he addressed them:
"Now start carrying corpses, and order the women to help you;
then straightway take care of the beautiful chairs and the tables,
clean them, washing them off with water and many-holed sponges.
440   But then, when you have put the entire house wholly in order,
bringing the handmaids out of the hall of the well-built palace,
there in between the round room and the faultless wall of the courtyard
put them to death with the fine-edged swords till you have bereft them
all of their life, so that they are forgetful of Aphrodítè,
445   who was with them as in secret they mingled in love with the suitors."
    So he spoke, and the women all came in a body together,
raising a piteous moan, pouring out great tears in abundance.
First they carried away the dead bodies of those who were slaughtered,
laying them outside under the porch of the well-walled courtyard,
450   propping them one on another; Odysseus himself gave orders,
spurring them on, and they carried them outside under compulsion,
then straightway took care of the beautiful chairs and the tables,
cleaned them, washing them off with water and many-holed sponges.
Then did Telémachos meanwhile, as well as the oxherd and swineherd,
455   carefully level the floor of the strong-built palace with shovels,
scraping it; maids kept taking the scrapings and putting them outdoors.
But then, when they had put the entire hall wholly in order,
leading the handmaids out of the hall of the well-built palace,
there in between the round room and the faultless wall of the courtyard,
460   they penned them in a narrow place with no way of escaping.
Thoughtful Telémachos then spoke out, thus broaching the matter:
"Certainly not by a neat clean death would I take away life from
women like these, who upon my head have been heaping disgraces,
also upon my mother, and sharing the beds of the suitors!"
465   So did he say, then, taking the rope of a blue-prowed galley,
fastened it on a tall pillar and threw it about the round storeroom,
stretching it high, so that down to the ground no feet would be reaching.
Just as it is when thrushes with long wings stretching, or pigeons
tangle themselves in a snare that has been set up in a thicket,
470   as they go in to roost—most hateful the rest that receives them—

so their heads in a line those women were holding, and nooses
went around all of their necks, so they would most pitifully perish.
Then with their feet they struggled a little, but no very long time.
    Leading Melánthios out to the portico, then to the courtyard,
475 there with the pitiless bronze they cut off his nose and his ears, then
tore out his privates and gave them raw to the dogs to be eaten,
also chopped off his hands and his feet in the wrath of their spirits.
    Finally, when they had cleansed their hands and their feet of the carnage,
they went into the house of Odysseus; the labor was finished.
480 Raising his voice, he spoke to his much loved nurse Eurykleía:
"Bring me sulfur, old woman, the cure of iniquities; bring fire,
so I can sulfur the palace with fumes; and Penelope meanwhile
you go order to come here along with her women attendants;
all of the handmaids now in the house rouse up to come hither."
485 Speaking to him made answer his much-loved nurse Eurykleía:
"Certainly this, my child, you speak as is fitting and proper.
But come now, I will bring you a mantle and tunic as clothing,
so that you may not stand as you are, with your great broad shoulders
covered with rags, in the halls; that surely would be a great scandal."
490 Speaking to her then answered Odysseus of many devices:
"First of all now, let a fire be made for me here in the palace."
    He spoke, nor was ignored by his much loved nurse Eurykleía;
quickly she brought him the fire and the sulfur, and straightway Odysseus
thoroughly sulfured with fumes the whole house, both dwelling and courtyard.
495 Then the old woman set off through the beautiful house of Odysseus,
taking the women his message and bidding them come in a hurry.
Out of the hall they came, in their hands all carrying torches.
There they gathered around, embracing and greeting Odysseus,
giving affectionate welcome by kissing his head and his shoulders,
500 taking his hands in their own; most sweet was the longing that seized him
then for lamenting and moaning: he knew them all in his spirit.

BOOK 23

Now to the upstairs chamber the old dame, cackling, ascended,
bearing her mistress the news that her much loved husband was inside.
Nimbly her knees rushed on, though her feet underneath kept stumbling.
Standing above her head, she spoke these words and addressed her:
5 "Come now, awake, dear daughter Penelope, so with your eyes you
finally see for yourself what all of your days you have longed for:
noble Odysseus has come and arrived home, late though his coming.
Yes, he has killed the presumptuous suitors, who always disturbed this
palace of his, insulted his son, and devoured his possessions."
10   Prudent Penelope then spoke answering words and addressed her:
"Mamma dear, you have been driven insane by the gods, who are able,
even if one is a sensible person, to make her quite senseless;
those who are simple of mind they set on the way of discretion.
Now even you they derange, though before your mind was well balanced.
15 Why are you mocking me, who have a heart so heavy with sorrow,
telling me this nonsense and awakening me from the pleasant
sleep that was holding me fast after covering over my eyelids?
Never have I slept such good sleep from the time that Odysseus
parted to see Evililion, that place not to be mentioned.
20 But come now, go away and return to the hall of the palace.
If it were anyone else of the women belonging to me who
came with a message like this and awoke me out of my slumber,
swiftly and hatefully I would have sent her away to return back
down to the hall; but in this, old age is for you an advantage."
25   Speaking to her made answer the much loved nurse Eurykleía:
"I do not mock you at all, dear daughter, but really and truly
noble Odysseus has come and arrived home, just as I told you:
he is the stranger and guest whom all in the palace insulted.
Yes, and Telémachos has for a long time known he was inside
30 but in his thoughtful discretion concealed the design of his father,

so that the violent deeds of the arrogant men he could pay back."

　　So she spoke, and the lady rejoiced, jumped out of her bed, then
gladly embraced the old woman and let tears fall from her eyelids;
raising her voice she spoke, and in these winged words she addressed her:
35　"Come, dear mamma, if you can indeed say this to me truly,
if he has really arrived back here in his house, as you tell me,
how has he managed to set his hands on the shameless suitors,
being but one, while they in the house stayed always together?"

　　Speaking to her made answer the much loved nurse Eurykleía:
40　"I did not see it or learn it, but I heard only the groans of
men being killed, while deep in a nook of the well-built chambers
we sat stricken with terror; the well-fitted doors were enclosing
us right up to the moment your son Telémachos called me
out of the room, for his father himself had sent him to call me.
45　Then I discovered Odysseus among dead bodies of slain men
standing, and they quite covered the hard-stamped floor all around him,
heaped up one on another—your heart would have warmed to behold him
spattered and fouled with the blood and the battle gore, much like a lion.
Now in fact they are all outside by the doors of the courtyard,
50　lying together; the beautiful house he is fuming with sulfur,
with a great fire that he kindled; and he sent me here to call you.
But come, follow along, so that both of you go on the way of
happiness deep in your hearts, since many the ills you have suffered.
Finally now this long-felt wish and desire is accomplished:
55　he has himself come back to his hearth still living and found both
you and his son in the halls; although they have done to him many
evils, on all of the suitors he took his revenge in his palace."

　　Prudent Penelope then spoke answering words and addressed her:
"Mamma dear, do not exult at it yet so greatly, nor cackle;
60　you are aware that to all in the house he would be most welcome
when he appeared, above all to myself and the son that we brought forth.
Nevertheless, this story is not the real truth, as you tell it—
no, some immortal it is who has slaughtered the valorous suitors,
angered at their heart-anguishing crimes and iniquitous actions;
65　for to no person who lives on the earth they showed any honor,
neither the base nor the noble, whatever man might have approached them;
so for their recklessness they suffer this evil; Odysseus
far from Achaia has lost his return and himself is lost also."

　　Speaking to her then answered the much loved nurse Eurykleía:
70　"Oh my child, what a word has escaped from the fence of your teeth now,

383

when you say that your husband who sits inside at the hearth will
never return to his home! Your spirit is ever mistrustful.
Come now, something besides I will tell you, a manifest token,
it is a scar that a boar inflicted on him with its white tusk,
75   which as I washed him off I noticed, and wanted to tell it
also to you yourself, but he covered my mouth with his hands in
great and resourceful astuteness and did not allow me to tell you.
But come, follow me now—my life I will hazard upon it—
if I am lying to you, by a death most piteous kill me."
80   Prudent Penelope then spoke out to her, giving an answer:
"Mamma dear, it is a difficult matter for you to interpret—
though you are most wise-minded—the schemes of the gods who live always.
Nevertheless, let us go to my son, so that I may behold those
dead men who were my suitors, as well as the person who killed them."
85   So she spoke, and went down from the upstairs room, in her heart much
pondering whether to stay well away as she questioned her husband
or to stand near him to kiss his head and his hands and to clasp them.
Finally, when she entered the chamber and crossed the stone threshold,
she sat then in the gleam of the firelight, across from Odysseus,
90   close to the opposite wall; he was sitting beside a tall pillar,
casting his eyes down, waiting to see if his virtuous wife would
say to him anything when with her own eyes she could behold him.
Long in silence she sat, and a daze came over her spirit;
sometimes full in the face she would gaze at him, thinking she knew him,
95   sometimes failing to know him who wore foul clothes on his body.
Scolding, Telémachos spoke to her these words, calling upon her:
     "Mother of mine, harsh mother, with unreconcilable spirit,
why do you thus withdraw from my father, and why are you not now
sitting beside him, asking him questions and making inquiry?
100   Other than you, no woman would thus with an obstinate spirit
stand so far from her husband, who suffering many afflictions
came in the twentieth year back home to the land of his fathers;
always in you is a heart that is more unyielding than stone is."
     Prudent Penelope then spoke answering words and addressed him:
105   "Oh my child, in my bosom the spirit is full of amazement,
nor am I able to say any word to him nor to ask questions,
no, nor to look at him straight in the face. If really and truly
he is Odysseus and he has arrived back home, we will surely
know one another, and that even better—for us there are tokens
110   which we, both of us, know of, but which are a secret from others."

So she spoke, and he smiled, much-suffering noble Odysseus;
straightway in these winged words to Telémachos he began speaking:
"Well then, Telémachos, let your mother examine and make her
trial of me in the halls: she quickly will understand better.

115 Now because I am so dirty and wear foul clothes on my body,
she dishonors me still and will not yet say that I am he.
Straightway now let us think of the best way matters could happen.
For somebody who kills but a single man while in the district,
even a man who does not have many avengers thereafter,

120 flees into exile, leaving his kin and the land of his fathers;
we have destroyed the supports of the city, the best of the young men
dwelling in Ithaka now; it is this I urge you to think of."
   Thoughtful Telémachos then spoke out to him, giving an answer:
"Look to these matters yourself, dear father, for yours is the finest

125 mind among men in cunning, as it is reported, nor is there
anyone else among men who are mortal who might be a rival.
We will be eagerly following you, for I do not imagine
we will lack courage at all, so far as we have any power."
   Speaking to him then answered Odysseus of many devices:

130 "Well then, I will now tell you the way I think is the best one.
Start out first by washing yourselves, then putting on tunics;
order the handmaids here in the palace to dress in clean garments;
next then, holding his clear-toned lyre must the godlike singer
furnish us rhythmical guidance in dance for a festival revel,

135 so that whoever was outside hearing would think it a wedding,
either a man who was walking the road or else one of the neighbors,
so that the widespread news not get to the town of the death of
these men who were the suitors, until we have made our departure
out of the house to our well-wooded farm; there, after arriving,

140 we will take thought of the schemes the Olympian then may provide us."
   So he spoke, and they carefully listened to him and obeyed him.
First they started by washing themselves, then putting on tunics;
also the women arrayed themselves; and the godlike singer
took up the hollow lyre, and he stirred up longing among them

145 both for the sweetness of song and the blameless pleasure of dancing.
Now the great palace about them resounded aloud with the feet of
men who were festively dancing and women in beautiful girdles.
Thus would say one of those who listened outside of the palace:
"Certainly, someone has married the queen who has been so much courted.

150 Miserable wretch! She did not hold out for the husband she wedded,

steadily keeping the great house up until he could return home."

So would one of them say, as they did not know what had happened.
Straightway the housekeeper, old Eurýnomè, there in his own house
bathed greathearted Odysseus and rubbed him with oil of the olive,
155 then threw garments about him, a beautiful cloak and a tunic.
Over his head did Athena suffuse great beauty and made him
taller to see than before, more mighty; the hair on his head she
made flow down in thick curls that resembled a hyacinth flower.
As when a man well-skilled at the task lays gold over silver—
160 one who was taught his craft by Hephaistos and Pallas Athena,
every sort of technique—and the work he achieves is delightful,
so upon him did she now pour grace, on his head and his shoulders.
He came forth from the basin, in form most like the immortals.
Then he again sat down on the armchair whence he had risen,
165 facing his wife as before, and he spoke these words and addressed her:
"You strange woman, the gods who inhabit Olympian dwellings
gave you a heart that beyond any womanly nature is stubborn.
Other than you, no woman would thus with an obstinate spirit
stand so far from her husband, who suffering many afflictions
170 came in the twentieth year back home to the land of his fathers.
But come, Mamma, and spread out a bed for me, so that alone I
may lie down, for the heart in the breast of this woman is iron."

Prudent Penelope then spoke answering words and addressed him:
"You strange man, I am not being proud, nor at all do I slight you,
175 nor am I overimpressed; I know very well what you looked like
when you departed from Ithaka once on the long-oared galley.
But come, make up the stout bedstead for the man, Eurykleía,
outside the well-built chamber, the one that the master himself built;
there, after bringing the stout bedstead, put bedding upon it,
180 fleeces beneath, then mantles and covers of shimmering fabric."

So she spoke to make proof of her husband; but straightway Odysseus
angrily spoke and addressed his devoted and virtuous bedmate:
"These are indeed, my wife, heart-anguishing words you have spoken!
Who can have put my bed in another place? Even for someone
185 very expert, it would be quite hard, unless one of the gods came
personally, who could easily put it elsewhere if he wished to.
No one of mortals who now are alive, even one in full vigor,
ever could easily change its position, because in the well-wrought
bed a great token was fixed—I worked on it; nobody else did.
190 Growing inside of the court was the long-leaved trunk of an olive

386

tree in the prime of its vigor, and it was as stout as a pillar.
So around this I constructed the chamber until I was finished,
building with close-set stones, and above I skillfully roofed it,
also put on the doors, well-jointed and fitting exactly.
195 Finally then I cut off the crown of the long-leaved olive,
trimmed the stump up from the root, then smoothed it around with a brazen
adze expertly and well, and I trued it straight to a chalk line,
fashioning it as a bedpost, and bored all the holes with an augur.
Starting from that, I worked on the bedstead until I was finished,
200 added adornments of gold and of silver and ivory inlays,
stretched on the bedframe a strapping of oxhide, shining with purple.
This is the token that I have declared to you: I do not know now
whether it still stands firm for me, woman, or whether already
someone has put it elsewhere, first cutting the trunk of the olive."
205   So he spoke; and the limbs and the heart inside her were loosened,
as she perceived to be certain the tokens Odysseus had shown her.
Starting to weep, she ran straight up to him then, and she threw her
arms on the neck of Odysseus and kissed his head and addressed him:
"Do not be angry at me now, Odysseus, for otherwise you are
210 far the most thoughtful of men; our afflictions the gods have assigned us,
those who begrudged it to us to remain here always together
taking our joy in our youth, then reaching the threshold of old age.
So do not now be angry with me over this nor resent it,
that when I saw you first I did not greet you as I now do.
215 For it is true that the dear heart deep in my bosom was always
chill with the fear that a man might someday come and beguile me
merely by speaking—for many men meditate evil devices.
Neither in fact would Helen of Argos, the offspring of Zeus, have
mingled in love and in bed with a man from an alien people
220 if she had known that the warlike sons of Achaians would bring her
back once more to her home, to the much loved land of her fathers.
It was a god who aroused her to do so shameful an action;
never before she had laid in her heart such hateful and reckless
folly, from which first came to us also affliction and sorrow.
225 Now, since you have already related a manifest token
as to our nuptial bed—which no other man has seen ever,
but you only and I and as well just one of the handmaids,
Áktoris, whom my father had given to me when I came here,
she who used to stand guard at the doors of the strong-built chamber—
230 you have persuaded my heart, although it indeed has been stubborn."

387

She spoke, stirring in him yet greater desire for lamenting;
he wept, holding his wife so virtuous, lovely, devoted.
Just as appears most welcome the mainland to men who are swimming,
those whose well-made galley Poseidon has smashed on the open
235 sea after it has been pounded by stormwinds and powerful billows—
few are the men who escape from the silvery sea to the mainland
swimming, and much salt scurf from the brine has encrusted their bodies;
then most welcome they go on the mainland, escaping from evils—
so most welcome to her as she looked on him was her husband;
240 neither at all from his neck she loosed the embrace of her white arms.
Now would the Dawn have shone forth rose-fingered as they were lamenting,
were other things not devised by the goddess bright-eyed Athena.
Keeping the course of the long night lingering, Dawn of the gold throne
she held away at the bounds of the Ocean, and she would not let her
245 harness the swift-footed horses that carry the daylight to people,
Lampos and Pháëthon, radiant colts who bring on the Morning.
Then to his wife thus uttered Odysseus of many devices:
"Not yet we have arrived, dear wife, at the limits of all our
trials, but still there is left for the future a measureless labor,
250 long and enormous and hard: all this I am bound to accomplish.
For it was prophesied thus by the seer Teirésias' spirit,
on that day I descended and entered the dwelling of Hades,
looking to find a return back home for myself and my comrades.
But come, let us to bed, dear wife, so that finally we while
255 lying together may take our delight in the sweetness of slumber."
Prudent Penelope then spoke answering words and addressed him:
"There will indeed be a bed for you finally, when in your spirit
you should desire, since it is the gods who have caused you to come back
here to your well-built house, back here to the land of your fathers.
260 But since you have perceived and a god put it into your spirit,
come, tell me of the trial, since later at least, I am certain,
I will be hearing, and it is no worse to be told of it straightway."
Speaking to her then answered Odysseus of many devices:
"You strange woman, and why do you urge me so strongly and bid me
265 speak of it? Nevertheless I will tell you and I will hide nothing.
Not in the least will your heart feel joy in it—neither do I feel
joy myself, so many the towns of mankind that he bade me
go among, bearing an oar in my hands, well-fitted for rowing,
traveling till I arrive at a place where the people have never
270 heard of the sea, and they eat no food that is mingled with sea salt;

nor in fact do they know anything about purple-cheeked galleys
nor of the well-fitted oars which serve as the wings of a galley.
This unmistakable sign he told me, and I will not hide it:
when on the road I am met by another wayfarer who says that
275 it is a winnowing fan I hold on my glistening shoulder,
straightway, when in the earth, he said, my oar I had planted,
making oblation of excellent victims to lordly Poseidon,
burning a ram and a bull and a sow-mounting boar in his honor,
then I should go back homeward and sacred hecatombs offer
280 there to the deathless gods, the immortals who hold the broad heaven,
all of them, one by one; then out of the sea will a death come
over me, ever so gently and easily; this it will be which
kills me, tired in a sleek old age; and around me the people
all will be happy and blessèd; he said this will all be accomplished."
285   Prudent Penelope then spoke answering words and addressed him:
"If it is true that the gods bring forth an old age that is better,
then there is hope that for you there will be an escape from afflictions."
     Such things then they spoke and addressed each one to the other;
meanwhile Eurýnomè and the old nurse made ready the bed with
290 soft bed coverings, under the light of the radiant torches.
When they had spread out thick soft bedding with speed and adroitness,
then back into her chamber to lie down went the old woman,
while Eurýnomè, serving as maid of the bedroom, conducted
them as they went to their bed; in her hand she was holding a torch up.
295 When to the room she had led them, she went back in; and the two then
came to the place most welcome in which was their bed of the old days.
     Then did Telémachos straightway, as well as the oxherd and swineherd,
stop their feet from the dancing; the women they made stop also;
then they went to their beds all over the shadowy palace.
300   Those two, when of delectable love they had taken their pleasure,
pleased themselves with the stories that they now told to each other—
how much she had endured in the halls, that splendor of women,
as she beheld the detestable company there of the suitors,
those men who for her sake had slaughtered his cattle and fat sheep,
305 many of them; there was much wine too drawn out of the wine jars.
Then Zeus-nourished Odysseus related the many distresses
he caused men, and the many he suffered himself in his sorrow.
All he related, and she was delighted to hear, nor did slumber
fall on her eyelids before he had told her of all that had happened.
310   So he began how first he had quelled the Kikonians, then had

389

gone to the fertile land of the men who feed on the lotus;
all that the Cyklops had done, then how he had taken revenge on
him for the valiant companions he ate, and he showed no pity;
how he had reached Aíolos, who received him kindly and sent him
315 onward, but he was not destined as yet to arrive in his own dear
fatherland; rather again did a stormwind, seizing upon him,
carry him over the fish-thronged seaway, heavily groaning;
then how to Laístrygónian Télepylós he had journeyed—
they had destroyed his galleys as well as his well-greaved comrades,
320 all of them; only Odysseus in his black ship had escaped them.
Then he related the guile and the many devices of Circè;
how he had then gone into the moldering palace of Hades,
seeking prophetic advice of the Theban Teirésias' spirit,
gone in his galley of numerous oarlocks and seen all his comrades,
325 also his mother, who bore him and nurtured him when he was little;
how to the voice of the Sirens of echoing song he had listened;
how he had come to the Wandering Rocks and to dreaded Charýbdis,
Skylla as well, whom never a man has escaped uninjured;
then too how his companions had slaughtered the cows of the sun god;
330 how high-thundering Zeus with a smoldering bolt of his lightning
struck at the hollow ship and the noble companions had perished,
all at one time; he alone had escaped from the terrible doomsday;
how he had reached the Ogygian isle and Kalýpso the nymph who
kept on holding him fast—she wanted to make him her husband—
335 there in her spacious cavern, and gave him nurture, and told him
she would make him immortal and ageless forever and ever;
nevertheless, she never persuaded the heart in his bosom;
how after suffering much he had reached the Phaiákian people—
they in their hearts as if he were a god then honored him greatly,
340 sent him away with a ship to the much loved land of his fathers,
giving him treasures of bronze and of gold in abundance and garments.
This was the last of the tales he told, when the sweetness of slumber,
loosing his limbs, came upon him, releasing the cares from his spirit.
      Then other things were devised by the goddess bright-eyed Athena:
345 finally, when she supposed that Odysseus had taken his pleasure
deep in his heart, of the bed of his wife and as well of his slumber,
straightway out of the Ocean the one born early at daybreak,
golden-enthroned, she aroused, to bring light among men, and Odysseus
out of his soft bed rose, and a word he spoke to enjoin her:
350 "Dear wife, we have already been glutted with manifold trials,

both of us—over my painful return back home were you weeping
here in the house, while Zeus and the other gods ever detained me,
wishing to come, in pains faraway from the land of my fathers.
Now since both of us thus have arrived in the bed that we longed for,
355　you for your part take care of the goods I have in the palace;
as for those cattle of mine that the arrogant suitors have ravaged,
many will I get back through raids; the Achaians will give me
others, until they have filled up every one of the steadings.
Now however will I go out to the well-wooded farm to
360　visit my excellent father, for he incessantly mourns me.
This is the charge I lay on you, wife, though you are sagacious:
since right away when the sun comes up will the rumor begin its
rounds about all those suitors, the men I killed in the palace,
going upstairs to your chamber along with your women attendants,
365　sit there and do not see anybody nor ask any questions."

　　　Thus, and his beautiful armor he put on over his shoulders,
wakened Telémachos straightway, as well as the oxherd and swineherd,
ordered them all to take up in their hands their weapons of battle.
They did not disobey him but armed themselves in bronze armor,
370　opened the door leaves, and went outside, and Odysseus was leading.
Light already was over the earth, but Athena, concealing
them in a night gloom, guided them rapidly out of the city.

BOOK 24

Hermes, Kyllenian god, then summoned the souls of the suitors
out of their bodies; the beautiful wand well-crafted of gold he
held in his hands, that he uses for charming the eyes of whatever
man he wishes, and others again he arouses from slumber;
5 stirring them up with it now he led them, and squeaking they followed.
As when the bats in the deepest recess of a marvelous cavern
squeak as they flitter about when one of them falls from the rock where
they in chains have been clustered as each holds on to another,
so they squeaked as they followed together; and Hermes the kindly
10 healer was leading them on, down over the moldering pathways.
Forth by the streams of the Ocean they went, and the White Rock Leukas,
then they went by the gates of the sun, and the country of dreams they
passed in their journey and quickly arrived in the asphodel meadow,
there where spirits are dwelling, the phantoms of men who are worn out.
15 There they discovered the spirit of Peleus' scion Achilles,
that of Patróklos and that of the noble Antílochos also,
then that of Ajax, the man who surpassed in beauty and stature
all of the Dánaäns other than Peleus' excellent scion.
So in a throng they surrounded Achilles; approaching the heroes
20 then did the soul of the scion of Atreus come, Agamemnon,
bitterly grieving, and others collected around, of the men who
perished with him, encountered their doom in the house of Aigísthos.
First did the spirit of Peleus' son speak out to the other:
"Atreus' son, it was you we thought to be dear beyond mortal
25 heroes all of your days to Lord Zeus the great thunderbolt-hurler,
since you were lord over men who were many and mighty in valor,
when in the land of the Trojans Achaians were suffering sorrows.
Yet upon you also it was destined to come very early,
ruinous doom, which nobody who has been born can escape from.
30 Would that as you were enjoying the honor of which you were master,

you in the land of the Trojans had met your death and your doomsday!
Then would a funeral mound have been heaped by all the Achaians;
so for your son also you had won great fame for the future;
now instead it was doomed that a death most shameful should take you."

35   Speaking to him then answered the spirit of Atreus' scion:
"Peleus' fortunate son, most like the immortals, Achilles,
you who perished in Troy, far distant from Argos—around you
others were killed, the best sons of the Trojans and of the Achaians,
as over you they fought, while you in the turbulent dust lay
40 greatly, the greatest of heroes, your skill as a horseman forgotten.
We kept fighting the whole day long, nor at all had we ever
put any stop to the battle, if Zeus with a storm had not stopped it.
When we had carried you down to the galleys, away from the battle,
we placed you on a litter and cleansed and anointed your handsome
45 body with pure warm water and unguents; and many the hot tears
there around you did the Dánaäns pour forth, cutting their hair off.
Out of the sea then came your mother, with her the immortal
sea nymphs, hearing the news; and the marvelous cry that arose spread
over the seaway, and all the Achaians were seized with a trembling.
50 Jumping up now, they would have gone onto the hollow galleys
if they had not been stopped by a man most learnèd in old lore,
Nestor—before this too his advice had been seen to be noblest.
He with benevolent wisdom addressed them, giving them counsel:
'Hold back, Argives, do not take flight now, youthful Achaians;
55 it is his mother who comes from the sea, and with her the immortal
sea nymphs, so as to be here and care for her son who has perished.'
So he spoke; the greathearted Achaians were kept from their panic.
Standing around you then, the old man of the sea's dear daughters
raised up piteous moans; in ambrosial garments they dressed you.
60 Then all nine of the Muses in lovely antiphonal voices
sang you a dirge; there you would have seen not one of the Argives
who was not weeping, for so the clear song of the Muses aroused them.
Seven days, then ten more, in the night and as well in the daytime,
you were bewailed by the gods undying and men who are mortal;
65 then on the eighteenth day, to the fire we gave you; around you
many a fine fat sheep we slaughtered, and crooked-horned cattle.
So in the clothes of the gods you were burned, and with many an ointment,
also with much sweet honey; and many heroic Achaians
danced in their armor, surrounding the pyre on which you were burning,
70 both foot soldiers and horsemen; and great was the clamor that rose up.

But then, after the flame of Hephaistos had fully consumed you,
early at dawn we gathered your white bones together, Achilles,
into the unmixed wine and the unguent—a jar had your mother
given, of gold, two-handled; she said it had been Dionýsos'
75 gift, and that it was the work of the glorious craftsman Hephaistos.
It is in this that your white bones lie now, brilliant Achilles,
mingled with those of the perished Patróklos, Menoítios' scion,
while Antílochos' bones lie apart; it was he that you honored,
after the death of Patróklos, the most of all other companions.
80 Then around these bones we of the sacred army of Argive
spearmen heaped up a funeral mound, an enormous and faultless
tomb overlooking the broad Hellespont on the point of a headland,
so that it might be observed by men far out on the seaway,
both by the ones now living and those who will live in the future.
85 Then your mother, beseeching the gods to grant beautiful prizes,
set them up for a contest amidst the most noble Achaians.
You in your time have attended the funerals many heroic
men are accorded—whenever, because of a king who has perished,
young men dress in their loincloths and ready themselves for the contests—
90 but far more in your heart, seeing these things, you would have wondered,
such were the beautiful prizes for you set up by the goddess
Thetis of silvery feet; to the gods you were dearly belovèd.
So even though you are dead, your name is not lost, but forever
noble renown you will have among all of the peoples, Achilles.
95 But what pleasure did I have, when I had wound up the warfare?
For as I came back home, Zeus planned me a wretched destruction
under the hands of Aigísthos and those of a murderous bedmate."
        Such things then they spoke and addressed each one to the other.
Then came up and approached them the messenger, slayer of Argos,
100 leading the souls of the suitors who had been killed by Odysseus.
Wondering, those two went straight up to them when they beheld them;
then did the soul of the scion of Atreus, great Agamemnon,
know Melanéos' belovèd offspring, far-famed Amphimédon;
he was a guest-friend of his, in Ithaka keeping his dwelling.
105 First did the spirit of Atreus' son speak out to the other:
"What have you borne, Amphimédon, that you come under the dark earth,
all of you choice young men and of similar years? Nor would he choose
otherwise who was selecting the noblest men of a city.
Was it Poseidon who brought you down as you sailed in your galleys,
110 raising against you towering billows and terrible stormwinds,

or on the dry land were you destroyed by enemy fighters
when from the fields you were driving their cattle and beautiful sheep flocks
or when over their city you fought them and over their women?
Answer me what I am asking—I tell you, I am your guest-friend.
115 Or do you not remember when I came there to your palace,
with godlike Meneláos, that I might stir up Odysseus,
so he would follow to Ilion then in the well-benched galleys?
We were a whole month passing across the entire broad seaway,
then we barely persuaded Odysseus the sacker of cities."
120   Then Amphimédon's spirit in turn thus spoke and addressed him:
"Atreus' glorious son Agamemnon, lord of the people,
all those things I remember, belovèd of Zeus, as you say them,
and about all these things I will tell you exactly and fully,
what was the baneful end of our death, how it was accomplished.
125 We were then courting the wife of Odysseus, who long had been absent;
she would neither reject nor accomplish the odious marriage—
rather was planning for us our death and the blackest of doomsdays.
This is another deception that she in her spirit invented:
putting her great loom up in her chamber, she set about weaving
130 delicate fabric of amplest measure, and thereupon told us:
'Young men, suitors for me, since noble Odysseus has perished,
wait, hold off from the marriage you urge upon me, until I can
finish the mantle, lest all of the yarn be uselessly wasted.
It is a burial robe for the lord Laërtes, for when he
135 falls in the ruinous doom of his death so long in the mourning,
lest in the town some woman among the Achaians reproach me
that this man who acquired so much should be lying unshrouded.'
So she spoke, and the valorous spirits in us were persuaded.
Then each day she would weave at the loom, enlarging the fabric,
140 while each night she undid it, when torches she had set beside her.
So three years by her craft she fooled and convinced the Achaians,
but when the fourth year came with the passing of hours and of seasons,
with the decline of the months, when many a day was completed,
finally one of the maids spoke out who knew of it plainly,
145 so that we came upon her undoing the glorious fabric.
Thus she completed the cloth unwillingly, under compulsion.
When the great fabric was woven, she made a display of the mantle,
washing it first—in splendor the sun or the moon it resembled.
Finally then by a mischievous spirit Odysseus was guided
150 out to the bounds of his land where the swineherd lives in a cabin.

Thither arrived also the dear scion of godlike Odysseus,
he with a dark-hued galley returning from sandy-soiled Pylos;
those two, when they had plotted a baneful death for the suitors,
soon went up to the glorious city, but it was Odysseus

155 who came last, with Telémachos going before as the leader.
Later the swineherd brought him—he wore foul clothes on his body;
he had the look of a beggar, an ancient and miserable vagrant,
propped on a staff, who was wearing the vilest of clothes on his body;
nor was a one of us able to recognize him as the man who

160 suddenly made his appearance, not even the older among us,
but we began to assail him with evil rebukes and with missiles.
Nevertheless for a time he endured, in the halls of his own house
being assaulted and being rebuked, with a resolute spirit;
but when the purpose of Zeus who carries the aegis aroused him,

165 then with Telémachos he made off with the beautiful weapons,
stowed them away in a chamber and bolted the door to secure them.
With a resourceful cunning of mind, his wife he directed
then to set up for the suitors the bow and the silver-gray iron—
so ill-fated we were—as a contest, starting the slaughter.

170 Nor was a one of us all, when the great strong bow we attempted,
able to fasten the string—we were far too weak to achieve it.
But when the great bow finally came to the hands of Odysseus,
straightway raising our voices, we all of us shouted together
not to allow him the bow, no matter how much he was talking;

175 only Telémachos urged him to do it and gave him the order.
Taking it into his hands, much-suffering noble Odysseus
easily fastened the string to the bow, then shot through the iron;
he stepped onto the threshold; the swift-flying arrows he poured out,
dreadfully glaring around him, and King Antínoös struck down.

180 Then also at the others he shot the maleficent missiles,
aiming them straight at the men; and they dropped down one by another.
One of the gods, it was manifest now, was assisting the fighters;
for in the palace at once, they, guided by furious passion,
killed one after another; and miserable was the groan which

185 rose from the heads thus stricken; the whole floor ran with our lifeblood.
Thus, Agamemnon, we were destroyed, whose bodies are lying
still uncared for even till now in the halls of Odysseus,
since not yet do our friends in the house of each one of us know it,
those who, washing away the black gore from our wounds, may lamenting

190 lay us out on our biers, since this is the prize of the perished."

Speaking to him then answered the spirit of Atreus' scion:
"Fortunate child of Laërtes, Odysseus of many devices,
great indeed was the virtue the wife you won was endowed with!
Such was the excellent wisdom in faultless Penelope's spirit,
195   noble Ikários' daughter! How well she remembered Odysseus,
that same man she had wedded! And so the renown of her virtue
never will die: about constant Penelope will the immortals
make for the people on earth a delightful song in her honor.
Not thus, those evil deeds Tyndáreos' daughter concocted,
200   killing the husband to whom she was wedded; and hers will a loathsome
song be among mankind, and an evil repute does she bring on
all of the female sex, even one whose acts are of virtue."
     Such things then they spoke and addressed each one to the other,
while in the depths of the earth they stood in the dwelling of Hades.
205   Out of the city the others had gone; at the beautiful well-worked
farm of Laërtes they quickly arrived, the estate that Laërtes
once had acquired for himself, when he worked very hard to reclaim it.
Here was his house, and around it on every side ran a cabin,
inside which would the slaves who were bonded to work as he wanted
210   eat their dinners, and sit at their leisure, and go to their slumber.
There was as well an old woman of Sicily here, who would kindly
care for the old man out on his farm faraway from the city.
Thereon Odysseus addressed this word to his son and the servants:
"You now go on ahead to the well-built dwelling and enter;
215   straightway slaughter a pig for our dinner, the one that is finest;
meanwhile, I will myself go put my father to trial,
if in fact he will recognize me, with his eyes he will know me,
or if he might not know me, as I have been gone for a long time."
     So he spoke, and he gave to his servants the weapons of warfare;
220   quickly they went on into the house then. Meanwhile Odysseus
went up close to the fruit-rich orchard to put him to trial.
Dolios he did not find when he went in the great plantation,
nor any slaves, nor a one of his sons—at the time they had all gone
outside so as to gather some rubble and brush for the orchard
225   wall they would build; and the old man superintended the errand.
Only his father he found inside of the well-worked orchard,
digging around a young tree; and the tunic upon him was squalid,
mended with patches, disgraceful; and leggings of oxhide were fastened
over his calves, all patched, to afford him protection from scratches;
230   gloves he wore on his hands on account of the brambles; above he

had on his head a rough goatskin cap, increasing his sorrow.
Then, as he noticed him there, much-suffering noble Odysseus—
seeing the man worn down by old age, in his heart great sorrow—
stood still under a great tall pear tree, letting his tears fall.

235   Then he began to revolve his thoughts in his mind and his spirit,
whether to kiss and embrace his father and tell him his story,
all of it, how he had come and arrived in the land of his fathers,
or to ask first about everything and to put him to trial.
So as he pondered the matter, the best course seemed to be this one:

240   he would at first by bantering mockery put him to trial.
Thinking of these things, noble Odysseus directly approached him.
Keeping his head bent downward, around a young tree he was digging;
then his illustrious son, as he stood at his side, so addressed him:
      "Old man, certainly you do not lack the expertness to tend this

245   orchard, but it has been cared for well; there is nothing at all here,
never a plant, no fig tree or vine, nor an olive tree either,
neither a pear tree nor a leek bed in the garden uncared for.
Something else I will tell you; do not take anger to heart now:
you are yourself not cared for at all well—to add to your wretched

250   old age, you are disgracefully scurfy; your clothing is squalid.
Not on account of your laziness, surely, your master neglects you,
nor is there anything slavish at all to behold in your body,
either appearance or size, for you look like a man who is kingly.
Yes, you look like a person who, when he has bathed and has eaten,

255   sleeps in a soft bed soundly, for this is the right of our elders.
But come now, tell me this and recount it exactly and fully:
What man's servant are you? Whose orchard is this you are tending?
Truthfully speak to me now about these things, so that I know well
if this really is Ithaka I have arrived in, as that man

260   told me, the one who encountered me now as I came here—
not very clever at all, for he had no patience for either
telling me all of his story or hearing my word as I asked him
after my dear guest-friend, if he lives and is still in existence,
or he has died already and dwells in the palace of Hades.

265   For I say to you plainly, and you take notice and heed me:
There was a man I entertained once in the land of my fathers
when he arrived at our place—no other man ever appeared more
welcome to me, of the strangers who came from abroad to my household.
He in birth, he declared, was of Ithakan parents; his father,

270   as he informed me, was Lord Laërtes, Arkeisios' scion.

I then brought him along to my house, and I well entertained him,
kindly befriending him there—in the house were abundant provisions—
offered him also the gifts of a friend, as was fitting and proper.
Gold well-wrought and refined I presented to him, seven talents,
275 also a wine bowl wholly of silver, embellished with flowers,
twelve wool mantles to be worn single, as many thick blankets,
so too as many fine cloaks, and as well the same number of tunics;
then beyond this four women I gave to him, skillful in faultless
work and attractive, and he could himself choose those that he wanted."
280   Speaking to him then answered his father, while letting his tears fall:
"Stranger, indeed you have come to the country of which you were asking;
arrogant men, however, and reckless are those who possess it.
Fruitlessly you have bestowed those presents, the many you gave him;
if in the Ithakan land you had come on the man yet living,
285 he would have sent you away with an ample exchange for your presents—
good hospitality too, as is right when a man has begun it.
But come now, tell me this and recount it exactly and fully:
how many years is it now from the time when you entertained that
miserable man as your guest—my son, if he ever existed,
290 so ill fated, whom far from his friends and the land of his fathers
either at sea fish may have devoured, or perhaps on the mainland
he has been prey for the birds and the wild beasts; nor did his mother
mourn him and give him a shroud, or his father, we parents who bore him;
nor did his bedmate, constant Penelope, wealthy in bride gifts,
295 mourn for her husband who lay on his bier, as is fitting and proper,
after his eyes she had closed, since this is the prize of the perished.
Truthfully speak to me now about these things, so that I know well:
Who are you? Whence do you come? What city is yours, and what parents?
Where in fact is the swift ship anchored that carried you hither?
300 Where are your godlike comrades? Or have you arrived on another's
galley as passenger now, and they left you behind when they left here?"
     Speaking to him then answered Odysseus of many devices:
"All this I will indeed now tell you exactly and fully.
I am from Álybas, where I live in a glorious palace;
305 I am the son of Apheídas, the son of the lord Polypémon;
as for my own name, it is Epéritos; but I have now been
driven by some god here from Sikania—I did not want it.
Out by the fields my galley is anchored, away from the city.
But with regard to Odysseus, it now is the fifth of the years from
310 when he started from there and departed the land of my fathers,

so ill fated; and yet as he went away, birds of good omen
flew to his right, so that I was rejoicing in them as I sent him;
he too rejoiced as he left, and the hearts in both of us hoped that
we would be meeting in friendship and proffering glorious presents."

315   So he spoke; a black cloud of distress enshrouded his father;
taking the grimy and ash-gray dust into both of his hands, he
poured it over his face and his white hair, heavily groaning.
Then in the other the heart was aroused—already a piercing
pang in his nostrils struck as he looked at his own dear father.

320 Quickly he leapt up, kissed and embraced him; and thus he addressed him:
"I am he—yes, it is I, dear father, of whom you are asking,
I have returned in the twentieth year to the land of my fathers.
But keep holding yourself from your wailing and tearful lamenting.
For I say to you plainly—though great is our need to act quickly—

325 I have indeed just slaughtered the suitors inside of our palace,
punishing their heart-anguishing crimes and iniquitous actions."
    Then in answer Laërtes addressed him, speaking in these words:
"If you in fact are Odysseus, my own child, who have arrived here,
tell me a sign very clear to me now, so that I am persuaded."

330   Speaking to him then answered Odysseus of many devices:
"First then, here is a scar—with your eyes take notice and see it—
which in Parnassos a boar inflicted on me with its white tusk
when I had gone there, for you and the lady my mother had sent me
there to Autólykos, Mother's dear father, in order that I might

335 get those gifts he had promised to me with a nod when he came here.
Come, I will also speak of the trees in the well-worked orchard,
which of them you once gave me—about each one I would ask you,
when as a child I followed you over the garden, and while we
went among these same trees you named them and told me about them.

340 Thirteen pear trees you gave to me then, ten apple trees also,
fig trees forty in all, in the same way named me the fifty
vine rows which you would give me, with each one bearing its grapes at
different times, all sorts and varieties clustered upon them,
when from the heavens the seasons of Zeus bring weight to the branches."

345   So he spoke, and his limbs and the heart inside him were loosened,
as he perceived to be certain the tokens Odysseus had shown him.
Quickly his arms he flung on his own dear son and began to
fall in a faint; much-suffering noble Odysseus received him.
When he recovered his breath and the strength came back to his spirit,

350 once more starting the talk, he spoke these words as an answer:

"Oh father Zeus, even still you gods are on lofty Olympos
if it is true that the suitors have paid for their reckless outrage.
Now in my mind I dreadfully fear that the Ithakans all will
soon come here and attack us and then moreover will send out
355   messengers everywhere to the Képhallénians' cities."
        Speaking to him then answered Odysseus of many devices:
"Take heart—do not allow these matters to trouble your spirit.
Now let us go to the house which lies here close to the orchard;
I sent Telémachos there, as well as the oxherd and swineherd,
360   well in advance, so that they might quickly prepare us a dinner."
        So having spoken of this, to the beautiful house they proceeded.
Finally, when they arrived at the house well-built as a dwelling,
they found Telémachos there, as well as the oxherd and swineherd;
much roast meat they were carving, and glistening wine they were mixing.
365   Meanwhile there in his house the Sicilian woman attendant
bathed greathearted Laërtes and rubbed him with oil of the olive,
then threw about him a beautiful mantle; and straightway Athena
stood close by and augmented the limbs of the shepherd of people,
made him taller than he was before, much stouter to look at.
370   He came forth from the basin; at him did his dear son marvel,
seeing a man who resembled the deathless gods in appearance.
Raising his voice he spoke, and in these winged words he addressed him:
"Father, assuredly one of the gods who live always has made you
in your appearance and size much taller and stronger to look at."
375   Thoughtful Laërtes in turn spoke out to him, giving an answer:
"Oh Zeus, father of all, and Athena as well and Apollo,
just as I was that time, as the Képhallénians' ruler,
I took Nérikos' strong-built fort on a cape of the mainland,
would that yesterday I had been such in the halls of our palace,
380   bearing upon my shoulders my armor, to stand there and ward off
all those men who were suitors; so I would have loosened the limbs of
many of them in our halls—you would have rejoiced in your spirit."
        Such words then they spoke and addressed each one to the other.
Then when they had completed the work and had readied the meal, they
385   took their seats in orderly rows on benches and armchairs.
Then to begin they were putting their hands to the meal, and approaching
them old Dolios came, and with him were the sons of the old man,
quite worn out from their labor, because their mother had called them,
going to them—the old woman from Sicily, she who had raised them,
390   carefully tending the old man too, since old age had seized him.

When they had looked at Odysseus and recognized him in their spirits,
they stood there in the hall in amazement and awe; but Odysseus
started to speak and addressed him in words mollifying and gentle:
"Old man, sit at your meal, put out of your mind your amazement,
395   since we have long been eager to lay our hands on the victuals,
while we waited for you in the halls, expecting you always."
    So did he say; straight up to him Dolios ran as he stretched out
both hands; taking Odysseus' hand, on the wrist he kissed it.
Raising his voice he spoke, and in these winged words he addressed him:
400   "Dear lord, since back home you have come to us, who have desired it,
thinking no more it would happen—the gods themselves must have led you—
health to you! Heartiest welcome! And may the gods give you good fortune!
Truthfully speak to me now about these things, so that I know well,
whether already the prudent Penelope knows of it clearly,
405   that you have come back here, or a messenger should we dispatch her?"
    Speaking to him then answered Odysseus of many devices:
"Old man, she is already informed—why bother about this?"
    So he spoke; on a well-polished stool again sat down the other.
So also around famous Odysseus Dolios' children
410   made him welcome with speeches and took his hands in their handclasps;
then in order they sat beside Dolios, who was their father.
    So it was that they busied themselves in the halls with a dinner.
Rumor the messenger now went swiftly all over the city,
making report of the odious death and the doom of the suitors.
415   Hearing of it, they gathered together from every direction,
groaning and making lament in front of the house of Odysseus.
Taking the corpses away from the house, each buried his own man;
those of the suitors from different cities they sent to their own homes,
put them upon swift galleys of fishermen who would convey them.
420   To the assembly they went in a throng, much grieving in spirit;
then when they had collected and all were gathered together,
old Eupeíthes at once stood up; these words he addressed them,
for in his heart lay an unforgettable grief for his own dear
child Antínoös, who was the first to be killed by noble Odysseus.
425   Shedding his tears over him, he addressed them, giving them counsel:
"Friends, how enormous a deed this man has devised the Achaians;
some he carried away in his ships, men many and noble,
losing the hollow galleys and utterly losing the people;
others he killed on returning, the Képhallénians' best men.
430   Come now, let us, before he swiftly can voyage to Pylos

or to illustrious Elis, in which the Epeíans are rulers,
go to him. Otherwise we will be shamed in the future forever;
for these things are disgraceful for men of the future to learn of,
if on the killers of our own children and kinsmen we do not
435   take our revenge—as for me, in my heart there would be no pleasure
living, but I prefer quickly to die and to be among dead men.
So let us go, lest they get a start on us crossing the seaway."
      So he said, shedding his tears; compassion held all the Achaians.
Then came up and approached them the godlike singer and Medon
440   out of the halls of Odysseus, for now their sleep had released them.
There in the middle they stood, and amazement seized upon each man.
Raising his voice among them spoke Medon, sagacious and knowing:
"Listen to me now and heed me, Ithakans, for if Odysseus
planned these deeds, the immortals were certainly not unwilling.
445   I myself saw a deathless god who was taking a stance quite
close to Odysseus, and Mentor in every way it resembled;
then sometimes in front of Odysseus appeared an immortal
god encouraging him, other times agitating the suitors,
dashing about in the hall; and they dropped down one by another."
450   So did he say, and a green fear seized upon all of the people.
Then spoke also among them a hero, the old Halithérses,
Mastor's son—for alone he saw the before and the after—
he with benevolent wisdom addressed them, giving them counsel:
"Listen to me now and heed me, Ithakans, while I am speaking:
455   it is by your own cowardice, friends, these deeds are accomplished;
neither myself you obeyed nor Mentor the shepherd of people,
so as to make your sons put a stop to their senseless behavior,
they who wrought in their recklessness an enormous misdoing,
laying to waste the possessions and disrespecting the wife of
460   that most noble of men; they thought he would never be coming.
Now then, let it be thus, and obey me in what I advise you:
let us not go, lest some find evil that they themselves brought on."
      So he spoke; with a great war cry then leapt from the benches
more than half the assembly—the others remained there together—
465   for to their minds his speech was not pleasing, but they were persuaded
by Eupeíthes; and quickly they started to run for their armor.
Straightway, when in the glittering bronze their bodies were covered,
they all gathered together in front of the spacious city.
It was Eupeíthes who in their foolishness served as the leader;
470   vengeance he thought to exact for the death of his son, but he was not

destined to go back home but himself to encounter his doom there.

Meanwhile Athena was speaking to Zeus the great scion of Kronos:
"Father of all of us, scion of Kronos and sovereign ruler,
answer me what I will ask: What plan lies hidden within you?
475 Is it additional baneful battle and terrible strife you
yet will inflict, or between the two sides now establish friendship?"

Answering her in return spoke forth the cloud-gathering god Zeus:
"My child, why of these things are you asking and making inquiry?
Was this not the design which you yourself recommended,
480 so when Odysseus returned he could pay them back for their evils?
You do just as you wish; I will tell you what appears fitting.
Now that the suitors have been paid back by noble Odysseus,
let these pledge themselves with their oaths that he always be ruler.
Then for our part, as regarding their children's and kinsmen's slaughter
485 let us make them forgetful; and let them be friends of each other,
just as before; then let there be riches and peace in abundance."

He spoke, rousing Athena, as she already was eager;
speedily she came down from the summit of lofty Olympos.

Soon as the diners were quite satisfied with the heart-cheering victuals,
490 speaking among them began much-suffering noble Odysseus:
"Somebody go out now, see whether they might be approaching."

He spoke; Dolios' son went out as Odysseus had bidden,
went to the threshold and stood, and at once saw all of them nearby.
Straightway he spoke to Odysseus; in these winged words he addressed him:
495 "They are indeed quite close—let us arm ourselves very swiftly!"

He spoke, and they leapt onto their feet, then put on their armor—
three men still with Odysseus, and Dolios' six sons also.
Joining with them, Laërtes and Dolios put on their armor,
even as gray as they were—of necessity they would be fighters.
500 Straightway, when in the glittering bronze their bodies were covered,
then they opened the doors and went out, and Odysseus was leading.

Then came up and approached them Athena the daughter of great Zeus,
making herself like Mentor in speaking as well as appearance.
Seeing her there he rejoiced, much-suffering noble Odysseus;
505 quickly Telémachos then he addressed, his son so belovèd:
"This you will learn very shortly, Telémachos, when you have come there
where the most excellent men among those who fight are distinguished,
not to bring shame on the blood of your fathers, on us who in time past
were outstanding all over the earth in valor and manhood."
510 Thoughtful Telémachos then spoke out to him, giving an answer:

"You will observe if you wish, dear father, that I in my present
spirit will bring no shame on your blood, as you have suggested."
So did he say; Laërtes rejoiced, and a word he addressed them:
"Now what a day, dear gods, this is for me! Much am I gladdened;
515   here my son and my grandson are vying in courage and prowess."
Standing beside him then, thus spoke forth bright-eyed Athena:
"Son of Arkeisios, dearest by far among all of my comrades,
saying a prayer to the bright-eyed maid and to Zeus her father,
swing very swiftly aloft the long-shadowing spear shaft and hurl it."
520   Thus, and in him great power was breathed by Pallas Athena.
Then he, saying a prayer straightway to the daughter of great Zeus,
swung very swiftly aloft the long-shadowing spear shaft and hurled it,
so Eupeíthes it struck on the bronze cheek piece of his helmet,
nor was the spear held off, but the bronze of the tip went straight through.
525   Falling he crashed to the earth, and around him clattered his armor.
Then with his glorious son on the foremost men fell Odysseus;
both began striking at them with swords and with double-curved spear blades.
Now they would have killed all, no return to their homes would have given,
had not Athena, the daughter of Zeus who carries the aegis,
530   shouted in such a loud voice as to hold back all of the people:
"Hold back, Ithakan men, from the painful and burdensome battle,
so that without bloodshed you may settle and separate quickly."
Thus cried out to the people Athena, and green fear seized them;
out of the hands of the terrified warriors all of the arms flew,
535   all fell onto the ground at the sound of the goddess's shouting.
They turned back to the city, desiring to go on living;
vehemently then yelled much-suffering noble Odysseus,
gathered himself, then swooped on the men like a high-flying eagle.
Hurled by the scion of Kronos, a smoldering bolt of his lightning
540   fell in front of the bright-eyed maid whose father is mighty.
Then to Odysseus at once thus spoke forth bright-eyed Athena:
"Zeus-sprung son of Laërtes, Odysseus of many devices,
hold back, cease from the struggle of war's impartial contention,
lest wide-thundering Zeus son of Kronos be angry against you."
545   So said Athena, and he then obeyed her, rejoicing in spirit.
Now were established the oaths for the future between the two sides by
Pallas Athena the daughter of Zeus who carries the aegis,
making herself like Mentor in speaking as well as appearance.

List of
Proper Names
in the *Odyssey*

Since the rhythm of the verse is a primary consideration in this version, I have used accents, in the following list and in the text, on any transliterated Greek names that might cause problems in reading aloud. For this purpose, an acute accent (´) over a syllable indicates a major metrical stress—in a few names, it occurs twice. The grave accent (`) over the final *è*, as in *Alkándrè*, signifies that it is to be read as an unstressed syllable. The dieresis over the second of two contiguous vowels, as in *Alkínoös*, signifies that it is to be read separately, not as a diphthong. The ending *-eus* should be pronounced as one syllable (*eu* is a diphthong); thus, *Odysseus* always has three syllables. Final *-es* should be pronounced as a separate syllable in all proper names except *Thebes*, for which I adopt the usual English pronunciation. In Greek names, *ch* always sounds like that in *school*. Several names (e.g., *Penelope*) are so commonly known as not to need marking; for such names as *Ajax*, *Circè*, *Crete*, *Egypt*, and *Phoenicians*, I have used the name familiar to contemporary readers.

This list will serve as a quick reference, citing the first occurrence of each name in the epic and occasionally two or more occurrences when these are widely separated. The few line numbers in boldface refer to the major appearance of a character when that comes after the first occurrence of the name. Some "significant names"—especially those whose meanings are the most important thing about them—are glossed in quotation marks in entries; this was often accomplished with the aid of the notes in the edition of W. B. Stanford. The index of proper names in the Loeb Classical Library edition of the *Odyssey*, edited by A. T. Murray, revised by George E. Dimock, has been of great help in compiling this list; those who wish more exhaustive references will find them there, though without annotation.

Achaia: region in Greece; used in Homer to signify all of Greece; 13.249.

Achaians: designation of all the Greeks at Troy under Agamemnon's leadership or of the Greeks in general; 1.61.

Ácheron: a river of Hades' domain; "River of Woe"; 10.513.

Achilles: greatest of the Greek heroes; 3.106; his shade appears at **11.467**, 24.15.

Adréstè: one of Helen's handmaids; 4.123.

Agamemnon: king of Mykénè; son of Atreus; leader of the Greeks at Troy; murdered by his wife, Klýtaimnéstra, and her lover, Aigísthos; 1.30.

Ageláos: a suitor; son of Damastor; killed by Odysseus; 20.321.

Aiaía: the island of Circè; 9.31.

Aíakos: father of Peleus; grandfather of Achilles; 11.471.

Aiétes: brother of Circè; son of Helios; 10.137.

Aigai: the place in Achaia where Poseidon has his palace; 5.381.

Aigísthos: son of Thyéstes; Agamemnon's cousin and murderer; Klýtaimnéstra's lover; 1.29.

Aigyptios: an old Ithakan; 2.15.

Aiolia: the island of the winds; 10.1.

Aíolos: (1) the keeper of the winds; 10.2; (2) grandfather of Kretheus; 11.237.

Aison: son of Tyro and Kretheus; father of Jason; 11.259.

Aithon: Odysseus' fictional self in the story he tells Penelope; 19.184.

Aitolian: a man from Aitolia, in central Greece, who tricked Eumaíos with a story; 14.379.

Ajax: (1) "the greater": son of Telamon; against him Odysseus contended for the arms of Achilles; 3.109, **11.543;** (2) "the lesser": son of Oíleus; 4.499.

Akastos: king of Doulíchion in Odysseus' tale to Eumaíos; 14.336.

Akróneos: a contestant at the games in Phaiákia; "top-ship"; 8.111.

Áktoris: one of Penelope's handmaids who stood guard at the chamber door; 23.228.

Alektor: father of the bride of Megapénthes; 4.10.

Alkándrè: an Egyptian woman; wife of Pólybos (2); gave Helen a basket; 4.125.

Álkimos: father of Mentor; 22.235.

Alkínoös: king of Phaiákia; "valiant of mind"; 6.12.

Alkíppè: one of Helen's handmaids; 4.124.

Alkmaíon: son of Ámphiaráos; 15.244.

Alkménè: wife of Amphítryon; mother of Herakles by Zeus; 2.120, 11.266.

Alóeus: husband of Íphimedeía; 11.305.

Álpheios: a river in the Peloponnese; father of Ortílochos; 3.489.

Álybas: unknown place from which Odysseus says he comes in the story he tells Laërtes; 24.304.

Amnísos: a city in Crete; 19.188.

Amphíalos: son of Polynéos, grandson of Tékton; a contestant at the games in Phaiákia who wins the jumping contest; "sea-girt"; 8.114.

Ámphiaráos: a soothsayer; son of Oïkles; one of the Seven against Thebes; second cousin of Theoklýmenos; 15.244.

Amphílochos: son of Ámphiaráos; 15.248

Amphimédon: a suitor; killed by Telémachos; 22.242.

Amphínomos: a suitor; son of Nisos; warned by Odysseus and killed by Telémachos; 16.351, 18.119, 22.89.

Amphion: (1) son of Antíopè by Zeus; cofounder of Thebes; 11.262; (2) father of Chloris; son of Iásos; ruler of Orchómenos; 11.283.

Amphithéa: wife of Autólykos; grandmother of Odysseus; 19.416.

Ámphitrítè: daughter of Ocean and Tethys; wife of Poseidon; 3.91.

Amphítryon: putative father of Herakles; husband of Alkménè; 11.266.

Amytháon: son of Tyro and Kretheus; 11.259.

Anabésineós: a contestant at the games in Phaiákia; "aboardship"; 8.113.

Anchíalos: (1) a Taphian; father of Mentes; 1.180; (2) a contestant at the games in Phaiákia; "seashore"; 8.112.

Andraímon: father of Thoas; 14.499.

Antikleía: daughter of Autólykos; wife of Laërtes; mother of Odysseus; 11.85.

Ántiklos: one of the Achaians in the Trojan horse; 4.286.

Antílochos: son of Nestor; killed at Troy; 3.112, 11.468.

Antínoös: son of Eupeíthes; one of the two leaders of the suitors; 1.383.

Antíopè: daughter of Asópos; mother, by Zeus, of Amphion and Zethos; 11.260.

Antíphates: (1) king of the Laistrygonians; 10.106; (2) son of Melámpous; grandfather of Ámphiaráos; 15.242.

Ántiphos: (1) son of Aigyptios; killed by the Cyklops; 2.19; (2) an older Ithakan; comrade of Odysseus; 17.68.

Apeírè: the homeland of Eúrymedoúsa; 7.9.

Apheídas: in the story Odysseus tells his father, the father of his fictional self, Epéritos; 24.305.

Aphrodítè: the goddess of love and pleasure; wife of Hephaistos; 4.14, **8.267**.

Apollo: the "far-shooting god"; son of Zeus and Leto; 3.279.

Ares: the god of war; lover of Aphrodítè, 8.115, **267**.

Arétè: wife of Alkínoös; queen of Phaiákia; "she who is prayed to"; 7.54.

Arethoúsa: the spring beside which Eumaíos pastures the swine of Odysseus; 13.408.

Arétias: father of Nisos; grandfather of Amphínomos; 16.395.

Arétos: son of Nestor; 3.414.

Argive: designation of the people of Argos or, more often, of all Greeks; 3.132.

Argo: the ship on which Jason, in earlier times, made his voyage to King Aiétes; 12.70.

Argos: (1) the dog with eyes all over its body set by Hera to watch over Zeus's paramour Io—disguised as a cow—but put to sleep and killed by Hermes; 1.38; (2) a city and region in Greece; the word can also refer to the Peloponnese or to Greece in general; 1.344; (3) the old dog of Odysseus; 17.292.

Ariádnè: Minos' daughter; carried away by Theseus but killed by Artemis in Dia; 11.321.

Arkeisios: father of Laërtes; grandfather of Odysseus, 4.755.

Arnaios: a beggar in Odysseus' palace; nicknamed "Iros" by the suitors; 18.5.

Artákia: a spring in the Laistrygonian country; 10.107.

Artemis: the goddess of hunting; 4.122.

Arýbas: father of the Phoenician woman who took Eumaíos from his father's house; 15.426.

Asópos: father of Antíopè; 11.260.

Asphálion: an attendant of Meneláos; 4.216.

Ásteris: the island between Ithaka and Samè where the suitors wait in ambush for Telémachos; 4.846.

Athena: the goddess of intelligence and of battle, Odysseus' patroness; 1.44.

Athens: the city; 3.278.

Atlas: the Titan who holds up the heavens; 1.52.

Atreus: father of Agamemnon and Meneláos; brother of Thyéstes; uncle of Aigísthos; 1.36.

Autólykos: father of Antikleía; grandfather of Odysseus; 11.85, **19.394**.

Autónoë: one of Penelope's handmaids; 18.182.

Boëthoös: father of Eteóneus; 4.31; 15.95.

Boötes: a constellation; 5.272.

Boreas: the north wind; 9.67.

Centaurs: people of Thessaly, half-man, half-horse; fought with the Lapiths; 21.295.

Chalkis: a stream in the western Peloponnese near the Álpheios River; 15.295.

Charýbdis: the whirlpool Odysseus encounters or the goddess who inhabits it; 12.104, 23.327.

Chios: an island in the Aegean Sea; 3.170.

Chloris: wife of Neleus; daughter of Amphion; mother of Nestor, Chromios, Periklýmenos, and Pero; 11.281.

Chromios: son of Neleus and Chloris; brother of Nestor; 11.286.

Circè: a goddess dwelling on the isle of Aiaía; sister of Aiétes; 8.448.

Crete: an island in the Mediterranean; 3.191.

Cyklops, Cyklópes: a gigantic and savage island dweller, especially Polyphémos, and the race to which he belongs; 1.69, 9.107.

Cyprus: an island in the eastern Mediterranean Sea; 4.83.

Damastor: father of Ageláos; 20.321.

Dánaäns: designation of the Greeks at Troy or of the Greeks in general; 1.350.

Deïphobos: a Trojan; son of Priam; later known as the husband of Helen after the death of Paris; 4.276.

Delos: an island in the Aegean Sea sacred to Apollo; 6.162.

Deméter: the goddess of fertility; sister of Zeus; lover of Iásion; 5.125.

Demódokos: the singer of tales at the Phaiákian court; 8.44.

Démoptólemos: a suitor; killed by Odysseus; 22.242.

Deukálion: father of Idómeneus and of (the fictional) Aithon; 19.180.

Dia: an island in the Aegean Sea where Artemis killed Ariádnè; 11.325.

Díokles: son of Ortílochos; lord of Phérai (1); 3.488.

Diomédes: a Greek leader; son of Tydeus; 3.181, 4.282.

Dionýsos: the god of wine; 11.325, 24.74.

Dmetor: son of Iásos, the ruler of Cyprus, according to Odysseus in the tale he tells the suitors; 17.443.

Dodóna: the oracle of Zeus in northwestern Greece; 14.327.

Dolios: Penelope's old manservant; father of Melánthios the goatherd and Melántho the handmaid; fellow worker of Laértes in the orchard; 4.736, 17.212, 24.222.

Dorians: inhabitants of Crete; 19.177.

Doulíchion: an island near Ithaka (probably modern Lefkas) from which many suitors come; 1.246.

Dymas: a Phaiákian; father of Naúsikaä's girlfriend to whom Athena likens herself; 6.22.

Echenéos: the oldest Phaiákian man at the court of Alkínoös; 7.155.

Echéphron: son of Nestor; 3.413.

Échetos: the harsh ruler of a mainland kingdom in western Greece; 18.85.

Egypt, Egyptians: the country and its people; 3.300.

Eídothéa: daughter of the sea god Proteus; helps Meneláos; 4.366.

Eileíthyia: the goddess of childbirth; 19.188.

Elátos: a suitor; 22.267.

Elátreus: a contestant at the games in Phaiákia; "helmsman"; 8.111.

Elis: a mainland city and region in the western Peloponnese; 4.635.

Elpénor: a companion of Odysseus; falls from Circè's roof and dies; 10.552.

Elysium: the pleasant plain where dwell those whom the gods favor; 4.563.

Enípeus River: Tyro's paramour, to whom Poseidon once likened himself; 11.238.

Epeíans: inhabitants of Elis; 13.275.

Epeíos: the builder of the Trojan horse; 8.493.

Epéritos: Odysseus' fictive name in the tale he tells his father; 24.306.

Ephiáltes: brother of Otos; son of Íphimedeía by Poseidon; a Giant who rebelled against the Olympian gods; 11.308.

Ephýrè: the place where Ilos lives; Odysseus went there after a poisonous elixir; 1.259.

Epikástè: mother of Oídipous; 11.271.

Érebos: the dark place where the spirits of the dead go; 10.528.

Eréchtheus: a hero and early ruler of Athens; 7.81.

Erémboi: people visited by Meneláos on his journey; 4.84.

Erétmeus: a contestant at the games in Phaiákia; "oarsman"; 8.112.

Erínyes: the Furies, avenging goddesses; 11.280.

Eriphýlè: wife of Ámphiaráos; for a bribe, she caused her husband to fight as one of the Seven against Thebes, though he knew he would be killed, 11.326.

Erymánthos: a mountain in Arkadia in the northwestern Peloponnese; 6.103.

Eteóneus: an attendant of Meneláos; 4.22, 15.95.

Ethiopians: a distant people whom Poseidon goes to visit; 1.22.

Euánthes: father of Maron; 9.197.

Euboía: an island just off the coast of eastern Greece; 3.175, 7.321.

Euénor: father of Leiókritos; 2.242.

Eumaíos: a swineherd; loyal to Telémachos and Odysseus; 14.55.

Eúmelos: husband of Íphthimè, Penelope's sister; 4.798.

Eupeíthes: father of Antínoös; leader of those who seek revenge for the death of the suitors; 1.383, **24.422.**

Euros: the east wind; 19.206.

Euryádes: a suitor; killed by Telémachos, 22.267.

Eurýalos: a contestant at the games in Phaiákia; jeers at Odysseus; "broad sea"; 8.115.

Eurybátes: the herald of Odysseus on the expedition to Troy; 19.247.

Eurýdamas: a suitor; killed by Odysseus; 18.297.

Eurýdikè: wife of Nestor; daughter of Klýmenos; 3.452.

Eurykleía: the old nurse of Odysseus; 1.429, 17.31.

Eurýlochos: a prominent companion of Odysseus; 10.205.

Eurýmachos: a leader of the suitors; son of Pólybos; 1.399.

Eurýmedon: king of the Giants; father of Periboía; grandfather of Naúsithoös; 7.58.

Eúrymedoúsa: the chambermaid of Naúsikaä; 7.8.

Eúrymos: father of Télemos; prophet of the Cyklópes; 9.509.

Eurýnomè: the housekeeper in Odysseus' palace; 17.495.

Eurýnomos: a suitor; son of Aigyptios; 2.21, 22.242.

Eurýpylos: a hero killed at Troy by Achilles' son, Neoptólemos; 11.519.

Eurýtion: a Centaur who became drunk and fought the Lapiths; 21.295.

Eúrytos: an archer; King of Oichália; father of Íphitos; kllled by Apollo; 8.224, 21.14.

Gaia: the earth; mother of Títyos; 7.324.

Geraistos: the southern promontory of Euboía; 3.178.

Gerenian: epithet of Nestor, from Gerenia in Messenia, to which he fled when Her-akles sacked Pylos; 3.68.

Giants: huge beings who rebelled against the Olympian gods; 7.59.

Gorgon: a monster of Hades (in later mythology, one of three sisters with but one eye and one tooth among them); "the Grim One"; 11.634.

Gortyn: a city in Crete, between Mt. Ida and the south coast, ten miles east of Phais-tos; 3.294.

Graces: in Greek, *Charites*; the goddesses who embody grace and beauty and attend Aphrodítè; 6.18.

Gyrai: a headland of uncertain location in the Aegean Sea; 4.501.

Hades: the lord of the dead; by metonymy, the realm he rules; 3.410.

Halios: son of Alkínoös; contestant at the games in Phaiákia; "seaman"; 8.119.

Halithérses: an old comrade of Odysseus who can interpret bird omens; 2.157, 17.68.

Hébè: daughter of Zeus and Hera; consort of Herakles on Olympos; 11.603.

Helen: wife of Meneláos; her abduction by Paris caused the Trojan War; 4.12.

Helios: the sun god, whose cattle Odysseus' companions kill; 1.9, **8.270**.

Hellas: Greece generally or, specifically, the country of Achilles; 1.344, 11.496.

Hellespont: the strait near Troy; the modern Dardanelles; 24.82.

Hephaistos: the god of metalwork; husband of Aphrodítè (in the song of Demódokos); "twice-lame cripple" (= lame in both legs); 4.617, **8.268**.

Hera: wife of Zeus; queen of the gods; 4.513.

Herakles: the mightiest of the mythical heroes; son of Zeus and Alkménè; 8.224, 11.267, 21.26.

Hermes: the messenger-god; son of Maia and Zeus; 1.38.

Hermíonè: daughter of Meneláos and Helen; 4.13.

Híppodameía: one of Penelope's handmaids; 18.182.

Híppotas: father of Aíolos; 10.2.

Hylax: a Cretan; father of Kastor (2); 14.203.

Hypereía: the land where the Phaiákians dwelt before migrating to Phaiákia; 6.4.

Hyperésia: the town in Achaia where Polypheídes lived and prophesied; 15.254.

Hypérion: father of Helios; this word seems usually to be an epithet of Helios and is translated "High Lord"; only in book 12 does the word clearly appear as a patronymic; 12.176.

Iardános: the river in Crete where the Kydónians live; 3.292.

Iásian: epithet of Argos; 18.246.

Iásion: paramour of Deméter; killed by Zeus; 5.126.

Iásos: (1) the ruler of Orchómenos; father of Amphion, who begot Chloris; 11.283; (2) the ruler of Cyprus; father of Dmetor; 17.443.

Idómeneus: the ruler of Crete; hero of the Trojan War; 3.191.

Ikários: father of Penelope; 1.328.

Ikmálios: the maker of Penelope's chair; 19.57.

Ilion: Troy, city and country; 2.18.

Ilos: son of Mérmeros; king of Ephýrè; 1.259.

Ino: a sea nymph; daughter of Kadmos; here a goddess known as Leukothéa, who helps Odysseus; 5.333.

Iólkos: the realm of Pelias in central Greece; 11.256.

Íphikles, also known as Phýlakos: Lord of Phýlakè; owner of the cattle that Melámpous drove away; 11.290.

Íphimedeía: wife of Alóeus; paramour of Poseidon; mother of Otos and Ephiáltes; 11.305.

Íphitos: son of Eúrytos; friend of Odysseus, whom he met in Messénè and gave the bow used in the contest; 21.14.

Íphthimè: Penelope's sister, whose phantom Athena sends to Penelope in a dream; 4.797.

Iris: the messenger-goddess; 18.7.

Iros: nickname of Arnaíos, the beggar who fights Odysseus, so called after Iris; 18.6.

Ísmaros: the home of the Kikonians in Thrace; 9.40.

Ithaka: one of the Ionian Islands off the west coast of Greece; home of Odysseus; 1.18.

Ithakos: the builder of a fountain on Ithaka, by the path to the city; 17.207.

Ítylos: son of Zethos and of Pandáreos' daughter, the nightingale (Proknè?); killed by his mother; 19.522.

Jason: son of Aison; leader of the expedition of the Argonauts; 12.72.

Kadmos: father of Ino; founder and ruler of Thebes; 5.333, 11.276.

Kalýpso: the nymph who dwells on the island of Ogygia; daughter of Atlas; Odysseus' entertainer and paramour for seven years; "concealed/concealer"; 1.14.

Kassandra: daughter of Priam; captured by Agamemnon when Troy was taken; killed by Klýtaimnéstra; 11.421.

Kastor: (1) half-immortal son of Leda and Tyndáreos; brother of Polydeúkes; 11.300; (2) a Cretan; son of Hylax; Odysseus pretends to be his illegitimate son in the story he tells Eumaíos; 14.203.

Kaúkones: the people Athena-as-Mentes says she will visit on account of a debt; 3.367.

Képhallénians: the people of Képhallénia, not explicitly connected by Homer with the island later called Képhallénia (modern Kephalonia), which is here called Samè or Samos; the mention of a Képhallénians' district in 20.210 perhaps refers to a region on the mainland opposite Ithaka; in 24.355, the word apparently designates all the subjects in Odysseus' (and formerly Laërtes') domains.

Keteían: perhaps refers to the Hittites of Asia Minor; describes the comrades of Eurýpylos, whom Neoptólemos killed; 11.520.

Kikonians: the people of Ísmaros in Thrace, which Odysseus sacked; 9.39, 23.310.

Kimmerian: the people who dwell near Hades' domain, in a dark and mist-covered land; 11.14.

Kleitos: son of Mantios; carried away by Dawn because of his beauty; 15.249.

Klýmenè: a heroine seen by Odysseus in Hades' domain; 11.326.

Klýmenos: father of Eurýdikè; 3.452.

Klýtaimnéstra: wife of Agamemnon; paramour of Aigísthos; 3.266, 11.422.

Klytios: father of Peiraíos; 15.540.

Klytonéos: son of Alkínoös; contestant at the games in Phaiákia; "ship-renowned"; 8.119.

Knossos: the city in Crete ruled by Minos; 19.178.

Kokýtos: a river in Hades' domain; a branch of the Styx; "River of Wailing"; 10.514.

Krátaïs: mother of Skylla; 12.124.

Kreion: father of Mégara; 11.269.

Kretheus: grandson of Aíolos (2); husband of Tyro; father of Aison, Pheres, and Amytháon; 11.237.

Kronos: father of Zeus; 1.45.

Krounoi: a place, probably springs, on the west coast of the Peloponnese; 15.295.

Ktésios: son of Órmenos; king of the island Syria; father of Eumaíos; 15.414.

Ktesíppos: a suitor; throws a hoof at Odysseus; killed by Philoítios; 20.288.

Ktímenè: youngest daughter of Antikleía; sister of Odysseus; 15.364.

Kydonians: a people of Crete; 3.292, 19.176.

Kyllenian: epithet of Hermes, from Mount Kyllénè in Arkadia, where he was born; 24.1.

Kýthera: an island off the coast of Lakedaímon in the Peloponnese, sacred to Aphrodítè; 9.81.

Kythereía: an epithet of Aphrodítè, from the island sacred to her; 8.288.

Laërkes: a smith at Nestor's court in Pylos; 3.425.

Laërtes: father of Odysseus; husband of Antikleía; 1.189.

Laistrygonians: gigantic cannibals living in Télepylòs who destroy all of Odysseus' galleys except his own; 10.82.

Lakedaímon: a region in the southern Peloponnese whose capital is Sparta; 3.326.

Lamos: the founding king of the Laistrygonians; perhaps "glutton"; 10.81.

Lampétië: daughter of Helios and Neaíra; with Phaëthoúsa, she tends the cattle of the sun; "radiant"; 12.132.

Lampos: one of the two horses that draw the chariot of Helios; "radiant"; 23.246.

Laódamas: son of Alkínoös; contestant at the games in Phaiákia; 7.170.

Lapiths: the people ruled by Peiríthoös; fought with the Centaurs; 21.297.

Leda: wife of Tyndáreos; by him, mother of Kastor, Polydeúkes, and Klýtaimnéstra; by Zeus, mother of Helen; 11.298.

Leiódes: a suitor skilled as a prophet; killed by Odysseus, 21.144.

Leiókritos: a suitor; son of Euénor; killed by Telémachos; 2.242, 22.294.

Lemnos: a city and island in the Aegean Sea; favored by Hephaistos; 8.283.

Lesbos: an island in the Aegean Sea where Odysseus wrestled with Phílomeleídes; 3.169.

Leto: consort of Zeus; mother of Apollo and Artemis; 6.106, 11.318.

Leukas: the "White Rock" on the way to Hades' domain; 24.11.

Leukothéa: another name for Ino, the sea nymph who helps Odysseus; "white goddess"; 5.334.

Libya: Africa in general; 4.85, 14.295.

Lotus-eaters: a people Odysseus and his men visit; 9.83.

Maia: consort of Zeus; mother of Hermes; 14.435.

Maira: a heroine seen by Odysseus in Hades' domain; 11.326.

Máleia: the extreme southeastern promontory of the Peloponnese; 3.288.

Mantios: son of Melámpous; grandfather of Theoklýmenos; "soothsayer"; 15.242.

Marathon: a village and plain of Attika, near Athens; 7.80.

Maron: son of Euánthes; priest of Apollo at Ísmaros; gave Odysseus the wine with which he makes the Cyclops drunk; 9.197.

Mastor: father of Halithérses; 2.158, 24.452.

Medon: the herald in the palace of Odysseus; saved by Telémachos; 4.677, 22.357.

Megapénthes: son of Meneláos by a slave; 4.11, 15.100.

Mégara: daughter of Kreion; wife of Herakles; 11.269.

Melámpous: a soothsayer who won Neleus' daughter Pero for his brother Bias by driving Íphikles' cattle from Phýlakè to Neleus in Pylos; great-grandfather of Theoklýmenos; 11.291, 15.225.

Melanéos: father of Amphimédon; 24.103.

Melánthios, or Melántheus: son of Dolios; goatherd who insults Odysseus; 17.212.

Melántho: daughter of Dolios; handmaid of Penelope; sleeps with Eurýmachos; 18.321.

Memnon: the handsomest of men; son of Morning; killed Antílochos at Troy; 4.188, 11.522.

Meneláos: son of Atreus; brother of Agamemnon; husband of Helen; 1.285.

Menoítios: father of Patroklos; 24.77.

Mentes: chief of the Taphians, to whom Athena likens herself when she comes to Telémachos; 1.105.

Mentor: son of Álkimos; one of Odysseus' oldest companions, whom he left in care of his household and to whom Athena often likens herself; 2.225.

Mérmeros: father of Ilos; 1.259.

Mesaúlios: a servant of Eumaíos; 14.449.

Messénè: a region in the southwestern Peloponnese where Odysseus met Íphitos; 21.15.

Mimas: a promontory of Asia Minor opposite Chios; 3.172.

Minos: son of Zeus; father of Ariádnè; king of Crete; judge in Hades' domain; 11.322.

Minyan: inhabitants of Orchómenos in Boiótia and Iolkos in Thessaly; 11.284.

Moulios: the herald of Amphínomos; 18.423.

Muse, collectively Muses: daughter of Zeus; goddess and inspirer of singers; 1.1, 8.63.

Mykénè: (1) a city in the Peloponnese ruled by Agamemenon; 3.304, 21.108; (2) a heroine renowned for her excellence; 2.120.

Mýrmidons: the people ruled by Achilles, by Achilles' father, Peleus, and by Achilles' son, Neoptólemos; 3.188.

Naíades: nymphs of springs and other running water; 13.104.

Naúbolos: father of Eurýalos; "ship-launcher"; 8.116.

Naúsikaä: daughter of Alkínoös and Arétè; rescuer of Odysseus; 6.17.

Naúsithoös: son of Poseidon and Periboía; father of Alkínoös; "swift ship"; 6.7.

Nauteus: a contestant at the games in Phaiákia; "shipman"; 8.112.

Neaíra: consort of Helios; mother of Lampétiè and Phaëthoúsa; "new (dawn)" (?); 12.133.

Neion: a mountain on Ithaka; 1.186.

Neleus: son of Tyro by Poseidon; brother of Pelias; father of Nestor; 3.4.

Neoptólemos: son of Achilles; 11.506.

Nérikos: probably a town on Leukas (then still attached to the mainland); captured by the young Laërtes; 24.378.

Nériton: a mountain on Ithaka, 9.22.

Néritos: the builder of a fountain on Ithaka, by the path to the city; 17.207.

Nestor: hero and sage of the Trojan expedition; son of Neleus; ruler of Pylos; 1.284.

Nisos: father of Amphínomos; lord on Doulíchion; 16.395.

Noëmon: son of Phronios; friend of Telémachos, to whom he lends his ship; 2.386.

Notos: the south wind; 11.289.

Ocean: the water surrounding the world; 3.1.

Odysseus: the hero; son of Laërtes and Antikleía; father of Telémachos; "angry, hating, hated, odious" (see 19.407–9); 1.21.

Ogygia: the island of Kalýpso, where Odysseus remained seven years; 1.85.

Oichálian: from Oichália, the town in Thessaly from which Eúrytos came; 8.224.

Oídipous: son of Epikástè; killed his father, married his mother, and ruled in Thebes; 11.271.

Oïkles: son of Antíphates; father of Ámphiaráos; 15.243.

Oinops: father of Leiódes; 21.144.

Okýalos: contestant at the games in Phaiákia; "swift sea"; 8.111.

Olympos: a mountain in Thrace; home of the gods; 1.102.

Onétor: father of Phrontis; 3.282.

Ops: father of Eurykleía; 1.429.

Orchómenos: a city of the Minyan people in Boiótia; 11.284.

Orestes: son of Agamemnon and Klýtaimnéstra; killed his mother and her paramour Aigísthos to requite the slaughter of his father; 1.30.

Oríon: the hero loved by Dawn; killed by Artemis; now a constellation; 5.121, 11.310.

Órmenos: father of Ktésios; 15.414.

Orsílochos: Idómeneus' son, whom Odysseus pretends to have killed in the story he tells Athena; 13.260.

Ortílochos: son of Álpheios; father of Díokles; entertained Odysseus in Messéné; 3.489, 21.16.

Ortýgia: "Quail Island" (perhaps Delos), where Artemis killed Oríon; 5.123, 15.404.

Ossa: a mountain in Thessaly that Otos and Ephiáltes wanted to pile on Olympos; 11.315.

Otos: brother of Ephiáltes; son of Íphimedeía by Poseidon; a Giant who rebelled against the Olympian gods; 11.308.

Paiéon: the god of medicine; Egyptians are said to be of his race; 4.232.

Pallas: cognomen of Athena, perhaps from Greek *pallo*, "brandish (a spear)"; 1.125.

Pandáreos: father of the nightingale (Prokné?) and of daughters seized by stormwinds; 19.518.

Panópeus: a town in Phokis, between Orchómenos and the Kephisos River; 11.581.

Paphos: a city in Cyprus with an important shrine of Aphrodíte; 8.363.

Parnassos: a mountain in central Greece, above Delphi; 19.394.

Patróklos: a Greek hero at Troy; Achilles' closest companion; 3.110.

Peiraíos: an Ithakan; son of Klytios; companion of Telémachos; 15.539.

Peiríthoös: a hero of earlier times; friend of Theseus; king of the Lapiths; 11.631, 21.296.

Peisander: a suitor; son of Polýktor; killed by Philoítios; 18.299.

Peisénor: (1) grandfather of Eurykleía; 1.429; (2) a herald in Ithaka; 2.37.

Peisístratos: son of Nestor; companion of Telémachos on his journey; 3.36.

Pelasgian: a people of Crete; 19.177.

Peleus: father of Achilles; 5.310.

Pelias: son of Tyro by Poseidon; brother of Neleus; king of Iólkos; 11.254.

Pelion: a mountain in Thrace that Otos and Ephiálté wanted to pile on Ossa; 11.316.

Penelope: wife of Odysseus; daughter of Ikários; mother of Telémachos; perhaps "bird of lamentation"; 1.223.

Periboía: mother of Naúsithoös by Poseidon; 7.57.

Periklýmenos: son of Neleus and Chloris; brother of Nestor; 11.286.

Perimédes: a companion of Odysseus; 11.23.

Pero: daughter of Neleus and Chloris; sister of Nestor; 11.287.

Persè: a nymph; daughter of Ocean; consort of Helios; mother of Circè and Aiétes; 10.139.

Perséphonè: wife of Hades; queen of the dead; 10.491.

Perseus: son of Nestor; 3.414.

Pháëthon: one of the two horses that draw the chariot of Helios; "shining"; 23.246.

Phaëthoúsa: daughter of Helios and Neaíra; with Lampétië, she tends the cattle of the sun; "shining"; 12.132.

Phaiákians: the people of Scheria, ruled by Alkínoös; 5.35.

Phaídimos: the king of the Sidonians who received Meneláos and gave him a wine bowl; 4.617, 15.117.

Phaidra: daughter of Minos; sister of Ariádnè; wife of Theseus; mother of Hippólytos; 11.321.

Phaistos: a city in Crete; 3.296.

Pharos: an island in the Mediterranean Sea near Egypt; 4.355.

Phéai: a cape on the coast of Elis in the Peloponnese; 15.297.

Pheidon: king of the Thesprotians; 14.316.

Phemios: son of Terpes; singer of tales in Odysseus' palace; spared by Odysseus; 1.154, 22.331.

Phérai: (1) a town in the Peloponnese; 3.488; (2) a town in Thessaly, where Íphthimè, Penelope's sister, lives with her husband, Eúmelos; 4.798.

Pheres: son of Tyro and Kretheus; 11.259.

Philoítios: the oxherd loyal to Odysseus; 20.185.

Philoktétes: son of Poias; Greek hero at Troy famous as an archer; 3.190, 8.219.

Phílomeleídes: a man of Lesbos whom Odysseus threw in a wrestling match; 4.343, 17.134.

Phoenicia, Phoenicians: a country and people on the Syrian coast of the Mediterranean Sea, known for trade and navigation; 4.83.

Phoibos: cognomen of Apollo; 3.279.

Phorkys: an old man of the sea; grandfather of Polyphémos; lives in an Ithakan harbor; 1.72, 13.96.

Phronios: father of Noëmon; 2.386.

Phrontis: son of Onétor; steersman of Meneláos; 3.282.

Phthia: a town in Thessaly, home of Achilles; 11.496.

Phýlakè: the Arkadian town ruled by Phýlakos, whence Melámpous drove the cattle; 11.289, 15.236.

Phýlakos, also known as Íphikles: lord of Phýlakè; 15.231.

Phylo: one of Helen's handmaids; 4.125.

Piéria: a region in Thessaly near Mount Olympos; 5.50.

Planktai: the Wandering Rocks; 12.61.

Pleíades: a constellation; "doves" or, from Greek *pleo*, "sail"; 5.272.

Poias: father of Philoktétes; 3.190.

Polítes: a companion of Odysseus; 10.224.

Pólybos: (1) father of Eurýmachos; 1.399; (2) an Egyptian; husband of Alkándrè; 4.126; (3) a Phaiákian craftsman; 8.373; (4) a suitor; killed by Eumaíos; 22.243.

Polydámna: an Egyptian woman; wife of Thon; 4.228.

Polydeúkes: half-immortal son of Leda and Tyndáreos; brother of Kastor; 11.300.

Polykástè: youngest daughter of Nestor; 3.464.

Polýktor: (1) the builder of a fountain on Ithaka, by the path to the city; 17.207; (2) father of Peisander; 18.299.

Polynéos: son of Tekton; father of Amphíalos; "many a ship"; 8.114.

Polypémon: father of Apheídas; 24.305.

Polypheídes: son of Mantios; father of Theoklýmenos; 15.249.

Polyphémos: son of Poseidon; the Cyklops whom Odysseus encounters; 1.70, 9.403.

Polythérses: father of Ktesíppos; 22.287.

Ponteus: a contestant at the games in Phaiákia; "seaman"; 8.113.

Pontónoös: the herald of Alkínoös; "sea-minded"; 7.179.

Poseidon: the god of the sea; son of Kronos; brother of Zeus; enemy of Odysseus; 1.20.

Prámneian wine: the wine into which Circè mixes food for the men she changes to swine; 10.235.

Priam: king of Troy; father of Kassandra, Hektor, and many other children; 3.107.

Prokris: daughter of Eréchtheus; 11.321.

Proreus: a contestant at the games in Phaiákia; "prow man"; 8.113.

Proteus: the shape-changing old man of the sea; father of Eídothéa; met and questioned by Meneláos; 4.365.

Prymneus: a contestant at the games in Phaiákia; "stern man"; 8.112.

Psyrian island: Psyra, an island north of Chios; 3.171.

Pylos, Pylians: a city and people in the southwest Peloponnese ruled by Nestor; 1.93.

Pyriphlégethon: a river of Hades' domain; a tributary of the Ácheron; "River of Blazing Fire"; 10.513.

Pytho: the sanctuary of Apollo on Mount Parnassos, later called Delphi; 8.80, 11.581.

Rhadamánthys: son of Zeus and Europa; brother of Minos; dwells in the plain of Elysium; 4.564.

Rheithron: a harbor in Ithaka; 1.186.

Rhexénor: son of Naúsithoös; brother of Alkínoös; father of Arétè; "breaking through ranks"; 7.63.

Salmóneus: father of Tyro; 11.236.

Samè, Samos: an island near Ithaka, probably Cephallenia (modern Cephalonia); 1.246.

Scheria: the country in which the Phaiákians live; 5.34.

Sicily, Sicilian: island in the Mediterranean and its inhabitants; 20.383.

Sidon, Sidonians: an important city of the Phoenicians and its inhabitants; 4.84, 15.118.

Sikania: old form of the name *Sikelia* (Sicily), though the singer of the *Odyssey* may have thought of the two names as signifying separate places; 24.307.

Sintians: the people of Lemnos whom Hephaistos goes to visit; 8.294.

Sirens: island creatures who with their singing enchant passersby to destruction; 12.39, 23.326.

Sisyphos: a hero tormented in Hades' domain by being forced to roll a stone uphill only to see it rebound; 11.593.

Skylla: monstrous daughter of Krátaïs; lives on the headland across from Charýbdis; 12.85, 23.328.

Skyros: the island in the Aegean Sea from which Odysseus took Neoptólemos to Troy; 11.509.

Sólymoi: the people dwelling around a mountain in Asia Minor, Mt. Sólyma, from which Poseidon sees Odysseus on his way back to Olympos from visiting the Ethiopians; 5.283.

Sounion: the extreme southeast headland of the territory of Athens; 3.278.

Sparta: a city and region of Lakedaímon, in the Peloponnese; 1.93.

Stratios: son of Nestor; 3.413.

Styx: the river in Hades' domain by which the gods swear; "Hateful River"; 5.185, 10.514.

Syria: an island near Ortýgia where Eumaíos was born and raised; 15.403.

Tantalos: a hero tormented in Hades' domain by never being able to reach the drink or food that he can perceive; 11.582.

Taphos, Taphians: a place in western Greece (perhaps the northern Echinades Islands or Corfu) and its inhabitants, known for navigation and piracy; 1.105, 14.452.

Taygétos: a mountain in Lakedaímon, favored by Artemis; 6.103.

Teirésias: the Theban prophet in Hades' domain who counsels Odysseus; 10.492.

Tekton: father of Polynéos; grandfather of Amphíalos; "shipwright"; 8.114.

Télamon: father of Ajax (1); 11.543.

Telémachos: son of Odysseus and Penelope; 1.113.

Télemos: son of Eúrymos; a prophet of the Cyklópes who foretold that Odysseus would blind Polyphémos; 9.509.

Télephos: father of Eurýpylos; 11.519.

Télepylós: the city of the Laistrygonians; 10.82, 23.318.

Temesian: from Temesa (perhaps a place in Cyprus), which was renowned for its copper; 1.184.

Ténedos: an island in the Aegean Sea near Troy where the returning Achaians made sacrifices; 3.159.

Terpes: father of Phemios; 22.330.

Thebes: (1) a city in Egypt; 4.127; (2) a city in Boiótia, in eastern Greece; 11.263.

Theoklýmenos: son of Polypheídes; a soothsayer in flight from Argos, whom Telémachos takes to Ithaka on his ship and who foretells the doom of the suitors; 15.256.

Theseus: the hero and king of Athens; 11.322.

Thesprotians: people of Thesprotia in northwestern Greece, ruled by Pheidon; 14.315.

Thetis: a sea nymph; wife of Peleus; mother of Achilles; 24.92.

Thoai: small islands, probably the southern Echinades Islands, near the Peloponnese; 15.299.

Thoas: son of Andraímon; Achaian warrior at Troy who, in the tale Odysseus tells Eumaíos, left his cloak behind; 14.499.

Thon: an Egyptian; husband of Polydámna; 4.228.

Thóön: a contestant at the games in Phaiákia; "swift"; 8.113.

Thoösa: a sea nymph; daughter of Phorkys; mother of Polyphémos; 1.71.

Thrace: a region north of Greece, frequented by Ares; 8.361.

Thrasymédes: son of Nestor; 3.39.

Thrinakia: the island of Helios, where his cattle were pastured; 11.107, 19.275.

Thyéstes: brother of Atreus; father of Aigísthos; 4.517.

Tithónos: consort of Dawn; 5.1.

Títyos: son of Gaia, the Earth; tormented in Hades' domain for having abducted Leto; 7.324, 11.576.

Trítogeneía: cognomen of Athena, of uncertain meaning; 3.378.

Troy, Troäd, Trojans: the city of Ilion in western Asia Minor, its territory, and its people, ruled over by Priam; 1.2.

Tydeus: father of Diomédes; 3.167.

Tyndáreos: husband of Leda; father of Kastor, Polydeúkes, and Klýtaimnéstra; 11.298, 24.199.

Tyro: a heroine of former times; daughter of Salmóneus; wife of Kretheus, to whom she bore Aison, Amytháon, and Pheres; paramour of Poseidon, to whom she bore Neleus and Pelias; 2.120, 11.235.

Zakýnthos: an island south of Ithaka (probably modern Zantè); presumably part of the dominions of Odysseus; 1.246.

Zephyr: the west wind; 2.421.

Zethos: (1) son of Antíopè by Zeus; cofounder of Thebes; 11.262; (2) husband of Pandáreos' daughter, the nightingale (Proknè?); father of Ítylos; 19.522.

Zeus: son of Kronos; ruler of the gods; "Father of gods and of mankind"; 1.10.